Imagery and
Consciousness

Imagery and Consciousness

PETER E. MORRIS
Department of Psychology
University of Lancaster
Lancaster

and

PETER J. HAMPSON
School of Psychology
Manchester Polytechnic
Manchester

1983

ACADEMIC PRESS
A Subsidiary of Harcourt Brace Jovanovich, Publishers

London   New York
Paris   San Diego   San Francisco   São Paulo
Sydney   Tokyo   Toronto

Academic Press Inc. (London) Ltd
24–28 Oval Road
London NW1

US edition published by
Academic Press Inc.
111 Fifth Avenue,
New York, New York 10003

British Cataloguing in Publication Data

Morris, P.E.
  Imagery and consciousness.
  1. Imagery (Psychology)
  I. Title   II. Hampson, P.J.
  153.3'2   BF367

  ISBN 0-12-507680-0
  LCCCN 82-074571

Phototypeset by Dobbie Typesetting Service, Plymouth, Devon
Printed in Great Britain by St Edmundsbury Press, Bury St Edmunds, Suffolk

For
Priscilla and Shelagh

Preface

There can be few famous philosophers or psychologists who have had nothing to say about the role that mental images play in our lives, and, from the founding of experimental psychology onwards, there have been many empirical studies of imagery. However, the 1970s and early 1980s have seen imagery become one of the most popular topics for theorizing and research in cognitive psychology. There has been an enormous amount of discussion about the part images may play in representing and allowing access to information within the cognitive system. More than in any other area outside the artificial intelligence field, psychologists interested in imagery have been forced to consider just what underlies the cognitive processes which they study.

While issues of the nature of the processes underlying imagery have attracted much attention, less research has been directed to more mundane questions such as when do images occur and what are their properties. There is a danger, without a grounding in such basic facts, that abstract issues of the underlying representation may not only remain insoluble for lack of appropriate data, but also the impression may be conveyed that research on imagery requires only contributions from intellectual giants who can extend the development of frameworks suitable for representing cognition. In reality, research is needed upon a whole spectrum of imagery phenomena.

In this book we have reviewed not only the fundamental issues on the nature of imagery, and research using recently popular paradigms, but also topics with a longer history, including individual differences in imaging ability, the many types of images which occur, and the contribution imagery can make as a memory aid.

Images are subjective experiences, and to report about them individuals must introspect. Through the years, introspection has probably attracted more criticism than any other technique which psychologists have used to collect data. Any consideration of mental images also raises many venerable philosophical disputes about the relationship of mental and physical processes. We have therefore

devoted an early section of the book to problems related to introspection and consciousness. We propose an account of the place of
consciousness in the cognitive system which we believe best describes
the many aspects of consciousness, including those of mental imagery.

We would like to thank the many people who have made the book
possible: the Psychology Department at Exeter University who
provided the facilities for Peter Morris to take sabbatical leave there
while writing his chapters; Joan, and Chris who typed several chapters
at Exeter; Sylvia and Anne who typed others at Lancaster, and Jean
and Mary who typed the remainder in Manchester. Their assistance
was invaluable. We would also like to thank Stewart Morris who
helped us break the convention of "words only" in most books on
imagery by providing many of the illustrations.

February 1983   PETER E. MORRIS
                                                   PETER J. HAMPSON

Contents

1
Imagery previewed

I Introductory remarks

We invite the reader to try some thought experiments. First of all, consider the front door of your house. On which side is it hinged? Does your house have windows? How many has it got? Ask anyone to consider simple questions like these and to reflect on the ways in which they answer them, and the replies are intriguing. To decide how many windows their house has, and on what side their door opens, people often claim that they need to "visualize", "imagine" or "see" their home with varying degrees of fidelity and vividness. On the other hand, when asked to decide whether their house has any windows or whether, say, motor cars have engines, they often claim just to "know" the answer, no image is apparently necessary.

Now consider these pairs of words: WHALE-CIGAR; NAPOLEON-DAFFODIL; STRAWBERRY-BASKET; and now these: JUSTICE-TRUTH; LOYALTY-FREEDOM; SORROW-PRECISION. Which set do you think would be the easier to remember? People often say that they can form mental pictures easily when given the first set, but have more difficulty doing so with the second. Does the image-arousing value of a word affect its memorability? Do images have to link up the names of objects to be useful? Do mental pictures help us to understand detective stories? Recently, psychologists have become very interested in these sorts of questions and answers. Mental imagery, once virtually banished from psychology while behaviourism was dominant, is now a respectable topic for serious enquiry.

To unpack the issues raised by these opening questions will take the rest of this book, but we can at least make a start here. To begin with, the very fact that people can reply to these queries shows that they can think and solve problems. We believe that this is not a trivial point but one worthy of deeper consideration. The nature of thought and its function are issues which have, of course, exercised the minds of philosophers and scholars for centuries, but until relatively recently little real progress has been made in understanding them. Perhaps one reason for this is that lately there has been a shift in emphasis from considering, primarily, the nature of thought, imagination and so on, to considering its function. Craik (1943) was one of the first psychologists to do this. He asked: what does thinking allow the thinker to achieve? What is it for? Arguing along Darwinian lines, he maintained that one function of thought, indeed one reason for its existence, is that it increases the chances that the thinker will survive. Taken on its own this insight was not startling; at one level all biological processes and properties exist because they have conferred ''survival value'' on their possessors. Giraffes have long necks, and blood clots when it is exposed to the air for this reason. Craik realized, however, that it was important to specify more clearly just how thought conveyed these advantages. His conclusion was simple but important. Thought aids survival by allowing organisms to anticipate events before they occur. By doing this, creatures which have this ability can maximize their commerce with the advantageous and minimize their exposure to the harmful. You can anticipate the consequences of running in front of a double decker bus, you do not need to perform the experiment itself! Craik and other psychologists (e.g. Miller *et al.*, 1960) have claimed that, to fulfil this anticipatory function, thought must not merely reproduce past experience but must be able to model reality actively. They agree that thinking involves the use of stored information (originally derived mainly through the senses) to symbolize reality, its transformation into new representations and a retranslation to relate the new symbols thus derived back to the world. The two vital elements in this process are (1) the ability to symbolize, and (2) the possibility of acting on stored symbolic representations. These notions are important and will recur frequently in this book.

A second lesson to be drawn from our initial thought experiments is that people make claims about the types of representations they use when thinking. Reference is frequently made to visual images, though as we mentioned, people do not always report the presence of these phenomena. Images are (just) one type of symbolic representation considered by Craik and others, and a greater part of this text is concerned with their structure and function. To cope with our thought experiments people often claim to have to use visual images. We must remind the reader, though, that images may well occur in other sensory modalities. Imagine the sound of a telephone ringing, the smell of roses, the feel of velvet or the taste of onions! Your experiences may not be particularly vivid, but the fact that you can conjure up these situations, however vaguely, demonstrates that ''thinking verbally'' and ''thinking visually'' do not exhaust the number of ways you can symbolize reality.

A third aspect of our thought experiments which easily escapes notice is that people are apparently able to report on the content of, and certain operations associated with, their mental life. They can introspect. As we shall see, introspection is usually presented as a notoriously bad psychological technique and most introductory textbooks list the traditional arguments against the use of this method. Introspection is said to be error prone because of its privacy, the inaccessibility of many cognitive processes, its distorting effect on those that are accessible, and many other problems (see for example Hilgard *et al.*, 1979). Despite its drawbacks as a method of psychological enquiry, which incidentally do not completely rule out its use as a source of data, introspection can and does occur. This in itself is interesting in that it reminds us that people are aware or conscious of some aspects of their mental life. Certain cognitive processes apparently have an inner experiential dimension as well as being amenable to external, information processing analysis.

As this book's title suggests, mental imagery and consciousness are closely linked. Theories about the structure and function of imagery quickly lead to theories of consciousness and vice versa. Like the study of thinking, however, the topic of consciousness has been played by a number of philosophical problems. There are some, though, who would argue that many of these are largely linguistic or conceptual (e.g. Ryle, 1949) and that consciousness is a non-problem. We believe that this is misguided, that it is possible to locate consciousness as a functional aspect of the cognitive system and will introduce a provisional model in Chapter 3 to illustrate this. For the moment, however, another *caveat* is necessary. A theory of consciousness can only give us insights into what a conscious system is like, it can only offer analogies as to how it functions. What it can never do is to tell us what it is really or essentially like to be a conscious system. A moment's reflection might convince the reader that this is so. The only thing that it is like to be a conscious system is to be another conscious system! Put another way, we believe that questions concerning the role or purpose of consciousness can be answered, whereas those concerning its true nature or essence cannot. We suspect that to ask a psychologist what *is* consciousness, rather than what is its function, is as misguided as asking a physicist what is the essential nature of energy rather than asking what are its properties.

Imagery can also be considered a phenomenon which stands at the intersection of memory and perception, where it can be used to aid conscious thinking and problem solving. As a perceptual phenomenon imagery owes its content and possibly also its structure to information originally derived through the senses. This implies no more than that we can have images of particular objects or events, and that at least some of the information underpinning our images of those events must, at some time, have been gained through perception. However, to have images of events that are not physically happening at the time we must also store this information. Imagery thus has memorial properties. Finally, in line with our functional analysis of thinking, images are used for a reason, for example, to help give directions, to picture old friends or to make poetry more enjoyable. If this common-sense analysis is correct, increasing our knowledge of imagery will also enrich our understanding of these associated cognitive processes. Also, the type of questions we ask about imagery should be determined by important, contemporary issues in cognitive psychology. So, one matter which is widely discussed at the moment concerns the form in which knowledge is represented in memory. Our notions of the structure of imagery must be examined in the light of this debate. If imagery and perception are related, do both processes behave in similar ways? Do they sometimes compete with each other? How do thought processes which use images differ from those that use other types of internal representations? These are just some of the types suggested by the three-way analysis of imagery but they indicate the general types of issues we will be considering. For the moment, though, we must defer a closer examination of them and examine briefly the historical background to contemporary imagery research.

II   The historical background of imagery research

Given that imagery appears to be a construct of such central importance it may come as something of a surprise to learn that it has, until recently, been studied in a rather patchy fashion. According to Paivio (1971) many fundamental ideas concerning the role of imagery in meaning and memory are to be found in early Greek writings. Plato's wax tablet model of memory asserted that "images" are copies of perceptions and thoughts and this rudimentary model of memory formed the basis for later stimulus-trace theories. Another line of enquiry demonstrated that imagery can have a significant mediational role in certain mnemonic techniques, and the poet Simonides is usually accredited with the discovery of one of the more important of such devices, the Method of Loci (see Yates, 1966; Paivio, 1971b; Morris, 1979 and Chapter 10). Yet although these ideas have a long history, it was not until the latter part of the nineteenth century that their more systematic study began. About 100 years ago, when Wilhelm Wundt founded the first psychological laboratory in Leipzig, psychology began to detach itself from philosophy. The new movement became known as Structuralism. Its epistemological roots were Associationist. Knowledge derived solely through the senses was believed to be stored in the form of "ideas" or mental atoms. New ideas were formed from associative groups of old ones, the principles of grouping being determined by similarity, contrast and contiguity. The most popular theory of mind adopted by these early psychologists was some version of parallelism: mental and physical events ran in synchrony but did not interact. In view of these twin philosophical assumptions, their two basic techniques, psychophysics and introspection, were sensible ones to adopt at the time. Psychophysics was (and is) an attempt to relate physical and psychological magnitudes in as direct a way as possible, though nowadays the metaphysical belief that the mental world and its laws mirror the physical world may not be so widely accepted. The second method, introspection, relied on the notion that all the important aspects of mental functioning are conscious. This technique initiated the more formal investigation of imagery, but also eventually led to its virtual banishment from psychology for 50 years or so. Classical introspection involved an attempt to discover the raw materials of mental life, not to make interpretations about them. To describe the object in front of me as a table would be to commit the stimulus error, to describe it as a brown trapezoid would be more appropriate. Wundt believed that this method was inapplicable to the higher mental processes which, for him, included perception as well as thought. Its proper application, he maintained, was in the realm of sensation, since this was uncontaminated by meaning. Indeed, Wundt could find no way of opening up the study of the higher cognitive processes.

Titchener (1896), however, was more willing to tackle thinking. He maintained that all cognitive activity was accompanied by images. In common with sensations, such images had the properties of quality, intensity, duration and clarity, but differed from sensations by virtue of their transparency. This latter term was meant to imply that images were less objective, less realistic and more easily destroyed than sensations. Titchener, therefore, equated thought with conscious content, which was reducible, in turn, to a series of mental images. He opened up imagery and thinking to introspective analysis, since conscious mental content was observable through the "mind's eye".

The approach was doomed to failure. Experiments performed by the Wurzburg school of psychology demonstrated that thinking can and does occur without any reportable, conscious content (see for example, Humphrey, 1951; Paivio, 1971b). This began the famous "imageless thought" controversy. Titchener rejected the possibility that thinking need not be conscious on the grounds that investigators who had failed to find mental images had simply not looked hard enough! For a time, science ended and polemics began. The outcome is well known. For these and other reasons, Watson (1913) came to the conclusion that images and other mental events were simply not valid objects of scientific enquiry. In addition, the technique of introspection was error prone and not open to public scrutiny. Statements about images should cease and the methods by which they had been studied should be discontinued, and the role previously attributed to images in memory and thinking was to be taken over by verbal responses. Insofar as thinking occurred at all it was to be equated with an internal vocalization or "sub-vocalization", more simply, thinking involved merely "talking to oneself" (Paivio, 1971).

Very quickly, Watson's behaviourist manifesto resulted in a marked diminution of the number of empirical studies involving imagery and a consequent increase in those concerned with verbal mediation. It did not, however, completely exorcise the imaginal ghost from the machine. During what has been referred to as the "period of behaviourist induced scepticism" (Cooper and Shepard, 1973, p.1) imagery research continued, albeit somewhat sporadically and images under other names appeared in even the most explicitly behaviourist theories. Paivio lists Tolman's (1948) cognitive maps; Hull's (1931) fractional anticipatory goal responses and Osgood's (1953) representational mediation process as examples. Leuba (1940) referred to images as conditional sensations and Skinner (1953) has described imagery as conditioned seeing! European psychologists, though, remained largely sceptical of behaviourism and, for example, Piaget continued to use the term "image" freely. However, in the English speaking world, only a few psychologists, mainly British, such as Bartlett (1932) resisted the behaviourist critique.

Eventually, the climate of opinion changed. It became clearer that many psychological theories could be simplified by making inferences from behavioural data about internal representations of the world. Miller *et al.* (1960) provided the first real manifesto for cognitive psychology, though they cautiously called themselves subjective behaviourists, and Neisser (1967) wrote its initial progress report. Paivio (1971b) was one of the first to take advantage of the new *Zeitgeist* though A. Richardson (1969) and Sheehan (1972a) were also among the first to welcome back the mental images. One psychologist, McKellar (1957), pre-dated them all with his interest in imaginal phenomena. However, it was Paivio's work which set the scene for much of the work in the late 1960s and early 1970s. Paivio's concern was to establish the importance of images as mediators underlying many different situations involving perception, memory, language and thinking. Notice that even in 1971 Paivio used the term "mediator" more freely than "representation", perhaps because of his neo-behaviourist background. *Imagery and Verbal Processes*, Paivio's book, which we shall consider in some detail below but will expand on later, had three main effects. First, it affirmed that imagery was worth studying and opened up many issues associated with the construct. Secondly, methods by which imagery research could be pursued were suggested to psychologists. Thirdly, a theoretical position concerning the role of images was presented.

Establishing the importance of images involved Paivio in many investigations in many areas. For example, one issue which has received considerable attention is the relation between words and images. Specifically, it seems to be easy to form images of certain words such as carrot, tiger or bus, but not to others such as truth, zeal or justice. An allied issue is the concreteness of words, the extent to which they refer to specific objects. Paivio and colleagues began the attempt to tease out the role of Imageability and Concreteness in free recall, paired associate learning, serial recall and other situations. This research is still continuing and is quite fully reviewed in Chapter 11. He also examined the speed with which people can form images and explored the relationships between images, meaning and comprehension, issues which will be taken up later. Finally, picture memory, mnemonics and individual differences were among the other topics he studied, as we shall see.

Paivio used three main techniques for studying imagery, which are still widely used. One way is to ask subject to form images and to see if the effects of manipulating strategies in this way are significant. Another approach involves varying the image arousing value of the stimuli used. An example of this latter method would be the use of words varying in imageability. Finally, the performance of subjects who vary in their abilities to image can be compared in a variety of situations. Paivio has repeatedly emphasized that these three techniques should not be considered as independent research strategies, but can (and should) be used in conjunction in many experiments. Hopefully, the evidence gained from one method will be supplemented by that derived from the others. The use of "converging evidence" in this way can be very helpful when studying a difficult phenomenon such as mental imagery. In parallel with Paivio, researchers such as McKellar (1957), A. Richardson (1969) and Sheehan (1972b) concentrated mainly on individual differences between imagers. Actually, this tradition has a long history and dates back to the work of Sir Francis Galton (see Galton, 1883). We believe that any general theory of imagery, indeed any general cognitive theory, must take account of individual variation, and so will consider these issues in Chapter 5.

During the last ten years, imagery research has increased in both scope and variety. While the issues raised by Paivio and colleagues are still being thoroughly explored, other concerns have recently emerged. One reason for this is that new methods have been discovered for studying imagery. The 1970s have seen the rise of chronometric or reaction time techniques in imagery research. The "new mentalism", as it has been called, seeks to use the same methods that are used in the rest of cognitive psychology to examine mental imagery. Previously, as we mentioned earlier, cognitive psychologists have used behavioural data, such as reaction times and error scores, to make inferences about internal processes which are often not open to introspection, and which are assumed to cause or produce the behaviours. For example, a psychologist interested in memory for verbal materials might make inferences about the type of encoding processes that have occurred from the variations in time spent by his subjects in studying the stimuli. Similar procedures are now being applied in imagery research (e.g. Kosslyn, 1980) with perhaps a couple of differences. First, the link between mental operations involving imagery and external behaviour is often less direct than that between, say, visual search processes and visual search times. Phenomena associated with imagery are more autonomous and need not result in any observable behavioural output. This means that the researcher who investigates imagery has to become adept at framing his questions about the construct in such a way that at least some behaviour is consequent on mental performance. Often, the techniques that have been tried involve the subjects making a response to say that they have finished a particular task, or replying "yes" or "no" in answer to simple questions about their images (see Kosslyn, 1980). These methods are not without their critics, on the grounds that they are too subjective and can be influenced by task demands. At other times the new reaction time methodologies more closely resemble "standard", cognitive psychological experiments (e.g. Cooper and Shepard, 1973). A second difference is that these techniques are being used to explore phenomena which very often have a conscious component. Whether or not this difference matters remains to be seen. Cognitive psychology may have come of age or it may have regressed to its origins!

Closely linked with the rise of the new methods has been a shift in emphasis by some researchers from considering whether or not images can act as mediators at all, to examining their structure and function (e.g. Kosslyn, 1980). In fact, new issues have been to some extent one cause of the emergence of the new techniques. To investigate the structure of imagery, it is often necessary to ask people to do things with their images; finding out how long some of these operations take can provide us with useful information. Reaction time methods allow us to do this.

Questions concerning the structure and function of images have led, in their turn, to a deeper examination of the theoretical status of the construct itself. Pylyshyn (1973) in a classic paper drew researchers' attention to weaknesses in the everyday, uncritical use of the concept. Pylyshyn's arguments will be considered in detail later, but to give the reader a flavour of his approach we will mention one or two aspects of it here. One complaint of Pylyshyn's is that to talk of "mental images" seems to imply the existence of "mental pictures" which require "seeing" by some internal mechanism. Images may not be pictorial at all, he claims, but are probably much more abstract structures. Also, going from images to words and back involves translation problems.

One of Pylyshyn's alternative types of representation, the "proposition", allows bridges to be made across modalities and provides, he claims, a better (less philosophically troublesome) way of supporting the "language of thought". Some, however, would say that this programme is ultimately reductionist and ignores the functional level of representations and processes (Kosslyn and Pomerantz, 1977; Johnson-Laird, 1980a). Throughout the 1970s this debate rumbled on, and its resolution at times seemed improbable (Anderson, 1978). We believe, however, that there is more room for optimism now than 10 years ago, since rather than deciding in favour of images and against propositions or vice versa, it may make more sense to ask when and in what circumstances, a particular type of representation is needed. It is important that this debate should be resolved as, far from being an esoteric academic matter, it has far-reaching consequences for our understanding of the fundamental ways in which knowledge is represented and used by the cognitive system — surely an important issue! Also, a satisfactory answer to these problems will not only affect neighbouring fields of enquiry within cognitive psychology such as semantic memory, language and perception but will have important repercussions for the Computer Simulation of the higher mental processes.

An issue raised by the imagery debate is the status of introspective reports and data and their place in psychology. It is interesting that a concern with such issues has also arisen in social psychology (e.g. Nisbett and Wilson, 1977). Consequently we wish to re-examine some of our beliefs and attitudes with respect to these data later. Once again, consciousness is closely linked with introspection which brings us back to one of the central themes of this account.

III   The structure of this book

This book is intended as an exploration and review of the areas we have mentioned. It is divided into three main sections. The first after this introduction deals with philosophical and meta-theoretical problems associated with the imagery construct. In particular a brief introduction to the philosophy of mind is provided and a position advanced with respect to consciousness. The role of the latter and points of attachment with other cognitive processes are discussed in Chapter 3, in which our BOSS-consciousness model is introduced. Chapter 4 begins the second section which is largely concerned with the subjective qualities and objective correlates of imagery. The various types of imagery are discussed in Chapter 4 and variations in individuals imagery abilities in Chapter 5. Section II is really a consideration of imagery "from within". The remainder and greater part of the book, Section III, is concerned with theories of imagery, its structure and function and its wider involvement in memory, perception and thinking. Throughout an attempt is made to relate the diverse empirical findings to our theoretical analysis expressed in Chapters 3 and 6.

Section I

Meta Issues

2
Philosophical and methodological problems

I Philosophical accounts of the mind–body relationship

For centuries philosophers have been concerned with the relationship between mental and physical events and processes. They have struggled to clarify the nature of the relationship between the mental and the physical in what is often termed the mind–body problem. A book like ours would be incomplete without some reference to their arguments. We are concerned with the role imagery plays in cognition, but this assumes that mental processes like imagery can influence behaviour. Some philosophers would want to deny this, or at least to point out that the common-sense views of what an image is and how it is used are misguided.

Some qualifications are necessary before beginning to examine the philosophical positions. For two reasons we are not attempting a thorough review of the mind–body issue. First, we are only concerned with the relationship between conscious experience and bodily states. For many philosophers the term "mind" refers to much more than consciousness. For example Armstrong (1968) defines a mental state as "a state of the person apt for bringing about a certain sort of behaviour". Clearly this may be something different from conscious experience. In Chapter 3 the processes of which we are conscious are discussed, and it will be clear that a very large proportion of psychological processes are unconscious. The meaning of the word "mind", as used by many philosophers, is closer to the concept of the cognitive system whose activities in processing information and determining and controlling behaviour are studied by cognitive psychologists. Secondly, a psychologist's expectations of any account of the relationship of mind and body may be different from those of a philosopher. Ideally, the philosopher would like to demonstrate that one account of the mind–body relationship is sensible while all others are self-contradictory in some way. For the psychologist it is necessary only for the account which he adopts to be free from internal inconsistencies and at least as plausible as other accounts. Psychologists would like to know the solution to the mind–body problem, but it is sufficient for their purposes to know that the philosophical position which is implicit in their approach to the study of mental events is not logically flawed. Beyond that, criteria other than those within the province of philosophy will be involved in determining which theories are preferred.

In the following discussion we will use the term "mental" to refer just to conscious events or processes. We are not concerned with wider concepts of mind.

A   The Problem

Why is there a problem over the relationship of mental and bodily events? The problem arises because conscious experiences are very different from physical "things". Mental experiences appear to be not locatable in the world in the same way as physical events. Your mental image may seem to be in your head, but no one would expect to find it if they started poking about in your brain. A pain may be described as in one's toe, but, while the cause of the pain — a blister say — can be observed by someone else on your toe, the pain cannot. Furthermore, if you are unlucky enough to have a toe amputated you may still feel pain in the non-existent toe. Conscious experiences are not "things in the world", but bodies are. How then can mental events come to influence bodily events, if indeed they do? The problem is made worse by the fact that conscious states are experienced by only one person. From this arise the many problems in interpreting the status of reports of conscious experiences. What is the nature of such reports and to what extent can they be trusted? This leads to the question of the nature of introspective reports, and the role they can or should play in psychology. The problems of introspection will be discussed in detail later since they are obviously central in the study of mental imagery. In this section, however, we will review the major accounts of the relationship between conscious experiences and bodily states.

There are two strategies for approaching the mind–body problem. One either assumes that minds and bodies are in some real sense different "things", in which case the problem becomes one of describing the relationship between them, or one assumes that the distinction involves a misunderstanding and that either the mind is really some property of the body, or vice versa, in which case one has to account for the apparently different properties of mental and physical processes. The former approach assumes a dualism of mind and body, while the latter are monist accounts.

DUALIST THEORIES

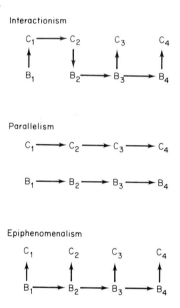

Interactionism

Parallelism

Epiphenomenalism

Fig. 1 The causal relationships between conscious and bodily events, according to three Dualist theories. Conscious events, C_1, C_2, ..., bodily events, B_1, B_2, ...; causal links ⟶.

B   Dualist accounts

1   Interactionism

Of the dualist accounts, the one which is most attractive to common sense is interactionism. Mental experiences are caused by bodily activities, and mental processes may themselves change body processes. So, for example, the physical changes in a decaying tooth will lead to the mental experience of toothache. Similarly, your mental decision to step outdoors leads to your body doing just that. Recently, Popper and Eccles (1977) have advocated an interactionist account. Nevertheless, interactionism has always been faced with several difficulties.

How do mental events come to cause physical changes? How do mental events which are immaterial and not locatable in space come to intervene in the normal causal sequence of the physical world? If mental events do change physical events this seems to imply that on occasions the physical laws which are believed to apply throughout the universe are suspended and the physical events are not predictable from the preceding physical conditions. The importance which one attaches to this problem depends upon one's opinion of the status of man in the universe. It may not worry those who believe that the universe exists so that man can act out the central part in some divine plan. However, it does usually worry those with less theological commitment who see the result of the scientific study of the biology, chemistry and physics of human beings as placing man as a product of the universal physical laws and not as the reason for the universe itself.

Interactionism has also to accept that no account of the relationship between physical events and the mental events that they cause can be given, beyond the bare causal statement. It is a causal relationship which appears to have no comparison in the rest of the world so that generalizations are difficult. And when, it may be asked, in the evolution of man did the interaction process arise? How could it occur? What chance mutation could suspend the physical laws and allow interactions to begin? Does the interference with the normal physical laws take place only in man, or in the higher mammals also?

2   Parallelism

Faced with problems raised by the causal relationship between mental and physical events, some philosophers (e.g. Leibniz, 1934) have suggested that the body and mental events do not causally interact, but run in parallel. Mental events cause other mental events and bodily events cause subsequent bodily events, but the two do not interact. This move seems to require unacceptable damage to the concept of causality. My toothache now has nothing to do with my bad teeth but results from some earlier mental event! Further, it is hard enough to swallow the idea of some Pre-established Harmony which allows the mental and the physical to run together. It is harder still to accept that with each evolutionary change which has affected the body the appropriate harmonious change in the mental flow has taken place for no apparent reason. Similarly it seems odd that when an external cause, such as an injection of chemicals changes our physiology in a novel way, mental changes also occur. Nor is any explanation of the existence of mental events provided in parallelism.

3   Epiphenomenalism

To those who wish to maintain a distinction between mental and physical events, while retaining the view that the physical laws are not suspended by the intervention of mental events, epiphenomenalism has been attractive (e.g. Huxley, 1894). Bodily events are assumed to cause mental events, but not *vice versa*. Mental events do not affect the body. Huxley described our conscious experiences as the smell above the factory.

The attraction of not having to give up the laws of physics when dealing with human behaviour should not obscure the problems of epiphenomenalism. It is no better than parallelism in its arbitrary use of causality. It accepts that my bad teeth cause my toothache but denies that my conscious decision to step outdoors causes my going out. Other, physical, concurrent factors are the ''real'' cause of my going out. Admittedly it is hard to conceptualize the ways in which mental and physical events might cause one another, but if causality is accepted in one direction the basic problem has already been incorporated into the account. If in the same sequence of events the mental and physical events occur in the same order it seems odd to say that the physical are causing the mental while denying that the mental cause the physical. Since it is not possible to empirically manipulate the events to establish empirically the relationship between the events, the *a priori* denial of the causal nature of the mental events seems arbitrary.

Popper has argued (Popper and Eccles, 1977) that epiphenomenalism is inconsistent with the theory of evolution. Epiphenomenalism holds that mental events have no biological function. It cannot, therefore, account for the evolution of consciousness which must be assumed to have occurred without being selected for any value to the organism. Wassermann (1979) has replied that this argument does not refute epiphenomenalism. Natural selection will act upon the physical mechanisms which control behaviour and which (according to epiphenomenalism) produce mental experiences as a by-product. More complex epiphenomena are consistent with the evolution of a more complex nervous system to control the flexibility of behaviour in the higher animals.

Accepting Wassermann's argument, Popper's criticism still highlights the big assumptions which must be made by the epiphenomenalist, namely that contrary to our everyday introspections our mental experiences are irrelevant to our behaviour, and that, by chance, the path of evolution has led to the evolution of brain processes which appear to be so consistent and coherent as to convince many people that these conscious experiences rather than the underlying physical processes are the essential "stuff" of life. Conscious experience may not be of importance, but consider the following joke:

> First the good news — after the operation you will go on doing everything that you did before. Now the bad news — but you will never regain consciousness.

Surely to the individual, conscious experience is more than just a by-product but is central to being a living human being. To the epiphenomalist this should appear a strange state of affairs. Many of the perceptual processes, such as size and shape constancy, the stability of the perceived world during head movements, and so on, could be interpreted as existing to improve the quality and consistency of conscious experience. Possibly these processes have evolved for accurate processing of the world, and the conscious experience has fortunately developed at the same time. Yet smells from factories, squeaks from machinery, and other sorts of epiphenomena normally result in a random mixture of effects. The quality of the conscious epiphenomena is, therefore, surprising if indeed consciousness is really an epiphenomenon.

C Monist approaches

1 Philosophical behaviourism

One attempt at a solution to the problems raised by the dualist accounts of the mind–body relationship is to argue that what is taken to be references to mental events in our everyday talk are, if properly understood, not references to private conscious experience but to observable aspects of behaviour. Since this has implications for our very concept of a mental image, we will deal in more detail with philosophical behaviourism in the later section on Introspection.

Gilbert Ryle (1949) in *Concept of Mind* presented the best known case for philosophical behaviourism. He argued that the dualist's distinction between body and mind, which he called "the dogma of the Ghost in the Machine" involved one big mistake. It represented facts about mental life as if they belonged to one logical type or category when they actually belong to another. One of Ryle's examples of a category mistake is of a foreigner visiting Oxford or Cambridge who, having been shown the colleges, libraries, playing fields, etc., asks "But where is the University?". In fact, the University is not some other institution separate from what the visitor has seen. The University is just the way in which what was seen is organized. Ryle argues that dualists such as Descartes represented the mind as a thing different from, but in some ways similar to the body, so that man's behaviour would not be reduced to the mechanical cause and effect account which was coming to be accepted for the physical world. However, in maintaining that the mind was a thing they were committing the same error as the foreigner at Oxford.

> Somewhat as the foreigner expected the University to be an extra edifice rather like a college but considerably different, so the repudiates of mechanism represented minds as extra centres of causal processes, rather like machines but considerably different from them. (Ryle, 1949, pp.20–21)

Ryle proceeds to try to demonstrate that "when we describe people as exercising qualities of mind, we are not referring to occult episodes of which their overt acts and utterances are effects; we are referring to those overt acts and utterances themselves" (p.26). Ryle argues that words such as "intelligent" describe dispositions to behave in certain ways and not private mental acts. The extent to which Ryle is successful in so analysing concepts such as intelligences is beyond the scope of this book. What is important is whether, even if Ryle does give the correct account of most references to mental processes, his analysis properly captures what we are talking about when we speak of conscious experiences including images as well as pains and other conscious experiences. We will discuss Ryle's account of imaging in the section on Introspection. Here we will just note that many philosophers have maintained that Ryle does not deal satisfactorily with the contents of consciousness. After all his efforts it is just not possible to believe that references to conscious experience are either reducible to dispositions to behave in certain ways, or are logical errors. Critiques of Ryle will be found in Armstrong (1968), Locke (1968), Hannay (1971) and later in this chapter.

Like Ryle, Wittgenstein (1953) argued that we were making errors in understanding the language we use when talking of mental events. From his private language argument, which we discuss more fully in the Introspection section, he deduced that talk about mental experience was not talk about private sensations, but was really based on criteria open to all to observe such as the person's behaviour. We describe later why we do not accept this argument. Like Ryle, Wittgenstein and his followers are driven by their efforts to avoid dualism into strange claims about the status of mental experience. Nevertheless, their efforts help to clarify what can and is being said about mental experience.

2   Identity theory

If the behaviourist's attempt to account for mental states is unsatisfactory then we can turn to one of the more popular solutions to the mind–body problem in recent years. It maintains that consciousness is a brain process (Place, 1956). Proponents of the identity theory (e.g. Smart, 1963; Armstrong, 1968) wish to maintain that those mental experiences which are not easily analysed as dispositions on a behaviourist account are actually brain processes. We cannot use the words that we use for describing mental experiences to replace descriptions of brain processes and *vice versa* because the words have developed with a different logic, but, nevertheless, as a matter of fact they are describing the same things. Examples of such identities are the statements that "a cloud is a mass of tiny particles in suspension" and "lightning is an electrical discharge". The meaning of the words cloud and lightning are not the same as tiny particles in suspension or electrical discharge, but it is a matter of fact that that is what clouds and lightning actually are.

When Place (1956) first proposed the identity theory he claimed that it was a reasonable scientific hypothesis, but since it is impossible to imagine a test which would go beyond showing a perfect correlation between mental events and specific brain processes to actually demonstrate their identity, later proponents of the theory have defended it on the grounds of its not being demonstrably wrong, while being more parsimonious than, for example, epiphenomenalism. The theory's attraction is its escape from the problems of the immaterial nature of mental events which arise for dualist accounts. Its weaknesses are its strong assertion of the relationship of mental and physical states, which can always be questioned, and the difficulty of maintaining that the properties of mental events are such that they could be brain processes. Popper and Eccles (1977) have argued that the Identity Theory shares with epiphenomenalism the problem of why consciousness should have evolved. However, if mental states actually are certain brain processes, and if those brain processes are selected by evolution, then so will be the mental states. What is not explained is why those brain processes that are actually also mental states should have been the ones to be selected, why the special category of brain processes that are mental states should occur in the first place, and why, if evolution works upon the brain states, the mental states should seem to be so coherent and consistent.

Much of the argument around the identity theory concerns what is required for two things to be, in fact, identical. If, however, by identity is means that for A and B to be identical, any property of thing A must as well be a property of thing B, then it is very doubtful if mental events and brain processes could be matched in this way (see e.g. Thomson, 1969, and Kripke, 1971).

3   Double aspect

The account of the body–consciousness relationship which we find most satisfactory is sometimes called double aspect theory. It maintains that mental processes are physical processes experienced "from the inside". It is possible to consider this to be one version of the identity theory, as do Popper and Eccles (1977), or as a form of epiphenomenalism, but we believe that it is best considered separately since it is more satisfactory than some common versions of these accounts.

The double aspect theory can be traced at least to Spinoza (d.1580) although there are many aspects of Spinoza's theory to which we would not subscribe, for example his panpsychism, the belief that all things are conscious if only in a rudimentary way.

We wish to claim that mental experience is what it is like to be a complex system such as a human being, functioning in a certain way. Brain processes are what are observable to someone examining the system, and conscious experience is what the system when operating feels like to itself. We will discuss in Chapter 3 which parts of the cognitive system we believe to be operating when we are conscious.

Among the advantages of this view are that it escapes from the problem of dualism by denying mental processes an *independent* existence while avoiding the denial of the importance or existence of mental states which underlie the identity theory and behaviourism.

Identity theorists do not wish to ascribe any properties to mental experiences which are not ascribable to physical processes. The double aspect theory does accept that mental experience cannot be reduced to physical descriptions. In the functioning of complex organisms as a result of the operation of those organisms' systems, *for* those systems, something new has emerged. It is best, however, not to think of what has emerged as purely epiphenomenal, since, for the organisms concerned, what they are conscious of is the functioning of their own cognitive systems, and that is not an epiphenomenon. It is necessary to recognize that the contrasting of mental and physical events as if they were the same sort of thing is a mistake because they are not comparable. Mental events happen in functioning cognitive systems while physical objects are the things which both may do the functioning and, for the purposes of the systems themselves, are constructs on the basis of which the world is processed and analysed.

The main problem for theories of the relationship of consciousness and the physical world that have arisen in the earlier discussions are: (1) the way mental and physical states are interrelated, given their different natures; (2) accounting for the apparent involvement of conscious mental decisions in the direction of our behaviour; (3) explaining the evolution of the coherent, consistent nature of consciousness. We have already discussed how the double aspect theory deals with (1).

It is also satisfactory in explaining (2) without the "ghost in the machine" of interactionism. If double aspect theory is correct, then the experience of conscious decision-making will be valid and not a mistake, as it would be if epiphenomenalism were true. For the individual, the conscious decision-making *is* the decision making by his or her system. Problem (3) is also minimized since if consciousness is the working of the system it will be coherent and consistent insofar as the system itself functions that way. Consciousness will evolve as parts of the system are selected for by evolution, and since only changes in the functioning of the system which lead to its more adequately coping with the world will be selected, so consciousness will evolve to be consistent and appropriate to the external world. Some problems still remain. Why should the functioning of the system lead to consciousness? Perhaps this is one of those questions which can only be answered by "because that is the way the world is". All explanations must be in terms of other accepted facts, and at the end of the analysis some facts must be taken as so without requiring explanation. Also, it is difficult to know what to expect about the emergence of experience in complex systems, since we only have evidence from the human case.

D   Conclusions

The importance that is attached to mental images will depend upon the status that mental experience holds. We have reviewed briefly the main alternative philosophical accounts of the relationship between mental states and bodily processes. We believe that Double Aspect theory gives the most adequate account of this relationship. If so, then reports of mental experience may play a valuable part in helping to understand cognitive processing since they are reports on that processing, as experienced by the system itself. It is not, however, necessary to accept the double aspect theory for mental images to be worth studying. Even if they are only epiphenomena, they are interesting epiphenomena since our conscious experience is of interest to us even if it plays no role in the way we behave. Also epiphenomenal mental images could serve as indications of the state of the cognitive system even if they have no part in its activities. The smell above the factory can tell you much about what goes on in the factory, even if it does not contribute to the processes inside!

For us to know about the mental states of others, they must report to us what they experience. There are limitations on, and problems with such reports, and it is to them that we now turn.

II   Introspection

A   The problem

To obtain information about someone else's mental images we have to rely upon their descriptions of their experiences. These descriptions can take many forms. They might be verbal descriptions or pictures drawn to represent the image, or simply the pressing of a button to signal the occurrence of an image. However, in all cases, the subject is reporting on experiences which are private to them. This raises problems over the reliability of such reports. Philosophers have questioned their nature and we will discuss Wittgenstein's private language argument later in the chapter. Psychologists in the behaviourist tradition have argued that only publicly observable phenomena are suitable for scientific study so that reports of mental experiences should be excluded from scientific examination (Watson, 1913, 1930; Skinner, 1953). In this section we examine the limitations upon reports of subjective experiences.

B   Early use of introspection in psychology

Studying one's own conscious experience is known as introspection. As a method of collecting data it has a chequered history in Psychology. When Psychology was established as an independent discipline in Germany — the traditional date being the opening of the first psychological laboratory by Wilhelm Wundt at Leipsig in 1879 — it was differentiated from other disciplines as being the scientific study of consciousness. Under carefully controlled conditions, Wundt and his associates required their subjects to describe their conscious experiences when undertaking very simple tasks, such as listening to a metronome. A strong philosophical tradition, stretching back at least to Aristotle, but developed by the British Empiricists including Hobbes, Locke, Hume and John Mill, held that consciousness was composed of raw sensations which became attached to other sensations because they either occurred together in time or were similar to one another. If this was so, it would seem a sensible activity to try to examine and separate sensations to discover the exact conditions which led to their occurrence and their associations with one another. Such analysis was taken to its extreme by Titchener (1908) who demanded that his subjects describe their mental experiences in terms which were not tainted by reference to the object being perceived. If, for example, a subject was asked to introspect upon his experience while looking at a table, his report would be rejected by Titchener as committing *the stimulus error* if it included references to "brown *top*" or "curved *leg*" since "top" and "leg" he considered to be words appropriate for describing the stimulus but not for the raw sensations of which each perception of the table was composed. Titchener proposed that mental experiences should be analysed into simpler and simpler components until they could be decomposed no more, at which point one had reached the level of raw sensations (Titchener, 1908).

C   Assumptions underlying the early introspective research

The analytical introspections with which psychology began required several strong assumptions to be true before the method was worthwhile. The philosophical speculations of the British Empiricists had to be well founded. Even if conscious experience was really the result of sensations being joined through association, it was also necessary that the result could be unpacked again through careful introspection. It might, for example, have been the case that the sensations were not joined in some way analogous to bricks in a wall, but through some sort of mental chemistry, as John Stuart Mill speculated. Just as the end-product of the combination of hydrogen and oxygen in the form of water shows quite different properties to those of the elements of which it is composed so the product of the combinations of sensations might not be decomposible just by inspection of the result. Another assumption was that subjects possessed, or could acquire, a vocabulary suitable for describing their sensations. The errors in these assumptions highlighted the limitations of the introspective method, but also led to a too hasty complete rejection of introspective data.

D   Limitations on introspection

It became obvious before the First World War through the work of psychologists at Wurzberg (see Humphrey, 1951) that many tasks set to subjects are solved without the processes leading to the solution being open to introspection. If asked, for example, to classify *cat* and one responds ''animal'' such conscious experiences as can be reported as occurring before the answer is given are clearly trivial compared to the unconscious processing that must underlie the response. Conscious experience is not explicable solely in terms of associations with other conscious sensations. What is and what is not accessible to introspection is an important question that we will consider later, especially in Chapter 3. The recognition that introspection could not supply all the information necessary to understand consciousness was one of the reasons why the method became discredited. Another was the shift from asking questions about consciousness to asking first about what determines behaviour and later to questions on the nature of cognitive functioning.

The move from the study of consciousness to the study of behaviour as the main object of psychology was justified for many reasons irrelevant to the purpose of this chapter, but at least some of the enthusiasm with which behaviourism was greeted followed from the failure of analytical introspectionism. Not only had little of value come out of the thirty odd years between Wundt's founding of his laboratory and Watson's public launching of Behaviourism in 1913, but the intervening years had produced many disputes between distinguished practitioners of introspection. As Boring once wrote when discussing introspection:

> there is always to be remembered that famous session of the Society of Experimental Psychologists in which Titchener, after a hot debate with Holt, exclaimed: "You can see that green is neither yellowish nor bluish!" and Holt replied: "On the contrary, it is obvious that a green is that yellow-blue which is exactly as blue as it is yellow." (Boring, 1946)

The problem was not that there were disagreements, but over the means of resolving the disagreements. Since Holt and Titchener had no access to the other's conscious experiences all sorts of possibilities were open and unresolvable. They could believe that the other was incompetent at introspection, or was lying for some reason, or perhaps really did have a different experience. Such problems will always exist when using introspection and are not restricted to situations where disagreements occur. Agreement can appear to occur when the subject is lying and perhaps reporting what he believes the experimenter wishes to hear or through inaccurate reporting by the subject. Even so, while the probability of error is higher with introspective data than with some other forms of data in psychology this is not by itself sufficient grounds for its total rejection. Something is better than nothing, and the alternative is to dismiss conscious experience as being completely unsuitable for study. It is usually possible to limit the likelihood of error. It would be possible, for example, to check that Holt and Titchener agreed in the way they used the names of the colours they were discussing. Other evidence for their being likely to lie could be found, and their accuracy in reporting publicly available events could be assessed. It is worth remembering that the reliability of data is a matter of degree. In the last analysis *all* reports of empirical results are open to doubt and deception or error.

It is sometimes argued that the act of introspection will interfere with the processes which are introspected upon, and change them to the point of making the report worthless. Wundt maintained such an argument against the Wurzburg Imageless Thought research

(Humphrey, 1951). There can be little doubt that there is a genuine danger here, and that there are limitations to what can be attended to at any time. However, unless one accepts that the Imageless Thought controversy was itself a demonstration of the dangers, there seem to be no well known examples of introspections critically distorting psychological processes and Ericsson and Simon (1980) found little evidence of alterations in performance in "think aloud" tasks. Advocates of Introspection have always instructed their subjects to regard it as a form of retrospection, and to carry out the task first, then to base their reports upon memories of the experiences which accompanied the task. As such, it involves all the problems of testimony, which will be discussed later. Even so, there seems to be no reason for rejecting introspection because of its potentially interfering effects, while accepting the results of decision tasks, such as pressing one of two keys to indicate whether a string of letters is a word. Such tasks provide the building blocks of cognitive psychology, but like introspections, they incorporate a potentially interfering response with the decision whose latency is being measured.

E   Types of introspections and their limitations

While the use of introspection in psychology has increased again, following its decline during the 1930s–1950s, arguments still occur over its suitability as a method of collecting data. Self reports have been strongly criticized in recent years by, for example, Nisbett and Wilson (1977) and Evans (1980a,b,c). Before turning to these critiques, it is worth drawing some distinctions between different types of introspection and self reports.

One important distinction is whether the person making the report is trying to *describe* their conscious experience, or to *explain* either that experience or their behaviour. It is very easy to slip between these two purposes. The reporter may believe (perhaps correctly, so far as it goes) that the conscious experiences of, say, seeing a road sign, or deciding to turn left were the reasons for subsequent actions. However, because so much of our behaviour is determined by factors not available to introspection there are many occasions when the contents of consciousness has little or no relevance. People often do not know how they did what they did, and are not aware of the processes underlying perceiving, remembering and thinking. If this was not so there would be little need for psychological research. Since people can often explain their own behaviour, both psychologists and their subjects frequently consider it reasonable to ask subjects why they behaved as they did. However, to request that a subject tries to explain their behaviour is not to ask for introspections, even though introspections may be mingled in the answer that is given. Answers to these sorts of questions are, perhaps, best termed *self-hypotheses* (Morris, 1981a). They will incorporate the subjects' observations of their past behaviour and expectations derived from many sources. They may be useful to psychologists, but they are far from the reports of conscious experience which constitute introspection.

Several types of reports do qualify for the label ''introspection''. The differences between them, while not so clear as those between self-hypotheses and introspections, are worth noting, since they may relate to the reliability and value of the introspections.

The most respectable form of introspection has been called the method of impression by Woodworth (1931). Woodworth describes it as ''Apply a stimulus and ask your observer what impression he gets''. This method, coming originally from physics and physiology and the study of light, sound and the sense organs, never fell into quite the same disrepute as other introspections. There were several reasons for this. One is that the method worked for simple reports on well controlled stimuli. It was possible to develop an elaborate psycho-physics linking conscious sensations to physical input (Stevens, 1951). The experiences were open to everyone and were agreed upon by virtually all subjects. The reports were simple, usually stating whether or not two experiences differed, and there was no need to train subjects to teach them to use words which were not already part of their normal vocabulary. None of this, however, alters the fact that the reports were of conscious experiences, private to the individuals in the sense that no one else could examine the experiences upon which the reports were based.

Some behaviourists from Watson onwards rationalized their use of introspections by terming them ''verbal reports'' and claiming that as such they did not differ from other behaviour. Such reports were, obviously, behaviour. However, to treat them as reports implied that they were reports of something, which was to more or less concede the introspectionist's case, while to deny that they were reports seemed bizarre to all but the most committed behaviourist. In reality, many psychologists who called themselves behaviourists and who were impressed by the arguments against the introspective approach of Wundt and Titchener were willing to use the method of impressions, and even more dubious "verbal reports" if they provided sensible, consistent data. Woodworth and Sheehan (1965) noted that in 1958, 44% of research papers in the major American Psychology journals made some use of impression and verbal report.

The behaviourist critique of introspection was developed against the analytical techniques of Wundt and his followers. Such analytical introspections where the trained introspector is necessary and the object is to separate out the elements of the conscious experience was based upon, as we have already commented, strong and incorrect assumptions about the nature of conscious experience. However, even if one admits that it was misguided, boring and sometimes led to disputes which were difficult to resolve, it is not obvious that analytical introspective research was especially different from some subsequent approaches in these respects. Nor does this justify the condemnation of all careful introspection by trained subjects, so long as those involved are aware of the inherent weaknesses of the method, which will be discussed more fully in the next section.

A final type of introspection is the subject's report of their plans, intentions and strategies. These have been the source of much recent debate. Some social psychologists (e.g. Harré, 1979; Gauld and Shotter, 1977) see such reports as a fundamental building block of a realistic psychology, while others (Nisbett and Wilson, 1977; Evans, 1980a,b,c) have collected considerable research which shows that subjects are often unaware of the reasons for their behaviour.

Morris (1981a,b) has analysed the research on which Nisbett and Wilson and Evans base their arguments. The subjects' reports upon which they found their arguments are self-hypotheses rather than introspections. This does not, of course, alter the conclusion that the subjects were unaware of some of the factors influencing their behaviour. The Nisbett and Wilson experiments do not extend to intentional behaviour (see Morris, 1981a); those upon which Evans bases his case have serious methodological weaknesses, described in detail in Morris (1981b). Neither critique successfully demonstrates that people cannot make useful reports upon the plans, intentions and strategies which they are consciously aware of adopting. Several reports of valuable research using such reports of strategy choices will be found in the later chapters of this book.

As a rough generalization, introspections about the conscious awareness of physical stimuli and strategies and intentions seem to be possible, and in some circumstances provide data for the psychologist.

However, psychological processes between these, which seem to represent a low and a high level of cognitive functioning, do not appear to be open to introspection. In the next chapter we will try to clarify what is and what is not consciously perceived. Next, however, we turn to some of the other limitations on introspection.

F   Language limitations on introspective reports

One of the major limitations to introspective reports is the need to communicate the experience in some form that can be understood by others. We may be aware of all sorts of subtle qualities in our conscious experience, but while we may be able to introspect them, we may not be able to convey what we experience in an adequate introspective *report*. The limitations upon what can be said about one's conscious experience follow from the problem of teaching that a given word is used to refer to a particular mental experience. Since only the person having the experience is aware of the experience itself the teacher has to use clues that are available from the situation and the learner's behaviour. In ordinary life this does not present too many problems, and children will use words like "hot", "like" and "hurt" before they are two years old. Nevertheless, the way in which words referring to conscious experiences have to be learnt set several restrictions on what can be said when introspecting.

The first limitation is that names of mental states can only be learned where the mental experience coincides regularly with evidence that is available to others. Pains coincide with cut knees and burned fingers so that it is easy to know when it is appropriate to speak of them (see Fig. 2). However, names cannot be taught for mental experiences which are not so connected with some reliable signs. Two points are worth noting here. First, although a link between external evidence and a mental experience is necessary before it can have a name which others will understand, this does not mean that the evidence and the sensations need always coincide, and the external evidence cannot replace the person's report of his sensations. Bumps and burns may be necessary when the word "pain" is taught, but once a child has learned to attach the name to the experience which usually accompanies such accidents it can be used whenever the sensations occur. Secondly, the evidence used in the teaching of a name for a mental experience need not be the behaviour of the individual, and will probably never depend just upon the individual's behaviour. When, for example, teaching the word

Fig. 2   The girls (A and B) may have different conscious experiences when the stone falls on their fingers. However, they can learn to label such feelings as "hurting" and can use the term later, even if there is no visible evidence that they are in pain.

"hot" to a child who has just touched a hot cup of coffee, it is necessary not only to observe that the child pulls away its hand and cries, but also to know that the cup is hot. For an example of the small part observation of behaviour need play in teaching mental state names, imagine teaching an adult the meaning of "after-image". The point remains, however, that some external evidence must exist before one can begin to teach a name of a mental state, so that the mental state must have quite a high probability of occurring in the situations when you expect it to occur if its name is to be taught. It is possible to stretch the range of vocabulary applicable to mental experiences by analogies to other experiences, as the jargon of wine-tasting and musical appreciation illustrate, but the words used in the analogies must themselves be learned and are therefore limited.

Another limitation that results from the way in which names for mental experiences must be learned is that it is not possible to compare the nature of experiences which people call by the same name. We cannot discover whether you experience pains and tickles and so on just as we do. We learn to call the mental experience that accompanies cuts and burns a pain, but what we actually label pain may be different in nature from one to another. All that is consistent between us is that we use the word "pain" to signal that we are talking about the experience that occurs with cuts and burns etc. Of course, given our considerable similarities one to another in our physiology it may be reasonable to assume that our experiences are similar. People do not often make remarks about their experiences which seem odd to us, as would be the case if their mental states differed markedly from our own. Even so, since we are not able to go beyond either naming mental experiences as "one of those which happen when . . ." or describing them in terms which are learned from shared experiences where the use of the words can be checked and corrected, as in naming colours, it is not possible to convey to others the quality of what we experience.

A final limitation from the way words are acquired is that for words to exist in the vocabularies of subjects in experiments requiring introspections those words must have been previously taught to the subject. For them to have been acquired in everyday life the particular mental experiences must have been sufficiently important in the lives of the subject's linguistic community for names for them to be evolved and taught. We need to tell others about our pains, but there will be insufficient interest in the subtler aspects of experience for an appropriate vocabulary to have developed. Of course, within the limits of what can be taught, new terms could be acquired by subjects in psychology experiments, but in practice such time-consuming activities do not take place.

G   Other limitations on introspections

So far we have considered the problems with introspection which arose in the history of psychology and which follow from the restrictions on describing mental experience. There are other factors that will contribute to inaccuracy of reports which are common to any reports which subjects make. Introspective reports are based on the memories which subjects have for the experiences they had. As with all such testimony, for something to be recalled it must have been initially encoded, and what is encoded and retrievable depends on the activities of the subject at the encoding stage (e.g. Morris, 1978a). As with the memory reports of eye-witnesses, it is likely that accuracy will be highest with free narrative recall, but then much may be omitted by the subject. If questions are asked, these may bias the responses and influence what is recalled (see e.g. Bull and Clifford, 1979). Then there is the traditional problem of the extent to which paying attention to one's experiences during a task may interfere with and alter the way the task is performed. This will be discussed further in Chapter 3.

To maximize the accuracy of subjective reports one would attempt to meet the following conditions.

1   The report should be possible in ordinary language or in terms that can be easily taught.

2   The report should be made as soon as possible after the experience which is being reported.

3   Demand characteristics should be minimized by avoiding direct questioning whenever possible, by making any questions as neutral as possible, and by not communicating the purpose of the experiment through a transparent experimental design.

4   The subjects should clearly understand that they are being asked to report their experiences, and not to speculate on how they undertook the given task.

5   Subjects should be aware that they may not have any relevant experiences to report, and that this is not a failing on their part.

Given these principles the most obvious likely errors should be minimized, but may and will, of course, still occur. That is inevitable with introspective data. However, its value should outweigh its failings.

We do not wish to debate whether introspective reports can be described as data suitable for scientific study, since we believe that attempts to define the limits of what is called scientific are of little relevance to anyone other than those interested in the meaning of the word "science" itself. What is important is that one should attempt to obtain the most reliable information possible, and that the information is sufficiently trustworthy for it to be used to develop and then test hypotheses without too great a fear of inherent weaknesses invalidating the whole activity. The result may or may not be describable as science, but it will lead to an increase in our knowledge.

H   Philosophical objections to the basis of introspection

In the previous section we mentioned that Ryle and Wittenstein have argued that it is quite misleading to consider reports of mental experiences, such as mental images, as reports of private objects or events experienced only by the one person. Since in the rest of the book we will often treat subject reports in this way it is necessary to explain why we do not accept the arguments of Ryle and Wittenstein.

1   Ryle

Imagining is one activity that provides problems for Ryle. Because it is the theme of this book, and because it illustrates the efforts of a behaviourist philosopher to analyse talk about conscious experience without admitting the existence of events of a special nature, and because some psychologists still accept Ryle's account (e.g. Evans, 1980a,b), we will discuss Ryle's treatment of imagery in some detail.

Ryle argues that imagining is not the seeing of mental pictures. "Having a mental picture of Helvellyn . . . is actually a special case of imagining, namely imagining that we see Helvellyn in front of our noses . . ." (p.242). While not denying the appropriateness of visualizing as a proper and useful concept, Ryle claims that the use of such terms does not mean that there is some sort of picture which we contemplate: "Roughly, imaging occurs, but images are not seen" (p.234).

Ryle begins by pointing out that there is a difference between seeing and visualizing; the latter can be done in the dark or with shut eyes, while we can see only what there is to be seen. The difference, he says, is often marked by putting inverted commas round "see" when talking of imaging. Also, adjectives like "vivid", "faithful" and "lifelike" may be used of "seeing" one's childhood home, but not of seeing what is in front of your nose. So, according to Ryle, a person who "sees" something knows that he is doing something "totally different in kind from seeing" (p.233). The fact that in deliriums etc. people may think they are seeing when they are only "seeing" does not obliterate the distinction any more than problems distinguishing an authentic from a forged signature removes the distinction between signing and forging.

Ryle claims that when talking of images, we inadvertently subscribe to the theory that "seeing" is seeing after all, and accept that there is a genuine likeness which is seen as oil paintings are seen.

Ryle's distinction between seen and "seen" is quite inadequate to prove that they are "totally different in kind". The fact that seeing and "seeing" are very much alike is implied by the use of the same word when describing both. Certainly the conditions under which they take place differ and everyone sensibly acknowledges the fact. The inverted commas around "see" indicate that we do not intend claiming that what we are "seeing" is out there in the world, but that does not show that the *experiences* of seeing and "seeing" differ in themselves. Ryle's only grounds for claiming a difference is his claim that words like "vivid", "faithful" and "lifelike" are used of images but are inapplicable to seeing. This argument collapses when it is recognized that such adjectives are used of representations, a class which includes pictures, statues and models as well as some mental images. Many things which are seen, if they are representations, can be described as "faithful" etc. What is more, not all images are representations. If I happen, perhaps after a blow on the head, to "see" coloured patches, that image is not of anything, and words like "faithful" and "lifelike" would be quite inappropriate. Even Ryle's forgery example tells against him, because what is interesting there is that the end results of signing or forging may be indistinguishable even though the processes of production may differ. Just as in seeing and "seeing" there is a difference between signing and forging which should not be obscured, yet the products of signing and forging, and of seeing and "seeing" may be the same.

Ryle tries to ridicule the view that visualizing involves seeing something by taking the example of a child who imagines her wax doll smiling: "the picture of the smile is not where the doll's lips are, since they are in front of the child's face. So the imagined smile is not on the doll's lips at all. Yet this is absurd" (p.235). It is absurd if you agree with Ryle in rejecting the existence of both images and percepts. If, however, one accepts that the perception of the doll's face is the result of processes which produce and include a conscious percept, then there is nothing odd in suggesting that the child's percept is modified by a "top-down" intervention (Norman, 1976) in the processing which leads to a percept of a doll which is smiling.

Ryle argues that images are analogous to mock murders. Mock murderers pretend to, seem to, commit murders but there are no actual murders taking place, and questions about, for example, the disposal of the victim are spurious. Similarly, Ryle argues, "There is no answer to the spurious question 'Where do the objects reside that we fancy we see?' since there are no such objects" (p.237).

Of course, Ryle is trivially correct when he argues that what goes on when we imagine that we see a tree differs from actually seeing a tree in that no tree exists. This, however, no more disposes of the existence of mental images than the following argument disposes of the existence of oil paintings. Where, one might say, when looking at the Mona Lisa, is this woman I fancy I see? A spurious question, of course, since even when paintings are of objects, the objects do not receive some strange existence of their own. However, if this argument disposes of the existence of the Mona Lisa, then the visitors to the Louvre are in for a surprise. What it illustrates is that Ryle's argument has nothing to say about the existence or otherwise of the representation itself—whether a mental image or a painting.

Not only do Ryle's arguments fail to dispose of the existence of mental images, they contain within them references which seem to assume that images exist in at least some reasonable use of "exist". Even mock murders involve some action which mimics the real thing. A mock murder is not a real murder, but it is a real event. Words like "faithful" and "lifelike" which Ryle uses of images assume a comparison between a representation and the real thing. If the representation does not exist, then no comparison can be made and the words are inappropriate. With the existence of the representations already implicit in Ryle's account it is not surprising that his arguments come to nothing.

2   Wittgenstein and the private language argument

Wittgenstein's (1953) cryptic style has always made it difficult to be sure exactly what he was and was not saying. What follows may not do him justice, and it certainly omits many of his important insights. It will, we hope, nevertheless explain why we do not accept that the private language argument demonstrates the impossibility of reporting on private objects.

The argument may be summarized as follows.

1   A language must have publicly checkable rules.
2   A private language would not have publicly checkable rules.
3   A private language is impossible.
4   Any reference to "private objects" such as mental images of which only one person can be aware would involve a private language.
5   Reference to private objects such as mental images is impossible.

The rules must be publicly checkable, according to Wittgenstein, because if they were private there would be no difference between a rule being kept and the person merely thinking it has been kept. Appealing to memory will not help, "Always get rid of the idea of the private object in this way: assume that it constantly changes but that you do not notice the change because your memory constantly deceives you" (Wittgenstein, 1953). Memory is not a check because "Justification consists in appealing to something independent" (p.265).

There are many points at which the argument may be criticized. The basis for (1) is that there must be a difference between a word being correctly and incorrectly used. However, it does not necessarily follow that for a language to be used it must be possible to *detect* all, or even any errors. Of course, if many errors occurred communication would break down. However, that merely shows the desirability, not the necessity, of checks. The superiority of public checks can also be questioned since it is possible to doubt the reliability of any public or private criteria in the way Wittgenstein invites us to doubt our memories.

It is not clear exactly why Wittgenstein believed (4). He appears to have believed that references to private objects would not be open to public checks. He remarked that "An 'inner process' stands in need of outward criteria" (p.580). Here it is worth distinguishing between what is required for the meaning of a word to be taught, the meaning itself and the thing to which it refers. To teach the name of a private object it is necessary to have grounds for believing the learner possesses (is experiencing) the private object. However, the means required for the teaching of the name are not its meaning. We may need to see a child touch what we know to be a hot cup and withdraw its hand swiftly and start to cry before we can say "I expect that hurt" etc. The meaning of hurt, pain etc. are not the criteria I need for teaching, but the private experiences, for which I wish to teach the name. By pain we mean the sensation I get when I am wounded that makes we want to cry etc. It is possible to check the use of words like ''pain'' since if they are used by someone only when laughing and never when injured, we would doubt their knowledge of the meaning of the word. The use of the words is, therefore publicly checkable. Since it is possible to reject both (1) and (4), it is not necessary to accept the conclusion (5). Other reasons for doubting the argument are the dubious alternative accounts of talk about private experience into which Wittgenstein and his followers such as Malcolm (1959) are forced by their conclusions, but they are beyond the scope of this book (see e.g. Locke, 1968).

3
Consciousness

In Chapter 2 we concluded that the most satisfactory account of the status of consciousness was that it was what it was like to be the human cognitive system while in operation. In this chapter we will develop this idea, and try to locate more precisely which parts of the system are involved when we experience what we call consciousness. One major reason for the chapter is to try to place mental imagery in its proper context. We hope that by relating conscious experience to aspects of the functioning of the cognitive system it will be possible to understand the nature of the different types of mental images that we will discuss in later chapters.

A further purpose of the chapter is to clarify the issue of when introspective reports may be of use in helping to explain cognitive processing. It is obvious, as we pointed out in Chapter 2, that we are not conscious of many of the processes that go on within our cognitive systems. Under pressure from experimenters, or even deluded by their mistaken expectations about their knowledge of their own cognitive systems, subjects may appear to report on the contents of their consciousness when they are actually offering guesses as to what they think they ought to experience. If it is possible to identify situations in which introspection may be worthwhile and those when it will not, it will help to avoid unnecessary erroneous reports.

I What are the features of consciousness?

As the first step to linking consciousness with cognitive activity we will begin by listing some of the properties of the contents of consciousness. The purpose is not to try to give a complete account of all the aspects of consciousness, which would be an enormous undertaking. Rather, it is to highlight the type and range of elements of consciousness that need to be captured by any adequate attempt to deal with its role. It will then be possible to see how well some other accounts of the place of consciousness capture these aspects.

To begin with the most obvious, but also, as will be seen later, one of the sometimes overlooked components of consciousness, we are conscious of perceiving the external world. We are aware, unless we unfortunately suffer from some damage to our perceptual systems, of several different types of information about the external world. We experience a visual array extremely rich in details of texture and colour. However, the most immediate feature of this experience is that we see a three-dimensional world of objects. In so far as we can analyse our experiences for the properties that objects possess, such as their colour, this is, in a sense, secondary. We do not see the world as composed of physical objects made up from simple sensations, as might be expected from the British Empiricist tradition in philosophy, but as physical objects which have certain properties.

Information from the other senses does not seem to have the same richness as that from vision, but nevertheless, sounds are usually heard as more than just raw noise. We hear dogs barking, cars passing, and so on. Similarly, tastes, smells and sensations of touch are usually experienced as *of* something.

Some psychologists have made a distinction between cognitive processes and their products, and have argued that we are only ever conscious of the products of cognitive processes. Neisser (1967) for example, says of perceptual processing "The constructive processes themselves never appear in consciousness, their products do" (p.56). Similarly, Mandler (1975) states "There are many systems that cannot be brought into consciousness, and probably most systems that analyse the environment in the first place have this characteristic. In most of these cases, only the products of cognitive and mental activities are available to consciousness" (p.245). This process/product (or process/content) distinction has attracted criticism (Smith and Miller, 1978; White, 1980) because the terms are sufficiently vague for the interpretation of any given example to be classified as a process or a product as it suits the classifier. For example, Smith and Miller (1978) claim that Nisbett and Wilson (1977) accept "knowledge of prior idiosyncratic reactions to a stimulus category" (Nisbett and Wilson, 1977, p.258) as mental content and available to the individual, while describing as a process, and unavailable to subjects, the influence of the presence of other people upon helping behaviour (cf. Latane and Darley, 1970). Smith and Miller comment that the only reason for labelling the first as content and the second as process is that people may, in general, be able to report on the first but not the second. In other words, Nisbett and Wilson's argument is circular.

Nevertheless, even though it is not possible to give exact criteria for distinguishing a product from a process, and even though this could lead to confusions and deceptions, we should not miss the central point which the distinction attempts to capture. We know that considerable processing and analysis must go on of which we are not conscious, and the content of consciousness seems most appropriately described in terms of elements which must represent a high level of analysis and integration of information. The degree of our lack of awareness of the process underlying conscious perception is best illustrated by imagining attempting to simulate the processes (perhaps on a computer). Using just our knowledge from our introspections we would not know where to start. The difficulties encountered by those who have tried to model the perceptual processes confirms that in general we do not have access to the processes. If, however, we had to check the adequacy of some attempted simulation by comparing its products to our own experiences, we would not feel this to be an impossible, nor, probably, a difficult task. For example, if a computer simulation outputs visual displays to represent the form a visual experience was predicted to take under some circumstances, we would have no problem in comparing the actual experiences we had with the computer output and commenting upon the accuracy of the simulation. So while it would be a mistake to overemphasize the process/product distinction it does help to illustrate the nature of some of our conscious experience.

As well as those experiences which seem to come directly from the external world there are those which, while often initiated by external causes are not experienced as "things out there". These include the phenomenal aspects of emotions, the feelings that go with anger, fear, happiness and so on. They also include experiences which appear to share some of the properties of externally initiated experience, but which we normally know are not of things out there. These are the experiences such as mental visual images, tunes "in one's head" and what is sometimes called sub-vocal speech. This name is misleading because it is not speech that is some way *below* normal speech as a whisper might be. The individual ''hears'' it loud and clear, and no one else would hear it whatever amplifiers were used. Here the term ''mental voice'' will be used.

There are also conscious experiences which are linked to our bodily state, such as feeling hot, or tired or hungry; and there are more specific experiences, including pains associated with parts of our bodies.

Thinking and decision-making are to an extent interwoven with some of the types of mental experiences already mentioned, including the mental voice, mental images and emotions. However, there is more to the conscious experience of thought than the occurrence of mental words and images. William James (1890) remarked upon the flights and perches of thought, where the conclusions of a piece of thinking were available for introspection while the processes which led up to the conclusion seemed to pass so quickly, like the flight of a bird, that they could not be reported in detail. As with our perceptions of the external world, there is a worthwhile distinction, however difficult to pin down exactly, between what is the conclusion of a process, which may be introspectible, and the process itself, which frequently, if not always, is not. We are often aware of decisions we have taken, and of the current object of our behaviour, but it is not so easy to introspect upon how the decision was made.

If we turn from the contents to the more general features of consciousness there are several frequently noted aspects which should be captured by any good account of consciousness. One is the unitary nature of conscious experience, in that, for all its diversity, it has a coherence and consistency which, as was remarked in Chapter 2 must always puzzle an epiphenomenalist. Another is its continuity, except during those parts of sleep when one is not dreaming, and, of course, sleep and dreams must also be accounted for. During waking hours, we are aware of planning what we are going to do, of monitoring what we are doing and of fantasizing what could be done.

Breaking this continuous flow of higher cognition is very difficult, although diverting it into new channels is, as everyone knows, all too easy and daydreams can occur at most times (Singer and Antrobus, 1972). The control of these thought processes is one object of meditation and relaxation therapies, and it is often suggested that these techniques do not so much stop the processes as side track them into a small loop line (see e.g. Mandler, 1975 and Ornestein, 1972). Meditation and deep relaxation require considerable practice. One result of skill in the techniques is awareness of properties in things commonly experienced which have not been noticed before. These and other altered states of consciousness received much attention during the 1960s and 1970s and discussions of consciousness in many modern introductory textbooks (e.g. Hilgard *et al.*, 1979) are largely devoted to subject reports of changes in their conscious experience following drugs, meditation or sensory deprivation. It may, however, be misleading to place too much emphasis upon these experiences when trying to give an account of consciousness. Any such account should be able to incorporate these findings, but it need not assume that they are central to the functions with which consciousness is associated. One of the features of all the techniques which lead to altered states of consciousness is that they all involve an interference with the usual conditions in which we are conscious. What is experienced is probably the result of the cognitive system functioning abnormally. Evolutionary selection can hardly be imagined for altered states of consciousness that follow meditation or sensory deprivation!

One commonly recognized feature of consciousness is that new tasks seem to require our full conscious attention while well practised tasks can often be carried out without our being aware of them. When learning to drive one is aware of having to concentrate upon too many new skills, steering, changing gear and so on. It is often difficult also to listen to the driving instructor, and rarely possible to carry out a conversation with him. Skilled drivers, however, can drive while thinking of something else so that afterwards they cannot remember any details of their road. They can carry on conversations and may only cease them at particularly difficult situations, such as new, busy roundabouts. For a well practised skill, attempting to consciously follow how it is done may lead to its deterioration, a fact exploited by Steven Potter (1948) in the Primary Hamper of *Gamesmanship*. Here the purpose is to draw your opponent into consciously examining the highly skilled act which is the basis of their superior performance, such as their golf or tennis swing. Why learning a new skill should at first appear to require conscious attention, and later to be independent of it or even inhibited by it, is an important point with which any theory of consciousness must cope.

One aspect of consciousness which interested both William James and Wilhelm Wundt was the way that one component of current conscious experience may be attended to and seem to be particularly clearly perceived, while other elements might be only vaguely experienced. Wundt called the clear perception through attention *apperception*.

In Chapter 2 we concluded that introspections seemed more reliable for reports of the impressions that stimuli make and for accounts of strategies and intentions than for describing the cognitive processes of perceiving, remembering and thinking. This is captured within the BOSS account. The method of impression enquiries about the conscious experience of information made available for BOSS; questions about strategies and intentions tap the information which BOSS itself records of its own decisions and instructions. The processing which leads up to the display of this information is not introspectable, and efforts to draw subjects into commenting on such processes lead to the errors by subjects chronicled by Nisbett and Wilson (1977) and Evans (1980a,b,c).

II   Cognitive processes not consciously experienced

There is evidence from many sources that much processing can go on without conscious awareness. In their review of perception without awareness Dixon and Henley (1980) refer to eleven different areas of research including subliminal perception, binocular rivalry, selective attention and visual search. There is a vast amount of evidence for the influence of stimuli which are not consciously perceived upon other perceptions and on behaviour. The following are just a selection of examples.

Using dichotic listening, where subjects have to repeat the message being played to one ear they cannot normally report the words played concurrently to the other ear (e.g. Moray, 1959). However, when the words in the unattended ear come from a class which has previously been associated with electric shocks, even though the subjects cannot report the words, they do show galvanic skin responses which do not occur to control words (Corteen and Wood, 1972; Forster and Govier, 1978). The early work of Corteen and Wood suggested that semantic generalization occurred in the non-attended channel, so that words from the same category as those originally conditioned, evoked a response. Forster and Govier, however, demonstrated that only words which were phonemically similar produced any responses. This implies that non-attended material is processed though maybe not so thoroughly as attended. Whether or not deeper processing of non-attended material following practice occurs, remains to be seen. That the unattended message must be processed to a considerable degree though is shown by the way that subjects will switch to shadowing the message in the "unattended" ear if the message they are shadowing is switched to that ear during a meaningful sentence (Treisman, 1960). Subjects will then return to the correct ear at the end of the sentence, and are unaware of their changeovers.

A subliminal stimulus word, "happy" or "sad", will influence the perception of a neutral face (Somekh and Wilding, 1973). While words which are not consciously perceived can disambiguate other words (e.g. Henley, 1976) they can also increase the time taken to respond to another word (e.g. Lewis, 1970; Treisman et al., 1974). The increase occurs in tasks where the unattended word may compete with the response word. We are rarely conscious of more than one meaning of a homophone or homograph at any given time. However, several behavioural indicators suggest that both word senses are activated (Conrad, 1974; Warren and Warren, 1976).

When summarizing research on unconscious processes in reading, Allport (1979) concluded that "the experimental results . . . very clearly indicate . . . that *activation of lexical or semantic demons is not in itself a sufficient condition for conscious perception a word*" (p.79).

Just as we are not conscious of much that goes on when processing stimuli during perception, we are also not conscious of the processes which control our actions. We may be aware of planning our actions at a gross level such as going to post a letter, standing up from a chair, and so on. However, we have very little awareness of the complex and subtle processes which control these actions. Even a simple action such as picking up a cup from a table requires the integration of current perceptual information with already existing programmes for controlling arm and hand movements, and the construction of an appropriate motor response for this particular situation. We are aware of none of these processes. In discovering how they take place, introspections are rarely examined by experimenters since they have been found to be of little or no value. It is through the study of practice, the availability and type of feedback, and the patterns of errors that the processes have to be investigated (see Harvey and Greer, 1980, for a recent review of motor control). By studying the form and distribution of errors in skills such as typing, speaking or writing it is possible to identify the hierarchical structuring involved in constructing the response (e.g. Shaffer, 1975). Subjects are not aware of such structuring, though they may be able to explain pauses in speaking as resulting from searching for a word.

It is interesting that people *are* able to report on the accuracy of some action like throwing a dart even when they are not able to see the result (Henderson, 1975). It would appear that the results of the comparison of expectancies and the actually occurring intrinsic feedback can be consciously experienced.

III   Models of the cognitive system

If we are to locate consciousness within the cognitive system we need to know how that system operates. However, there is little agreement among cognitive psychologists upon how the human cognitive processes function. There is not even agreement upon the terms in which the system should be described. Most cognitive psychologists prefer to investigate small aspects of the system which they believe they can model with some hope of success, and leave to the future the determination of its overall structure. There have, however, been some general themes common to many accounts of the system, and these will be sketched in this section as a prelude to reviewing a number of accounts of the place of consciousness in the system.

Until relatively recently most models of the processing of input to the system have been represented as flow charts between a succession of boxes which represent either processes or structures in the system which carry out the processing. What goes on in the boxes has often been only vaguely specified. An example of such a model is the Pandemonium model of item recognition (Selfridge, 1959). Perhaps best known of all such models was the modal model of memory of the 1960s (Murdock, 1971) illustrated in Fig. 3 where information passed through sensory memory to short-term memory and on to long-term memory. It was gradually recognized, however, that the system is not so passive as such models assume. Processing of inputs does not just involve the analysis of the stimulus, step by step, working from

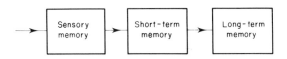

Fig. 3   The modal model of memory

peripheral analysers of the physical stimulation up at last to a construction of the stimulus. In addition to the latter, which Norman (1976) has called "bottom-up" processes, there are what he calls "top-down" processes where the system generates hypotheses about the likely input, and directs the analysis to test whether the hypothesis is correct. One result of the recognition of the importance of higher level processes was Neisser's (1976) proposal of a perceptual cycle where input from the environmental continuously influences the schema which the cognitive system brings to analyse the input, while the schema themselves determine expectations about the world and are selectively open to new input from the world. This view led Neisser to an account of imagery to which we will return later.

A general trend in the models which followed the early information flow accounts was to postulate a general purpose, limited capacity central processor. The analogy with the structure of digital computers helped to encourage this, and interpretations of performance with competing tasks have frequently incorporated a limited capacity central processor (e.g. Moray, 1967; Kahneman, 1973). Some recent models of memory and problem solving also include such a device (Hitch, 1980; Ericsson and Simon, 1980). However, the evidence for such a central processor is not compelling. It is possible to interpret studies of attention in other ways (Allport, 1980).

Recently, production systems have been popular as the building blocks of some cognitive models (Allport, 1979, 1980). In its basic form a production system has two main components, a long-term memory and a data base. The long-term memory consists of *condition* → *action* (if → then) rules or productions. The data base represents the system's current active knowledge. A production rule is activated if its *condition* is matched by the current state of the data base. When activated the *action* can be applied to the information in the data base. So, a production for a gear change while driving might be *IF: the car is in third gear; and going faster than 25 mph; and the road is clear; and I am accelerating THEN: depress clutch; move gear stick to bottom right position; release clutch.* If the IF condition is fulfilled then the THEN action can be carried out.

Production systems can compute anything computable (Anderson, 1976) and they have been used to model language recognition (Reddy, 1975), problem-solving (Newell and Simon, 1972) and memory (Anderson, 1976). Such systems are especially attractive for their ability to handle very large amounts of informal information acquired piece meal. One major feature is that there is no executive system.

Those productions which have access to the most important or best data or resources take control.

While production system models emphasize the value of processing which is based upon a large number of components all of equal status, others have pointed out the value for the cognitive system that would accrue from a hierarchical structure. Broadbent (1977) claims that Craik, Bartlett and the other early workers on information processing assumed that the human processing system operated on many levels, some modifying or controlling the operations of others. Craik, writing in the 1940s, pointed out that when the Commander-in-Chief of Fighter Command orders a sweep over some area, he does not have to add that Spitfire number so and so must have so many gallons of petrol, have loaded guns, cleaned plugs and so on. These are delegated to subordinates. Craik (1966) argued that in just the same way, for rapidity and certainty of action certain units of activity such as walking, using words, or balancing should be delegated to lower levels. Koestler (1967) has reviewed the way in which all organic systems appear to be hierarchically organized, including human physiology.

It may be that some combination of the hierarchical control structure of systems which within themselves function heterarchically with no prior dominant organization, in the manner of production systems, will eventually provide the best accounts of cognitive structure. At the present time the issue seems likely to remain unresolved. The complexities involved in simulating sufficiently rich, varied and adaptive human behaviour are such that it is unlikely that the strengths and limitations of different systems in providing a complete model of human cognition will be fully tested.

IV   Some accounts of the place of consciousness in the cognitive system

In this section we will discuss only those theories on the place of consciousness which refer to models of the cognitive system. We will concentrate upon more recent and influential speculations. Nevertheless, the reader will see similarities to Freud's concept of the ego (e.g. Freud, 1927), and few of the authors quoted below would disagree with James' remark in 1890 that "The distribution of consciousness shows it to be exactly such as we might expect in an organ added for the sake of steering a nervous system grown too complex to regulate itself" (p.144).

In the days of information flow models of cognition, the fact that the contents of consciousness had the property of appearing as a product of complex processing suggested that "conscious awareness is itself rather late in the sequence of mental processing" (Posner and Boies, 1971, p.407). While some psychologists held this view, others believed that we could be conscious of processes taking place very early in the system. The iconic image (Sperling, 1960; Neisser, 1967) was regarded as a mechanism for holding input while it was awaiting processing, and the iconic image itself was often assumed to be consciously perceived so that reports of the conscious perception of the stimulus were used in some methods of estimating the duration of the icon (e.g. Haber and Standing, 1969). Given that the conscious experience in such experiments was always of some categorized item (letters etc.) while the information in the icon is pre-categorical, this was always a dubious assumption, and it has been convincingly attacked by Coltheart (1980).

Several of the proponents of a separate short-term memory system (e.g. Waugh and Norman, 1965) argued that consciousness and the short-term store were closely related in that short-term memory was memory for information still in consciousness — a view derived from William James (1890).

According to Mandler (1975), who discussed the "Uses of Consciousness", consciousness intervenes in the testing of potential actions. "It is possible for the cognitive system to call for the testing of specific outcomes while temporally blocking the output from the system as a whole" (p.53), so that various outcomes can be compared. He claims that one of the functions of the "consciousness mechanism" is to bring two or more previously unconscious mental contents into juxtaposition. "The phenomenal experience of choice, as a matter of fact, seems to demand exactly such an occurrence. We usually do not refer to a choice unless there is a "conscious" choice between two or more alternatives" (p.53). He asserts that ". . . practically all novel relational orderings require that the events to be ordered must be simultaneously present in the conscious field" (p.54).

Mandler also claims that consciousness participates in the retrieval of information from long-term memory, and in the construction of storable representations of current activity. He points to conscious coding activities such as the formation of mental images. He also emphasizes limitations upon the capacity of consciousness, and links these with limitations upon attention. He notes that "Consciousness (or attention) is highly selective" and that "attention theorists have been concerned primarily with the filtering mechanisms that reduce the sensory information to the few chunks of information that reach consciousness'' (p.58).

In summary, Mandler emphasizes both the limited capacity of consciousness and its executive role in planning and controlling behaviour.

Posner (1978) links consciousness with a central processing system of limited capacity. He argues that ''conscious awareness is a discrete event that plays a specific role within the stream of information processing'' (p.180). Earlier, he specifies that this ''discrete event'' is related to central processor functioning when he suggests that ''the central processor can be viewed as an isolatable system related . . . to the ability to provide introspective reports'' (p.152). Posner distinguishes ''active attention'' from other forms of information processing, and implies that attention, consciousness and the functioning of the limited capacity central processor are essentially the same things. He reviews several experiments where interference can be demonstrated between two tasks, and attributes this interference to competition for the central processor, or the need to switch attention. He has less evidence to link phenomenal experience with the central processor. He does, however, point to studies of visual dominance as evidence that one code can control awareness. In these studies, distortions of the visual information, by prisms for example, lead to incorrect reports of the position, size or shape of objects which the subjects can both see and feel. Such evidence though is hardly conclusive in linking consciousness, attention and the postulated central processor.

Posner (1978) discusses the reasons for the evolution of a conscious control mechanism. One role, he suggests, is to inhibit pathways in the nervous system so that action patterns can be suppressed. Another role is to co-ordinate the activity of processing systems which are modality-specific (e.g. visual and auditory). A third ''role for consciousness'' Posner suggests is to abstract patterns of behaviour that have been acquired for a particular function and to use them in new ways.

Accounts such as Posner's are not restricted to psychologists but are sometimes offered by physiologists. So, for example, John (1976) asserts that

Consciousness is a process in which information about individual modalities of sensation and perception is combined into a unified multidimensional representation of the state of the system and its environment and is integrated with information about memories and the needs of the organism, generating emotional reactions and programs of behaviour to adjust the organism to its environment (p.4).

Some comments upon the accounts of Mandler, Posner and John are necessary. First, while they all point to complex processes which must be carried out by the cognitive system, we have little more evidence than their own assertions that consciousness itself is central to these functions. Certainly we are conscious of some aspects of thinking and planning, and to suggest that all attending and decision-making was unconscious would be bizarre. Nevertheless there is a danger of over-emphasizing the executive place of processes of which we are conscious. For one thing, this ignores the very rich visual, acoustic, tactile etc. conscious experience of the world, which may be used in making decisions, but is not *prima facie* the result of executive functioning.

Secondly, these accounts emphasize limited capacity. It is true that in some situations the cognitive system has problems coping with all the input information. It is also true that we can consciously attend to only part of the input information. But to claim, as Posner (1978) does, that "the key to understanding the nature of conscious attention is its limited capacity" (p.153) can be misleading. It may be true of attention, but it is not necessarily true of consciousness. Against the emphasis upon limited capacity by these cognitive psychologists should be placed the richness and variety of, especially, visual experience. The visual world of which we are conscious at any given time is so full and varied in its objects with their colours, tones, component parts and so on that it is virtually impossible to know how to describe it as limited in capacity.

Thirdly, there is a tendency for Mandler, Posner and John to use the term "consciousness" as if it referred to a particular part of the cognitive system, rather than as a result of the functioning of the system. So Mandler (1975) writes of "Some Uses of Consciousness", "the functions of consciousness" and says that "consciousness makes possible" the modification of long-term plans etc. Posner (1978) writes of "consciousness as a mechanism" (p.181). The danger is that this will lead to an emphasis upon consciousness rather than upon the cognitive processes which result in consciousness. Then it becomes very difficult to make any progress, since consciousness is not something we know how to incorporate into our theorizing. It *may* be necessary to give consciousness so central a place, but as yet no one has suggested either *how* consciousnes makes possible any sort of cognitive functioning which could not be carried out by an unconscious system, nor, indeed, any way in which consciousness *per se* could contribute at all! To discuss the uses, functions and mechanisms of consciousness without having any idea of how consciousness, as opposed to the cognitive processes which are taking place when consciousness occurs, actually contributes to the functioning, is at best, misleading. It is misleading because it mistakes the nature of consciousness. Consciousness is not a "thing" which can play a causal role in cognitive processing, it is the experience of the processing itself.

The models which have been considered so far as those which claim an executive, integrative function for consciousness. One alternative account is that of Shallice (1972). He links consciousness with the functioning of action systems. Shallice sub-divides the cognitive system into perceptual, motivational, effector systems, and a set of action systems. In Shallice's terms, action systems are systems which "operate so as to attain a goal, by means of output to effector units or other action systems". They are the control systems, similar to Miller *et al.*'s (1960) TOTEs which control actions such as hitting, running, and drinking. At any one time, one action system will be strongly activated and dominant while others will be inhibited. The efficiency of an action system's operations depends upon its level of activation, with the minimum necessary for normal functioning depending on its complexity and the extent to which it has been learned. Action systems have their goal set and are activated by selector input which may come from the perceptual or motivational systems or from other action systems. This selector input must be stored in a memory so that the goal and activation of the action system are retained without requiring continual input and so that subsequently the appropriate action systems may be activated and their goals set after this particular system's action is complete. Shallice postulated that selector input to dominant action systems are stored in a memory.

Shallice suggested that consciousness is identical with the selector input to the dominant action system. When one is conscious of X a certain action system is receiving selector input which represents X. Shallice suggests that percepts are the result of selector input from the perceptual system, while intentions are selector input from a previously dominant action system. The lack of conscious content of much processing occurs, according to Shallice, because an action system only requires selector input at the beginning of its operation, it can operate with little or no input. We are not conscious of processes connected with lower level skills as those are always directly controlled by effector units. The automaticity of skills results from their initially requiring maximum activation but with practice less activation is required.

Shallice himself notes several weaknesses of his model. He acknowledges that no account is given of many types of experiences "such as the consciousness of relation or doubt or expectation. Nor have aspects of consciousness such as the complexity of conscious perception been considered". These omissions are more serious than Shallice seems to suggest. It is far from clear how the theory copes with emotions. One would expect the external events causing emotions to be the input to the action systems, rather than the emotions themselves (whatever they may be in Shallice's model). If consciousness is, indeed, equivalent to the selector input (a concept left very vague by Shallice) to the dominant action system, then one should only be conscious of the causes and goals of one's actions. A possible interpretation of the theory is that, since we are conscious of the selector input to just the one dominant action system, then we should be conscious of only one thing at a time. But at this moment I am conscious, not only of my pen as I write, but of my other hand beside the pad, my wrist watch on its wrist, the page of writing, the carpet on the floor beyond the table, the sound of rain outside, and so on. Many of these are irrelevant to the dominant action system controlling writing. Someone listening to a symphony concert or watching television may sit without acting, but are surely not unconscious. The same is true of dreams. This problem remains even if Shallice were to extend his assumptions so that the selector input to *any* action system is considered identical with consciousness. The point is that much of what we are conscious has no obvious connection with actions. Of course, the meaning of action could be extended to include seeing and hearing, but the result would be to reduce acting to merely processing and any attraction which the model possesses vanishes with its specificity.

Shallice's model avoids the postulation of a central processor with obvious advantages in not having to specify how such a processor fulfils all the complex functions ascribed to it. On the other hand, it is not easy to see how Shallice's model can cope with some of the functions that Mandler and Posner locate in the central processor. Shallice explicitly ignores the learning of actions and implicitly ignores the complexities of the selection of goals and the choice of actions. Constant conscious attention seems to be required when learning many new skills. This does not translate easily into Shallice's model, nor is there any suggestion in the model of how such skill acquisition is accomplished. As it stands, there seems to be no part of the model which will allow for the suspension of already acquired action systems while new ones are acquired or while the possible outcomes of actions are considered. The evaluation of possible actions, the suspension of action systems so that new ones can be acquired, the application of action systems to novel situations or their adaptation to situations which differ from those for which they were initially acquired, all of these suggest the need for a higher part of the system with the executive functions Mandler and Posner discuss.

Like Shallice, Allport (1979, 1980) champions the production system as the appropriate building block for models of the cognitive system. As such he does not accept the need for a central processor, and argues instead for processing depending upon the shared activities of many systems. Because there is considerable evidence as reviewed earlier, that many elements involved in perceptual processing can be activated without conscious awareness occurring, he does not wish to link consciousness with any particular processing "demons". The output from productions are, in the "pure" production system, made available in the one central data base. During perceptual processing information made available by some productions is interpreted by others, and the results of the integration re-entered into the data base. Allport (1979) suggests that conscious identification of stimuli depends upon information made available at the appropriate level of integration in the data base. Allport does, therefore, consider consciousness during perception, which gives problems in the Mandler, Posner and Shallice accounts.

Finally, in this section, some reference to Ericsson and Simon's (1980) attempt to give an account of the processes underlying verbal reports should be made. They do not specifically refer to consciousness, and their object is to provide a theoretical setting for research on verbal reports of cognitive processes. They propose a central processor which controls and regulates the non-automatic cognitive processes. The central processor "heeds" or "attends to" a small part of the information in sensory stimuli and long-term memory. This information is entered into a short-term memory (STM) where it is available for only a limited time. It is this information in STM which is "heeded" and which is used as the basis for verbal reports. Since Ericsson and Simon do not refer to consciousness specifically we can only guess, assuming that they do not wish to totally avoid using such terms, that they would suggest that consciousness is associated with either the central processor, or the STM, or both.

V   The BOSS-consciousness model

The previous section indicated that accounts of the place of consciousness in cognitive processing have often focussed upon the executive, control processes and have tended to understate ordinary conscious perception. In this section an attempt will be made to outline the place of consciousness which minimizes these shortcomings. The intention is to avoid making too many assumptions about the form of the cognitive system, since the state of cognitive psychology means that any such account would perish in the rapidly eddying tides of fashions for cognitive models.

For the cognitive system to function efficiently, it does seem likely, as Craik (1966) and Broadbent (1977) have argued, that it is hierarchically organized. This is not a claim for special structures controlling different levels but a claim about the way the system will function. Functionally, at the crude levels of knowledge which we currently possess, there is no important difference between the conception of a control system as a separate entity, and a subset of productions which have the requirement of high-level integrated input from the data base as their condition rule, and high-level instructions as output.

With Mandler and Posner we suggest that consciousness is associated with the functioning of the highest levels of the hierarchy of control of behaviour. We do not want to use the term "central processor" since such a system need not be the one responsible for overall control. We will instead refer to the BOSS sub-system which we define as that in overall control of the person's actions, controlling decisions about the main purposes of our behaviour. The components of the system which BOSS supervises we will refer to as the EMPLOYEE sub-systems. So, BOSS decisions will determine the main aims of my actions, on the basis of information supplied by Perceptual EMPLOYEE systems and carried out by motor EMPLOYEE systems.

Our proposal is that one is conscious of the information that is made available to the BOSS sub-system. We are not conscious of the functioning of BOSS, as seems to be implied by Mandler (1975),

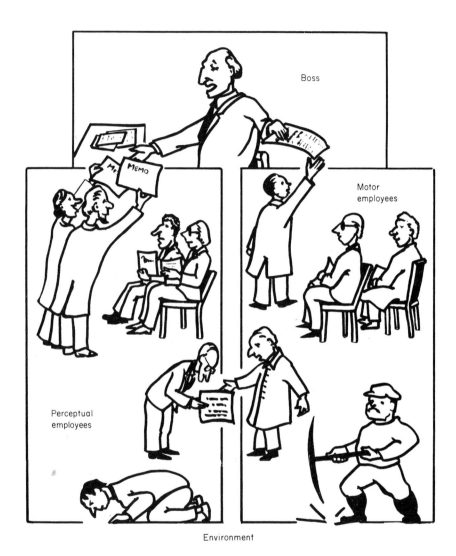

Fig. 4 The BOSS-EMPLOYEE model. BOSS directs intentional activities and novel processes. Consciousness is hypothesized as being associated with the information currently being made available to BOSS. See Fig. 18 for a more schematic representation of the model.

Posner (1978) and possibly Ericsson and Simon (1980) but of the information which is supplied to BOSS including, of course, the outputs of BOSS own processing which can serve as input for its future activity. If consciousness was the operation of BOSS itself one would expect that we would be aware of the mechanisms by which decisions about what we do are taken. Introspection suggests that while we are often aware of needing to take a decision, and of the intention that we are pursuing at a given time, we are not aware of how the decisions are made or of the processes which produce the decision.

Our position is similar to that of Allport (1979) in maintaining that consciousness is related to the display of information that has been already processed and integrated to a considerable degree. It differs from Shallice's (1972) in not requiring that the information of which we are conscious be directly linked with some dominant action system. It differs from Ericsson and Simon (1980) in emphasizing that it is information on the input side of BOSS processing of which we are aware, rather than merely the results of processing, as they imply.

The aspects of consciousness outlined in the earlier section in the chapter will be considered to show how they fit with our proposal.

Central to our position is that the information of which we are conscious is in a form appropriate to the functioning of BOSS. That is, it is processed to the point where it is in the format suitable for analysis and decisions about the overall direction of the system. We are conscious of chairs, tables, the sound of cars drawing up outside etc., and this is the sort of level of integration of input stimulation that is necessary for decisions on the actions we are to take. We believe that the cognitive system has evolved to maintain a supply of information to BOSS in those dimensions where changes in actions are most likely to be acquired, i.e. visual and acoustic information. So, during wakefulness, the perceptual EMPLOYEE systems maintain a stream of processed, categorized information to BOSS. From this input to BOSS, some will be relevant to the particular activity which BOSS is directing at that time. The processing of this special information by BOSS we believe gives rise to the experience of focal attention which has been studied by Wundt, James (1890), Posner (1978), Triesman and Gelade (1980) and others. That part of conscious experience of which we are most clearly aware and upon which we feel that we are concentrating is that which BOSS is currently using in its control activities.

Emotions are generally ignored by cognitive psychologists and have not been discussed in earlier attempts to place consciousness. Nevertheless they are an important component of experience. We suggest that the experience of emotions is the experience of information being made available to BOSS on the internal state of the person's system. Misattributions of the causes of emotions (see e.g. Antaki, 1981) arise because there is no necessary connection between the report of the state of the system and the reason for its being in this state. Emotional information is made available to BOSS when some high level decisions on overall control are necessary. These may involve taking evasive action of a novel kind, as with fears, or prolonging the situation as with pleasures. Freud (1927) noted that pains have the quality of impelling change to a high degree(!) while pleasurable sensations do not. He, however, attributed this difference to amounts of psychic energy. We suggest that we become aware of being thirsty, or hungry, or too hot etc. when the BOSS system may be required to direct complex behaviour such as finding a restaurant or taking off some clothing. We are not conscious of low level activities which normally maintain our homeostatis. Sometimes, BOSS may need to ignore the input to follow more urgent ends. So we sit feeling hungry through an important meeting. Sometimes, no BOSS action can eliminate the problem, as with pain from an incurable illness.

A problem for all theories which equate emotions with information about the state of the system is to explain why pains are unpleasant. Why are they not simply like the appearance of a warning light, an emergency signal to which the system responds without the need for the dimension of suffering? We believe that the dual aspect account goes some way towards explaining this problem. Since conscious experiences *are* the functioning of the system itself, the conscious awareness of pain is of the compulsion of the warnings of its urgency for BOSS and its unpleasant contents. Why they should have the form they have remains, probably by its very nature, beyond explanation, but at least the urgency and importance of conscious experiences of emotions for the system itself becomes comprehendible.

As the main theme of this book is the place of mental images they will be examined in detail in Chapter 4. They are, however, to be regarded as the display of information for BOSS which has not been primarily initiated by direct external stimulation. They will differ in the situations which led to their display and in the quality of the information that is made available, but this will be discussed further later.

Inner speech, with its use of words, illustrates the high level of functioning with which consciousness is associated. Words are not, of course, just marks on paper or sounds, but tokens, one of those in which the cognitive system operates, which stand for rich stores of related information. We are rarely conscious of the activation and use of this information which involves EMPLOYEE systems concerned with word recognition and comprehension. But the tokens are available to BOSS to aid its activities.

The perches and flights of thought, on our account, occur because the flights are the processing of information in EMPLOYEE or BOSS systems while the perches correspond to the display of the result of processing to BOSS to aid its further activity.

The coherent, continuous nature of consciousness presumably occurs because of the display for BOSS of information which is continuously being updated. The qualitatively different experiences of vision and the other senses suggests that the information is displayed in a sensory specific form for BOSS, though, of course, abstract information can also be made available. Even though the system will incorporate all the information into an integrated model of the world, the different senses provide input in different forms, reflecting the nature of the physical stimulation upon which they depend, and the information which they can derive from it. The continuous stream of thought reflects the continuous activity of BOSS during wakefulness. There is always feedback from BOSS processing in the form of awareness of intentions, the results of speculations, or imaginative exercises triggered either by BOSS or by other sub-systems. During sleep it is assumed that most of the system shuts down, except during dreaming, when information is displayed that has been activated in memory often by the immediately preceding display. With BOSS doing little to direct the sequence of display, and with no external control over the input, the result is a sequence of constructions which successively re-activate similar information in memory, but which are given some coherence by some active processing. The result is the momentarily meaningful, but continuously rambling by association, experience of dreaming.

The automation of skills and the concurrent decline in conscious involvement is presumed to occur because as a skill develops programmes to control the performance are constructed. Initially, with no appropriate main programme to link together the already existing sub-skills of which most new skills will be composed, BOSS must be involved in directing each part of the action. When the skill is well developed not only does it no longer require the involvement of BOSS' flexible control of behaviour, but the output from processing does not need to be displayed to BOSS until it is completed, if at all. The skill becomes a new EMPLOYEE sub-system.

To some readers the BOSS-consciousness model may seem to fall into the trap of postulating a homunculus or a ghost in the machine. This is however, not so. The weakness of "homoculus models" is that they simply replace the observable behaviour of the person by that of an equally complex and inexplicable "little man" who is held responsible for the observed behaviour, but whose own processes are not observable. None of these are true of BOSS. As a postulated control system it can be studied. Its capacities are severely limited. We assume that most cognitive processing goes on outside BOSS, and that it can only direct and regulate on a gross level. BOSS represents only one part of the whole cognitive system.

There is, however, another point associated with the idea of a homunculus as the locus of awareness in the system, and that is that most people can at times be self conscious, and observe, and feel surprised by their own behaviour and feelings. To deny this, as some philosophers and psychologists have appeared to do (Ryle, 1949; Neisser, 1976) runs the risk of excluding by *fiat* an important feature of experience. One positive aspect of the BOSS-consciousness model is that it provides an explanation for such experiences by locating consciousness with certain specific functions of the cognitive system, so that those that are not associated with consciousness can provide the input for the surprise and other elements of self awareness.

If consciousness is associated with the display of information for BOSS, then introspection about such information can reasonably be requested, even though they will still be open to the errors discussed in Chapter 2. It will not be possible for other processes to be introspected. It will be misleading if subjects are encouraged to produce attempts at introspection on other activities. Often the subject will resist, but if the task demands are sufficient, or the wordings of the request appropriately vague, then subjects may give guesses about their behaviour. In Chapter 2 we described such guesses as *self-hypotheses*. They may or may not be correct as descriptions of the causes of behaviour, but they are not reports of conscious experience.

In Chapter 12 we have included some further speculations about the BOSS-consciousness model. Now, however, we want to use the model as a framework to help to understand the types of imagery which occur, and the properties and functions of those images.

Section II

Qualities of Images

4
Types of imagery

I Introduction

In this chapter, the main types of images will be briefly examined. We
are here interested in properties of the images rather than the part that
images may or may not play in cognitive functioning. The latter will be
the theme of later chapters, and raises its own problems. Here,
however, we face the inevitable problem of making comparisons
between subjective experiences which are often difficult for the
individuals themselves to examine. The result must be open to error,
but, since it concerns common elements of our mental lives it is worth
undertaking.

Among the dimensions upon which mental images differ are three
which help to clarify the common distinctions between types of
imagery. These three dimensions are, firstly, the intentional/passive
role of the individual in the creation of the image, secondly, the
experience of the image as being out there as part of the real world, or
as existing "internally" in a different form from real objects, and
thirdly, the belief that what is being experienced is part of the real
world, or is created in some way by the individual's mental apparatus.
Of course, these distinctions beg many philosophical questions, but at
the common sense, conscious level they reflect the experience of the
person who is imaging and have therefore contributed to the commoner
classifications of images.

Probably the commonest type of imagery is that of some past
experience which is aroused from memory. Such memory imagery is
not experienced as out in the world; the individual is aware that it is of
his or her own creation. It does, however, span the intentional/passive
dimension, since such images may spontaneously occur or they can be

intentionally sought. Next, there is what we shall call imagination imagery. By this we refer to images which, while incorporating elements of past experience, are themselves newly composed and do not represent a memory of some specific past event. Like memory images, imagination images are experienced, for want of a better word, internally and do not appear as real to the person imaging. Often they will be voluntarily composed, for example, in response to the instructions to imagine scenes linking two or more items together which have often been given when studying the contribution of imagery as a mnemonic aid (see Chapter 10). Sometimes, however, the image may occur without conscious effort after its construction, perhaps in response to a problem which is proving difficult. A type of imagery with which everyone can become familiar and create at will is that of after-images· which follow exposure to a bright light, or prolonged fixation on one point. After-images are rarely mistaken for real world objects, but they are experienced as being ''out there'' in a way that memory and imagination images are not. Perhaps the best description of them is to say that they seem to be superimposed upon the real world, and only appear to be part of it in certain special circumstances, such as when a well formed after-image is seen against a plain background when it may appear to be upon the background itself.

Dreams contain many visual experiences which seem appropriate to be classified as mental images. While dreaming, the dreamer normally feels that the dream is really happening, so that dreams are best classified as experienced as real, ''out there'' images only marginally under the individual's voluntary control, although, when awake, we can usually distinguish what we have dreamt from reality. With dreams, we are moving onto the types of imagery which are especially difficult to study either because they are experienced by only a few people or because the conditions where they occur are not conducive to introspection, or both! Among these are hypnagogic and hypnopompic images which occur when falling asleep or waking up respectively. Hallucinations are, by definition, apparently out there in the world and are frequently assumed to be so by the sufferer. On the other hand, those very vivid visual images which a small number of young people and a very few adults can recall at will following the study of, for example, a picture, and which have been termed eidetic images, are seen as out in the world, but are not, usually, confused with things really existing.

In the following sections each of these types of imagery will be briefly discussed, and their status in the model described in Chapter 3 will be considered. A brief summary of this account of consciousness may be useful here. We have argued that the cognitive system is hierarchical, and have collectively designated those systems responsible for the overall control of the individual's functioning as BOSS. Consciousness, we claim, coincides with the input of information to the BOSS from lower-level, EMPLOYEE systems. There are memories and data bases of stored information which are accessible to BOSS and some EMPLOYEE systems. Normal conscious perception involves the transmission to BOSS of information from the external world, processed and selected to be relevant to the control functions which BOSS serves. Mental images occur when the information transmitted to BOSS is derived by the EMPLOYEE systems from the memory rather than from external input. Of course, as we discuss in Chapter 6, all perception involves some use of information from the memory. There are, consequently, situations, especially those involving ambiguous and insufficient externally supplied information, in which a distinction between perceiving and imaging is arbitrary. Normally, however, perception is dominated by external information *interpreted* with the aid of stored knowledge, while mental images are dominated by input from the memory.

II   Memory and imagination images

Memory and imagination imagery will be discussed together here for several reasons. One is that it is these types of imagery which are the topic of the rest of the book so that there is less need to deal with them in detail in this chapter. Secondly, few studies have tried to separate the two types of images, and, while logically distinct, memory and imagination images may represent ends of a continuum rather than distinct types. All memory images will probably represent a reconstruction rather than an accurate reproduction of the visual scene, and imagination images must draw on memory information. Even so, people can often report whether, in their opinion, the image which they have formed is a new construction (imagination image) or a remembered experience (memory image). Our personal introspections suggest that memory images appear to be more vivid than imagination images, but we do not know of any study which has properly investigated the question.

In terms of our account of imagery, the difference between memory and imagination images is mainly one of the organization of information in the memory. A memory image may be created for BOSS on the basis of data and rules already stored together as a packet in memory. Processing of related information may activate the packet in memory, and, if the current control processes in BOSS allow it, the image may be displayed. Memory search for a memory image is assumed to involve suppressing competing processes which might prevent the display, and thinking around the topic in the hope that an appropriate set of features will be activated in BOSS to match the retrieval codes of the memory packet. Imagination images require the selection and integration of several memory packets, usually in response to instructions from BOSS. Kosslyn (1980) has suggested that when a problem is encountered, parallel attempts at a solution begin *via* abstract and imaginal modes, with whichever is appropriate providing the solution. This is discussed in more detail in Chapter 9.

There is embarrassingly little information available to answer what seem to be the obvious questions about memory and imagination images, namely, when do they occur and what properties do they possess? In the past so much research on mental imagery has been dominated by the two questions, how do people differ in their imagery ability, and how do images contribute (if at all) to other cognitive functioning, that little careful work has been done on the nature of the images themselves.

There have been studies of the informational capacity of images (see Chapter 8) and the latency with which they are formed in certain limited situations, but almost nothing is known about when they naturally occur, whether they tend to be, as we suspect, relatively static etc. etc.

A *Image latency*

The latency with which memory and imagination images are formed depends, not surprisingly, upon what is to be imaged, although only a few of the many possible influencing factors have been experimentally examined. Several of these will be discussed in Chapter 8.

If subjects are required to press a button to indicate that they have formed an image of the referent of a concrete word, the mean latency is usually around one second (Morris and Reid, 1973; Tolman, 1917) but well practised subjects may require only 0·9 seconds (Simpson,

1970) while longer mean response times of 1·5 seconds and even
2·5 seconds have been reported (Moore, 1915; Paivio, 1966). Such
times do, of course, include that required for making the response.
Shorter estimates of latencies occur with very familiar material if
responding is removed either by subtracting the latency for a task
presumed to be a component of the imaging task, or by allowing a
series of images to be found. Simpson (1970) repeatedly tested subjects
with the same words until their speed at (a) reporting an image,
(b) reporting recognition of the word, reached an asymptote. He then
subtracted one from the other to obtain an estimate of 0·6 seconds for
image latency. This assumes that the processes underlying word
recognition are independent of those involved in image generation.
However, this is unlikely, since the codes for image creation may well
be activated during the recognition process. In one of a series of
experiments by Weber and his associates, Weber and Castleman
(1970) had subjects who claimed they could project images onto a blank
screen, go through the alphabet forming an image of each letter at a
time. A mean time of 13 seconds for the whole alphabet implies
0·5 seconds to image each letter.

The latency to image to abstract words, where the images usually
involve related objects (e.g. a church for "religion") is longer than for
concrete words, and reduces with repeated trials when the problem of
finding an appropriate object is reduced. So, for example, Morris and
Reid (1973) found mean latencies of 2·64 seconds and 1·88 seconds for
the first and second tests of abstract words. Images to pairs of concrete
words, where an image integrating the two referrents is required takes
about 2 seconds unless bizarre relationships are requested, when the
latencies may double (Morris and Reid, 1973; Morris, 1979). Subjects
report that for concrete single words or pairs of words the same image
recurs if they are tested some minutes later, but different images are
more common to abstract words (Morris and Reid, 1973).

B   Other properties of images

Our ignorance of the conditions under which images occur in normal
life is one aspect of a general neglect of what might be called the natural
history of memory. While the study of memory outside the very artificial
conditions which we impose in most memory experiments is, of course,
very difficult, avoiding the issue runs great risks of ignorance of the very
functions for which memory in general, and imagery in particular is adapted.

Most research which has been directed at the properties of images has involved efforts to specify individual differences in the vividness, control, or use of imagery. This research is reviewed in Chapter 5. If such research had provided clear-cut conclusions it might have been an appropriate forerunner to a study of the nature of images, since the range of the phenomena would be known. However, while the tests have revealed a range of willingness to describe images as more or less vivid or controllable, the tests have rarely been linked to performance, so that they can claim only face validity. Tests such as the Betts test of vividness, Gordon test of controllability or Richardson's of use of imagery do suggest that there may be a wide range of clarity, control and habitual adoption of imagery (see Chapter 5 and Richardson, 1969, 1977). This is supported by the differences between well known psychologists, with, for example, Titchener possessing such rich and frequent mental imagery that he both denied the possibility of image-less thought and searched for the images which carried the meaning of abstract concepts (see Humphreys, 1951) while Watson denied the occurrence of images themselves (Watson, 1930). On the other hand, there are some experimental situations, including mental rotation (Cooper and Shepard, 1973), backward spelling (Hampson and Morris, 1978), the describing of a skilled task (Annett, 1981) and reporting the number of windows in one's house (Shepard, 1966) where it is common for all those taking part to report having mental images. In testing many hundreds of subjects in imagery experiments we have encountered only one subject who genuinely appeared not to understand what we meant by mental images and who apparently did not normally experience them. Most people appear to have memory or imagination images and to do so under conditions which offer hope of classification and prediction.

There have been differing suggestions as to when images occur. Kosslyn's (1980) theory has already been mentioned. An older and by no means incompatible hypothesis is that spontaneous imagery often occurs when subjects are baffled or puzzled in their thinking. Reviewing the literature relevant to this claim, Sheehan (1972) found a "quite clear consensus" that this was so. Betts (1909) who put forward this hypo-thesis described images "as an army of helpers rushing to the mind's assistance" (p.53). Whether the images so formed actually play a functional part in the processing will be discussed in Chapter 9.

During memory tests for pictures or scenes mental images assumed to be of the original will often be reported. Bartlett (1932) describes many such reports. From his experiments on the recall of the five faces of members of the armed services he concluded that the occurrence of a visual image "is followed by an increase in confidence entirely out of proportion to any objective accuracy that is thereby secured". Jenkin (1935) also reported that imagery appeared to boost confidence without influencing accuracy. In Jenkin's experiment the girl who reported the most imagery was the most confident, and the one most often wrong! In Chapters 10 and 11 the considerable benefits from the use of imagery as a mnemonic will be reviewed. However, such memory improvement appears to follow the voluntary formation of images. Very little research has examined the accuracy of images themselves and the place they play in the overall phenomena of remembering visual information. Current research by the first author suggests that recall of visual information from a film is much more accurate when subjects report that it is based on a mental image. There is too little evidence in the studies of Bartlett and Jenkin to reject imagery as an irrelevance. Many studies of accuracy and confidence in other situations have found little or no correlation between subjects in their confidence and accuracy. That is, subjects who rate their confidence in their recall higher than others do not, in fact, recall more accurately (e.g. Clifford and Scott, 1978; Deffenbacher et al., 1978). There is, normally, a reliable relationship between confidence and accuracy within the reports of each subject, so that for subjects those memories in which they are most confident are the most accurately remembered. It is when one subject is compared with another that the relationship breaks down. This may be a result of the problem comparing individuals on their subjective experiences, discussed in Chapter 2.

C   Objective indicators of imaging

There have been, especially in the days when behaviourism still encouraged scepticism about imagery, many attempts to link behaviour or physiological changes to imaging, so that the latter could be used as an indication of the occurrence of imagery. At best, this would, of course, have had an element of pulling oneself up by one's boot straps because the final evidence for the occurrence or non-occurrence of images would have to be the subject's own report. Nevertheless, clear, observable evidence of imaging would be useful when, for example, subjects may be distracted if they have to make a report, and would, anyway, help to quieten the sceptic in the way that dreams were made more respectable by the discovery of REM states (see below).

Unfortunately, no completely reliable objective indicator of imaging has been found. This probably results as much from the nature of the available physiological measures as it does from the elusiveness of imagery-linked states. Since much of the physiological research has been directed towards identifying individual differences between people in the imagery they use, the bulk of that research is reviewed in Chapter 5.

Singer (1966) and Singer and Antrobus (1965) reported minimal eye movements during images, unless the task involved the imaginary following of moving objects. This fits with everyday observations of subjects who report they are imaging and would make sense in that if the eyes are fixated the amount of new, competing external information is kept to a minimum. However, even if this is the normal behaviour while imaging, not only would it not be sufficient in itself to show that imaging was taking place, but both Hale and Simpson (1970) and Bower (1971) had subjects either fixate or move their eyes during imaging with no difference in latency, reported imagery vividness or amount recalled. The normal pattern of eye movements can thus be easily changed without obvious detriment and does not appear to be important to imaging activity.

Several electroencephalogram (EEG) investigations have reported a relationship between imaging and the suppression of alpha activity (8–13 cycles/second) recorded by electrodes over the occipital region of the brain which is involved in visual perception. Alpha activity is usually increased by closing the eyes, suggesting a relationship between visual processing and the suppression of the alpha rhythms. Kamiya and Zeitlin (1963) in an early experiment on biofeedback requested subjects to suppress their alpha activity, which most subjects reported they did by forming visual images. However, Kamiya (1969) also found that subjects reported that alpha suppression required considerable concentration and it is hard to separate effort and imagery. Simpson et al. (1967) found more alpha suppression to a verbal than to a visual problem, and later determined that the visual problem was easier than the verbal, suggesting an arousal or effort explanation.

Gale et al. (1972) tried to minimize arousal as a conflicting variable by presenting words that varied in their imageability and asking subjects, after reading the word, "to close their eyes, relax, and see if the word suggests mental pictures . . . . Do not worry if nothing comes to your mind . . . . Do not make any effort to force the images into your mind . . . . If they do not come, do not worry, but do not think of anything else." In this condition there was a highly significant suppression of alpha activity to the easily imageable words. However, with tasks which demanded the manipulation of imagery, more alpha suppression accompanied the task which was rated as harder to visualize. Morris and Gale (1974), using a set of words which varied across the range of Imageability (I) rather than extreme groups, did not find a significant correlation between I and alpha suppression, although the total amount of imagery which subjects reported did correlate with alpha suppression. Several more EEG studies are described in Chapter 5. Overall, although there are repeated hints that imaging leads to alpha suppression, the picture is so clouded by other covariables that far more sophistication in psychophysiology is required before reliable conclusions can be drawn. In general, the behavioural and physiological covariables with imagery are interesting, but not, apparently, of central importance in imaging itself.

D   Separating memory images and imagination

One question that has attracted the attention of both philosophers and psychologists is how the individual knows whether he or she is experiencing an image or a percept. The problem was particularly pressing upon the Empiricist philosophers with their emphasis upon the importance of sensations in the formation of the mind. Hume (1748) began his *An Enquiry Concerning Human Understanding* by distinguishing percepts and images upon the basis of their "force", "violence" and "vivacity". Images were to him simply fainter, less intense, than percepts. This has rarely seemed adequate to explain the infrequency with which percepts and images are confused. Some philosophers and psychologists have objected to the dualist, ghost in the machine, implicit assumption of an inner soul which observes a constant picture show and decides on the basis merely of vividness, which came from external stimulation and which from its own imagination. Ryle (1949), Wittgenstein (1953) and Neisser (1976), for example, reject the problem itself as misconceived. However, hallucinations do sometimes deceive, and there is a tradition of research from Kulpe (1902) and Perky (1910) which examines subjects' ability to discriminate images from projected stimuli.

The procedure begun by Kulpe (1902), developed by Perky (1910) and studied in detail by Segal (1971) involves projecting faint stimuli on a screen before the subject and examining the subject's ability to discriminate the objective stimulation from images which they may be instructed to form. Kulpe's subjects often attributed to external stimulation sensations which must have been produced by "noise" in their perceptual system. Perky's subjects all failed to detect external stimuli while imaging. Segal (1971) summarizes a long series of investigations of the Perky effect. Using signal detection techniques, imaging was found to reduce the sensitivity of detection of external signals, with visual imagery specifically interfering with visual signals, and other forms of imagery (e.g. auditory) having much slighter effects.

Rather than deny the image/percept problem, which then leads to an "hallucination problem", it is simpler to point to (a) the rich information potentially available from those cognitive processors which could signal the source of their input (external or memory), (b) the part played in instigating images by the system itself, and (c) the evidence available to the system from processing over time and in a context. There is no reason to assume that BOSS receives the visual or imaginal information independent of information on the input's source. Such information could come from the processors themselves, or from BOSS's record of its direction to produce images, or by calculating the likelihood that a given experience can be externally produced in the current context of perceiving the environment. Such rich sources of information must surely be adequate to classify the BOSS input. If they are not adequate through flaws in the system or the poverty of information about the environment (which characterizes the Kulpe/ Perky paradigm), then errors may occur.

Those aspects of memory and imagination images which have received considerable attention in recent research will be considered in later chapters. We will turn now to after images.

III   After images

If a coloured shape is fixated for, say, 30 seconds, and then one transfers one's gaze to a blank white wall, a brief image in the original colour may be seen, followed after a second or so by an image in the complementary colour to the original. The first image is known as a positive after image, the latter as a negative after image. The negative after image may persist for several seconds, and seems to move as one's gaze shifts. If a coloured field fills all one's view, perhaps from a coloured light or by looking through a coloured filter for some seconds, white surfaces will appear the complementary colour when the coloured field is removed.

Negative after images appear to result from fatigue or adaptation within the visual system, possibly at the retina, while positive after-images may result from persistence of the original effects of the electro-chemical stimulation. As such, they differ from the other images discussed in this book which are constructed by the cognitive system. We will consequently discuss them only briefly here. A discussion of early research will be found in Woodworth (1938) and more recent research in Richardson (1969).

Fig. 5 Fixate a point between the man's eyes for about 20 seconds, then look at a plain surface. A light after image of the face should appear, and look larger the farther away the surface on which it is "projected".

After images are influenced by the intensity, duration, size, colour and position on the retina of the original stimulation. Some people can require practice with quite powerful stimulation before first becoming aware of their after images, and the time to become aware of an image declines with practice (Reinhold, 1957). This may reflect perceptual processes which minimize what would normally be distracting and irrelevant visual noise.

One property of after images is that described by Emmert in 1881 (see Boring, 1942). The more distant the surface on which an after-image is projected, the bigger it appears. Emmert's law states that the judged size of an after image is proportional to the distance of the surface upon which it is projected. This is a size constancy effect resulting from the after-image covering a fixed area of the retina. A real object, to cover that fixed amount, would have to increase in size proportional to the distance it moved away.

That some central processes, beyond the retina, are involved in after images is suggested by the Bocci image, named after its "discoverer" in 1900, B. Bocci (see Sumner and Watts, 1939). This effect, known according to Day (1958) at least since Newton's time, involves fixating a bright stimulus for 30 seconds or so with one eye. An after image may then develop in the other eye.

Some well known psychologists including Wundt have reported subjects who claimed to have after images following imaging a bright colour patch for some time (see Richardson, 1969; Kulpe, 1902; Oswald, 1957). Barber (1971) has questioned these and similar results following hypnotic suggestion, arguing that the reports of the student subjects in the hypnosis experiments resemble those which might be based upon an elementary knowledge of after images gained from introductory texts, rather than the more complex reality of actual after images. Barber argues that the reports result from suggestion. We are here entering a very difficult area where perhaps only those able to experience such effects for themselves (if they do occur) are likely to be fully convinced. Certainly, neither of the authors can maintain an image for anything like the time which would be required to produce an after image. But this may not mean more than that we, and many others, do not possess the full potential in imaging ability.

The visual sensory or iconic memory classically demonstrated by Sperling (1960) is, like the after image a transient result of external stimulation, with some researchers (e.g. Long, 1980; Sack, H., 1978) suggesting that icons are simply very weak after images located in the retina. The iconic image will not be discussed here because it lasts for a period of less than a second in all but the most exceptional conditions, because it appears to be a part of percepton rather than of the re-collection or construction as are other images and because the iconic image itself is probably not consciously experienced (Coltheart, 1980). Good reviews of research on iconic imagery will be found in many places (e.g. Wingfield and Byrnes, 1981).

IV   Dreams

Dreams have always fascinated man. Divine revelation of the future during dreams is common throughout the Old and New Testaments of the Bible, an idea that has attracted adherents up to the present day. Others, most notably Freud (1900), have seen in dreams the closest approach that consciousness can make to the unconscious. The study of dreams seems to have attracted some of the most grandeose theorizing but supporting evidence is necessarily sparse.

Dreams are certainly worthy of attention. They do, for example, demonstrate how rich conscious experience can be with little, if any, external input. However, they also provide some of the most unreliable data that psychologists encounter. At best, the recall of a dream occurs some time after the dream itself. Most dreams appear to be so rich in ever changing content that it is surprising if much can be remembered accurately, and even more surprising if it can be adequately communicated to another person. We suspect that most published accounts of dreams tend to minimize the inconsistency of dream sequences. Even for dreams there will be an effort after meaning in their recall (Bartlett, 1932). It is also rarely commented that while most cognitive processes seem to be bizarrely functioning during dreams, those which produce memories are assumed to be sufficiently normal to produce an accurate record. While noting some of these problems with dream reports, Cohen (1979) interprets them in the opposite way to ourselves, arguing that many dreams may be less bizarre than commonly believed. He agrees with Snyder (1971) who described the typical dream reports collected in sleep laboratories as "remarkably mundane, plausible, sedentary and uninteresting to anyone, with the possible exception of the dreamer" (p.528). The problem of discovering what dream reports leave out, which would resolve our differences with Cohen and Snyder, is of course virtually insuperable, and illustrates the difficulty of theorizing about dreams.

Within our account of imagery we assume that during most stages of sleep both the BOSS and some EMPLOYEE systems cease to function fully. During dreams, however, information is retrieved from the memories by EMPLOYEE systems, and displayed for BOSS, but BOSS does not control and direct processing as during waking hours, and the result is that the display (the dream), is a succession of constructs activated in the memory by related information, or by the needs and general state of the individual. So, dreams will reflect what is active or activated in memory, and may wander like free associations, may dwell upon recent events, or may be stimulated by the wishes, needs, fears and frustrations that are currently dominant.

Here, we will outline three approaches to the nature of dreams which have attracted twentieth century psychologists: the psychoanalytic, the physiological and the memory-consolidation or selection hypotheses. We do not intend to do more than introduce these approaches here.

The psychoanalytic approach developed from the work of Freud in, for example, *The Interpretation of Dreams* (1900) and in the writings of other psychoanalysts from Jung onwards. Dreams have, for the psychoanalysts, a purpose. Freud (1911) described them as the guardians of sleep, working to rob stimulation that occurs during sleep of its reality. According to Freud, during sleep, unconscious, repressed forces come closer to consciousness than during waking life, and determine the content of dreams. A careful analysis of the manifest dream content which the dreamer reports for its latent contents which underlies the symbolism in which the dreams cloak the forces may provide considerable understanding of the unconscious processes which may be shaping or warping the individual's behaviour. "Dreams" wrote Freud, "are the royal road to the unconscious." A proper examination of the psychoanalytic account of dreams is not appropriate here. Most psychologists are sceptical about the psycho-analytic interpretation of dreams for reasons usually associated with problems of verifying the interpretation given (Morris, 1972). Never-theless there is evidence to support some Freudian claims (Kline, 1982). It is worth noting that even if the full Freudian version of the cause of dreams is rejected, there is nothing incompatible in modern theories of cognitive psychology and semantic memory with the phenomena claimed by Freud. If dreams reflect those parts of memory which are currently activated by the ongoing state of the person, then those frustrations and wishes of the psychoanalytic account will influence dream content. Some aspects of symbolism may reflect spreading activation within a semantic network. If the everyday actions of the individual do not match the elements of the data base activated through frustrated needs or wishes, then they may not be retrieved for display to BOSS during waking hours, but the many hours of sleep with little or no BOSS direction may allow them to be retrieved. Failure to retrieve during waking life need not be the result of repression but of the incompatibility of waking life with the memory code. Repression may, of course, also occur, but it is extremely difficult to demonstrate (Morris, 1978).

The physiological approach to dreams examines the correlates of physiological activity and dreaming. Aserinsky and Kleitman (1953) noticed that periods of sleep were accompanied by rapid eye movements (REM) and electroencephalogram (EEG) records which were closer to the records during wakefulness than the normal slow waves of sleep. Dement and Kleitman (1957) found that subjects who were wakened during REM sleep produced significantly more dream recall (on 80% of occasions) than those wakened during slow wave sleep (7%). Most measures of the autonomic nervous system showed greater activity during REM (see Grosser and Siegal, 1971). Dreams, especially those involving visual imagery, appear to occur mainly during REM. People who claim that they do not dream will usually report dreams if awakened during REM (Goodenough et al., 1959). REM sleep occupies about 25% of the average adult's sleep (Williams et al., 1964) and increases in frequency as the night progresses, with the stages of sleep interchanging, but overall, more periods of REM occurring. Infants spend 50% of their sleep in REM sleep, with the amount dropping to the adult level slowly over years, and declining throughout life (Roffwag et al., 1966). When deprived of REM sleep for several nights both animals and man appear to "make up" by having more REM sleep on subsequent nights (Dement, 1960). It has been suggested that REMs involve the following of visual images by the eyes during dreams. There have been reports of appropriate eye movement patterns and dream reports (e.g. Dement and Kleitman, 1957) but a review of the nature and circumstances of REM makes this doubtful (e.g. Berger, 1969) and the research on imaging during wakefulness reviewed earlier in this chapter suggested that imaging is related to minimal eye movements.

The study of REM sleep does not, in itself, conflict critically with psychoanalytic accounts of dreaming, although an explanation of the need for guardian dreams in opossums, who show a higher percentage of REM than man (Berger, 1969), may require ingenuity! However, some workers in the biological tradition have suggested physiological bases for the activities associated with REM, and from which dreams may result as a coincidental correlate. Berger (1969), for example, argues that REM is the result of periodic innervation of the occulomotor system to maintain binocular co-ordination. Snyder (1966) has claimed that the period of sleep by an animal species has been evolutionarily selected to balance feeding and avoidance of activity, and that REM provides periodic arousal for "sentinel" purposes. Other maintenance functions of REM have been suggested. However, it is enough to note the possibility that dreams may be an epiphenomenon of sleep, rather than serve a function.

The memory consolidation hypothesis asserts that during REM sleep the retention of recently acquired memories is consolidated. The hypothesis does not imply that this is the only purpose of REM sleep, nor that consolidation, whatever that might involve, can take place only during REM, but simply that consolidation is intensified during REM sleep. Animal studies have supported the claim (reviewed by Fishbein and Gutwein, 1977; McGrath and Cohen, 1978) but it is difficult to eliminate alternative hypotheses which focus upon passive effects of sleep such as slowing decay or reducing interference as opposed to the positive contribution to consolidation supposed to come from REM sleep. Tilley (1981), using human subjects, found better recall of a list of words when REM rather than non REM sleep occurred between learning and testing. However, he also found higher arousal following REM, and speculated that this may have maintained the memory trace.

If correct, the memory consolidation hypothesis might require a physiological rather than a psychological explanation. Nevertheless, the hypothesis can be handled by our account of dreams. If dreams represent the re-activation of the most easily activatable entries in the data base, which will tend to be recent entries, and if, as with remembering during wakefulness, such activation increases the ease with which that entry can be accessed in future, then the dreams of REM sleep should lead to the strengthening of recent memories.

Finally, in contradiction to the consolidation hypothesis, Evans and Newman (1964) drew an analogy between dreaming and computers, and suggested that dreams reflect the scanning and sorting of "programmes" in the human brain in which information is examined for its value while the human is "off-line", i.e. asleep, and unnecessary recent input is cleaned off. They equated dreams with the material being cleaned off, so that one would expect dreams to be of unimportant information which is then forgotten. This contrasts with our suggestion that dreams reflect a free association route through currently active entries in memory, which we would expect to be strengthened rather than erased. Evans and Newman (1964) do, however, illustrate the possibility of cognitive theories of dreaming which are more positive in their attitude to dreams than that which we have adopted.

V   Hypnagogic and hypnopompic images

The term hypnagogic derives from Greek and means leading to sleep. It was first applied to images which accompany the drowsy state before sleep by a Frenchman named Maury (1861), and in English by Gurney (1886) in *Phantasms of Living*. Many reports of phantasms do occur either as sleep is approaching, or as waking occurs. The images which accompany the latter have been called hypnopompic (Myers, 1903) but we will ignore the distinction until later.

Reviews of hypnagogic and hypnopompic imagery will be found in Leaning (1925) and Schacter (1976). McKellar (1957, 1977) has surveyed large groups of students and found about 65% reported having experienced hypnagogic images in some modality. As with dreams, there are problems in investigating hypnagogic imagery resulting from the state in which they occur. Some people fail to notice such images until their attention is drawn to them.

Common features of reports of hypnagogic images are their antonomy and their vividness. McKellar's subjects reported they were "like nothing I have seen in art of life"; they resembled "scenes from the kind of travel books I don't read" and, wrote one subject, they always contained "faces of people unknown to me". Details are often vividly experienced. Leaning (1925) reports an image of "a white road and an avenue of trees, every detail—trees, leaves, trunk, cart-ruts, pebbles—microscopically clear". Faces, either ugly or beautiful, are especially common, according to Leaning. As well as meaningful images, however, there are reports of patches and flashes of light and geometric forms. The images appear to follow their own course, independent of the wishes of the person experiencing them, frequently changing in shape and size and lasting only briefly.

Leaning (1925) estimated that about a third of the population had at some time had a visual hypnagogic image. McKellar (1977) reports visual hypnagogic imagery by 61% of the women students and 48% of the men in his sample of 400. However, far fewer people experience such images regularly. Only 12 of McKellar and Simpson's (1954) sample of 182 students claimed to have visual hypnagogic images often or regularly.

Foulkes *et al.* (1966) awakened subjects immediately after they had fallen asleep and questioned them on hypnagogic states. They found reports of the experience of hypnagogic images to correlate with less rigid authoritarian personality types as measured by the California Personality Inventory and the TAT. Reports of dreams following awakening during REM sleep did not correlate with those obtained in the hypnagogic state.

While the content of hypnagogic states seem to differ in some ways from dreaming, we assume that, in our account of imagery, the processes resemble one another. The experience results from random activity in the EMPLOYEE systems and the data base. Perhaps, however, hypnagogic states are more influenced by the recent activation and fatigue in the perceptual EMPLOYEE systems. This

Fig. 6   After a long period picking blackberries, images of them may occur later prior to sleep.

would be an inappropriate explanation for hypnopompic states, since the perceptual systems have been largely inactive during sleep. However, many reports of hypnopompic imagery are difficult to separate from dreams, and may be essentially the same but with different degrees of BOSS activation.

One type of hypnogogic activity which does strongly suggest failure in the perceptual systems is that of perseverative imagery. These follow prolonged concentration upon some visual task involving similar stimuli. It was first reported following a day working at a microscope by a nineteenth century German anatomist, F. G. J. Henle (see Ward, 1883). On closing the eyes to rest, often several hours later, clear images of the objects studied appear. Hanawalt (1954) describes such images following a day's blackberry picking. He and his wife noted that the blackberries imaged were "large, purple tinged, luscious and profuse", — idealized in fact and relatively free from leaves and thorns. Similar images have been reported after strawberry picking (McKellar, 1957). The present first author has experienced such images several hours after blackberry picking — much to his surprise — and can vouch for their apparently idealized form, though the images while vivid seemed rather blurred. One can speculate that constant attention to a task involving a vast range of stimuli, but all evaluated on criteria of quality, leads to the creation of a perceptual stereotype related to those studied by Rosch (1976) and Posner (1973).

VI Hallucinations

With hallucinations we reach the extremes on the dimensions of imagery with which we introduced this chapter. The term "hallucination" derives from references to apparitions in the sixteenth century (Sarbin and Juhaz, 1967) but, while the word is loosely used today, the current meaning is probably best captured in the criteria used by Vernon (1963) to classify a visual hallucination (quoted by Richardson, 1969; p.101):

> (1) the experience must have an "out-thereness", just like any visual experience of the real world, (2) the one experiencing the hallucination must be able to scan, to attend selectively to, the various parts of the experience, (3) it must not be producible at the will of the subject, (4) the subject must not be able to terminate it, and (5) it must, for all purposes, "fool" the observer with its realism (1963).

Richardson himself describes an hallucination as "... a percept-like experience, whose objective reality is assumed without question" (1969, p.113).

Such hallucinations are commonly associated with schizophrenia, but that relationship is neither necessary nor sufficient. Many ordinary, healthy people experience hallucinations at some time, and most could be led to do so in appropriate conditions. Sidgwick's (1894) census of hallucinations involving thousands of people found at least one hallucinatory experience reported by almost 10% of the sample. Menninger (1949) found a similar percentage. Medlicott (1958) lists many famous persons who had experienced hallucinations, including Raphael, Schumann, Goethe, Descartes, Sir Walter Scott and Dr Johnson.

Sensory deprivation, stroboscopic stimulation, hypnosis and the so-called hallucinogenic drugs such as mescaline and lysergic acid diethylamide (LSD) can produce visual hallucinations in many but not all individuals (e.g. Holt, 1972; Barber, 1971; McKellar, 1972).

In a sensory deprivation experiment by Bexton *et al.* (1954) 14 of the 22 subjects reported visual hallucinations ranging from spots of light and geometric patterns through to visual scenes and "cartoons". The hallucinations tended to disappear when subjects carried out difficult tasks such as mental arithmetic. Eleven of the sixteen subjects in the sensory deprivation study by Zubreck *et al.* (1961) experienced hallucinations, and Heron (1961) claimed that some subjects were so confused by their hallucinations that they did not know whether they were awake or asleep. McKellar (1977) describes some examples of "hallucinations" during crystal gazing. These probably do not deceive the individual as is required by a rigorous definition of hallucination and the experience is closer to hypnagogic imagery, although the form of the crystal-gazing images and hypnagogic images by the same subjects differed markedly.

Within our model of imagery we assume that hallucinations represent a presentation to BOSS of information in visual format derived from the memory but with a breakdown in the systems which indicate the internal source of the information. So two conditions are required, the generation of the image and the suspension of normal feedback and evaluative processes. Sensory deprivation or crystal gazing encourage such conditions by reducing the demands on BOSS to cope with the environment (from which there is very little novel input), and the external information against which input to BOSS can be compared. An inappropriate image is contextually obviously out of place in perception of the normally rich visual environment, but less so against monotonous input to which the EMPLOYEE systems will fatigue or habituate. Activity in BOSS should help to reduce hallucinations, as Bexton *et al.* (1954) have observed.

VII   Eidetic images

The phrase "eidetic image" was invented by Jaensch (1909), a German psychologist, deriving it from the Greek word *eidos*, meaning that which is seen. He used the term to describe images which, for the imager, resemble percepts, but which, while perceived as "out there" are not, like hallucinations, mistaken for the real world, perhaps because they are usually under the voluntary control of the imager. Such images were described as early as 1819 by Purkinje (see Kluver, 1926).

The usual method of studying eidetic imagery (see Richardson, 1969 and Haber, 1979 for reviews) has been to first draw the attention of the subjects to their imagery by a session evoking after-images. Then the stimulus for the eidetic image is placed before the subject who is instructed to inspect it carefully. After 10–40 seconds the picture is removed, leaving a plain mat, and the subject is asked to report anything that they see upon the mat. Reports of vivid images of the picture from some subjects follow after anything between a few seconds to a minute. This technique has been criticized by Ahsen (1977) for its homogeneity between experiments. Ahsen argues that the eidetic is found in all people but its utilization depends upon the conditions and personal history. While we know of no evidence for this generalization, a wider range of test conditions does seem desirable.

Using the conventional test methods, eidetic images are almost exclusively restricted to children, and even then to only a small fraction of those tested. Haber and Haber (1964) found only 12 of a sample of 151 elementary school children (ages 7–12) to be classifiable as eidetics. These 12 were able to obtain an image of each of four pictures that they were shown, most of them scored 8 or 9 out of 9 on a test of detail recalled and all seemed able to scan their images. Using these sort of criteria, Richardson (1969) estimates that 6% and 9% of children, respectively would have been classified as eidetic in the large-scale studies of Teasdale (1934) and Morsh and Abbott (1945). Paivio and

Cohen (1977) classified 8·6% of their sample as eidetic using similar criteria.

Teasdale (1934) found a trend from 12·5% eidetics among children in their eleventh year, declining steadily to only 2·1% among those aged 13. However, Haber (1979) questions the reliability of the claim that eidetic imagery declines with age. In the only longitudinal study of eidetic imagery (Leask *et al.*, 1969) over the ten years between the ages of 5 and 15 only one of twelve children failed to remain eidetic. Haber (1979) also queried the reason for the existence of eidetic imagery. No relationship has ever been found between eidetism and any intellectual ability, skill or abstract reasoning potential. Nor have neurological studies supported early claims that eidetism was stronger in brain-damaged subjects. Paivio and Cohen (1977) factor analysed the performance of their subjects, and found a separate eidetic factor independent of ability on either spatial ability or normal imagery vividness.

The small numbers of eidetic individuals, and its restriction, with a few exceptions to be discussed later, to childhood, raises the difficult question of whether or not reports of eidetic imagery result from the demand characteristics of an experiment in which a strange and authoritative adult first shows a picture and then sits waiting for a minute or so having demanded that the child describes what they see out there on the projection mat. Children have long been recognized as more susceptible to leading questions than adults (e.g. Stern, 1939), but even a percentage of adults might fabricate their responses under these conditions (cf. Asch, 1956). Some of those who have studied eidetic imagery have come to this conclusion (e.g. Traxel, 1962). The demand characteristics are clear in Haber's (1979) description of the experimental procedure which he had used. After several trials using after images, which will have set the child to expect to report images the experimenter moved on to pictures. The exact instructions were:

> "When I take the picture away, I want you to continue to look hard at the easel where the picture was, and tell me what you can still see after I take it away."

Under these sorts of demands, it is, perhaps, not surprising that a proportion of children tell the experimenter what he wants to hear. The problem is complicated by the need to separate eidetic imaging from less dramatic normal memory imaging—a distinction which is not always obvious in Haber's (1979) writing. As Ashton (1979) points out, anyone asked to describe the image of a friend's face will do so in much the same way that eidetic children do. That is, they will use the present tense, changing when the image fades (see also Hunter, 1979).

Of course, the nature of the phenomenon may make it impossible to provide convincing proof to the non-eidetic sceptic. However, some support for the reality of eidetic images may come from studies where the information in the eidetic image is used subsequently. Supola and Hayden (1965) found that over half of their eidetic subjects reported a composite picture when two pictures which when superimposed formed an unexpected composite were scanned successively. None of the non-eidetic subjects reported the novel composite. Gengerilli (1930) described a 15-year-old girl who was able to judge perfectly whether the eidetic image of a circle was greater or smaller than a given square. She reported doing this by "placing" the circle image over the square. She said "It's just like placing a real circle on top of a square." The ability to superimpose stereoscopic pictures without the aid of a stereoscope has been claimed for the occasional adult (Jaensch, 1930; Stromeyer and Psotka, 1970). Allport (1924) found three children who knew no German but could spell the word *Gartenwirthschaft* either forwards or backwards after seeing it printed above a shop in a picture of a street scene.

On the other hand, detailed recall by eidetikers is extremely rare (Stromeyer and Psotka, 1970) and most cannot carry out the letter square test (e.g. Woodworth, 1938) where subjects who have been shown a 6 × 6 square of letters are asked to "read-off", say, diagonals (Leask *et al.*, 1969). Haber (1979) reported that only 4 of 23 eidetic children could form a composite image of two pictures, and that the criteria of especially good recall of the pictures shown had to be abandoned as a criteria for eidetic imaging since eidetic subjects did not appear to be especially accurate. Doob (1965) has found greater confidence and vividness in recall by eidetic subjects, but not necessarily more accuracy. Merritt (1979) reported that tests published in several newspapers and magazines and probably taken by more than a million people failed to identify one person who could combine two patterns as had been claimed for Stromeyer and Psotka's (1970) subject.

Jaensch (1930) believed all young children to be eidetic, and Piaget and Bruner have both seen imagery as having an important role in children development. However, the evidence for a special eidetic imagery ability in all children which is lost through disuse or the development of abstract thought is not substantiated by available evidence. If, at best, a figure of 10%–15% is the most that we can give for the proportion of eidetism then its explanation may be easier to seek in divergent functioning or even abnormal functioning rather than a common process.

The best documented adult eidetic individual is Shereskevskii (S), described by Luria (1968). S's consciousness from early childhood had been dominated by visual imagery as real to him as his perception of the actual world. This enabled him to carry out dramatic memory feats such as the memorizing in 3 minutes of a table of 50 numbers arranged in columns so that he could recall them equally well in any direction. He became a stage memory expert, using naturally the imagery mnemonics such as the place method, where items to be remembered are imaged along a familiar street (see Chapter 10). The vividness of his imagery is illustrated in many of his conversations with Luria. For example, when describing his use of the place method he commented "Take the word egg . . . . It was so easy to lose sight of it; now I make it a larger image, and when I lean it up against the wall of the building, I see to it that the place is lit up by having a street lamp nearby" (p.37). Discussing the dentist, he said:

"I used to be afraid to go. But now it's all so simple. I sit there and when the pain starts I feel it . . . it's a tiny orange-red thread . . . . I'm upset because I know that if this keeps up the thread will widen until it turns into a dense mass . . . . So I cut the thread, make it smaller and smaller until it's just a tiny point. And the pain disappears" (p.107).

This passage centres around the interrelationship for S of several senses; S's reports often reveal the interrelationship of images and other senses, i.e. synaesthesia. Most of his consciousness seems to have been so related. Particular images accompanied any given sound: he once remarked to Vygotsky "What a crumbly, yellow voice you have" (p.25). Synaesthesia is not uncommon in normal individuals, McKellar (1968) found it in 21% of his student sample, Galton (1883) describes many instances, and as a student Skinner (1976) wrote a long note on synaesthesia describing the colours associated with letters, thinking he could trace the influence of a coloured alphabet book from his childhood! However, it is rarely so dominating.

The domination of images in his life and their interweaving with reality caused him many problems, leading to concrete thinking and difficulty in separating imagination from reality. Luria concludes that:

> Indeed, one would be hard put to say which was more real for him: the world of imagination in which he lived, or the world of reality in which he was but a temporary guest (p.118).

Within our account of imagery, we can speculate that S was unusual in the ease with which visual information activated in memory could obtain access for display to BOSS. For most people external input normally has priority, but for S the two seemed to compete. He does, also, seem to have had a better memory store of the rules which generate visual images. This might, in part, have been the cause of his unusual subjective experience, or, perhaps a result of them. The more common cases of eidetic imagery perhaps also reflect a good visual store, along with the ability to combine imagery with external input so that the image appears to be projected onto the external world. More than any of the other imagery states, however, eidetic imagery remains mysterious.

VIII   The interrelationship of types of imagery

Are people who frequently experience one type of imagery likely to report other types also? That would seem to be so for Shereshevskii, but he was a unique individual. Awareness of one type of imagery would be expected to facilitate awareness of other types, and personality characteristics which might predispose some people to report imaging might increase their reporting of any imaging. However, Holt (1972) describes a study in which 25–28 subjects were interviewed about their imagery experiences and their replies were then reliably scored by two judges. The study examined the vividness of imagination imagery, hypnagogic imagery, eidetic imagery in childhood, imagery in dreams, daydreams and sensory deprivation. None of the correlations between reports of these variables reached 0·4 and most were much smaller. Holt (1972) concluded that "There is a real possibility that the many types of imagery usually distinguished have a good deal of intrinsic independence."

IX   Conclusions

This chapter's review is, as we stated at the beginning, intended only to illustrate what is known about the many types of imagery. In recent years more attention has been directed towards the role, if any, of imagery in cognition, and we will turn to that in the next Section. Many of the types of imagery which have been described here are hard to study experimentally, and this has, in part, contributed to their relative neglect. Some of the phenomena are hard to accept by anyone who has not experienced them. Some may indeed result from suggestion and compliance. The first author did not have any time for Freudian symbolism in dreams until, very soon after splitting up with a girlfriend of several years, he dreamt that he and she were inside the London Post Office Tower which was falling down! He did not believe that hypnopompic or hallucinatory images could be vivid, until once waking from an evening doze he ''saw'' an enormous green spider in the far corner of the ceiling, which moved its legs for perhaps a second before vanishing instantly. We mention these simply to illustrate that scepticism needs to be tempered with a willingness to accept that there may be more in the claims of some imagers than can usually be tested in our own experience. What is very rare or non-existent for one individual may be very common to another. There do seem to be individual differences in imaging, and it is to these that we turn in the next chapter.

5
Individual differences and dimensions of the image

When considering any cognitive process, the psychologist must eventually turn his or her attention to the problem of individual differences, and, as far as the study of imagery is concerned, this area of research has had a long history. In fact it was speculations about variations in imaging which, in the last century, began the wider investigation of the structure and function of the image, and were part of the general attack on human mental abilities and their measurement (e.g. Galton, 1883). Work on individual variation, however, is plagued by a number of theoretical and methodological difficulties in any area of psychology, and imagery is no exception. We shall be considering several of these difficulties in this chapter, but for the moment we wish to make two general points which will serve as a sort of *leitmotif* in the sections which follow. They are these: Research into individual differences in imagery abilities has been trapped, perhaps by its history, into concentrating on a limited number of dimensions of the image which, ultimately, might not be of any great importance. Second, there has been too little attention paid to the integration of such work into a general model of imagery. In the last analysis the concept of individual variation as a cognitive skill is theoretically cleaner if it can be related to some more general aspect of processing. Scores on difference measures can then be seen as parameters which specify the operating characteristics of the particular system under consideration. To illustrate this, consider for a moment the engines which power, say, a small hatchback, a medium-sized family saloon and a powerful sports car. Generally speaking the basic workings of these systems are very similar. All three, however, differ in various

91

ways. The compression ratios, rate of fuel consumption of acceleration, maximum speed and power developed are unlikely to be the same. These variations in performance though do not mean that different underlying systems or processes are involved, they simply indicate that there is a certain flexibility in the number of ways the same general process can be physically realized. By altering the cubic capacity, timing ratios, value settings and so on, engines can be designed to meet desired performance specifications. Therefore observed individual differences in performance between engines can be understood in physical terms because they are directly related to underlying functional characteristics of this type of system. An additional point worth noting is that the fact that one car's engine might be coloured green and another blue is less useful information about whether a car is worth buying than knowing the performance characteristics of the two engines. It is likely that the study of those imagery dimensions which can be linked to underlying functional processes will be of more use in predicting performance on other tasks than those dimensions which bear no such relation.

The first two sections of this chapter document the two major dimensions of the image which have been studied, vividness and control, and chart some of the main subjective and objective attempts to measure them. Included in the second section is a consideration of "one off" studies of individuals with super-normal and often quite spectacular imagery abilities. These studies, though obviously restricted in their wider applicability, are easier to exempt from our two general criticisms. The dimensions studied have often been quite varied, and serious attempts have been made to relate them to the general case. The behavioural correlates on other tasks of the individual differences mentioned in the first section are also reviewed in the second, and a general critique and consideration of the area presented in the third.

I   The dimensions of the image and their measurement

A   Vividness

A natural starting point when investigating a construct with such intriguing phenomenal properties as imagery is to try to assess its vividness. The implicit assumptions are that firstly, images vary in their vividness or brightness, secondly that people can assess, albeit subjectively, this vividness and thirdly that those with more vivid imagery have, in some ill-defined sense, "better" imagery. Unfortunately, as we shall see shortly, the accurate measurement of this dimension has been sullied somewhat by attempts to measure it which lump together image *vividness* and image *clarity* without any *a priori*, let alone empirical, reasons for so doing. Amount of detail and subjective intensity of images may co-vary, but the necessary data to demonstrate this are not yet available.

The historical background of attempts to measure individual differences in symbolic habits has been well reviewed by Richardson (1969) and Paivio (1971b) and so we shall not dwell too long on such details here. Originally attempts were made to classify individuals into imagery types on the basis of the vividness and clarity of their imagery in various sensory modalities (see Woodworth, 1938 for a discussion). The assumption was that people with highly vivid imagery in one modality would make extensive use of that form of processing and less of others. The first systematic investigator of individual variation in imagery ability was Galton (1883) who asked his subjects to imagine some particular, everyday object, such as a breakfast table and to answer questions about its qualities. Although it was an early instrument, Galton's Questionnaire was surprisingly detailed and included questions concerning the colour, definition and brightness of visual images. While Galton quickly discovered that pure imagery type did not exist, he did find a wide range of vividness reported by subjects who had been asked to form an image of their breakfast table, and was surprised that many of the scientists in his sample reported little use of visual imagery.

As Paivio (1971b) points out, later investigators did not recognize that most people experience all types of imagery to some extent and persisted in attempts to describe typologies (e.g. Fernald, 1912). Eventually the type approach was abandoned, perhaps no bad thing, since its underlying logic, at the time, was muddled. Basically, it rested on the unproven assumption that habitual use of imagery correlated with high imagery ability, yet it is logically possible for those with poor quality images to persist in using them (though see Richardson, 1977b). For some tasks, they may have no alternative.

The majority of subsequent "vividness" questionnaires are related to Galton's original measure. In 1909, Betts produced a 150 item test which represented an extension in terms of the number of items, but was essentially constructed on similar lines. Betts' test assessed imagery in seven modalities including kinaesthetic, and organic, as well as the more common, visual, auditory, gustatory, olfactory and cutaneous. Subjects were asked to rate their images on a 7-point scale which referred both to clarity and vividness. One major finding was a positive correlation between the different modalities. As Paivio (1971b) points out, this clearly does not support the notion of imagery types.

Two tests which have been widely used in recent years are those by Sheehan and Marks. A shortened version of the Betts test *The Questionnaire upon Mental Imagery* (QMI) has been developed by Sheehan (1967), it is 35 items long but still assesses all 7 modalities. Ashton and White (1980) found that Sheehan's version of the QMI produced sex differences as an artifact of the ordering of the questions, and they have produced a revised version (White *et al.*, 1978). Marks (1973) has developed a short test of visual imagery, the Vividness of Visual Imagery Questionnaire (VVIQ).

B   Image control

It has not escaped workers in the individual difference field that images have dynamic as well as structural properties. They can be deformed and altered in various ways and, occasionally, may appear to alter themselves without the imagers volition being involved (Chapter 4, McKellar, 1957). Do people vary in their ability to perform operations with their images? Certainly the speed and accuracy with which mental rotations can be executed varies between subjects, as anyone who has done experiments in this area can testify. One of us (Hampson, 1979) found a great deal of subject variability in such a task. The measurement of people's ability to control their imagery has been attempted by Gordon (1949) who produced the Test of Visual Imagery Control (TVIC) subsequently revised by Richardson (1969). The TVIC requires the subject to imagine a motor car and its occupants undergoing various transformations and deformations. Here are the first few items.

1   Can you see a car standing in front of a house?
2   Can you see it in colour?
3   Can you now see it a different colour?
4   Can you now see the same car turned upside down on its roof?
and so on. In Richardson's version the response is either "Yes",

"No" or "Unsure" and the sum over all the items is used as an index of control.

C   Criticisms of subjective measures

A number of criticisms have been levelled at the use of subjective measures such as the tests of vividness and control which we have just considered. First of all, when a person is asked to rate the "clarity and vividness" of his imagery he is faced with severe criterial difficulties. To begin with, how does he know at what level of vividness to rate his image? The experimenter may have in mind a much stricter or a more lenient, definition of "perfectly clear and vivid", say, than his own. The problem is compounded when two or more people respond to a particular test item, what *absolute* standard could possibly be used (see Chapter 2)? Second, without some theoretical rationale for assuming that imagery abilities remain relatively constant over time, it is hard to see how test–retest reliability could be established, though split-half, or alternate version methods have been employed (see White *et al.*, 1977b for a review). However, subjective measures can be criticized most heavily on grounds of validity, though perhaps because of their obvious *face* validity, these problems have only surfaced in the last ten years or so. There are, of course, many complex issues concerning test validity (see e.g. Jackson and Messick, 1967a). Here, however, we will concentrate on just one. The issue can be put quite simply: Do subjective questionnaires of imagery measure what they purport to or are subjects' responses on these tests contaminated by, for example, a social desirability factor? This is not unknown, even for commonly used tests. Jackson and Messick (1967b) found that over 50% of the variance in responses to the Minnesota Multiphasic Personality Inventory (MMPI) could be attributed to social desirability and acquiescence, and that these overwhelmed other factors. DiVesta *et al.* (1971) discovered that responses to the Betts' and Gordon's tests correlated highly with performance on the Marlowe–Crowne Social Desirability scale (Crowne and Marlowe, 1964). Urging caution, Ernest (1977), in her review, points out that more recent work has shown lower and less general correlations between self-ratings and social desirability. For example, Richardson (1977a) has found that male responses to the QMI are contaminated by social desirability whereas females' are unaffected and that the Gordon's test and his own Ways of Thinking (WOT) Questionnaire, to be discussed later, are reasonably free from response bias (see Richardson, 1977b). Furthermore, attempts to manipulate scores on the Betts' and Gordon's tests, by suggesting that performance on them is related to such socially desirable qualities as intelligence and creativity, have been relatively inconclusive (Durndell and Witherick, 1976). Nevertheless, the possibility that acquiescence, as distinct from social desirability, may be making a major contribution to the test variance should be further examined.

Despite these problems the psychometric properties of the Betts' and the Gordon's tests are reasonable, considering their nature. White *et al.* (1977b) have reviewed the reliability and validity of these and other measures and the Betts QMI in particular has been given a fairly clean bill of health. As far as the Gordon's test is concerned, they report that it has adequate though not impressive test–retest reliability with estimates ranging from $r = 0.6$ (White and Ashton, 1976) to $r = 0.84$ (McKelvie and Gingrass, 1974) but that studies of its internal structure (White and Ashton, 1977) show that it may well measure four as opposed to a single dimension of imagery ability. Experimenters must be extremely cautious when interpreting the TVIC in view of the latter finding.

D   Objective and performance measures

If the experimenter believes that the problems of the subjective measurement of imagery abilities outweigh its advantages he can always turn to the so-called "objective" tests. Paivio (1971b) and Ernest (1977) have both reviewed the major varieties. Objective measures are usually standardized tests, or sub-tests, designed to measure visual-spatial abilities, whose scores can be interpreted as indicating imagery ability. A typical test is Flags (Thurstone and Jeffrey, 1956) in which the subject has to indicate whether two flags are in the same orientation or whether one member of the pair has been turned over to show its reverse. Other tests mentioned by Paivio and Ernest are the Minnesota Paper Form Board (MPFB) (Likert and Quasha, 1941); Space Relations (Bennett *et al.*, 1947) and the Primary Mental Abilities Space Test. One problem with the use of these devices is that although they are often well standardized and generally have very good psychometric properties, it is not at all clear what *imagery* abilities are being assessed. However, as Paivio has pointed out, one important factor identified by these devices may be what Guilford (1967) has termed "cognition of figural transformations'' (CFT) defined as the ability to handle changes or alterations in visual information, including variations in such sensory qualities as colour, its location and changes in the spatial arrangement of the parts of objects. Tests which load heavily on this factor, e.g. Flags and the MPFB, when used to assess imagery, may be measuring imagery control. So far as we are aware, there is no standardized test which could conceivably be measuring vividness; nor can we envisage the form that such a test would take. The only possibility seems to be to find other behavioural indices which correlate highly with subjective assessments of vividness and then use these to predict the latter. By hitching the cart of a performance measure onto the horse of a subjective assessment in this way, though, the researcher cannot assume that his final instrument is psychometrically ''clean''. If anything it is likely to be worse than the original, subjective test.

E   Intercorrelations between tests

Several studies have looked at interrelationships between the various measures of imagery ability we have discussed so far (see for example Paivio, 1971b; Ernest, 1977 for reviews). The general finding seems to be that whereas self ratings and spatial, ''objective'' measures both correlate well amongst themselves (e.g. Ernest, 1976; Morris and Gale, 1974), self-ratings such as the QMI and spatial measures are often found to be poorly intercorrelated (Ernest, 1976; Richardson, 1977b). Some studies have, on the other hand, found a small but significant correlation between the TVIC and Space Relations and Flags (Ernest, 1976). Also, as Ernest points out, some experiments have shown that subjects who obtain extreme high and low scores on the Betts test perform significantly better and worse respectively on Flags (Durndell and Wetherick, 1976). There are, of course, two ways of interpreting such correlations though this is rarely made clear. Evidence that subjects score highly on two measures of imagery, one a performance test, say, the other a self-rating questionnaire could be taken to mean either (1) that the two tests are different ways of measuring the *same* imagery ability, and that those who do well on the one will tend to do well on the other, or (2) that the two tests happen to measure *different* imagery abilities, but that subjects who have a certain level of one tend on average to have a similar level of the other. Where correlations between spatial tests and the TVIC are concerned we suspect that the former applies, both tests probably tap subjects ability to handle information about *changing* spatial relationships. As for correlations, such as they are, between tests of vividness and spatial measures, it is more likely that different aspects of imagery are being assessed. Work investigating the functional neuroanatomy of the visual system as well as more general evidence from visual perception suggests that the visual system may treat identity and location information separately (cf. Lindsay and Norman, 1977) and most contemporary theoreticians in imagery accept the basic distinction between a representation and the processes (often guided by spatial information) which use it (Kosslyn, 1980; Pylyshyn, 1973; though see Baddeley, 1976, and Neisser, 1976 for alternative views). It is our belief that self reports of vividness, if reliable, tap aspects of the image or representation, whereas measures such as the TVIC and spatial tests are mainly assessing its control processes. If this is correct, the TVIC should be a reasonable predictor of performance in, for example, mental rotation experiments, the QMI, on the other hand, might provide better estimates of memory performance. We shall explore some of these issues shortly.

F   Processing preference

Recently, there has been renewed interest in whether or not individuals differ in their reliance on imagery in a particular sensory modality. So, for example, Richardson (1977a,b) has suggested that subjects can be categorized as being predominantly ''visualizers'' or predominantly ''verbalizers''. This resembles a weak version of the typological approach, claiming that people have different cognitive styles and that extremes on the visualizer–verbalizer dimension may index different performances on other cognitive tasks. Paivio (1971b) has constructed an 86 item Individual Differences Questionnaire (VVQ). He claims that the instrument is unaffected by social desirability, has an acceptable test–retest reliability and has a number of behavioural experiential and physiological correlates. For example, as will be described further later in the chapter, Richardson has shown that visualizers are more likely to exhibit regular breathing patterns than verbalizers. He has also investigated the link between this discussion and laterality of eye movements. It has been believed for some time that verbal type questions, which are assumed to involve the left hemisphere, elicit right lateral eye-movements whereas visuo-spatial questions, assumed to involve the right hemisphere, elicit left movements (e.g. Kinsbourne, 1972). Richardson (1977a) has shown that verbalizers make significantly more left, eye-movements than visualizers. However, as he has since shown (Richardson, 1978), other variables such as the sex of the experimenter and subject can also affect the direction of gaze break.

G   Other tests

There are a number of other measures not as widely used as the ones we have reported here. For information concerning these the reader is referred to Paivio (1971), Ernest (1977) and White *et al.* (1977b).

II   Imagery ability and performance

A   Correlates of vividness and control scores

The student of the behavioural and cognitive correlates of individual differences in imagery abilities is faced with a multitude of papers demonstrating relations between performance on imagery tests and a bewildering variety of other measures. To review all of these studies in the space available is both impractical and probably unproductive. We feel it is more helpful to the reader if we select a representative set of studies for consideration and introduce some means of categorizing them (for additional information see Ernest, 1977; White *et al.*, 1977b). Our solution to the latter problem has been to divide up the studies into those concerned with global aspects of the person, such as age, sex and personality, those relating to cognitive processes, perception, memory, problem-solving and so on, and those which correlate with arousal and behaviour change. While this division is by no means hard and fast, it does demonstrate that an individual's imagery ability can have important consequences at the level of information processing and behaviour, and may itself in turn be a product of wider dispositional factors such as mood or general state of health. The relationships between image vividness, control and cognitive performance are, of course, especially important as far as this book is concerned, and we have done our best, in this section, to give due consideration to those studies which have a direct bearing on the issues such as the function and nature of imagery which we will consider in more detail in Chapters 7, 8 and 9.

1   Subject variables

Differences in imagery ability appear to depend on a variety of dispositional and other factors. One of the earliest observations was that females report greater degrees of vividness than males (Galton, 1883) and as White *et al.* (1977b) point out, this finding receives support from several studies (Schmeidler, 1965; Michael, 1966; Sheehan, 1967) though some surveys have found no significant differences (Hiscock and Cohen, 1973; White *et al.*, 1974). The reason for these differences, if indeed they exist at all, is not clear, though White *et al.* speculate that females might employ more lax criteria when evaluating their images than males. An alternative explanation which they offer is that females may devote more neural tissue to processing images than males. The reason for this is that men may be more rigidly hemispherically specialized than females, who may be able to generate and process images using *either* hemisphere. However, when Ashton and White (1980) randomized the order of the questions on the QMI, the sex difference which they had discovered in the study by White *et al.* (1977b) almost disappeared. They suggest that the difference was an artifact of the original test in which questions on each type of imagery were blocked together.

As well as possible sex differences in imagery abilities there appear to be age-associated changes. Galton argued that imagery vividness increases with age and this claim has received recent support from White *et al.* (1977a). Perhaps, vividness increases as a concomitant of practice at dealing with images.

It should come as little surprise to the reader that interactions between personality and imagery ability have attracted the attention of researchers. The personality dimension that has received most consideration in this as in other areas is that of introversion–extroversion as measured by the Eysenck Personality Inventory (EPI). The most common finding, with the occasional exception (e.g. Morris and Gale, 1974), has been that introverts generally report more vivid imagery than extroverts (e.g. Gralton *et al.*, 1979). This fits in well with the *general* notion that introverts are less stimulus-oriented and somehow more inner directed than extroverts, but there is a theoretical gap between the specific argument that the cortical arousal levels of the two groups differ, with introverts higher than extroverts, to the finding that the *content* of their mentation is also different. In any case, the relationship between this dimension and imagery abilities may not be so clear cut. Recent work by Stricklin and Penk (1980) has examined the link between, sex, image vividness, image control, extroversion and neuroticism (N). They found a significant negative correlation between control and neuroticism scores in females but not males, but males with high neuroticism tended to have very vivid, organic imagery (imagery for internal bodily sensations). The relation of extroversion to the other dimensions was a little more complex. In their low N groups, introverts had more vivid imagery than extroverts, whereas in high N groups extroverts had more vivid imagery than introverts and, apparently, had the highest vividness of all four E, N groups. Any simple equation of vividness and introversion should be viewed sceptically in the light of these findings.

2   Cognitive correlates

Variations in imagery ability can be shown to have important consequences on a variety of cognitive tasks from the input of information, perception; the storage of information, verbal learning and memory; and the mental manipulation of information, thinking, creativity and mental operations. Carole Ernest's (1977) review provides excellent coverage of many of these areas and so we shall offer only a representative sample of studies here.

The interaction between imagery ability and perceptual processes has been investigated indirectly for the most part. Many of the experiments cited in Ernest (1977) and Paivio (1971b) demonstrate the facilitating effect of imagery vividness, a preference for using imagery, and skill in manipulating images on visual recognition tasks (Ernest and Paivio, 1971b; Ernest, 1977). The assumption behind this work seems to be that high imagery ability can aid recognition by helping with the encoding of the items to be memorized. More direct evidence of imagery's involvement in perceptual processes is provided by the finding that high imagers surpass low in the identification of frag- mented words and pictures (Ernest, 1977). From the point of view of any theory which construes perception as an interaction between bottom-up processes and top-down processes which working alone can also support imagery, it would be interesting to look for correlations between subjects' ability to comprehend visually certain illusory figures and their imagery powers. It is known already that the ease of voluntary reversal of the Necker cube is related to visual imagery control (as measured by the TVIC) (Gordon, 1949; Richardson, 1977b), but it would be interesting to see if similar effects obtain in the case of, say, the wife–mother-in-law figure or the detection of indistinct forms. We might expect that in the latter situation image *vividness* would be an important factor, whereas in the disambiguation of stimuli the ability to retrieve alternative images rapidly and efficiently might be more central.

The ability of high imagers to profit from interactions with information provided by the environment is suggested by work on incidental learning. Several studies indicate that vividness, control and spatial ability (as measured by objective tests) can all be used to predict performance on tasks involving unexpected recall (Sheehan and Neisser, 1969; Morris and Gale, 1974; Ernest and Paivio, 1971). Perhaps high imagers are able to indulge in more extensive, top-down processing of the stimulus so that at a later date they can use not only the cues provided by the experimental situation to aid recall, but also memory for their own constructive operations (cf. Kunen *et al.*, 1979). Less clear-cut conclusions can be drawn from studies of intentional learning. Using stimuli such as block designs (Sheehan and Neisser, 1969), photographs of faces (Rehm, 1973) and letters formed by two, successively presented, dot patterns (Wagman and Stewart, 1974) no links have been found between image vividness (measured by the QMI) and memory. The VVIQ has proved more useful, however, and Marks (1973a,b) has used it to predict recall of both the identity and location of pictorial information. Recently, using her as yet un-published Visual Elaboration Scale, Slee (1980) has shown that imagery ability correlates best with the retrieval of visual appearances, i.e. information about the physical properties of objects. Ernest summarizes the objective test literature as showing that high spatial imagery facilitates memory for forms, colours and pictures and that *low* imagery females are apparently better in remembering unrelated lists of words.

One area that is ripe for investigation is the relation between imagery ability and cognitive processes believed to depend on imagery for their successful operation. The many and various tasks we will review in Chapters 7, 8 and 9 may be easier for people with high than with low imagery abilities. One such task is, so called, mental rotation, where, in a typical experiment (e.g. Cooper and Shephard, 1973) a subject is successively presented with two patterns at different orientations, and has to decide whether the stimuli are identical or whether the second is a mirror image version of the first. The general finding is that response times increase in proportion to the difference in orientation of the two patterns. One implication which is often drawn from these studies is that subjects must perform a mental rotation on an image of one of the two stimuli before a match can be computed with the other (see Chapter 8 for more details). If this explanation is correct in principle, it suggests that an important factor in these tasks is the ability to transform and manipulate images. Does the ability to control one's imagery predict how well one is likely to perform in a mental rotation experiment? There is some evidence that it may. Snyder (1972) has shown that image ability as measured by the TVIC is related to mental rotation speed, higher control, faster rotation, whereas there is no relation between the Betts QMI and rotation performance. There are many other situations in which the active use of imagery has been studied (see especially Chapters 7, 8 and 9). For example Kosslyn (1980, 1975), in a series of experiments, has asked subjects to use their images to answer questions about the properties of objects. Does imagery ability correlate with speed of response on these tasks? Also, people take finite amounts of time to generate images (e.g. Morris and Reid, 1973), do people with higher imagery abilities take less time to retrieve or construct images? There is some evidence to support this (Rehm, 1973). Can habitual visualizers form visual images faster than verbalizers? These questions have still to be answered more fully.

Representations and processes, of course, form the basis for the activities of problem solving and reasoning, and some work has been done to link skill in these areas with the level of subjects imagery. For example, Shaver et al. (1974) have shown that imagery ability can be used to predict performance on three-term series problems. A typical example of the latter, discussed in more detail in Chapter 9, takes the following form (if A is larger than B, and C is smaller than B is C smaller than A?). Some workers (e.g. Huttenlocher, 1968) have argued that subjects use mental imagery to solve these problems, while others (e.g. Clark, 1969) have proposed a more abstract, linguistic explanation. Shaver et al.'s study provides "converging evidence" for the use of imagery in these situations. By manipulating instructions to foster the use of imagery and examining the effects of imagery ability they have shown that performance improves when subjects are encouraged to use images and when subjects have high imagery ability as assessed by a variety of measures. Recently, Johnson-Laird and Steedman (1978) (see also Johnson-Laird, 1980a,b) have developed a general theory of syllogistic reasoning which asserts that mental models (image-like representations) have an important role to play in the evaluation and testing of logical arguments. We will discuss the details of their model in Chapter 9, and so will simply say here that it would be interesting to see whether imagery ability is an important factor in the solution of classical as well as transitive syllogisms.

Finally, an area of cognition that has had something of a chequered history is the study of creativity. A lot of this research has been in the psychometric tradition, and perhaps because of the intractable and elusive nature of the associated phenomena, there is a dearth of good, *process* accounts. Anecdotally, however, the importance of imaginal representations and processes has often been emphasized (e.g. Khatena, 1976; Richardson, 1969) but the exact role, if any, that imagery plays has yet to be determined. One study by Ernest (1976) found a small though significant correlation between image vividness measured with the QMI and the Alternate Uses and Unusual Uses tests, but Durndell and Wetherick (1976) found no such relation though there was a link between image control (TVIC) and divergent thinking test scores. For a recent review of the area the reader is referred to Forisha (1978) (see also Forisha, 1981).

3   Arousal and behaviour

Several attempts have been made to use psychophysiological measures as objective indices of imagery (see e.g. Zikmund, 1972 for a review). Briefly, three main parameters have been considered: first, change in breathing pattern, with visual imagery associated with regular rates of breathing, and verbal-auditory imagery with an irregular span; second, electric activity of the brain, with early studies suggesting that visual imagery blocks or attenuates the alpha rhythm; third, eye movement activity has been associated with waking and sleeping visual imagery.

Golla and Antonovitch (1929) found a correspondence between breathing rhythm and the type of imagery which subjects reported habitually using, with those classified as visualizers having more regular breathing patterns than those who predominantly used auditory–verbal images. The difference presumably reflects the subjects inclination to talk to themselves. Since that early study several others have reported more regular breathing patterns for subjects who either report more frequent or more vivid imagery (Wittkower, 1934; Paterson, 1935; Short, 1953; Chowdhury and Vernon, 1964; Richardson, 1977). While breathing rhythms have emerged as the most reliable external correlate with subjective reports of visual imagery use, they do not allow the identification of particular instances of imaging. In part this is because the measure is necessarily too gross, but the visualizer–verbalizer difference is found both when the subjects are resting or when they are solving problems that appear to lead to their imaging activities (Short, 1953; Richardson, 1977). An intriguing possibility, that would have delighted J. B. Watson, is that implicit or anticipatory movements of the larynx and tongue might be associated with the verbal mediation of thought which thus disrupt regular breathing. The implication being that verbal imagery can be used as a method for rehearsing *future* behavioural output, and that the rehearsal is carried out even to the extent of preparing a motor program.

Golla *et al.* (1943), Walters (1953) and Short (1953) classified subjects as visualizers and verbalizers, and found that visualizers characteristically showed less alpha activity in their EEG. These studies usually involved a classification of the EEG unaided by filters and analysers with the subject's imagery type known to the experimenter so that they raise doubts of experimenter bias. Nevertheless, others have found more alpha suppression during tasks designed to produce imaging (Mundy-Castle, 1957; Slatter, 1960). As we discussed in Chapter 4, subsequent studies of EEG and imagery (e.g. Gale *et al.*, 1972; Morris and Gale, 1974) have produced equivocal results in which it is difficult to separate changes that accompany increases in arousal from the actual influence of imaging itself. With Paivio (1973) we must conclude that the evidence is inconclusive.

Several other physiological measures have been linked with imagery, but the problem is that these measures are usually sensitive to any change in arousal, so that observed differences may reflect imaging, greater arousal produced as a result of imaging, or arousal for quite independent reasons. Colman and Paivio (1968) observed quicker Galvanic Skin Responses to concrete than to abstract I words, though the magnitude of the response did not differ. Colman and Paivio (1969) also found greater pupil dilation for abstract than for concrete words. Colman and Paivio (1970) found few differences in pupil dilation when subjects were learning paired associates of concrete or abstract words, but the latency of the pupil's response was longer for abstract pairs. However, Kahneman (1973) reviews many studies of pupillary dilation and concludes that they are related to the effort and/or arousal of the subject, and there is no obvious way of separating imaging from effort in these studies.

Lorens and Darrow (1962) suggested that increases in oculomotor activity when solving certain problems were associated with the presence of visual imagery. Also, Antrobus *et al.* (1964) and Singer and Antrobus (1965) found an increase in eye movements when subjects were asked to imagine dynamic as opposed to static situations. Under conditions of *spontaneous* imagery however, subjects reported more visual imagery immediately after periods with few eye movements. The use of Rapid Eye Movement activity to index dreaming has been described in Chapter 4.

The initial equation of REM sleep with dreaming and hence with visual imagery experience has proved too simplistic. REMs have been discovered in subjects with lifelong blindness (Gross *et al.*, 1965) and decorticate organisms (Jeannerod and Mouret, 1963). Also dreams have been reported in non-REM stages of sleep (e.g. Foulkes, 1962). More interesting are recent experiments which demonstrate a significant relation between subsequent ability to recall dreams and waking image vividness (Hiscock and Cohen, 1973; Richardson, 1979). The strength of the dreaming experience may well contribute to its memorability, assuming, of course, that the vividness of waking and dreaming imagery are themselves correlated.

It is well established that there has been separate specialization in the right and left hemispheres of the brain for different types of processing, although confident specification of the specialization may be premature (see Chapter 7). Specialization for language production and sequential processing has taken place in the left hemisphere. Consequently, a style of thinking or a type of problem may require more activity in one hemisphere than the other. Temporary hemispheric dominance has been suggested as accounting for different tendencies to break eye-contact to the individual's left or the right when they are faced with, respectively, spatial or non-spatial problems. Kinsbourne (1972) and Kocel *et al.* (1972) found that the majority of subjects made left lateral eye-movements when faced with questions such as which way the Queen's head faces on a coin, which is of the type which commonly leads to report of imaging, while the majority looked to the right when at non-spatial tasks. Some subjects showed a strong preference for one direction of break, which matched their reported styles of tackling the problems, with visual images or words. Richardson (1977a, 1978a) found conflicting evidence on eye movement in different experiments and he reviews several other studies which have failed to obtain the expected results. One problem which the first author has noticed when trying to collect eye movement data is that subjects will exploit any available distinctive feature in the room and move their fixation to it while solving the problem, so that a completely plain background to the experimenter is required. At best, the phenomenon is fragile and not central to imaging.

4   Manipulation of images

Somewhat old fashioned studies of mediation used to suggest that images and words and other implicitly mediating responses could function as "internal" stimuli (e.g. Osgood *et al.*, 1957). More cognitive approaches describe images and words as symbolic *representations* or models of reality (e.g. Craik, 1943; Miller, Galanter and Pribram, 1960). Both have in common the notion that images can be used in place of objects, as a "surrogate" or "simulated" world. Consequently it is interesting to enquire whether the possession and skilled manipulation of vivid images can have real behavioural consequences. Many behaviour modification techniques seem to depend on the client's ability to form and maintain mental images, not only in those treatments based largely on classical conditioning (e.g. Bandura, 1969; Wolpe, 1973) but also in more flexible ones based on operant conditioning (see Cautela, 1977 for a comprehensive review). Speaking about systematic desensitization, Wolpe (1973) has claimed that poor imagery may be more of a hindrance than a help in achieving successful treatment. Imagery ability may be an important factor that the clinician should consider before suggesting a therapy to his client. Any work which tries to ameliorate people's imagery could have immense therapeutic value, though up to now the evidence showing that improvement might be feasible is limited but encouraging. White and co-workers have pioneered this research. White (1978) demonstrated first that images can produce affective responses by showing that the degree of vividness of people's images of food and their ability to increase or decrease salivation were significantly related. His results suggest that the mental image can be construed as an *internal* stimulus to which the subject can respond, in an affective manner, as he or she would to an external stimulus. In the case of imagery, the strength of the reaction is related to the vividness of the image. This, in turn, suggests that the law of stimulus strength, the more intense the stimulus the greater the response to it, might apply to internal representations of events as well as to the external events themselves, and that self-generated imagery could be useful in controlling other autonomic functions. Does this then mean that those with weak images will be unable to use the various techniques of behavioural control and autonomic modification? Not necessarily. Walsh *et al.* (1978) have been investigating methods for improving imagery with some success. Essentially, their approach is to persuade the subject to pay more attention to his imagery, to examine it for details and deficiencies, and to attempt to flesh out poorly defined and sketchy images. They have evaluated their technique by using salivation as an index of effectiveness. Their major prediction, that imagery training would significantly affect only those whose imagery was initially poor, was confirmed. They concluded that their training technique has now to be tested in a therapeutic setting. If positive results are obtained, these will unquestionably demonstrate the importance of first considering variations in imagery ability before suggesting treatment options to clients, and may also lead to better prognoses for those with poor imagery. For a recent review of clinical uses of imagery see Strosahl and Ascough (1981).

A final area of interest relating images and behaviour is the study of so-called mental practice. This is a method of attempting to improve one's skill in performing a particular action by covert, imaginal rehearsal. For example, a tennis player might imagine herself perfecting her service while relaxing at home in an armchair, or a golfer could mentally try out his drive while sitting on a bus! The issue at stake is not whether people indulge in such mental activities, for simple introspection and anecdotal reports lead us to suspect that they are practised frequently, but whether mental rehearsal can lead to subsequent behavioural improvement. Early studies (reviewed by Richardson, 1969) found that mental practice did result in better performance, but Smyth (1975) has found little or no effect. It may, once again, be necessary to consider individual difference variables here. Start and Richardson (1964) discovered that people with high vividness and high control were much more likely to profit from mental practice than those with, in descending order, low vividness, high control; low vividness, low control; high vividness, low control. The latter group may experience little benefit from mental practice, because their vivid imagery is attention compelling, but difficult to transform. The possibility that other imagery modalities as well as the visual might be important in mental practice has been raised by Smithells and Marks (1977). They have shown that vividness of visual imagery (as measured by the VVIQ) is a good predictor of the efficacy of mental practice, but so is the vividness of kinaesthetic imagery (measured by the QMI). The type of skill and the degree of practice may be additional important factors controlling the effectiveness of mental practice. Perhaps imagining the execution of a stylized ballroom dance would be effective whereas trying to do the same for the smooth, controlled movements needed to remain upright when skiing would not. Also, because there is no feedback from the real world about the success of a mentally practised skill, imagery is unlikely to be of use in developing new skills. However, where a degree of competence already exists, mental practice may maintain the integration and co-ordination of the skilled performance.

B Single subject studies

Every now and then the psychological community stumbles across individuals with exceptional abilities in some area of cognition or behaviour. Several such people have been studied in the imagery literature. On the one hand there are reports of children with so-called photographic or eidetic images (see Haber, 1979; and Chapter 4) but more pertinent to the research considered in this chapter are studies of adult subjects with outstanding imagery powers. Of these, perhaps the most well known is Luria's subject, S (Luria, 1967) some of whose abilities we briefly described in Chapter 4.

The story of S is fascinating. One day he appeared at Luria's laboratory having been referred by his employer, the editor of the newspaper for which he worked as a reporter. When each morning the editor handed out lists of addresses and assignments to his subordinates, he noted, with some surprise, that S never made any notes. On questioning S, he found that he could repeat his instructions verbatim. Luria, over the next thirty years, was able to study S's remarkable memory. When presented with lists of numbers, letters or words he was able to repeat them back without error even when they were 70 items long. This seemingly infinite capacity memory apparently showed little forgetting. Retention was still perfect months or even years later.

Two main factors underpinned S's memorial abilities. The first was a set of mnemonic techniques which were under S's strategic control. For instance he made extensive use of the Method of Loci (see Chapter 10) when remembering lists of objects. Occasionally he would make mistakes but, somewhat paradoxically, these were more often due to the vividness and concreteness of his memory than its schematic nature. So, when trying to remember the word *egg*, he failed because he had imaged one against a white background with which it blended, and a pencil became indistinguishable from the set of railing among which it was stored. As Luria reports, S initially used very literal and highly articulated images in these techniques, but later, when he became a professional, stage mnemonist, he began to use more schematic images which were often idiosyncratic and apparently bizarre. The second cause of S's ability was not under his control but was evoked by the to-be-remembered stimuli. Synaesthesia, the experience of a stimulus in one sensory modality producing effects in another, was a common aspect of S's cognition. Mild synaesthesias are reasonably common in most individuals, certain colours are often described as warm or cold, and sounds as bright, and presumably this metaphorical use of language is prompted by sensory effects, but in S's case these effects were extreme. A tone of 3000 Hz and 128 dBs produced the experience of "a whisk broom that was of a fiery colour, while the rod attached to the whisks seemed to be scattering off into fiery points" (1975, p.26). Voices also evoked synaesthesic reactions. The psychologist Vygotsky was described as having "a crumbly yellow voice" (p.26), and the composer Eisenstein had a voice like "an entire composition, a bouquet" listening to him for S "was as though a flame with fibres protruding from it was advancing right toward me" (p.27). S found Eisenstein's voice so interesting that he failed to follow what he was saying! Subsequent retesting of the sensory effects associated with standard stimuli resulted in essentially similar reports from S, indicating that his synaesthesias were relatively stable. Some people's voices did give him trouble, though, and he would then experience difficulty recognizing them on the telephone, not because of a bad line, but because their voices changed subtly maybe twenty or thirty times in the course of a day, resulting in S experiencing them as different and distinct.

Forgetting could be a problem for S. As a stage mnemonist he frequently gave two or three performances each evening and was worried that items from the earlier ones might disrupt recall in the later. One early, apparently successful approach he employed to forget, was to erase material from the blackboard he used in his act and then to cover it mentally with an opaque film. Before the start of the next performance he would mentally uncover the board and then imagine himself crumpling up the opaque film and throwing it away. Another rather naïve technique, which failed to work, was to write down events he wished to forget on pieces of paper then burn or destroy the scraps. The simplicity and literality of S's intellect is noticeable here; he believed that since many people make and retain notes to remember things, the destruction of records should obviate forgetting. Finally, he discovered that a good way to make the recall of information difficult was simply to tell himself that he did not want to recall it. Luria points out that this, the most successful of his techniques, may have worked for S because he was fixating on the *absence* of images.

We mentioned in the previous section that images may elicit certain affective responses in the imager and be used to control autonomic functions. These phenomena were particularly marked in S. Luria reports that S could raise the skin temperature of one hand while simultaneously lowering that of the other. To do this S claimed that he imagined that one hand was on a hot stove, and the other was holding a piece of ice. By imaging himself running after a train he could raise his pulse rate and then lower it by picturing himself relaxed in bed falling asleep. These general abilities proved useful to S when he experienced pain. When at the dentist he was having his teeth drilled he imaged the pain, as it was just beginning, as "a fiery orange-red thread" (p.107). S remarked that if the drilling continued the pain would grow and the thread widen into a dense mass. His simple expedient was to "cut the thread, make it smaller and smaller, until it's just a tiny point. And the pain disappears" (p.107). Another successful strategy was to imagine the pain inflicted on another and S would merely observe!

Stromeyer and Psotka (1970) and Coltheart and Glick (1974) have studied two other people with outstanding though different visual imagery powers. Stromeyer and Psotka's subject was presented with two quasi-random dot patterns which when fused resulted in the perception of a square. The patterns were presented to separate eyes on different days and the subject was still allegedly able to retain sufficient information from the first stimulus to conjoin it with the second. Unfortunately, as Baddeley (1976) has pointed out, this person does not appear to have been studied since and, we understand, has proved difficult to trace (Richardson, 1978b). A wide ranging search has failed to identify anyone else with a similar ability (Merritt, 1979).

The abilities of Sue D'Onim, (O), Coltheart and Glick's subject are less dramatic and extreme. Ms D'Onim, when tested, showed a remarkable proficiency in backward spelling and a greater ability than normal at reporting letters in iconic memory experiments. When it came to manipulating her images O has great difficulty. Coltheart and Glick claimed that the backward spelling proficiency and the low level of skill in manipulating images were related. The resistance of O's images to disruption allowed the former and caused the latter. We agree with Baddeley that O's imagery is merely a rather extreme variation from the norm, and can be understood within a normal framework. Whether the same is true of Luria's S is doubtful.

Reports of two subjects with more obvious verbal than visual abilities have appeared in the literature. Hunt and Love (1972) have studied a mnemonist, V.P., who from an early age evidenced a considerable ability to memorize poems and other verbal materials. When tested, he was able like S to remember large matrices of numbers but did not seem to rely on visual imagery. Whereas S appeared also to profit from synaesthesia, which may have allowed items to be multiply encoded, V.P. claimed never to have experienced such phenomena. Instead, he relied more on multiple linguistic or semantic encodings, and his wide knowledge of languages. V.P. himself attributes his skills to his upbringing in the Judaic tradition with its accompanying stress on the value of rote learning.

The late Professor Aitken of the University of Edinburgh has been studied by Hunter (1962, 1977a). Unlike V.P. and S, Aitken not only possessed a remarkable reproductive memory but was also a very talented mathematician which undoubtedly demanded more creative, intellectual skills. Hunter (1977a) faced with what he describes as "a sprawling mass of evidence about Aitken's talents" (p.156), has attempted to crystallize and explain these in terms of an all-pervading interest in meaning. As he points out, Bartlett's (1932) phrase "effort after meaning" is a reasonable description. What were Aitken's skills? Basically, like S he was able to reproduce accurately long lists of numbers and words and to recall facts and events in sufficient detail that he was frequently used as a source of information in meetings — a role that he did not enjoy. Hunter (1962) was able to check on the accuracy of Aitken's memory over a period of years by examining his recall of material originally presented to him by Sutherland (1937) of Edinburgh University. His accuracy was astounding. When asked to recall Bartlett's "War of the Ghosts" story which he had read in the 1930s, though, he did respond with a shortened and slightly inaccurate version. When Hunter checked the earlier transcripts, however, he discovered that Aitken had been presented with the very version which he recalled 27 years later. Unlike V.P. and S, Aitken's skill seemed to rest on what Hunter describes as "conceptual mapping" rather than "perceptual chaining". If Aitken felt that information was meaningless he would be most reluctant to commit it to memory.

Can anything be learned about imagery from Aitken's abilities? In terms of direct emphasis on and information about images probably not much. Aitken made less frequent use of visual images than S and, besides, as Hunter indicates, everything we have learned about him can be explained from our current knowledge of the "design features of memory" (p.162). Where Aitken's data are useful is in their illustration of the relative importance of underlying organization and control processes in skilled cognition compared with the representations of thought. Neither images nor words alone provide sufficient bases for sophisticated intellectual achievement. Indeed, part of S's problem by comparison, was that his abstract conceptual processes were less powerful than his other literal representational skills.

III   Concluding remarks

Research on individual differences in imagery abilities has increased our knowledge of the imagery system. We hope that this is self evident from the studies we have described. As well as informing us about individual difference *per se* many of these experiments can contribute converging evidence for the involvement of imagery in a variety of situations. Though they only suggest that this "involvement" is functional and it cannot be ruled out that, say, reported vividness is epiphenomenal, this circumstantial evidence can be quite impressive. Problems do exist, however, and we must consider some of these here.

One obvious drawback is that this research has concentrated largely on the visual modality. It is true, of course, that the visual sense is believed to be central or dominant and worthy of special consideration, and that some tests, such as the QMI, do assess auditory, gustatory, olfactory and other types of imagery but the importance of the visual may have been overemphasized. Perhaps one result of this bias has been that a limited number of image dimensions have been studied. The most compelling and immediate phenomenal aspect of a visual image, its vividness, has been construed as the prime source of individual variance. The same assumption is then made about imagery in other modalities. No attempt, to our knowledge, has been made to investigate the control of auditory or other images. Even within the study of visual imagery there are a host of properties and processes which may vary between individuals and may be *within* individuals too. Before images appear in awareness, they must be retrieved, constructed, or be cued in some way, as we mentioned earlier, variations in these abilities have not been systematically investigated. Once they have been retrieved images can be transformed, or may apparently transform themselves. They can be rotated, expanded, contracted and otherwise deformed (e.g. Cooper and Shephard, 1973; Kosslyn, 1980). To suggest that a single dimension, control, can cover all these situations may be misleading. It is possible that people who excel at rotating their images may be slow in altering image size, alternatively, control may be a general factor. By examining the performance of subjects across a battery of RT experiments this issue could be resolved.

Images in other modalities may have qualities as yet undiscovered. One important issue must be the relation between verbal imagery and verbal rehearsal. Baddeley and Hitch (1974) have argued that there exists, in working memory, an "articulatory loop" or slave system, which can store speech responses prior to their omission, and take the load off the central processor. Baddeley (1976) goes on to suggest that articulatory coding might be more important than acoustic in working and STM. Is verbal imagery equivalent to the operations of the articulatory loop? If it is, different processes may be involved when people image (rehearse) words compared with when they imagine themselves listening to a symphony concert. To describe the former type of imagery as verbal and the other as auditory may not be too wide of the mark. Individuals may differ in their verbal compared with their auditory imaginal skills.

For auditory, visual and other types of imagery, a variable about which little is known is the typicality and constancy over time of particular images. The work of Eleanor Rosch (e.g. Rosch, 1973; Rosch and Mervis, 1975) would suggest that the most frequent image associated with, for example, the word "sheep" will be a prototypical or standard version. But do people always retrieve such images? We can imagine sheep on the fells, toy sheep advertising rugs, pantomime sheep and sheep on the butcher's slab! We need much better data on the stereotypical and prototypical nature of people's imaging through time, the studies which do exist (e.g. Gordon, 1950) are largely anecdotal (though see Reese, 1977; Morris and Reid, 1973).

As a guide to whether a particular dimension on which individuals differ is worth investigating we believe that it is important to discover whether the process or property is functional. Consider the case of typicality we have just mentioned. If, as some researchers have argued (e.g. Pylyshyn, 1973), the surface or conscious image has no real involvement in the stream of processing, that is, it is only useful in so far as it is a token of an underlying abstract type, then the issue of the particular form of the surface image may not matter. On the other hand if both types and tokens are functionally implicated in cognition, prototypically must matter. The point is that the relevance of a dimension cannot be demonstrated from individual difference studies alone. The reasons for studying a given process derive from our theories about the basic structure and function of the imagery system. We reiterate the point made at the start of this chapter, individual differences should really be studied within the framework of a general model.

There is a deeper reason why the integration of individual difference research and studies of imagery's structure has not been fully achieved. Difference testing is a part of the general area of psychometrics, a tradition which has been noted for its *lack* of theory and rather pragmatic approach to the existence of cognitive processes and structures. Intelligence and other aptitude tests, if standardized, measure abilities with respect to a statistical norm or central tendency, not in relation to any underlying model. Also, the test movement has made extensive use of factor analysis. This powerful technique can simplify data, but it does not automatically solve theoretical problems. Gilham (1978) comments that factors have primarily a mathematical significance and are "like human beings . . . born with no name although there is usually one waiting for them, which may not fit their character very well" (1978, p.117). Levy (1973) has pointed out that *facet* analysis, which allows a systematic description of the processing operations tapped by test items, can be used as an alternative. The psychometrics of imagery, however, have been mainly explored factor analytically. An extended discussion of the limitations of traditional methods of studying individual differences, the benefits of a well formulated functional model, and the contribution that individual's variations can make to understanding cognition will be found in Sternberg (1977).

Nature and Function of Imagery

6
Theories of imagery

What is a mental image like? So far we have looked at several different types of imagery and examined some of its experiential aspects, but we have not really considered its nature. One possibility is that images are like internal pictures or snapshots of things in the world. After all, the man in the street's notion of imagery and the etymology of the word "image" itself suggest that images might be *simulacra* or *re*-presentations of things seen, heard or otherwise experienced. Another possibility is that imagery is much more abstract than this, more like a description of something than a photograph of it. A yet more radical alternative is that images as such do not exist, but only the processes of imagining. The latter view leads to the conclusion that imagery is a type of mental role-playing or pretending to see, hear or whatever. During the last decade variations on these positions have emerged in a debate which has been marked by the almost religious fervour of those engaged in it. These issues are, of course, ones which cannot be ignored by any serious student of imagery since discovering the basic form of imagery will constrain the ways in which it can be used to explain performance in a variety of situations. The debate has wider ramifications, too. As part of the more general concern with how people retain and use any knowledge they have gleaned from the world the outcome of the "imagery debate" affects theories of representation in, at the very least, the study of perception and memory, but probably language as well.

A basic problem for newcomers to this area is that they are faced with an overwhelming and often confusing variety of labels for the different theories and models. For example, systems which assert that the image is in some ways a pictorial type of representation have been variously referred to as analogue, mental picture, holistic, radical image and computer graphic approaches, to name but a few! While we are aware that the term is not approved by everyone in the field we propose to refer to these as Picture Theories. The alternatives to Picture Theories can be divided into two groups. On the one hand there is the general orientation that images are rather more abstract than pictures, this position and its variations have been severally labelled: propositional; descriptive; abstract and anti-image. We have opted for the general term Description Theories for this sub-group. On the other hand imagery can be construed as a form of imagining, acting "as if" something were seen, or pretending to see. Role Playing Theories is our label for these approaches. As in the rest of the book, most of the discussion will be confined to the visual modality though other sensory systems will be referred to as and when appropriate. In the first section we will try to introduce the three approaches as impartially as possible. In Section II we will assess the theories, looking for similarities and differences between them with a view to offering a revised model, presented in Section III, which relies heavily on our discussion of consciousness in Chapter 3.

I   Theories of imagery

A   Picture theories

These theories rely to a greater or a lesser extent on the notion that an image is like a picture in the mind and that processing an image is akin to dealing with, seeing, rotating or generally manipulating the imagined object. Because of the effect of the criticisms of workers who disagree with this basic assumption (e.g. Pylyshyn, 1973; Neisser, 1976), later picture theories have become more sophisticated than the earlier ones.

One of the first though still very influential accounts is Paivio's dual code theory (see especially Paivio, 1971). According to this approach people remember and think about things they have experienced with the aid of words and images. Images, Paivio claims, are better than words for representing the way things look or appear. Because they resemble the objects or events they stand for in a very direct way, images are said to have the property of *concreteness*. Also, just as a picture of a landscape can display trees, mountains, rivers and cottages all at once so an image can tell us a lot about the relationships between one object and another and between the various parts of a given object because it can represent information in a spatially parallel fashion. Words can also be used to refer to perceivable objects, e.g. "carrot", "daffodil" and "elm tree", they too can be concrete, but unlike images certain words are more abstract in their reference, e.g. "truth", "pleasure" and "advice". We will explore the effects of word concreteness on memory in detail in Chapter 11, for the moment it is sufficient to note that such a dimension exists. Words and images, because of their different natures, it is also argued, have to be used in different ways, and are supported by different processing systems. With their origin in spoken language, words are dealt with by the verbal-auditory system and images by the visuo-spatial. Images permit parallel processing (in both spatial and operational senses of the term) of their various aspects; words, tied as they are to the temporal stream of verbal processing, allow sequential or serial processing only. This division of labour does not mean that the two systems must function independently. We can after all describe our images in words, however imperfectly, as we do when we tell a friend about a quaint town we saw on holiday and we can form mental pictures from descriptions as we might when reading about the appearance of one of Jane Austen's heroines. Indeed, Paivio (1971b) claims that when both codes, or types of representation, are used in certain memory tasks, performance will be facilitated compared with when only one is employed. This "dual code theory" has been extensively tested by Paivio and his colleagues (see Paivio, 1971b, and Chapter 11) and has received a certain amount of support.

So much for the global form of Paivio's theory, but what is the image itself like? Paivio (1975b) has stated that images are "analogue representations" originally derived from perception. Exactly what is intended by this is not clear, but we interpret it as meaning that visual images consist of stored information about the surface, physical structure and appearance of objects and events, gleaned originally through perception, and organized to resemble those objects or events. Yuille and Catchpole (1977) have criticized Paivio's views on these matters on the grounds that he gives the impression that images and words alone provide sufficient bases for knowledge, without postulating any extra mediating, transforming or interpreting *processes*. Wittgenstein (1953) illustrated this problem by saying that a camera does not contain knowledge merely because it contains exposed film. To re-present or transfer the world inside our heads does not tell us anything about it. Yuille and Catchpole's charge that Paivio is guilty of a naïve Lockean type of empiricism is valid but may be a little severe. Paivio does admit that images can be used in a dynamic fashion to aid thinking and problem solving and recognizes that their parallel representation of information affords parallel processing. Implicit in the model is the idea that ways of dealing with images, to derive new representations from old, are needed. Control processes as well as representations of the world are necessary in any information processing approach. Unfortunately this insight is not made fully explicit in Paivio's theory.

A model advanced by Shepard (1975) has sharpened up the representation-process distinction and has particularly clarified the notion of representation (see also Podgorny and Shepard, 1978; Shepard and Podgorny, 1979). Shepard argues that problems of representation arise more frequently with images than with words because the link between a word and the object to which it refers is obviously arbitrary whereas those between an image and its referent are not. The word "cat" stands for a small feline creature in English, but the French manage quite well with "chat", and if a linguistic community decided to use the word "plink" for the animal provided they did so consistently, no problems would arise! Images, however, are not only assumed to stand for objects but also to embody information about their appearance and structure. Shepard has argued that images are an example of a general class of representation which he calls "first-order isomorphisms", while words are "second-order isomorphisms". These terms, borrowed from linear algebra, sound forbidding but the distinction is simple and worth making. Iso-mosphisms are relations between representations and their referents. In both cases it is assumed that mental symbols (representations) uniquely specify their objects, i.e. each representation stands for one and only one different object. Without this assumption confusion could arise. If, for example, someone had exactly the same mental event when he was thinking about, say, a train as when he was thinking about a cabbage then he would not be able to distinguish mentally between the two! First and second order isomorphisms differ in that first order (images) are internally structured to resemble their referents whereas second order are not. An image of a square does not merely stand for a square but, in some sense, retains the information that a square has four sides of equal length which join at right angles in a particular topological arrangement. The word "square" alone fails to represent anything about the object's geometry. As well as, or because of, the two types of isomorphism Shepard also claims that various control processes are needed for the system to use its words and images. His concern then has not only been with the form of representations but also with their transformation (see Chapter 8).

Unfortunately, like Paivio's, Shepard's (1975) model does not specify precisely what the image is like. Is it pictorial, for example, or much more abstract? In fact there is no reason why even a first order representation should be a mental picture. Shepard actually sympathizes with the view that a visual image is more like a percept than a picture, but fails to state unequivocally what form he believes perceptual representation to take. Shepard's term, "first-order isomorphism", is often read as "pictorial image" but to do so risks ignoring alternative interpretations.

Shepard's and Paivio's accounts point to the distinctions between words and images but neither tell us much about the mechanics of the image itself. In a series of publications over the last few years, Kosslyn and his colleagues have described a model of the imagery system which is far more detailed than any comparable pictorial theory (Kosslyn, 1975, 1978, 1980, 1981; Kosslyn and Pomerantz, 1977; Kosslyn et al., 1979). The system has undergone several revisions and was originally proposed in terms of a particular concrete analogy, a computer generated visual display (Kosslyn, 1975), but recently has been translated into working computer simulation (see especially Kosslyn, 1980; also Kosslyn, 1981). It is easier to understand the computer simulation, however, by first considering the earlier "graphics model". Kosslyn (1975) rejected a simple picture metaphor on the grounds that images are not replays or re-appearances of unanalysed sensation but are often already partially interpreted. What can be imaged is determined by what can be perceived and how it was perceived. Images, for Kosslyn as for Shepard (1975) are more like percepts than pictures. Thus as an alternative to the picture theory, Kosslyn (1975) suggested that images are the end products of constructive processes (see Chapter 3). Consciously experienced images, in one version of the theory, are put together from underlying, abstract, long-term memory representations which in turn are more like descriptions of objects' appearances than appearances themselves. This conscious, or surface image then bears the same relation to its abstract substrate as a cathode ray tube display does to the computer program which generates it. A mental equivalent of the computer's visual display unit (VDU) supports the image not by displaying unanalysed pictures, but by maintaining representations similar to those which occur in perception.

One test of an analogy or model's strength is to see whether it can be used to make any empirical predictions about the modelled phenomena. Even Plato's simple wax tablet model of memory, for example, can be used to derive notions about trace interference and decay (cf. Marshall and Fryer, 1978). Kosslyn's (1975) system is quite good in this respect as he has indicated. For instance, just as VDU display fades unless re-activated or refreshed so too images will decay unless actively maintained. The VDU's area is finite in size and thus limits the amount of information that can be plotted within it. Also the definition of the screen limits the "density" or amount of information per unit area. The image display space may be similarly limited in capacity. Another type of capacity limit which might affect the graphics display could be a restriction on the amount of underlying, abstract information which can be activated at once. Similarly the long-term memory descriptions, from which images are produced, may limit the rate of production and total amount of information finally displayed. Capacity restrictions such as these affect the quality of information in the image. Very small or detailed properties of objects may be too poorly represented for imagers to spot them unless they improve their display in some way. TV pictures or graphics can be rescaled, as when a camera "zooms in" on an object. Perhaps the imagery system can do the same.

The reader will have noted that to speak of "spotting properties" and "re-scaling" images seems to imply that Kosslyn's (1975) model includes mention of certain processes which operate upon the image, once it has been constructed, as well as processes which are involved in the construction itself. This is indeed the case. In the graphics models a processor which Kosslyn unashamedly calls the "mind's eye" is able to access selectively all or part of the information currently on display. So for example, one mind's eye property that has been extensively investigated by Kosslyn's research group is "image scanning" (Kosslyn et al., 1977; see also Chapter 8). Shifting the focus of one's visual attention across real objects takes a finite amount of time. It will take longer to scan all the way up Nelson's column from bottom to top than to scan only halfway up. Similarly it may take some considerable time to find a friend's child in a large school photograph if the child is to be found at the extreme right of the picture and scanning starts at the left. Kosslyn's graphics model raises the issue as to whether images obey similar laws, so that long scans across images of, say, Nelson's column might be expected to take longer than short scans. The mind's eye is also strongly implicated in property checking or feature detection especially, as Kosslyn (1980) has tried to establish, where the relation between object and property has not been explicitly considered previously. Questions such as "Does an elephant have toenails?" might need to be checked with imagery whereas those such as "Does an elephant have a trunk?" would probably not. Kosslyn and Pomerantz (1977) claimed that the mind's eye need not imply that there is an homunculus or little man in the head doing the seeing, but that there simply exists a perceptual parsing system or set of processes that can search for interpreted parts of the image. We are to take the graphics metaphor literally but not too literally!

Kosslyn and Shwartz (1977) have refined, extended and formalized the earlier model in a recent computer simulation (CS) which has been well reviewed by Kosslyn (1980), together with supporting empirical data which we shall consider later (a shorter though quite comprehensive treatment can be found in Kosslyn, 1981). To describe this system in complete detail is beyond the scope of this book but we can highlight its main features. The simulation retains the most important basic postulate of the graphics account which is that surface images are generated from more abstract representations. Also, as before, the properties of the surface image, which is plotted as a series of points in a visual buffer, or *surface matrix*, are constrained by its display medium. The underlying representations are specified in more detail in the CS model. A distinction is made between *literal* encodings which specify how an object looked and provide inputs for the image construction process and *propositional* encodings which describes objects or scenes and can be used to organize the construction process. A rough and ready distinction is that literal encodings tell us *how* something appeared and propositional tell us *where* its various features are to be found. The exact format of literal encodings remains unspecified in the model though propositional encodings are "abstract, languagelike discursive representations, corresponding roughly to simple active declaritive statements" (Kosslyn, 1981, p.52). They are more like descriptions than pictures.

Surface images must be generated from literal and propositional encodings and this important set of operations is clearly worked out in the simulation. A process known as PICTURE is the basic means for doing this. PICTURE translates literal encodings about the appearance of objects and their parts into a surface image. With the help of a process known as PUT which accesses the propositional encodings the right things are plotted in the right place. Sometimes several literal encodings may need to be built together. Image an elephant. Now give it some wings. Where did you put the wings? Probably somewhere on its back rather than its belly. In this case a FIND process locates the position or part where the new information is to be plotted. An overall IMAGE process co-ordinates all these operations.

Following its construction, an image can be inspected and transformed. To check an image, LOOKFOR finds a description of the target part or objects and with the help of FIND inspects the surface image for its presence. To find tusks on your imaged elephant you need to be able to recognize them when you see them! Sometimes the sought part may not be directly available on the surface image in which case a feature may need scaling up, using ZOOM, or the whole lot brought into view, using PAN, or a distant section moved across, with SCAN. These, of course, are operations performed by the mind's eye in the earlier graphics model.

Transformations have several properties. First, they operate either on the underlying representations and thereby produce variations in the surface image or work directly on the surface image itself. This latter assertion is a very strong claim, since it means that the consciously, experienced image has a function. Second, when transformations are applied to the surface image they can affect the entire contents of the display space as when zooming in to a particular feature, in which case they are said to be *field general* or they can apply to specific aspects of the display, as when expanding a particular feature relative to others, in which case they are *region bounded*. Finally the majority of modifications involve incremental modifications of aspects of the display space, these are *shift* or *continuous* transformations as is the case with the ones we have just mentioned. A less obvious though equally important mode of transformation is to replace one image display with another. These *blink* transformations, as Kosslyn (1980) has called them, operate directly on the data base. Both Kosslyn and the present authors (Hampson and Morris, 1978b) have found evidence supporting the existence of blink transforms though we referred to them as "iterations" (see Chapter 8).

We have examined Kosslyn and Shwartz' (1977) simulation in some detail because it is the most sophisticated picture theory currently available. The crux of this approach is that images are quasi-pictorial only in so far as they display emergent properties which cannot be deduced from a more abstract underlying description. Processes such as SCAN and ZOOM operate on the surface image in the Kosslyn and Shwartz model and derive information from it. A further implication, which is now argued less forcibly than previously by Kosslyn, is that images are similar to the representations used in perception and that some of the processes operating on images are analogous to perceptual ones. However, whether or not the conscious image has a functional role to play is what really separates the pictorial theories from those we must now consider.

B   Non-pictorial models

1   The critique of the description theorists

During the past decade, considerable impetus has been imparted to imagery research by the criticisms and suggestions of workers who have rejected pictorial theories, most notably Pylyshyn (1973, 1975, 1980, 1981) but also Kintsch (1977) and Anderson and Bower (1973). The issues raised by these psychologists are not always easy to understand, but it is well worth making the effort to grasp them. Pylyshyn's work, possibly the most influential and considered in detail here, is really *meta*-theoretical in character. Much of it is a concern with what general kind of imagery theory is possible. It is a way of quartering the field before theory building proper begins.

Those who are critical of pictorial theories have been at pains to remind other researchers that all imagery theories depend upon one among several meanings of the concept "representation". To illustrate their point, consider the definition of the verb "to represent" which is offered by the *Concise Oxford English Dictionary*: "(to) call up by description or portrayal or imagination, (to) figure, (to) place a likeness before the mind, or senses . . .". This definition includes at least the following four alternatives: (1) representing is equivalent to describing how something looked; (2) representing is like viewing a picture; (3) representing involves imagining, pretending to see, or acting as if one were seeing; (4) representing is akin to fashioning or fabricating, e.g. sculpting. The particular interpretation adopted will constrain the class of admissible models of representation. Pylyshyn claims that analogue or pictorial theories are based on an inappropriate notion of representation, since they have adopted the position that "representing is like viewing a picture". The difficulty with this idea is that the image-as-picture metaphor pushes the problems of perception inside the head. A fully fledged pictorial image needs a fully grown homunculus to interpret it.

Can this *impasse* be avoided by siding with Shepard (1975) and Kosslyn and Pomerantz (1977) who state that the image is percept-like not picture-like, and also claim that the image is a spatially extended, analogue representation? The problem here, according to Pylyshyn, is that the representations underlying perception may be quite unlike these images. Following the discovery by Hubel and Wiesel (1963) of feature analysers and growing sophistication in the computer simulation of vision (e.g. Roberts, 1965; see Oatley, 1978 for a good review) it has become commonplace to argue that the perceptual system provides us with descriptions rather than pictures of the world. Thus, the weak argument against the Imagist position is that images-as-pictures run into the same problems as picture-percepts, both need to be reprocessed before they can be interpreted. The strong argument is that the information used when imaging is originally derived from perception and that this information is more like an abstract description than a spatially extended picture. The weaker argument asserts that the picture theory leads to an infinite regress; the stronger asserts that the regress can be avoided by using structural descriptions as a basis for imaginal representation.

Most of Pylyshyn's other criticisms are derived from the basic, metatheoretical point concerning representation. For example, the picture metaphor suggests that what is retrieved during imaging is an unstructured signal or pattern which is then further processed by the perceptual system, images are raw *inputs* to perceptual processes. Pylyshyn (1973) has claimed that this is wrong on several counts. For one thing, storing raw images would place an enormous load on the brain's resources. Also, since we can image at will parts of scenes or objects we must be addressing interpreted aspects of the wholes to retrieve the appropriate elements. Related to this is the fact that our images are often sketchy and fleeting with missing parts. These absent elements, however, are not arbitrary segments, like torn off corners of photographs, but are coherent, interpreted features. For example, my image of the window of the house I lived in 5 years ago is schematic because I cannot recall the number of separate panels, and I have chosen to image it with three, the rest of my image is normally structured (see Palmer, 1975). Finally, images are better considered as the outputs of rather than the inputs to the perceptual system. This last idea leads directly to the position that the experience of imagery has no functional part to play in the stream of processing. It is an epi-phenomenon, or as Pylyshyn says the cognitive cart and not the horse. Direct or "Privileged Access" to cognitive processing is limited and the conclusion follows that introspective reports should not be given much weight as data.

Having replaced image-as-picture with image-as-description, Pylyshyn (1973) was led to support a neutral code position against dual code theory. The end-product of all perceptual processing, whether visual or verbal, is considered to be an amodal, abstract representation. This "interpretation" of the world, though harmlessly dubbed a "description" is not necessarily linguistic or verbal in character but is perhaps best understood as the underlying meaning of a scene or event. This description can then be used to aid thinking, problem-solving or just plain daydreaming. Several possible candidates for the job of representing information in such an abstract manner were originally suggested by Pylyshyn (1973). They included propositions, list structures, networks and procedures. However, the details of and distinctions between these various alternatives are less important than what they have in common. To get the feel for how descriptions in general differ from pictorial theories examine how, in Fig. 7 a and b, the same scene is represented by the two types of system, noting that both are hypothetical examples and should not be read as precise models. For example, as we saw earlier, in any reasonably sophisti-cated pictorial theory the surface image is assumed to be constructed from an underlying, abstract representation, and in practice the structural description would doubtless be much more complex. Moreover both systems, abstract and pictorial, require processes as well as representations and these are absent from our diagram. However, despite these drawbacks the essential distinctions are clear. Pictures stand in place of, or *re*-present things, descriptions on the other hand, tell us what the things are and how they are related.

Recently, Pylyshyn (1981) has advanced some new and rather different criticisms of pictorial models. These seem to have been prompted by two factors. First, a considerable amount of new empirical data has been generated about images since the publication of his classic 1973 paper and a lot of this work has been directly addressed to contentious issues in the imagery debate. Second, in an effort to refine their own models and to respond to criticism, pictorial theorists such as Kosslyn (1980) have produced more sophisticated systems which have been formalized as computer simulations as we saw above. We shall consider some of the many experiments in

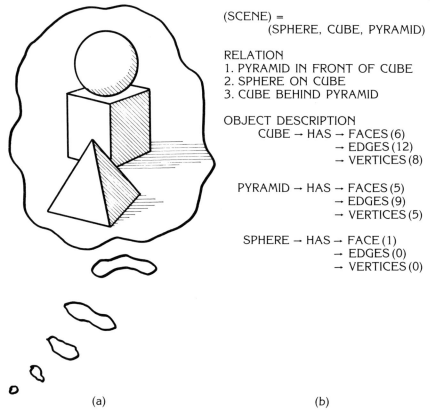

(SCENE) =
        (SPHERE, CUBE, PYRAMID)

RELATION
1. PYRAMID IN FRONT OF CUBE
2. SPHERE ON CUBE
3. CUBE BEHIND PYRAMID

OBJECT DESCRIPTION
        CUBE → HAS → FACES (6)
                         → EDGES (12)
                         → VERTICES (8)

    PYRAMID → HAS → FACES (5)
                         → EDGES (9)
                         → VERTICES (5)

    SPHERE → HAS → FACE (1)
                         → EDGES (0)
                         → VERTICES (0)

(a)   (b)

Fig. 7 (a) A simple pictorial representation. In more sophisticated models the surface image would be constructed from an underlying abstract representation (cf. Kosslyn and Shwartz, 1977). (b) An abstract description (grossly oversimplified).

Chapter 8, but it is worth noting here how the imagery debate has undergone a shift in character. As was stated in the opening remarks of this section, the earlier discussions were about what *general* form an imagery theory should take. Now, there is, as Kosslyn (1981) has noted, a move in the direction of debating the adequacy of *specific* theories, and a more healthy concern with collecting new data which will set constraints on such theories.

Pylyshyn's (1981) new arguments are both a concession and a challenge to pictorial theorists. In general he has accepted the results of many of the studies which *can* be used to support a model such as Kosslyn and Shwartz (1977). Perhaps because of its links with perception, he admits, imagery might well in some sense mimic or model operations with objects. His challenge though is whether an "analogue" or spatial medium such as Kosslyn's "display space" need be postulated to predict imagery effects. It could be, for example, that such things as the demand characteristics of the experiments themselves rather than intrinsic properties of the cognitive system cause people to respond as they do. Or, perhaps subjects know tacitly or explicitly how a corresponding perceptual operation could be performed and act as if they were doing the same with imagery. These and other criticisms have been considered by Kosslyn (1981) and will be discussed further in Chapter 8.

Proponents of propositional models sometimes argue that images are unnecessary as a means of retrieving information. They maintain that images must be constructed on the basis of stored rules, probably in a propositional form. If, they argue, the information exists, as it must, in the rules from which the image is composed, then there is no need to go through the process of image formation before the information becomes available. We will discuss the limitations of this argument further in Chapters 9 and 10, but we will explain here briefly why we believe it to be misleading.

The argument assumes that because information exists within the system that it must, therefore, be available for use. There are both empirical and theoretical reasons for doubting this. Much research, especially by Tulving and his associates (e.g. Tulving and Thompson, 1973) has shown that what can be recalled from memory depends on the match between currently available retrieval cues and the form of the entry in memory. If these do not correspond sufficiently the stored information does not become available. Memories seem to be stored in packets, cells (Posner, 1973) or records (Norman and Bobrow, 1979) which correspond to the processing activities at acquisition. These packets must be accessed by appropriate retrieval cues, and the information within them cannot be retrieved piecemeal, or be processed until retrieved. So, if information is input in a visual form, and processed in terms of the physical objects that are perceived, recall may require accessing a package of rules which correspond to the original processing, and which involves displaying an image in a quasi-visual form before elements of the package can be further analysed. Access to the package will depend on appropriate retrieval cues for the packet as a whole, and not for some small set of its parts. So, for example, to "remember" the number of windows in your house, a memory packet which contains visual memories of your house will need accessing, if you have not previously considered the question of the number of windows (see Chapter 9). Access to the visual memory will be via codes relating to memory for your house, not via the concepts of number and window. Without accessing the memory packet in this way the information will not be usable.

Another argument for the unavailability of information existing in memory is that even if the information, in raw propositional form, could be accessed, this would not mean that it could be used. Its use will depend on the existence of appropriate operators. In Chapter 10 we argue that the imagery format may allow operations upon the displayed information for which operators (probably perceptual) exist, but for which no operators will have been developed to interpret the raw propositions, prior to their application in the construction of the image. It is not sufficient for information to exist if the means to interpret it are not available.

2 Role playing models

Picturing and describing do not exhaust the various ways of defining the concept of representation; as we noted earlier, "fabricating" and "imagining" are plausible alternatives. Until recently the latter two possibilities have received little or no emphasis in psychology, though since the publication of Ryle's (1949) seminal book *The Concept of Mind* they have been discussed extensively in philosophy. Ryle has argued cogently that the familiar truth that people report seeing things in the mind's eye or hearing things in the head does not constitute proof that there really are things seen or heard. He reminds us that just as stage murders are not real homicides and have no (real) victims, so too seeing things with the mind's eye involves neither things seen nor seeing. Although this sounds like the propositional critique, Ryle is lead to a different conclusion. As he writes:

> a person picturing his nursery is, in a certain way like that person seeing his nursery, but the similarity does not consist in his really seeming to see the nursery itself, when he is not really seeing it. He is not being

a spectator of a resemblance of his nursery, but is resembling a spectator of his nursery. (1949, p.248)

Since its proposal Ryle's theory has been challenged by several philosophers and we have already criticized it in Chapter 2. Although we shall not consider these criticisms again, it is interesting to note that some of Ryle's ideas have been revived in a recent theory advanced by Neisser (1976). To understand Neisser's approach, it is important to realize that it is part of a more general account of perception and cognition. Neisser's aim has been to reconcile the notions of information pick up of Gibson (1966) with the information-processing approach typified by Neisser (1967) in his earlier book. The two paradigms may be caricatured as the studies of *what* information is processed and *how* it is processed respectively. His solution was to offer the "perceptual cycle" as a new, unifying theory, a somewhat Piagetian model with three elements. The first, the information sources in the world, afford classes of data which may be used by a particular organism. The usable data are picked up by cognitive structures known as schemata, provided that these are in a state of anticipation of readiness. A schema's anticipations are equivalent to a set of hypotheses about the world. The cognitive system gains *knowledge* by noting whether or not its schemata's expectations are realized. Another way to understand this is to compare these anticipations to *formats* in a computer programming language which specify the form information must be in before it is accepted. A second function of the schemata is to control the output or the exploration system, the final element in Neisser's model which further samples the first element, the information in the world. In this way a schema also acts as a plan (cf. Miller *et al.*, 1960).

Neisser accounts for the phenomena of imagery in a way which is both sophisticated and simple, and, at the same time, emphasizes its link with perception. He argues that having an image is equivalent to *imagining* or pretending to see. It is an anticipation or readiness to perceive, not the retrieval of a mental picture or a perceptual description, and it occurs when the schemata normally used for perceiving are used out of the context of their normal cycles. These "disconnected" schemata are used purely in their anticipatory mode and in this way the cognitive system acts "as if" it were perceiving without actually doing so. We can clarify this rather abstract idea with an example. When someone says that he is imagining Blackpool Tower, this does not mean that he is inspecting a mental picture of the famous landmark, but rather that he is reminding himself of what it would feel like actually to see the tower, were it in fact present. Note that if he were (miraculously) to find himself suddenly in Blackpool, his perceptual system would be primed to accept "tower-specifying-information" without more ado! Or, more plausibly, if approaching the resort by motor-car in a fog, he would be more likely to spot the building before another occupant of the vehicle who was not imaging it at the time.

Neisser's theory is interesting. It neatly solves, or dissolves, the problem of the link between imagery and perception and sidesteps the debate about the nature of representation. It is, however, beset by certain difficulties which we shall consider shortly. It is illuminating to note though that a model has been advanced which replaces the constructs of stored representations acted upon by control processes with a non-storage metaphor based on structural change of schemata, in the tradition of Bartlett (1932), Piaget (1971), and, especially, Ryle (1949).

II A comparison of the theories

So far we have outlined in some detail the major theoretical orientations in imagery research. Our aim now is to see what, if anything, is common between the approaches and what is a source of disagreement. We hope also to resolve at least some of these controversies and to suggest a set of criteria from which we can construct a coherent imagery theory. As yardsticks for the theories three issues have been selected: first the relation between imagery and perception; second, the general problem of representation and third the status of consciousness and introspection in the various models. These are topics pertinent not just to the study of mental imagery, but also to the wider debate on the representation of knowledge.

A Imagery and perception

Many theories of imagery have been constructed around the assumption that imagery and perception are related. This is especially true for models such as the one proposed by Neisser (1976) who has derived an account of imagery from an explicit theory of perception. Similarly, the accounts of Kosslyn (1975), Shepard (1975) and others are often used to claim that images and percepts are related in some way. Non-pictorial theories, too, can be used to assert that the processes are linked. Pylyshyn (1973) suggested that images are the abstract outputs of, rather than the inputs to, perceptual processes, though recently he has proposed alternative possibilities (Pylyshyn, 1981). To claim some general equivalence like this, though, is not very helpful. Given that it is accepted that if images exist at all, it is not unreasonable to claim that they are partially supported by some of the mental structures and processes used in perception. The two vital issues are: how are these structures and processes to be characterized, i.e. what form does the parent perceptual theory take, and where does equivalence arise?

If we consider the problem of which perceptual theory to choose first, it should be evident to anyone who has flicked through even the most basic textbook on the subject that there is no general consensus among researchers as to which one is correct. One strategy, at this point, is to avoid both this issue and the question of equivalence, to concentrate mainly on the mechanics of imagery itself and to ignore, or at least play down, the wider questions of its position *vis-à-vis* perception. While this seems to be the stance of some contemporary theoreticians (e.g. Kosslyn, 1981), it is not one that we choose to adopt, since our aim is to present a reasonably integrated account of imagery and consciousness in cognition. However, rather than commit ourselves irrevocably to any one perceptual theory at the moment we believe that it may be more useful to ask what the majority of perceptual theories have in common. Hopefully such an analysis will give us a general framework within which we can then ask more specific questions about imagery–perception equivalence.

We can imagine the reader's eyebrow quizzically raised. What attributes *do* contemporary theories of perception share? Our claim is that the majority of, if not all, modern theories, with rare exceptions such as Gibson's (1966) account, embody a distinction between two types of processing often referred to as data-driven or bottom-up processing on the one hand and concept driven or top-down on the other (e.g. Norman, 1976; Oatley, 1978). Data-driven processing refers to those operations which start with the incoming information and continue through more and more complex analyses in an effort to deduce what is being perceived. To use the example of looking at a tree as a case in point: light from the object is focussed on the retina where it is not only transformed into neuronal impulses but is coded by physiological mechanisms (e.g. Cornsweet, 1970). After the retina, the information is passed, through various synapses, up the optic nerve eventually arriving at the visual cortex. At each level further encoding operations are performed until the object is pattern-recognized and seen as a tree. However, the human perceptual system appears at times to be able to anticipate what the results of these bottom-up processing stages will be. We can use our expectations as, for example, Neisser (1976) has cogently argued, to prepare ourselves to receive certain types of information. These top-down, high-level processes are guided by stored knowledge about the world and interact with data-driven ones. Theorists do differ about *how much* top-down, or bottom-up processing is needed for perception. Marr (1976), for example, claims that we should attempt a bottom-up analysis as far as is possible, whereas Neisser (1976) has concentrated more on people's expectations. The majority agree, though, that some mix of the two processing modes is essential.

We may now be in a better position to consider our second question. Where does the equivalence between imagery and perception arise? Put at its simplest, the issue becomes whether imagery has more in common with bottom-up or top-down perceptual processing. It is likely that the central, conceptually driven perceptual operations, drawing as they do on information stored in memory are more likely to be also used to produce images than are peripheral, data-driven systems. On grounds of efficiency alone, the imagery system need not apply bottom-up analyses to raw, undifferentiated replicas of sensations when it can conceivably use the already pre-processed representations marshalled by top-down processes (see Kosslyn and Pomerantz, 1977 for a similar view).

If this analysis is correct, the substantive issue becomes the nature of top-down processing and how it operates during imaging. It is here that we must tread warily. There have been several suggestions made as to how such central processes might operate many of which seem to mirror positions in the imagery debate (which is perhaps hardly surprising). The variations include using hypotheses about the incoming data (e.g. Gregory, 1973), matching stored propositional descriptions and using a tacit theory of optics (e.g. Falk, 1972), cueing an embedded series of frames or scene descriptions (e.g. Minsky, 1977) or synthesizing a percept or visual representation to match the incoming data (e.g. Neisser, 1967). The point to notice is that pictorial, description and role playing accounts can be accommodated by choosing the appropriate system. What is very clear is the fact that claiming that images are the interpreted outputs of perceptual processes, which are then "read" by higher order conceptual ones need not commit us to the notion that images are descriptions. Although anti-pictorial theorists often suggest that the perceptual system provides us with parsed structural descriptions, and point to computer simulations of vision (e.g. Roberts, 1965) to support their case, some Artificial Intelligence workers (e.g. Waltz, 1979) have argued that analogue-like structures may be "more natural for representing the scene portions generated by top-down processes" (p.570). Thus, top-down processing itself might employ spatial images. We shall return to this issue shortly.

There is at least one prediction that can be derived from all three major approaches to imagery, pictorial, role-playing and descriptive, namely that imagery and perception can mutually interfere in certain circumstances. Neisser's (1976) model predicts that conflict will occur when a schema is used to perform an imagery and a perceptual task at the same time. Description theories could be used to argue that confusion may occur whenever spatial descriptions belonging to two or more separate tasks are manipulated in a common working memory. Finally, pictorial theories suggest that conflict can arise because both imagery and perception, at times, use the same processes and structures. We suspect that interference occurs at central, rather than peripheral processing stages since, as we intimated above, equivalence between imagery and perception is probably at this conceptually driven level. We shall explore these topics further too, in the next chapter when we consider empirical studies of interference effects.

B   Representation and process

Although it is generally accepted that there is some equivalence between imagery and perception, it is something of an understatement to assert that there is obviously considerable disagreement among researchers about the nature of the representations and processes used in imagery and perception. Most models, though, whether pro or anti-pictorial, embody and share the assumption that some form of stored information is used by the cognitive system to stand in place of objects and events when thinking about and imaging the same. One model advanced by Neisser (1976) does not depend on this notion. Instead, as we saw earlier, the remembrance of objects and events involves structural change in parts of the cognitive system, the schemata, which are normally involved in perception, rather than the storage of information in some repository after it has passed through various processing stages. Imagery involves re-activating these structures out of their normal perceptual context. A question which arises here is whether or not Neisser's theory offers a viable alternative to more traditional storage models. If it does, it might be advisable to accept it on grounds of parsimony and elegance. If not, then we must take up some position in the analogue versus propositional debate.

1   Neisser (1976)

Unfortunately, Neisser's theory, though interesting and elegant, is plagued by a number of problems. We have discussed these in detail elsewhere (see Hampson and Morris, 1978a) but will consider the main ones here. One of the difficulties with the theory concerns the nature of "anticipation". It will be remembered that when imaging the schemata are used "as if" perceptual information were forthcoming without having their expectations fulfilled. Difficulty arises in distinguishing between the anticipations of imaging and more general forms of expectation. For example, on returning home one may expect to see one's wife without actually imaging her. There appears to be something qualitatively different about imaging from being merely in expectation or readiness, and this is the conscious experience of having an image. Unless the experience of imaging is used to differentiate the two types of expectation, it is hard to see how the anticipations of a dormant schema differ from those of one actively used for imaging. Another weakness in the theory concerns its explanations of schema modification and imagery manipulation. In a normal perceptual cycle schemata modify themselves by interacting with an information source, but when operations are performed in an imagery mode no such external source is available. Assuming that the schemata *can* modify themselves when imaging, i.e. that the system has the capacity to learn by performing certain mental operations, as when imagining one's house and counting its windows, then three possibilities exist. First, perhaps image manipulation occurs when the schemata switch through a pre-existing set of expectations. If this is the case, then no new knowledge is ever gained imaging, as the system merely "goes over old ground". This seems to be counter-intuitive. Second, maybe the schemata modify themselves when imaging, though how this could take place without an information source is never made clear. Third, one way out of the dilemma would be to have a higher order schema supply information about the imaged object to a lower order one, but this would be equivalent to reintroducing stored representations, a strategy Neisser wanted to avoid. A final difficulty with the model concerns its treatment of introspection. Neisser argues that when describing imagined objects, we are not reporting on our mental experience, but instead are describing what the real object would look like if it were actually present. However, the fact that people use real-world descriptive terms when introspecting does not imply that they are actually describing real world objects. What other terms could they possibly use? Also, when introspecting, people often use terms inappropriate when describing the actual objects involved, for example they speak of "fuzzy", "vivid" and "lifelike" images. A simpler supposition is that they are describing the quality of their mental experience rather than an external object.

In a very fair paper, Neisser (1978) has replied to some of these criticisms, and has admitted the weakness of his theory in some respects, especially its treatment of introspection and mental rotation (for further discussion see Hampson, 1979). Unfortunately, these are not minor problems and for this reason it may be better to consider the alternative, storage models.

2   Storage models

As well as agreeing on the necessity for some form of internal represen-tation most theorists recognize that there is an intimate relationship between representations and the processes which use them. In general the more complex a representational system the simpler the procedures which use it, and vice versa. This trade-off, long recognized by computer scientists, has only recently been considered by imagery theorists, and has been used by Anderson (1978) to demonstrate that questions of representation are fundamentally undecidable using behavioural data alone. To understand what is meant by "trade-off", consider two libraries: in one the books are stored in alphabetical order of their authors' names, in the second the books are stored according to colour. In the first library, a retrieval process is most easily steered by using the authors' initials. In the second, though the organization is conceptually simple, retrieving a book by a particular author is exceedingly difficult, it might even be necessary first to telephone the publishers to ask the colour of the book's dust cover and then search exhaustively in the particular area. Similarly with imagery, at one extreme a raw, uninterpreted image will need a highly complex interpretive system, whilst the already interpreted description will require a simpler set of processes to "understand" it.

Exploiting this trade-off, Anderson has attempted to show that representation-process pairs in an image or picture theory are functionally indistinguishable from representation-process pairs in a more abstract system. His proof is designed to show that translation between the systems is possible without loss of explanatory power. However, as Johnson-Laird (1980a) has pointed out this proof only holds under certain specialized conditions. In particular, it depends on the assumption that perception involves a one-to-one mapping of objects onto their internal representations, i.e. that both images and propositions faithfully mirror their referents. To create a stable, internal model of the world it is more likely that our perceptual system has evolved to produce a many to one mapping of objects onto representations.

Johnson-Laird (1980a) goes on to demonstrate that far from being equivalent images (or as he prefers, "mental models") and propositions are quite different entities. His argument is complex but the crux of it is that whereas some theorists have claimed that propositions, or descriptions are *too* powerful in that they can, in principle, represent anything and everything (cf. Kosslyn and Pomerantz, 1977), Johnson-Laird has shown that, for certain states of affairs, propositional systems are not powerful enough to represent them unambiguously. This ambiguity can then be resolved, only with the aid of a mental model. As an example consider the relation of transitivity. It might be thought that from the statements "A is to the left of B", "B is to the left of C", "C is to the left of D", it can be

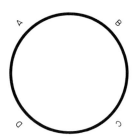

Fig. 8 The interpretation of descriptions depends on the context. The normal deduction that, if A is left of B, B is left of C and C is left of D; therefore A is left of D is invalid if, for example, they are seated round a circular table.

deduced unambiguously that "A is to the left of D". But is this so? What if A, B, C, and D are persons seated in sequence around a circular table but in such a way that A is on the immediate right of D (see Fig. 8). The indeterminacy of the description is easiest to resolve by reference to a spatial array or mental model, which may have to represent in *token* and therefore sometimes arbitrary fashion, aspects of the general *type* of description.

The critical reader could well protest that the ambiguity in the above description could be resolved by adding more qualifying descriptions and that the mental model itself might simply be the sum of the additional descriptions which are needed to do this. To make this claim, argues Johnson-Laird (1980a), is to miss the point that models and descriptions or propositions differ on a number of criteria of which the most important is their function. Propositions tell us what is happening and what exists in the world, and are therefore true or false with respect to states of affairs. One way of defining a proposition is to say that it is a function which takes a state of affairs as its argument and outputs a truth value. Abstract descriptions like these, then, need objects or events to work on. When used by the cognitive system they refer not directly to objects or events but to internal representations of them. They are, in a sense, parasitic upon mental models, which, in turn, should be understood as *analogical* representations because they mirror the relevant structural aspects of the world (see our earlier discussion of Shepard's 1975 theory). It is possible that both models and propositions are ultimately represented in the same common format, or machine code, but this tells us little since in the last analysis both could be reduced to changes in the neuronal substrate.

These functional differences led Johnson-Laird (1980a,b) to suggest that mental models, rather than propositions, underlie perception by providing the prototypical information about objects that allows the perceiver to interpret the "primal sketch" or output of data driven processes. As we noted earlier some AI workers such as Waltz (1979) have drawn similar parallels between top-down processes and analogical representations. These suggestions are interesting in the light of our equation of images with some aspects of top-down perceptual processing. Especially since Johnson-Laird has claimed that images correspond to the consciously perceivable aspects of mental models. Two substantive issues for imagery theory are thus when and how does top-down processing result in the production of images, rather than operating in a "cognitively silent" fashion? To address this question we believe that it is essential to consider how consciousness is involved in both imagery and perception.

C   Consciousness and introspection

Theories of imagery differ greatly in the role they ascribe to consciousness, and the credence they give to introspection. These issues are not entirely separable from the questions about the nature of representation since, leaving aside Neisser's model, description theories assert that the most basic level of representation may well be non-conscious. On the other hand, the surface or conscious image is given an important part to play in pictorial models. As for introspection, this finds little favour in propositional models, but is used with caution in the alternative accounts.

Johnson-Laird points out that it is still possible for description or propositional theorists to resist his argument that models and propositions are not necessarily equivalent. To do this they must exploit the computer analogy further. During the past 30 years or so there has been a growth in what are known as "high-level" programming languages such as FORTRAN, ALGOL, POP-10 and so on, which allow the programmer to interact with the machine in a more natural, though still somewhat constrained way than he could otherwise. The important point to note is that the machine does not execute its programmes in these languages, but first translates or "compiles" them into machine code, its own internal language, which simply tells the device how to shift bits of information from one storage location to another. Description theorists could similarly argue that irrespective of the high-level programming language in use, be it expressed in "images" or "analogues" or whatever, the most basic, irreducible language is the machine code, and this must be propositional. We side with Johnson-Laird (1980a) in believing this argument to be misguided since details of how a "representation is represented" (Kennedy, 1978) need not worry us here; it is the meaning rather than the format of the representation which is important (see Chapters 8 and 9). The machine code approach itself is misleading in two ways. First of all it invites further reduction since it is difficult to see why we should not translate the internal code itself into statements about neurophysiological and ultimately, biochemical processes, the reader's image of a table is, in one sense of the term, the *result* of neurophysiological processes save that this reductionist strategy has been frequently challenged (e.g. Putnam, 1973). Second, to reduce a high-level description into machine code causes us to lose sight of the *function* of the original representation. Demonstrating that a spatial array can be translated down into propositions or descriptions and then claiming that these are the fundamental units of representation is to miss the point that the particular propositions chosen were constrained by the original mental model's job. Moreover, this function is only apparent at the appropriate level of explanation, an array is only an array at the level at which it operates as one. Therefore, when in programming languages and in introspection we speak of manipulating arrays and such like, we are dealing with functional explanations at a *psychological*, not a computational level.

Using high-level representations may be facilitated by systems which possess an overall planning process to initiate and check the results of their various operations. Indeed this superordinate system might also be able to describe some of its own workings; these reports would then reflect the functional inner-language, or instructions which the system itself uses to plan and check its actions. Introspective protocol of this nature would of course use certain real world descriptive terms and would describe the experience of the system by analogy with perception. Executing a mental task would be said to feel "as if" a comparable perceptual task were being performed. This level of description would be functional as far as the system as a whole was concerned since it would allow it to continue planning and monitoring by rooting or grounding its current, mental activity in knowledge gained previously through perception. A control function of this nature would operate as a single and effective type of "reality check". The point we are making is that the superordinate system may harmlessly be described as conscious and that one of its important functions may be to monitor the stream of processing. We have explored some of these issues already in Chapter 3 but will have to consider them in more detail in relation to imagery shortly.

III   Toward a theory of imagery and consciousness

If our conclusions formed by comparing existing models of imagery are correct, then our own theory must be constrained in several ways. As these constraints are really a set of criteria around which various models can be constructed, it is useful to list them before describing our model. We suggest that the following are useful guidelines for theory construction: (1) A theory of imagery is always related to a particular theory of perception. (2) If the current view that perception depends on concept-driven as well as data-driven processes is accepted, imagery probably has more in common with the former than the latter. (3) Imagery and perception may interfere in certain circumstances. (4) Reasons can be advanced for rejecting non-storage models of imagery (e.g. Neisser's 1976 model) and accepting that information about states of affairs is stored in the form of internal representations. (5) Internal representations are operated on by various control processes, these will be involved in encoding, storage and retrieval and also in the derivation of new representations from old. (6) While the exact nature or format of representation has been the subject of much disagreement, it is by no means established either that propositions are viable alternatives to images or that the two are equivalent. A strong case can be made for the necessity of representations which function as mental models and representations which function as abstract descriptions or propositions. (7) A functional level of explanation precludes the reduction of models (high-level languages) to propositions (the machine code). (8) It may be more economical to store propositions in LTS, especially when the relations represented are indeterminate, and then to construct mental models from these underlying descriptions. (9) A model constructed from an indeterminate description will be arbitrary in either the number or the arrangement of its elements or both. (10) Consciously experienced images probably correspond to those aspects of models that can be perceived in the objects which they represent. (11) The use of high-level representations suggests the need for an overall control system which flexibly directs and monitors demanding cognitive tasks.

With these criteria in mind we are now in a position to put forward our theory of imagery. The model we describe is a particular version of the general approach which we outlined earlier in Chapter 3, and is similar to one advanced by Hampson (1979).

In Chapter 3, we introduced a general model of cognition which we labelled the BOSS-consciousness theory. The basis of this approach was that some central, control system is needed to explain the diverse phenomena of consciousness, introspection, automaticity and the interlinking of cognitive processes. A basic distinction was drawn between central, BOSS processes and the EMPLOYEE systems, and it was argued that the function of BOSS is to control the EMPLOYEE systems to make sure that they function in support of the main program or plans of the overall system. To do this, we claimed that a considerable degree of cognitive processing will go on without BOSS being any the wiser, and that when BOSS *is* informed about the action of its EMPLOYEE systems it will be in a format suitable for BOSS's operation. (Using Dennett's (1979) terminology BOSS can be said to have *public access* to some of the operations and products of its EMPLOYEE systems.) One of the characteristics of BOSS processing, we noted, was its intentionality, and its suitability for performing novel tasks. Consciousness is equivalent to the reception of information made available to BOSS and introspection involves reporting on this information.

The role of BOSS-consciousness in imagery depends on its specific links with top-down, perceptual processing. Although we believe that BOSS is presented with high-level information about the appearance and structure of the world, to say that BOSS-consciousness "perceives" the world in this way does not imply that BOSS programs are in total control of the perceptual process. For most of the time, the perceptual EMPLOYEE systems may well run without BOSS involvement, even when they are engaged in top-down operations. After all, most adult humans are *skilled* perceivers and one well known characteristic of their skills is automaticity, or as we noted in Chapter 3, their partial independence from BOSS programs. A notable feature of perception is its seemingly effortless operation, an aspect which frequently leads beginning psychology students to consider it as needing little or no explanation! Normally, then, perception looks after itself, drawing information from memory to interpret pre-processed data interlinking with the systems which produce responses and obediently feeding its findings to BOSS-consciousness where they may be used or ignored. At times, however, this smooth, "silent" system may encounter difficulties. When the incoming stimulus information is poor, as when walking in mist on the hills, or when the perceptual decisions are difficult, as when driving through heavy traffic, BOSS-consciousness may have to take more direct control of top-down processing. In our foggy day example, the primal sketch, or output from the data-driven processes might be insufficiently rich for the top-down processes to use it unaided. When this happens, BOSS-consciousness could recruit additional data to help top-down processing by interrogating memory about a similar walk performed in good weather and directing the retrieval of information about the appearance of the paths and crags at the time. Similarly, BOSS-consciousness programs are likely to take more direct control of the perceptual motor systems when driving in the rush hour. It may not be enough merely to perceive that the object in front is a bus, especially if the fact that it is masking a dangerous junction is not also evaluated. Often what is not directly seen in such cases is at least as important as what is. By taking a more active role in perceptual processing BOSS-consciousness can make up for any inadequacies in the incoming data, in certain cases supplementing it with perceivable aspects of its own mental models.

According to this view, imagery is the limiting case of perception without any stimulus information. Or, to put it another way, it is equivalent to the perceptual system working in a purely top-down mode, normally under the direct control of a BOSS program. Humans and possibly some other mammals have learned this trick of perceiving without stimulus data. We believe that this occurs when BOSS interrogates the memory data base for information about the appearance and structure of an object or event, and accepts the result. To supply the data in a way that BOSS programs can deal with and expect, a visual image will have to be constructed. This whole process of interrogating the data base and constructing a mental image is what it means to engage in top-down processing, or to use a mental model, in an imagery mode. Once the imageable aspects of the model have been set up in this way they can be used as an input for further BOSS programs, by suggesting further explorations of the data base which will, in turn, produce yet new inputs. Operations initiated by BOSS can thus be monitored in an appropriate format by BOSS programs.

It is interesting to note that our theory incorporates a distinction between mental models and propositions. We believe that the perceivable aspects of models are representations expressed in the sort of high-level language which BOSS deals in and are uniquely suited to allow it to plan further processing. On the other hand, it may be necessary to store information in propositional form on a long-term basis on the grounds of economy. It may also be the case that important operations on representations are conducted on these propositions, in the machine code as it were, but this does not detract from the fact that these operations will be constrained by the high-level representations delivered to BOSS as their products. The processes must function as if they are working on spatial arrays and as far as

BOSS is concerned, this is what they are doing. A further implication is that BOSS may control its own processing by giving itself instructions derived from descriptions of its images. These descriptions may, in suitable circumstances, be available to external observers as verbal reports on BOSS's functioning. Another distinction we have drawn is between images and their parent mental models. The latter when used to support top-down processing in perception need not be directly controlled by consciousness. Neither need their workings be totally open to inspection. Mental models, which may incorporate information specifying what can be done with them as well as including links with other models, embody more information than images. Images as we keep stressing are the perceivable aspects of models, and are organized in a suitable format for BOSS programs.

To keep the information displayed in a mental image and the underlying knowledge in its model continuously available it is likely that some reactivation or reconstruction will be needed. Unless something is done to refurbish the image it is probable that it will fade or decay with time. There are at least two ways in which the system could maintain its images. BOSS could continue activating the appropriate underlying model which would result in a refreshed image. Alternatively the surface image itself could be reactivated by a systematic BOSS procedure. In Kosslyn and Shwartz' (1977) simulation a process known as REGENERATE operates on the display matrix in this way. Another possibility which combines these two possibilities is that a BOSS program scans the image to locate parts which need refreshing and then interrogates the data base for more information about the areas in question. The image display would allow checks to be made on parts which require regeneration. Maintaining an image could be described as *visual* rehearsal, and it is interesting to speculate that similar effects of maintenance and elaborative operations, contrasting simple refreshing and deeper processing of the representation, may occur with images as they do with words (cf. Craik and Tulving, 1975). BOSS consciousness could be said to be involved in a spatial working memory, a visual equivalent of the "articulatory loop" (see Baddeley and Lieberman, 1980).

The specificity of mental models means that the images delivered to BOSS will be in the form of tokens rather than types. This property of arbitrariness has often attracted the attention of philosophers but the lack of generality of solutions to problems obtained using specific images is frequently offset by their heuristic strength. Images can be scanned, rotated and and otherwise manipulated. Also if the same task initially requiring imagery is performed several times information about the results of previous operations can be directly stored. This will allow the system to avoid bothering to construct and operate on images. For example when first asked what a square would look like if rotated through 45 degrees, a person may need to generate and rotate an appropriate image, before discovering that the result is a type of diamond shape. If asked the same question five minutes later it is reasonable to expect that the answer could be retrieved directly from memory. The more often an imagery operation like this is performed the less likely it will need to be performed subsequently. This is because the probability that the outcome of previous operations has been stored in descriptive form, will have increased accordingly.

The involvement of the non-conscious, EMPLOYEE data base in imagery and perception as well as the BOSS system means that similarities between imagery and perception should be found at levels other than the phenomenal. From what we have said these similarities should not be at the early, data-driven stages of processing except, maybe, where these are interacting with or primed by top-down ones. Whenever such levels of equivalence are found, it should also be possible to demonstrate that modality specific interference arises when imagery and perception compete for common processes and structures. Finally, wherever a subsidiary task, whether visual or verbal, is performed at the same time as an imagery task, and uses BOSS programs, more general, resource limited interference effects should arise. The result will be that either the imagery or the subsidiary task or both will suffer. Inter-modality as well as intra-modality conflict is possible according to our theory. These ideas will be explored in more detail in the next chapter.

7
Images and words: Evidence for separate processing systems

I   Introduction

The differences between what we see and the words we use are so
obvious and apparent to the man in the street that he would be unlikely
to believe that the two have any similarities. Nevertheless there is a
commonly held view, deriving from propositional accounts (e.g.
Anderson and Bower, 1973; Pylyshyn, 1973) that all cognitive
representations underlying perception, language and thinking, are
abstract and independent of the original form in which the information
was received. So far we have assumed that the visual and verbal modes
in general and visual and verbal imagery in particular are dissimilar.
While believing that it is really up to those who think otherwise to
justify their claim we shall attempt, in this chapter, to show that a case
can be made for a degree of functional independence between the two
major processing systems. The point, of course, is the *extent* to which the
modalities operate independently, and it might help the reader to use
two extreme positions on this issue as yardsticks. One notion is that the
visual and verbal processing systems function independently at all
stages including not only the encoding, but also the storage, manipulation and use of information to guide output. According to this view,
the obvious differences in *content* between visual and verbal events
imply that there must be a difference in *format* between their internal
representations. Words, images and their underlying memory
structure need to be supported by different types of processing systems.
Such a view resembles that of Paivio (1971b) and leads directly to the
position that meaning is represented as either mental words or mental

images; no deeper, more abstract code is needed. The other extreme is that the differences between visual and verbal processes are more apparent than real. Clearly, because of their different sensory sources, visual and verbal stimuli must be processed separately at relatively superficial, peripheral stages but after that information referring to these events is quickly coded into a neutral or common format. Because the mental representations underlying the two sorts of phenomena are not qualitatively different only one general information processing system is needed to deal with them. Meaning, according to this approach, is the abstract, amodal, common code which underlies the seemingly different inputs (cf. Anderson and Bower, 1973). While we believe that the extreme separate code position is unlikely on the grounds that somewhere in the system a common mapping function would still be needed to relate words and images, we also feel that the extreme common code view ignores the fact that it might be more efficient to process visual and verbal information separately at stages other than encoding. The peculiar character of visual events, their appearance and spatially extended nature may well require specialized processing that would not be applicable to more temporally organized verbal stimuli. Nevertheless while there may be a high degree of functional autonomy between the visual and verbal EMPLOYEE systems, at times more high level programs will need to accept and *co-ordinate* input from both. To the extent that such programs can accept processing output from either EMPLOYEE, they can harmlessly be dubbed "amodal" but note that this still does not preclude the existence of modality specific BOSS subroutines.

This modified dual code view receives some support from the studies we shall consider in this chapter. In the first section research supporting a general distinction between the two major processing systems will be introduced. In the second section we shall illustrate the links between visual imagery and the visual processing system and between verbal images and verbal processing with evidence from studies of selective interference. Finally we shall consider, how, in certain circumstances, images and percepts can combine.

II   Visual and verbal processes

A   Hemispheric differences

Converging evidence from studies of the brain injured, work with so called "split-brain" patients, and experimentation with normal subjects has suggested that the two cerebral hemispheres are differentially suited for dealing with visual and verbal information. As will become clear, however, we must be careful over the implications that are drawn.

Since the work of Hughlings Jackson (1880) it has been known that damage to the left hemisphere is more likely to result in language disorders than damage to the right. More recently, Newcombe's (1969) review of injuries caused by missiles or gunshots has demonstrated a clear distinction between injuries to the left and right hemispheres. Right-brain-injured patients were noticeably worse at tasks involving visual skills such as learning mazes, drawing, recognizing incomplete patterns and so on, than the left-brain-injured group. Left-brain-injured patients, on the other hand, were worse at tasks needing verbal skills, such as vocabulary, word fluency and spelling tests. There are some difficulties associated with studies of the brain-injured, for example, the effects of unilateral injury depend on the handedness of the victim (Rossi and Rosadini, 1965) and the age at which injury occurs (Lenneberg, 1967), but used cautiously studies of the brain-injured can provide useful information concerning the neuro-anatomical basis for the different processing systems.

A second body of evidence for functional asymmetry of the hemispheres is found in work done on patients following cerebral commisurotomy, that is the disconnection of the two hemispheres by cutting the corpus callosum which connects them (e.g. Gazzaniga *et al.*, 1962; Gazzaniga, 1970). Such operations have been carried out to control epilepsy in patients suffering frequent, severe attacks. The advantage in working with such patients is that it is possible to examine more carefully the responses of a *single* hemisphere to sensory input, whereas in normal subjects, the responses of a single hemisphere may be a joint function of sensory input and information received from its neighbour hemisphere. Split brain studies make use of the "neurological wiring" to transmit tactual or visual information to the right or left hemispheres, and then require patients to answer questions about what they have seen or felt. Figure 9 illustrates how the right visual field projects to the left hemisphere, and vice versa, so that, by showing pictures, words or objects to the right or left of the person's fixation point the information can be sent to one or other hemisphere. Figure 10 illustrates a typical demonstration where the patient is unable to report verbally anything about the picture projected to the right hemisphere, but can select the objects which are presented visually from among a set of items with the left hand. Moreover, Milner and Taylor (1972) have shown that complex tactile patterns are matched better by split-brain patients who use their left hand than by those who use their right hand to perform the task.

It is possible to study differences in the speed of processing, or the dominance of one hemisphere in normal subjects by presenting the stimuli to one of the hemispheres, and comparing the response to that for similar material when first received by the other hemisphere. This use of normal subjects avoids the limitations of using the small pool of split-brain patients, and a very large literature on hemispheric asymmetries has accumulated in recent years.

For the purposes of this book, the question is whether the collective hemispheric research demonstrates that there are two separate processing systems, one verbal and one visual. Early studies of split brain and other brain-damaged patients seemed to support this view. The patients with split brains could only describe verbally stimuli which were projected to the left hemisphere, while the right hemisphere seemed to be better for some non-verbal processing. As Gazzaniga and LeDoux (1978) comment, in the late 1960s and early 1970s ''There

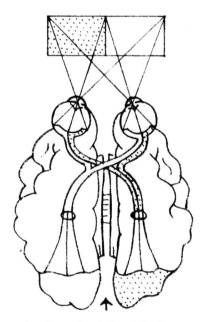

Fig. 9   Visual information from the right of the fixation point is projected to the left hemisphere of the brain while that from the left goes to the right hemisphere.

arose a barrage of popular and overdramatic accounts of the unique-
ness of mind left and mind right'' (p.6).

Rather than wishing to conclude that the right hemisphere is for
visual processing, and the left for verbal, several modern reviewers of
the field prefer to emphasize that lateralization is more a question of
degree rather than kind of processing (e.g. Beaumont, 1982; Bradshaw
and Nettleton, 1981; Gazzaniga and Le Doux, 1978). Gazzaniga and
Le Doux (1978) maintain that while the left hemisphere does usually
appear to develop a special language processing ability this is only
partially genetically determined since early brain damage can lead to
the right hemisphere taking over language processing. They argue that
the right hemisphere is better equipped for manipulospatial tasks, and
that this has been a confounding factor in some split-brain studies
which have shown better visual processing by the right hemisphere.

Fig. 10   Split brain patients are unable to name pictures of objects projected
to the right hemisphere of their brains, but they can select the objects from a
set of alternatives.

Bradshaw and Nettleton (1981) claim that the left hemisphere is better at sequential, analytic and time dependent tasks at the sensory (e.g. visual and auditory) and motor levels (control of limbs and speech apparatus), so that for example, some musical functions appear to be mediated by the left hemisphere. Spatial aspects, such as position of the limbs etc., they claim to be associated with the right hemisphere. We find it hard to accept that motor control will be grossly separated from spatial representation since the latter seems to be necessary for the successful operation of the former. Bradshaw and Nettleton describe the right hemisphere as possessing considerable powers of comprehension, and conclude that "there is a continuum of function between the hemispheres, rather than a rigid dichotomy, the differences being quantative rather than qualitive, of degree rather than kind" (p.51).

Both Gazzaniga and Le Doux (1978) and Bradshaw and Nettleton (1981) attribute the differences in hemispheric processing of visual and verbal stimuli to the specialization that the left hemisphere has undergone rather than a distinct division of verbal and visual functioning. However, while Gazzaniga and Le Doux believe this specialization to be for language production, Bradshaw and Nettleton see it as being for time dependent sequential analysis, which will often include language.

It was always obvious from the ability of split-brain subjects to name visually presented objects that visual processsng must go on in the left as well as the right hemisphere. It is reasonable to conclude that language is normally associated with the left hemisphere, although it is not easy to separate the motor-production systems from the semantic-cognitive systems. Theories of dual coding would hope that studies of hemispheric differences would have revealed separate semantic systems for visual and verbal material. This has not been reliably demonstrated, and visual processing certainly takes place in both hemispheres, although some specialization may occur in the right side.

B   Perception and memory

In addition to the functional differences between the cerebral hemispheres, there is more general psychological evidence to support a differentiation between visual and verbal processes. Posner and his colleagues have distinguished between visual and verbal *codes* when processing stimuli, and it is now feasible to refer to visual as well as verbal *memories*. We shall consider these in turn.

1   Visual codes

Posner and Keele (1967) provided evidence for the use of visually encoded information in letter matches when the inter stimulus interval was less than 1·5 seconds. They showed that subjects were faster at reporting that two visually identical letters (e.g. A–A) which were presented successively have the same name than if upper and lower case letters (e.g. A–a) were used. After this point the difference between nominal and physical matches disappeared, and the researchers concluded that matches were then based on the names of stimuli. However, it does not follow logically that because subjects do not appear to use a visual code after 1·5 seconds they are incapable of doing so. In a later study, Parks *et al.* (1972) asked subjects to perform a verbal shadowing task during the interval between the letters to hinder the formation of name codes. Under these conditions, the superiority of the physically identical matches persisted for some 8 seconds. Parks *et al.* concluded that subjects can maintain visual codes provided there is the incentive to do so.

Evidence that visual codes can be generated from verbal instructions has been advanced by Posner *et al.* (1969). They showed that when the first stimulus of a letter pair is presented auditorily and the second visually, subjects perform as if they generate a visual code for the first letter to match with the second. This process takes from 0·5 to 1 second. Slightly faster times were reported by Weber and Bach (1969) who used a different procedure. They asked their subjects to work through the alphabet, either by pronouncing each letter to themselves or by forming a clear visual image of each letter. The former task took around 150 ms per item, the latter took nearly 300 ms per item. Posner (1973) has argued that the subjective nature of the Weber and Bach tasks makes it difficult to compare their time estimates with times derived from letter matching experiments (see also Chapter 4).

We must be careful not to equate perceptual codes and images too closely with one another. It may be that what subjects maintain between test and retest in the Posner and Keele task, or generate from an auditory stimulus in the later experiments is akin to a visual image. Indeed, as Standing *et al.* (1970b) have shown, visualizing letters can affect the perceived clarity of visual letter stimuli. However, for matching tasks, a visual code simply construed as a set of expectations would suffice (cf. Neisser, 1976). In fact, Posner *et al.* (1969) were aware of this problem when they pointed out that though the visual code might be in the form of a visual image, it is probably better to think of it as a program for dealing with visual features. In terms of the BOSS-consciousness model, a visual code could involve the preparation of "early" perceptual systems by more central processes. For more information and a thorough summary of his work on codes see Posner (1978).

2   Visual short-term memory

According to the modal model of memory, popular in the 1960s, visually presented material was first encoded in a high capacity, fast decaying sensory store, translated into a verbal code during its stay in a short-term store (STS), and transferred to a long-term store (LTS) by means of rehearsal (e.g. Waugh and Norman, 1965; Atkinson and Shiffrin, 1968). There are now reasons to question this simple theory (see Morris, 1980a, for a brief review). For example, rejecting the emphasis on structures and storage locations, Craik and Lockhart (1972) suggested a "levels of processing" approach to memory, and argued that trace persistence was a function of how information had been processed initially, rather than depending on where the trace was retained. However, of more relevance to the study of imagery, is evidence which demonstrates that visual information need not be translated into a verbal code, but can be maintained in a visual equivalent of short term store. Posner's work, which we have just considered, can be interpreted as supporting a visual STS explanation and, as noted, the duration of the visual representation can be shown to be around 8 seconds, under appropriate conditions. Using a different technique, Phillips and Baddeley (1971) obtained a similar estimate for the forgetting characteristics of visual STS of computer-generated, block patterns, though some qualification is needed since forgetting rates have since been shown to be affected by exposure duration (Dale, 1973) and the complexity of the stimulus (Phillips, 1974).

Recently, psychologists have begun to investigate other character-istics of visual STM and their findings suggest that many of the important properties of verbal STM are also to be found in the visual system. So, for example, Bartram (1978) has shown that chunking can occur in visual memory, just as Miller (1956) did for verbal memory, though, of course, visual chunking is spatial and not temporal in nature. Also, Kroll et al. (1975) have demonstrated the existence of a rehearsal process in visual STM, equivalent to the verbal rehearsal first investigated by Brown (1958) and Peterson and Peterson (1959).

We suspect that this latter process involves using the perceptual-memory system in a top-down mode, and if continued for more than a couple of seconds, will necessitate the construction of a visual image. If this is true, a strong link between visual perception, memory and imagery is forged.

3   Visual long-term memory

It is obvious that we can retain information referring to things we have either seen or heard for long periods of time. For example, people easily recognize friends whom they meet infrequently, with greater or lesser degrees of accuracy they can describe the appearance of the house they lived in five years ago, remembering the gist and sometimes the exact words of a conversation they had last week presents few problems and some actors can recall long chunks from Shakespeare. What is not obvious and not easy to establish, is whether visual and verbal information is stored in the same code or format in LTS. One thing we can do is to investigate whether the *fate* of visual and verbal information differs after the encoding stage by showing, for example, that their forgetting characteristics are dissimilar. This is useful, for if memory for the two sorts of information was found to be identical, that is if it exhibited not only the same general functions, such as logarithmic forgetting curves or similar differences between recognition and recall but also shared the same parameters for these functions, on grounds of parsimony it would be foolish to claim that separate memory systems existed. If, on the other hand, memories for visual and verbal events are not identical, then the possibility that the two are represented differently cannot be ruled out. Indeed if a difference were found at the level of general functioning, for example taking an extreme and unlikely case, if verbal information showed *no* forgetting effects while visual information became less easy to retrieve with time, the case for separate visual and verbal LTMs would be greatly strengthened. A more likely occurrence is that the general memory functions will be found to be similar, but that their parameters will differ. If this is so, it is logically possible that separate memories exist *but by no means definite*. It could be, as the adage has it, that a picture *is* worth a thousand words but simply that a thousand words or equivalent are used to represent it in memory. What we have not got for long-term memory research is the equivalent of the shadowing or rehearsal prevention techniques used to occupy the verbal system in STS studies to show that visual processing can go unhindered. Similar techniques could, perhaps, be devised, but they have not been yet put into practice.

In Chapter 11 we review several studies which compare the recall of visual and verbal material. In general, pictures tend to be remembered better than the names of objects or descriptions of scenes. However, it can be argued that the reason for these differences lies not in two memory systems, but in one system in which visual information leads to a richer and more distinctive trace than verbal input. Forgetting parameters and interference techniques have not been adequately studied to tease out any subtle differences in the retention and recall of the two types of material. There are some studies, which we review in Chapter 11, which favour a dual code interpretation, but the issue is still far from resolved.

III   Interference studies

A   The general locus of interference

The visual and verbal processing systems which may be functionally independent, can be used in a variety of perceptual and cognitive contexts. Two questions now arise: First, what is the relation between these processing systems and the various types of imagery? Second, what happens when they are used to perform a mental and a perceptual task at once, or, for that matter, two perceptual or two mental tasks? In answer to these questions we suggest the following working hypotheses. (1) Visual imagery is supported by the visual processing system; verbal and auditory imagery by the verbal system. (2) Both the visual and verbal processing systems are limited in their capacity or currently available sub-routines. This means that performance on two tasks together may be worse than performance on either one alone when both tasks require access to the same mental processors. To substantiate these claims, we must consider some basic studies in selective interference which show that imaginal and perceptual processing in the same modality can conflict resulting in an increase in errors or response times on either or both of the tasks.

1   Visual processing

There is considerable evidence that concurrent or interpolated visual perceptual tasks can disrupt imaginal processing, and that concurrent imaging can interfere with perception. An example of the effects of perception on imagery has been provided by Brooks (1967). He suggested that since people often construct images to help them understand and remember description of spatial arrays, conflict might arise if the description is presented as a written rather than a spoken message. This is because in this situation the visual system is used to perform two separate tasks, to form a visual image, and to identify the visually presented words. Brooks found that recall for descriptions of spatial arrays of numbers was better when people listened rather than listened and read the descriptions. As we described briefly in Chapter 4, in a series of experiments, Segal and colleagues have shown that imaging can interfere with the perception of visual input (e.g. Segal, 1971; Segal and Nathan, 1964; Segal and Glicksman, 1967; Segal and Gordon, 1969). The early experiments of this group were designed as attempts to replicate the so-called "Perky effect". Perky (1910) asked the subjects, all trained introspectionists, to image common objects whilst looking at a small spot in the centre of a screen. At the same time, faint coloured pictures of the imaged objects were back projected on the screen without their knowledge. The pictures varied around the lower threshold of intensity, and oscillated slightly. Subjects were then asked to describe their imagery, but furnished descriptions which could well have referred to the projections, suggesting that skilled introspectionists could not distinguish images from percepts under special conditions. Segal and Nathan attempted to replicate this study using what they describe as the "pragmatic and suspicious" students who populated American campuses in the late 1950s and early 1960s, who, they claim, had not been "turned on" (sic.) and were often embarrassed when asked to describe their inner experience! These subjects proved to be too critical, and after only two or three images frequently noticed that stimuli were also present. However, by using a placebo introduced to their subjects as a relaxant, Segal and Nathan were able to demonstrate a tendency to report images of those who "reacted" to the placebo, and a converse tendency, to report perceptions, of those who failed to react. Extending these findings, Segal and Glicksman found that sitting subjects reported the presence of perceptions more than those lying in a supine position — a posture normally associated with relaxation and dreams. Later, using signal detection techniques Segal and Fusella (1970) demonstrated that visual images reduced the detectability of visual signals. Segal has interpreted these effects within the Piagetian framework of assimilation, incorporation of an external stimulus into an image, and accommodation, the modification of an image to cope with a percept. A related explanation, and one more in line with our BOSS-consciousness model, is to equate assimilation with predominantly top-down processing and accommodation with bottom-up processing. In the former the imaginal experience is dominant, in the latter the perceptual.

As well as conflict *between* visual imagery and visual perception, it would seem logical that there might be limitations in the visual system's ability to perform two tasks which are *both* perceptual or *both* imaginal. Studies of these situations are somewhat scarce, but Neisser and Becklen (1975) have shown that people can successfully attend to one of two superimposed video tape sequences, though the unattended sequence is effectively unperceived. Whilst no direct disruption of the primary task of "visual shadowing" occurred in this experiment, the inability of the visual system to follow both sequences at once was demonstrated. Neisser and Becklen argued that the unattended input is not filtered out, as some attention theories would predict (e.g. Broadbent, 1958), but is simply not synthesized (cf. Neisser, 1967; also Neisser, 1976). In our model, the top-down processes suitable for one perceptual event, were obviously unsuitable for the other. Finally, some of Kosslyn's (1975) experiments, which we will discuss in more detail in the next chapter, could be interpreted as evidence that two image representations can compete for scarce visual processing resources. So, a given image is pictured less clearly when processed at the same time as a complex image compared with when it shares the image space with a simple, neighbour image. To demonstrate further these effects of interference or competition *within* the imagery system it might be interesting to ask subjects to perform two or more transformations involving mental pictures at the same time. For instance, it could be that people would find it relatively easy to perform two mental rotations in the same direction, but take longer and make more errors when performing two rotations in different directions.

2   Verbal processing

Applying a similar analysis to the verbal system, it can be shown that the perception of auditory input can affect verbal imagery tasks, and verbal-auditory images may interfere with the detection of auditory signals. Similarly, we can look for interference within either imagery or perception in the verbal domain, as we did for the visual. So, for example, Brooks (1967) also found that when the description of the spatial array was replaced by a nonsense equivalent, by using *good*, *bad*, *quick* and *slow* instead of the spatial terms *up*, *down*, *left* and *right*, recall was easier for subjects who were allowed to listen to *and* read the message compared with those who merely heard it. This time, there was no conflict between the visual, reading task, and the verbal, memory task. Also Atwood (1971) found that auditory input interferes with memory for abstract verbal material, though this study is somewhat weak as we shall see later. Turning briefly to the effects of verbal or auditory imagery on perception, in the other half of their experiment Segal and Fusella (1970) found that auditory images made the detection of weak auditory signals more difficult. To illustrate this effect consider how sounds in the environment fade when you use verbal imagery, for example trying to put one's thoughts down on paper and simultaneously listen to a radio play is extremely difficult. Thus interference occurs between imagery and perception in the verbal as well as the visual system. Whether this interference is reduced following practice is not clear (cf. Neisser, 1976).

As for interference between two or more perceptual tasks involving verbal information, the enormous literature on selective and divided attention shows that there are frequently limits on our capacity to process multiple inputs at once (Kahneman, 1973; Norman, 1976). Those situations where two tasks can be carried on at the same time have helped clarify the nature of the underlying system (e.g. Allport, 1979, 1980). Until recently, much of this work has blurred the distinction between different processing systems. Finally, what about conflict between verbal imagery tasks? It is hard to find direct reference to these effects in the literature, but we believe this is because of the way that psychologists have partitioned their subject matter, for such phenomena do exist. The problem is that they have rarely been recognized as imagery effects, but have been classified under the general area of verbal memory. One early technique, used to investigate STS, which does not so much show conflict between two imagery tasks as depend on the fact that it occurs is, of course, rehearsal suppression. Brown (1958) and Peterson and Peterson (1959) discovered independently that people are unable to remember even the order of three letters if they are asked to perform a concurrent verbal task such as counting backwards in three's for perhaps 20 seconds. Several explanations have been put forward to explain forgetting in STS (see for example, Baddeley, 1976), but the assumption behind all of these is that the verbal-auditory system can only deal with a certain amount of information at once. More recent experiments along these lines are those investigating the so-called "articulatory loop" (e.g. Baddeley and Hitch, 1974; Hitch, 1980).

We feel that many of these diverse phenomena are interrelated, and a more general theory of attention or memory to link them would be valuable.

B   The nature of interference

So far we have demonstrated that various interference effects occur within the two major processing systems but have said very little about exactly where in the stream of processing these conflicts arise. We suggest that it is useful to consider interference as affecting either (a) the encoding and storage of representations or (b) the use of representations which are already formed. We will consider these in turn.

1   Forming representations

We can use our visual and verbal-auditory systems in a perceptual mode to take in new information from the world and to help us build new internal representations of it. These processes can be hindered under certain conditions. We have already mentioned the Brooks (1967) study and this can be used as evidence that visual perception interferes more with the construction of a visual image than with a verbal representation. Also, Atwood (1971) has attempted to show that modality specific interference occurs when encoding information. He asked half of his subjects to visualize relatively concrete scenes such as "a nudist devouring a bird" or "a pistol hanging on a chain", while the other half were to contemplate the meaning of relatively abstract phrases such as "the theory of Freud is nonsense" or "the intellect of Einstein was a miracle". After hearing each phrase all subjects were then required to perform one of three intervening tasks, after which they were asked to provide the last word of each phrase in response to the first noun. The intervening tasks were as follows: One group of subjects was presented with a visual "1" (or "2") and gave the verbal response "two" (or "one"). The second group received an auditory stimulus, "one" (or "two"), to which they responded "two" (or "one"). Finally, the third group received no interference in the presentation-test interval. Subjects presented with the visual stimuli had lower recall scores in the concrete condition compared with those presented with auditory interference. The reverse effect was found in the abstract phrase condition.

There are a number of methodological flaws in Atwood's study. To begin with, the phrases used in the concrete condition were somewhat bizarre. Since people take longer to construct unusual images (e.g. Morris, 1979), these atypical creations could have larger interference effects associated with them. Next, embedding the critical nouns within phrases, instead of using a paired-associate technique, increase the number of uncontrolled linguistic and semantic factors. Even the visual task contained a verbal component, since people in both interference conditions had to give a vocal response. There was a confounding of instructional set (''form images'' *vs* ''contemplate the meaning'') with the type of material (''concrete'' *vs* ''abstract''). Finally, the learning procedure itself was incidental and not intentional. However, in a much better controlled study, Jansenn (1976) has replicated and extended Atwood's work. He eliminated the confound between instructional set and type of material, and still found evidence for a modality specific interaction between interfering and primary tasks, with no evidence for any effect of either instructional set or, imagery ability. The interference effect itself was found for the free recall of single nouns as well as paired associates, and its magnitude decreased from High, to Medium to Low I nouns.

These results receive some support from a study by Klee and Eysenck (1973) which was concerned with the effects of interference on sentence comprehension. They presented sentences verbally with either visual or verbal distractors and discovered that concrete sentences were comprehended more rapidly with verbal than with visual interference, whereas abstract sentences were understood better with visual interference. Similarly, Sasson (1971) has shown that free recall for concrete sentences is disrupted when subjects view unrelated pictures after hearing them, whereas when they see pictures related to the sentences, recall is facilitated. Sasson presented the pictures at rates fast enough to rule out verbal processing. This effect of interpolated material was found on immediate but not delayed retention. Conversely, Sasson and Fraisse (1972) found that memory for abstract sentences is affected by interpolated abstract but not concrete materials. All these results do suggest that the two kinds of sentences are processed differently, but Eysenck (1977) points out that they may be a little implausible, since it is difficult to see how we *ever* remember concrete material as much of our waking life is spent in visual processing! Eysenck's criticism is a little unfair. We need not assume that concrete material is comprehended solely by using the visual system only that the visual system is implicated for these effects to occur. Perhaps forming a visual representation of a concrete sentence corresponds to the click of comprehension, but it may be possible to evaluate these sentences linguistically without resort to this visual check.

2 Manipulating representations

Once formed and stored, our representations can be retrieved and transformed to aid thinking and problem-solving. In the case of visual representations these transformations will be spatial in character, whereas those relating to verbal information will be more abstract and linguistic. There is evidence to show that the manipulation and use of internal representations can be disrupted by concurrent processes in the same modality. The experiments of Brooks (1968) are classic examples of these effects. Brooks showed that the use of visual imagery is hindered by a task requiring visual search, but not by a verbal task, whereas the opposite was found for operations on sentences. In a typical visual condition his subjects were asked to categorize the corners of block capital letters as either top or bottom corners or not. Three response conditions were used. In the first subjects responded verbally saying "yes" or "no" as appropriate, in the second they tapped out their answer, in the third, they responded by indicating *y* for "yes" or *n* for "no" using a spatial array of *y*'s and *n*'s. The general finding was that RTs and errors increased from verbal to tapping to pointing response modes. As for the verbal tasks, subjects were asked to categorize the words of sentences as nouns or non-nouns again responding in one of the three ways just mentioned. In this condition, it was verbal responding which produced the most disruption and visual the least.

Brooks confirmed and extended these findings in a further six experiments. Briefly, he showed that: (1) The degree of interference in the sentence condition varied as a direct function of vocal response difficulty. (2) Varying the amount and type of movement in the spatial response differentially affected spatial categorization: visually monitored movements disrupted diagram recall more than movement *per se* which, in turn, produced more interference than no movement. (3) The interference occurring in these tasks must be modality-specific since neither increasing the difficulty of a superimposed verbal task on a diagram recall–spatial response combination nor increasing the difficulty of a superimposed spatial response on a sentence recall–vocal response combination had any great effect (whereas a general capacity, or attention overload interpretation would predict a decrement in performance). (4) Recall of sentences is affected by articulatory responses; written presentation of the sentences did little to lessen the interference effect. This suggests that a verbal-articulatory code is used for the sentences. (5) Sentence memory is not disrupted by auditory feedback. Mouthing the responses did not result in significantly different interference effects from voicing them. (6) Tactual response monitoring produced significantly more interference than unmonitored input in the visuo-spatial task. Interference can result from visual or tactile monitoring of output.

Brooks explained these results in terms of interference between modality specific control processes, the systems which operate upon and use internal representations. He was careful not to specify too closely the parameters of a modality since letter categorizing was disrupted by visual and kinaesthetic monitoring.

C   Theoretical problems

Since these experiments were performed, two general theoretical issues have been raised concerning these, and other studies of selective interference. The first, specifically related to the Brooks (1968) study, concerns the nature of the interference in the diagram condition and asks if the interference which Brooks demonstrated is visual or spatial? The second is a more general problem concerning the argument for modality specificity. We shall consider these in turn.

1   Spatial *vs* visual interference

Despite Brooks' clear statement that the conflict produced in his studies arose between modality specific control processes and not representations, thus implying that the diagram interference was *spatial* in character, some investigators (e.g. Paivio, 1971b) have interpreted his results as evidence for a disruption of the image by *visual* interference. Baddeley *et al.* (1974) have investigated this issue in some detail. They showed that pursuit rotor-tracking seriously impaired performance on letter categorizing tasks, a finding to be expected if interference is spatial. Moreover, when subjects were asked to learn noun–adjective pairs which varied in concreteness (e.g. strawberry–ripe; bullet–grey *vs* gratitude–infinite; mood–cheerful) and to use a pursuit rotor at the same time no differential interference effects were found, though the concurrent task had a small but reliable *overall* effect on p-a memory. From these results, Baddeley *et al.* concluded that representations should be distinguished from their control processes and it is the latter that suffer interference in Brooks' type tasks. On the other hand, the p-a task required little manipulation of information, and so was unaffected by a spatial perceptual task. Thus, Baddeley *et al.* have demonstrated that a spatial perceptual task will affect imagery tasks involving transformations, but not those which merely involve retrieval of already stored information. Extending this logic: Baddeley (1976) suggests that the next step is to show that a purely *visual* perceptual task will not interfere with an imagery task in the way that a spatial task does. A study by Baddeley and Lieberman (1980) demonstrates this. Using the familiar task employed by Brooks (1967) in which subjects are required to memorize a message describing the position of members in an imaginary array, no interference was produced when subjects were asked to judge simultaneously the brightness of a fixed stimulus, but considerable conflict was produced when blindfold, they had to train a torch beam on a swinging pendulum which emitted a tone that changed when it was illuminated. From these studies and work by Byrne (1974), who demonstrated spatial interference when a matrix of abstract words is scanned, Baddeley has argued that since the locus of interference in these tasks is linked to spatial control mechanisms, then we can only safely conclude that the visual imagery system as a whole has spatial, and not visual characteristics. Baddeley is right to be cautious here, but it does not follow logically that because only spatial interference has been demonstrated, that imagery has no visual component. The crucial interaction of visual interference with a predominantly visual imagery task was not included in the Baddeley and Lieberman study.

We do not contest the argument that interference in certain imagery tasks is spatial. The findings of Baddeley and Byrne support this explanation. Also we have shown that perceptual responding conflicts with control processes which operate on the image once it has been produced, rather than with those involved in its production (Hampson and Morris, 1978b). What we reject, however, is Baddeley's suggestion that the imagery system has only spatial characteristics. There is in fact data available which suggests that imagery also has visual properties. As we mentioned above and as Baddeley and Lieberman (1980) recognize, Janssen (1976) has replicated Atwood's study, and provided evidence for visual–visual conflict. Also in an unpublished class experiment conducted at Manchester Polytechnic, one of us has shown that problems arise when people are asked to categorize imagined letters as "straight" (composed entirely of straight lines, e.g. A, T, Z etc.) or "rounded" (containing at least one curved line, e.g. R, C, S, etc.) if they are forced to point to an 0 for the straight and a 1 for the round letters. Both RTs and errors were greater in this condition than when the straight and rounded symbols were used for straight and rounded letters respectively. One possible explanation of this effect is that the processes used to detect straight lines in the imaged letters are the same as those used to detect straight lines in the environment. When the perceptual and imagery tasks both involve looking for the same type of feature the operation proceeds smoothly, but interference occurs when one task requires straight line detection and the other curve detection. However, an alternative explanation of this simple study is that some type of response competition is occurring and until this is ruled out our version must be regarded as tentative.

2 Modality specificity

A potentially more damaging attack on Brooks' interpretation of his results has been mounted by Phillips and Christie (1977). Questioning the logic behind Brooks' (1968) study, which is usually interpreted as evidence for modality specific interference, they pointed out that the design lacks any "no interference controls" and that without these precautions it is unreasonable to infer specificity in both modalities. This is because the performance of a no interference control group, say in the letter categorizing condition, might be better than that of groups who must perform a concurrent spatial or verbal task. Differences, in accuracy and speed found between spatial or verbal responding, could then result from different demands made on *general* purpose resources, with spatial responding making more than verbal. Admittedly, the cross-over effect with the sentence condition would suggest modality specific interference in the verbal domain, since otherwise it would be hard to explain why, in this condition, verbal responding, not spatial, used more general purpose resources. Even so, specificity, they argued, can only be inferred in one modality, not both. To test these ideas, they performed a series of five experiments using a visual STM paradigm of the type originally used by Phillips and Baddeley (1971). They found that reading visually presented digits between stimulus presentation and recognition test had little effect on performance, whereas adding digits did. Also, they discovered no significant differences between adding visually or auditorilly presented digits. In one experiment, the interpolated task involved processing patterns similar in structure to the test stimuli, in this situation interference was increased when subjects had to form representations of the intervening patterns which outlasted the icon. The amount of conflict produced depended on whether the interfering task was sensory or cognitive, with the latter producing more disruption than the former. Phillips and Christie interpreted their results as suggesting that interference does occur between perception and visualization, but that it results from competition for general purpose, not modality specific resources.

Phillips and Christie's results are intriguing and if their explanation is correct, they represent a severe challenge to the normal account of modality specificity. It is not clear, though, that we have to accept their interpretation. One of their arguments in favour of a general purpose resource limit rests on the fact that digit addition, an apparently non-visual task, conflicts with visualization. They claim that addition involves operations that are not automatic or pre-programmed and that these effortful transformations compete for a general purpose, limited capacity, central processor similar to the working memory system described by Baddeley and Hitch (1974) or the selector input in Shallice's (1972) model. Although they admit that it is possible that even verbally presented digits are added visually, Phillips and Christie maintain that this would further reduce any grounds for calling the visual processor, "special purpose". This argument is not watertight. In an interesting study Hayes (1973) has reported that subjects performing mental arithmetic often employ visual imagery, and Professor Aitken, the mental calculator whose prowess was reported by Hunter (1977), made extensive use of visualization techniques. At the very least, these studies demonstrate that frequent *spatial* manipulation occurs during mental arithmetic. On reflection, it is evident that visualizing is an eminently sensible strategy for people to adopt, for by using the imagery system as a temporary, and additional storage buffer, they can prevent the verbal system, presumably needed for more abstract manipulation, from becoming overloaded. The imagery and verbal systems may well interact during mental arithmetic, but each will transform and represent its information in the usual way. It is, therefore, not clear why any involvement of imagery in such tasks reduces the grounds for calling the visual processor special purpose. Indeed, it comes as no surprise that the manipulations described by Hayes' subjects are typical of transformations associated with more standard spatial tasks. Generality in the application of a processing system need not employ generality of its processing mode. We believe that an equally plausible explanation of this aspect of Phillips and Christie's results is that they have demonstrated interference between two imagery tasks, one the maintenance of a visual STM representation, the other the formation of imagery when adding digits. Without more evidence the issue is undecidable.

The other plank in Phillips and Christie's case is that "active" or "cognitive" representations produce more interference than "passive" or "sensory" ones, because the former, being more effortful, require central resources. First of all, evidence was found for this effect using similar visual patterns to the to-be-remembered items as potential interferers. Thus, one explanation is that this interference is still modality-specific but occurs only at higher levels of visual analysis. This might be the case especially since the higher perceptual operations of figural synthesis may well be of limited capacity and serial (cf. Neisser, 1967). However, recent evidence advanced by Anderson and Paulson (1978) supports a compromise position. Studying Identi-Kit type faces, they found that recognition times for faces and facts about faces increased as the number of component elements included in other study items increased. Particularly relevant was their finding that verbal information could interfere with pictorial information and *vice versa*, though this inter-modality interference was much less than the intra-modality variety. Applying these findings to Phillips and Christie's work and other interference studies, it could be that both modality specific and general purpose resource interference occur. There is no reason why they should be mutually exclusive (cf. Kahneman, 1973). The important question would then be not what *type* of interference was under investigation, but what *amount* of the two general types had been demonstrated.

In one sense we agree with Phillips and Christie that general purpose resource interference may occur, but we do not believe that this is evidence against modality-specific interference. The BOSS-consciousness model would in fact lead us to predict the possibility of both types of conflict. Modality-specific interference will occur whenever the perceptual employee system is used for two or more tasks at once, while general resource limits will obtain whenever BOSS is needed to control and monitor processing. In the case of imagery tasks,

BOSS's involvement is quite important, and, therefore, some amount of general resource deficit is to be expected when concurrent tasks are performed. Whether imagery tasks can become highly automated, so that they are performed solely by employee systems, and whether imaginal processes can become unintentional, so that BOSS does not need to supervise them is not yet known. If these effects do occur, though, an obvious prediction would be that in these circumstances, where BOSS is made redundant, resource interference will be reduced to a minimum. One more definite prediction, however, is that two tasks requiring more effortful, top-down processes will produce more mutual interference those involving predominantly data-driven analyses, some evidence for this from attention studies has been advanced by Eysenck and Eysenck (1979) and Johnston and Heinz (1978) for the verbal domain, but similar findings should also apply to the visual.

IV   Facilitation effects

An alternative, though related way to demonstrate the link between the various types of imagery and their parent, perceptual systems is to show that certain mental and perceptual processes can complement and support each other in favourable circumstances. These "facilitation effects" are really the other side of the coin from interference studies, since their interpretation rests on the assumption that a common processing system is used in such a way that interference effects are either minimized or avoided entirely, or even that performance is improved above normal levels. Facilitation effects are easiest to understand in the visual modality, and their existence is implicit in the BOSS-consciousness theory. At a rather obvious level, the interaction of concept-driven and data-driven processes in our model, and its affinities with Neisser's analysis-by-synthesis account of perception imply that most perceptual acts are partially supported by imagery-type processes. To borrow Wittgenstein's (1953) expression perception involves not just "seeing", but seeing something *as* something. This "seeing as" process is demonstrated in perceptual illusions, such as the duck-rabbit or the wife-old hag, where the ambiguous data are supplemented and interpreted by central conceptual processes. Also when the data are of poor quality central facilitation effects are brought to bear.

Less trivial effects can occur, however, when the cognitive system is performing a mental and a perceptual task at once. So, as we noted above, interference is minimized in Brooks' type problems when scanning and responding occurs in the same direction (Byrne, 1974; Hampson and Morris, 1978b). Also, as demonstrated by the work of Segal and Fusella (1970), signal detection can be improved by having an *appropriate* image, a situation akin to putting the right code in a state of readiness (Posner *et al.*, 1969) or having the right set of expectations for the stimulus (Neisser, 1976). In all these situations either the same representations (or codes) can be used for both tasks, or the set of control processes used in one situation can be employed in the other, or both. A way of labelling these effects is "facilitation by overlap".

Another type of effect we have labelled "facilitation by complement". This situation, a specific and more dramatic example of what happens all the time in perception, arises when data is of such poor quality that a supportive image is constructed to fill in the gaps. Although somewhat under-researched there is some data which suggest that these effects do occur. For example, Hayes (1973) in his study of mental arithmetic reports an interesting introspection of one of his subjects. A particular mathematical problem was printed in such a way that there was no room for the subject to project the answer mentally on the same card. To get around this difficulty the subject mentally attached a blank sheet of paper below the problem and proceeded to solve it without difficulty! Many engineering diagrams probably need this type of imaginal supplement at times. Horowitz (1970) has discussed some of these effects under the rubric of "hybrid images".

Similar facilitation effects presumably occur in the verbal domain, though, again they have not been highly researched to date. Perhaps priming effects should be considered under this heading. One clear demonstration of the latter (originally suggested by John Morton) is to listen to a piece of rock or popular music at high volume with or without the words in front of you. Without the transcript it is often difficult if not impossible to interpret the sounds, with the transcript the words become more intelligible. The written words allow the listener to form expectations for or synthesize the input when it arrives (Neisser, 1976, 1967). This may, in some circumstances, involve constructing an acoustic or articulatory image.

Finally, as we have remarked previously, the visual and verbal imagery systems can interact (see for example, Paivio, 1971b). The fact that this occurs can be taken as evidence for the independence of the two systems, strange though this may seem. By making use of the lower intermodality interference effects, additional temporary storage space can be employed in demanding cognitive activities.

8

Properties of the imagery system

In this chapter we move from considering studies which attempt to distinguish imaginal from verbal mediators and turn to those concerned with the structure of the imagery system itself. Our aims are to shed further light on the nature of images by examining the way in which they are generated, considering whether consciously experienced images have special properties and investigating the number and variety of their transformations. The work described in this chapter is particularly relevant to any discussion of the theories of imagery which we introduced in chapter 6, and so, in the concluding section, we will reconsider our model in the light of the data. Finally, the issue of the equivalence between imaginal and perceptual processes is re-examined.

I The nature of imaginal representation

A *Generating images*

Until psychologists started to discuss the nature of the imagery system, rather than merely look at the qualities and correlates of images, little attention was paid to the actual mechanics of image generation. When Paivio wrote his seminal book in 1971, one of the major issues was still considered to be the relation between images and meaning in verbal comprehension. Did people first understand words or phrases and then form images of their referents or did image production precede the comprehension process (see Chapter 1)? Only lately (cf. Kosslyn, 1980) have questions of image retrieval been considered in any detail. We will examine these issues in their historical sequence though it should be remembered that the comprehension studies are concerned with the implications of image generation rather than the process *per se*.

1   Image arousal and comprehension

Moore (1915a,b) was the first person to investigate this problem empirically. He presented concrete nouns to subjects and timed them under instructions to respond when either meaning or an image was aroused. He discovered that meaning was aroused more quickly than an image. Tolman (1917) repeated the procedure and found that individuals differed in whether meaning or image comes first. Paivio and Begg (1970) re-opened the case and argued that if imagery contributes to *reading* comprehension then indices of image generation and comprehension should be correlated though, in the light of Moore's findings, they doubted whether the conscious experience of imaging would occur before understanding. Given a correlation, however, imagery could still be involved in comprehension, they argued, since image-mediators need not be consciously experienced for them to be psychologically effective. In one of their experiments they presented sentences to people and measured their reading, comprehension, imaging and paraphrasing latencies. After adjusting for reading times, imagery, comprehension and paraphrasing were quite highly correlated (0·69 to 0·77). Moreover, contrary to the findings of the earlier research, imaging was faster than comprehending, though of course the earlier study used single words not sentences. In their second experiment, Paivio and Begg used both abstract and concrete sentences, and discovered that image latencies were significantly longer for abstract material though comprehension latencies were relatively unaffected by the nature of the stimuli. Overall, imaging took longer than comprehending, but for concrete referents there was little difference between the two latencies. From these results Paivio argued that whilst imagery and comprehension are not identical, they are related especially in the case of concrete material.

It can be seen from this study alone that data reflecting the supposed temporal order of imaging and comprehending should be treated with extreme caution. In the first experiment comprehension was supposedly slower than forming images, in the second supposedly faster. As Paivio himself points out:

> the absolute latency of imagery, as that of comprehension, depends on a variety of stimulus factors such as the length complexity, and abstractness of the stimulus materials as well as the precise experimental instructions and contextual cues. (1971, p.444)

Estimates of absolute latencies range from Tolman's of less than 1 second to Paivio's (1966) finding that subjects took 2·5 seconds to image the referents of concrete words, with Simpson (1970) reporting latencies of 0·6 seconds for well practised subjects (see also Chapter 4). Even more paradoxical at first sight is the fact that latencies obtained for concrete sentences in the Paivio and Begg study were not a great deal longer than latencies for single words. It is a distinct possibility, as Paivio recognizes, that subjects could have been generating images while the sentences were being read to them rather than waiting until reading was complete. If some subjects constructed images depicting only the first part of the sentences but had to wait to hear the whole of the sentence before understanding it, the discrepancy between the two Paivio and Begg experiments could be explained. To shed more light on this, therefore, we need to examine how images are produced or aroused before we can reach any decision on the comprehension issue.

2   The process of image arousal

In the discussion which follows, we will rely heavily on the work performed by Kosslyn and co-workers (e.g. Kosslyn, 1980; Kosslyn *et al.*, 1979) since this research group has been the only one to consider the production of images in any detail. Kosslyn's research strategy has been to tackle problems by working systematically through a decision tree, one issue at a time, ruling out in the process alternative classes of models. The first issue they investigated, which we shall consider later in this chapter, concerns whether or not images are epiphenomenal. The subsequent three questions centre around the generation of images.

A natural starting point for investigations of image retrieval is to try to discover in what form imaginal information is retained in LTS. Are the active and long-term memory representations the same, and hence, are images simply retrieved as a whole, or do the two states of the representation differ in format? This is an important consideration especially for those theorists who claim that the surface or active form of the image is functional and quasi-pictorial. To investigate this issue Kosslyn, Reiser, Farah and Fliegel (cited in Kosslyn, 1980) asked subjects to form images of detailed and undetailed black and white drawings of animals which they had previously seen. They found that detailed images took longer to produce than undetailed, and argued that this was because images are constructed from underlying, long-term units, and not retrieved wholistically. The authors ruled out an alternative interpretation of these results that both images took the same time to produce but the more detailed took longer to check or review after production, by having subjects image large and small versions of the detailed and undetailed drawings. The reasoning behind this was that larger images should take longer to check than smaller* if the production and subsequent review explanation were correct. Again, detailed images took longer to produce than undetailed, but the difference was unaffected by the size of the image, nor was there any *overall* size effect on formation times, a different finding from earlier work (Kosslyn, 1975).

Given that images are constructed rather than retrieved wholistically, what form do the underlying units have? Are images generated from organized and interpreted representations or merely put together from arbitrary units? In a very simple experiment, Kosslyn, Reiser, Farah and Fleigel have provided some evidence to support the former position. They presented to subjects geometric figures which were composites of simple shapes such as triangles, squares, rectangles, hexagons and parallelograms. The figures could each be described in one of two ways: either by referring to a few large, overlapping units, or in terms of a larger number of smaller contiguous elements. Subjects were asked to try to see the figures in terms of one of these descriptions, and, after covering up the stimulus, to form an image of it. Stimuli described in terms of a few units took less time to image than when they were described in terms of several parts. Using a slightly different approach, they manipulated pictures of animals so that subjects perceived them sequentially in terms of different numbers of units, by presenting line drawings of *parts* of the animal at a time. As before, there was a linear relation between image formation times and the number of underlying units. The type of long-term organization rather than the amount of information to be imaged appears to be the crucial factor affecting formation time.

The final issue investigated by Kosslyn and his associates concerns whether images can be constructed from both depictive and descriptive information or from depictions alone. In fact there was already considerable evidence to rule out the latter possibility before Kosslyn's group looked at this (see for example, Paivio, 1971b; Morris and Reid, 1973). Kosslyn has extended the earlier findings, which showed that people could form images of words' referents, and demonstrated that people can also form images from descriptions of scenes. The general

*Because of the distance effect (see Section IB)

conclusions to be drawn from all this work are that both the number of objects referred to in a description as well as the type of description itself can affect image construction times. So, Kosslyn and Gomez (cited in Kosslyn, 1980) and Beech and Allport (1978), using different techniques, have found that there is a linear increase in construction time with the number of to-be-imaged objects. As for the type of description, these studies fall into two subgroups. On the one hand there is a considerable body of research by Paivio (1971b), Morris (1972) and others which shows that the speed of image construction from a word is affected by the position of the word on the abstractness concreteness dimension. Moreover, Morris and Reid have also discovered that the *stability* of an image over time, that is whether or not the same image is constructed on successive occasions, depends on the concreteness of the description underlying the image with high concreteness resulting in more stable images. We have referred to some of this work briefly at the start of this chapter and in more detail in Chapter 11, to which the interested reader is referred. The second type of study, examining the effects of the relational terms used in descriptions, is more recent. We shall give only two examples of this work, for more information see Kosslyn (1980). In one experiment, Kosslyn and Gomez asked subjects to form images of arrays of capital letter X's, which they had previously seen, described either as "three rows of six", or "six columns of three", and although both descriptions referred to the same image few subjects realized this. More interesting was the fact that describing the array in terms of six columns resulted in longer construction times (4·076 seconds) than describing it as three rows (3·800 seconds). The second experiment demonstrated that subjects could use *stored* descriptive information to guide their construction of images. By first showing subjects a picture of the array, then providing them with a description of it and only then asking them to image it, Kosslyn and Gomez were able to show that the description affected image formation *per se* rather than perceptual organization. (In the first experiment subjects presumably knew that some segmentation of the array would be required.) As before columns took longer to image than rows.

Kosslyn has opened up the study of image construction. The data collected so far are compatible with a model in which the long-term form of the image is interpreted and descriptive rather than wholistic and pictorial. It would be interesting, given that some way of partialing out encoding times could be found, to compare image construction rates for statements which differed in propositional complexity. For example, we might expect that if image formation depends on the nature of the underlying propositions that descriptions such as "the man is sitting comfortably in the armchair attentively reading the newspaper" would be imagined faster than descriptions such as "the man is sitting in the armchair reading". Though whether the presumably small differences in construction time could be recorded with our present techniques is doubtful.

B   Properties of the surface image

Once an image has been retrieved or constructed it is often referred to as a "surface image" or "an image held in active memory". The crux of the theoretical debate, as we saw in Chapter 6, concerns the form of this surface image. A question frequently asked is, does the consciously experienced version of an image have a function to play in cognition by virtue of the fact that it possesses or manifests properties which cannot be deduced from a more abstract, underlying long-term representation? (e.g. Kosslyn, 1980; Kosslyn and Pomerantz, 1977). Such properties might include the possibility that the active image can be scanned or inspected in a manner analogous to the scanning of real objects, or that the image functions as a mental model which can be rotated, re-scaled and otherwise transformed. Once again, Kosslyn's research group has invested considerable energy in attempting to validate these emergent or privileged properties of imagery. Another way of looking at the issue is to take seriously the BOSS-consciousness account and the imagery theory introduced in Chapters 3 and 6. According to the double aspect account incorporated in the model, from the inside as it were, the conscious experience of having an image is what it is like to be the cognitive system while it is imaging. From the outside of the system, images are those perceivable aspects of mental models which are supplied as inputs to BOSS-consciousness programs. If this view is correct images have at least one function, namely that of supplying BOSS with information. The question then becomes *how* rather than *whether* they contribute to other cognitive processes. Our BOSS model leads us to expect images to contribute only to higher level processes, or at least tasks which are novel and relatively un-practised.

1   Scanning images

If consciously experienced images represent information in a spatially parallel manner then it might be possible to scan them. By scanning, we mean the sequential sampling or accessing of information from an image in a continuous way. Kosslyn (1973) was the first to investigate this possibility. He had subjects visualize line drawings of extended objects such as rockets and battleships and, after requiring them to focus their attention on a part of their image at one end, to scan across their representation to locate other parts. His main finding was of a linear increase in reaction time with distance traversed, and that subjects could just as easily scan from right to left as from left to right. Members of another group were not asked to use imagery but, instead, were required to memorize descriptions of the pictures and to describe a given end of the drawing before the property probe. Again there was an increase in RT with distance between initial focus and property, but this effect was much greater than in the imagery condition, and people found it much harder to work from right to left in the verbal condition.

Kosslyn concluded from these results that images depict information in a quasi-pictorial way which allows them to be scanned such that scanning time increases with *distance* travelled. Very soon a counter-argument was proposed. Lea (1975) pointed out that Kosslyn's experiment confounded the distance scanned on an image with the number of features encountered. Thus with an image of a battleship compare scanning from bow to stern, say, with scanning from bow to funnel. In the former case a greater distance is covered than in the latter, but also, more of the ship's parts are encountered in moving to the stern than stopping halfway. Lea's argument was that a propositional explanation of the scan effect, in which the image is represented as a feature list structure and scanning involves sequential retrieval of items from the list, was just as plausible as the analogue interpretation, and in a series of experiments he provided evidence to substantiate his claim. Lea's basic procedure was to ask his subjects to learn the identities and positions of objects in a circular array using imagery. He then named a particular object and asked them to respond with the name of the object (or something previously associated with the object) which was *n* steps away. The number of intervening objects, not the inter-object distance was the determining factor affecting scan times. There are several problems with this experiment (see Hampson, 1979; Kosslyn, 1980; Kosslyn *et al.*, 1978), but the most obvious one is that

Lea's subjects were not explicitly asked to use imagery and could have processed their representation in a verbally prompted, "round robin" fashion (cf. Weber *et al.*, 1972). In an attempt to clear up the controversy Hampson and Morris (1977), Kosslyn *et al.* (1978), and Beech (1978, 1979) working independently have eliminated the confound and still find evidence for a distance effect. For example, Kosslyn *et al.* (1978) performed a series of experiments in which the distance between stimulus attributes was varied while the number of intervening items was held constant. To do this they first had subjects memorize a schematic map of an imaginary island. Next they asked subjects to "stare mentally" at a named place on the island, designated on each trial as the focus. Following this a probe word was presented which on half of the trials named another location on the map. The subjects' task was to scan to the named object if it was present on the map and to press a button when they arrived. The general finding was that the greater the distance between two locations the longer it took subjects to respond. An important aspect of this experiment is that no intervening features were traversed between the focus and probe locations (see also Pinker and Kosslyn, 1978).

Since these data were collected, the mental travel experiments have been subjected to a second, potentially more serious criticism by Richman *et al.* (1979) who have argued that subjects' responses in these studies are affected by demand characteristics. They have shown that subjects who are asked merely to deduce the results of such experiments are able to do so, and suggest that people may be responding to implicit demands in the task. Kosslyn *et al.* (1979) question this interpretation and cite a study by Kosslyn and Joliceur and Fliegel to support their counter argument. A group of subjects was given statements such as "a bee has a dark head", asked to decide whether the statements were true or false and then to rate the degree to which they thought they had used imagery in evaluating them. From these data, Kosslyn *et al.* were able to collate a set of object-property pairs that needed imagery for their evaluation and a group which did not, with the proviso that the properties were located on an end of the object. Next, the items were used in an experiment with a new group of subjects. These people were required to image an object, to focus mentally on a particular end of it, and then to determine as rapidly as possible, without necessarily using their image, whether the object possessed a given property. The fixation point was varied such that on half of the trials it coincided with the end at which the property appeared and on the remainder it appeared at the opposite end. The data were interesting: for those object-property pairs previously rated as requiring imagery less time was needed to verify the property when it fell at the focus end, for those items rated as not needing imagery to evaluate, the distance between focus and property had no effect on RT. These results are difficult to explain in terms of demand characteristics, but they are a very good example of the use of "strategy reports" (cf. Morris, 1981a,b) to disambiguate reaction time data.

2   Image size effects and capacity studies

If the spatial display metaphor supported by the scanning studies is taken seriously it makes sense to ask a further series of questions about imagery's visual and spatial properties. One of the strengths of Kosslyn's research is that he has done just this. By exploiting his model to the full he has been forced to consider issues that might otherwise have remained unexplored. For example, parts of images which are subjectively small might be hard to detect, just as parts of objects which are subjectively small can be difficult to perceive, "large" images might require more processing capacity than small and might subtend a larger processing angle and so on. These hypotheses have been extensively investigated by Kosslyn, and we shall review only the major findings here (for more detail see Kosslyn, 1975; Kosslyn, 1978, and also Kosslyn, 1980, Ch.7, for a complete review). The basic procedure used in these experiments was to ask subjects to use their images to check whether objects, usually animals, possessed certain properties. In the 1975 experiment, Kosslyn showed that subjects took longer to verify the existence of features of subjectively small images. This effect occurred when subjects manipulated their image size either directly or indirectly. To illustrate the latter condition: when subjects were asked to image the target animal, say a mouse, next to an elephant, it appeared to be relatively small and therefore its properties took longer to spot, compared with when they imaged it next to a fly. In a later experiment, Kosslyn (1976) showed that small features of an image (e.g. a cat's whiskers) took longer to detect when subjects were asked to use imagery than large properties (e.g. a cat's head) even though the small properties were more highly associated verbally with the name of the animal than were the smaller properties. On the other hand, when no special instructions to image were given, the more highly associated items evoked faster responses.

Kosslyn's (1980, 1975) model of imagery also incorporates a fundamental limitation in the processing capacity of the imagery system. Implications of this are that the image display area itself may be limited in spatial extent, and that resources may be diverted differentially to different parts of the space depending on task demands and the subjects intentions. Kosslyn (1978), in a series of experiments, has tried to provide evidence to support the first of these possibilities in an ingenious if somewhat controversial experiment. The basic procedure involved asking people to imagine themselves moving closer to an object of a specified size until it took up their whole field of vision and had just started to "overflow". At this point, they were to cease their mental walk and to estimate their distance from the object. In a variant of this procedure, subjects were asked to image the longest possible non-overflowing time and to show with their hands how long the line would be at a certain distance away. A third technique involved timing subjects' scans of their longest imageable line. With all of these methods Kosslyn was able to estimate the angle subtended by line or object. The first general finding was that larger objects overflowed at longer distances. This result, of course, supports the notion of a limited image space. Next, the absolute size of the image space, as measured by the visual angle was shown to depend crucially on the stimuli and instructions. Kosslyn (1980) argues that the image space does not seem to have rigidly defined boundaries and that overflow occurs gradually. However, when the same criterion of overflow was used, very similar estimates of the "visual angle of the mind's eye", around 25 degrees, were obtained, using the three different procedures. This convergence is encouraging since this particular task is notoriously subjective, and was apparently too difficult for several subjects to do. Finally, the angles for vertical, diagonal and horizontal extents were broadly comparable which suggests that the image space is roughly circular (but see Finke and Kosslyn, 1980). Our feelings about this group of experiments is that they represent a brave attempt to measure a feature implicit in any analogue model of this nature, but that the results derived from them should be treated with caution on the grounds that the task is so unusual for the subjects.

The second issue, whether or not resources can be selectively allocated to different parts of the image space, was investigated earlier and reported in Kosslyn's 1975 paper. In one experiment, subjects were asked to image one of two matrices at one of two relative sizes next to the image of an animal. One matrix had four subcells, the other sixteen. The latter was considered to be more complex, and therefore to need more processing capacity than the former. If size alone was the main effect determining resource allocation, then imaging an animal next to a small matrix rather than a large one should have resulted in faster animal property verification. On the other hand if complexity was the main effect, then imaging an animal next to a 2 × 2 matrix instead of a 4 × 4 one should have resulted in speedier responses. In fact, evidence was found for both size and complexity effects.

The question of how much total information can be imaged simultaneously has been investigated by Beech (1976, 1977). He presented subjects with descriptions of arrays of objects, and instructed them to respond by saying "stop" when they could no longer image all the objects simultaneously. The objects were to be imaged in square pigeon holes, with the first named in a labelled base. An example of a typical description would be "base table, up match, up shoe, right doll" etc. After four practice arrays, thirty-five test arrays were presented at six rates (0·75, 1·25, 1·75, 2·5, 3·5 or 5·0 seconds per object), with three female and three male students in each condition. When a subject said "stop" he was asked to name the last object he had imaged before experiencing difficulty. He then rated his confidence that he had achieved "wholistic visualization" and that wholistic visualization could not be maintained if more objects were presented, using a 7-point scale. The limitation of visualization was found to be an inverted U function of presentation rate, with subjects imaging a maximum of 5·4 objects at a presentation rate of 2·9 seconds per object, and females imaging significantly more than males. Beech interpreted these findings as evidence that with each successive object imaged, there is a reduction in clarity of previous objects imaged, this process continues up to the limit of wholistic visualization. Increasing the presentation rate above the optimum reduces the time available to increase the clarity (consolidate) previous images. The effect of reducing the presentation rate "may in part be related to factors such as the decay of the image over time, or loss of concentration" (1976, p.1274).

Beech does not speculate any further how these limitations could arise, but it is interesting to attempt an interpretation of these findings in terms of Kosslyn's (1980) model. In this simulation of imagery, portions of the display are refreshed as they fade by a procedure called REGENERATE, which acts on the surface matrix itself point by point. Obviously, as the amount of information displayed increases less "dwell time" is available to REGENERATE successive portions of the display; thus, a point is reached where parts of the representation decay or fade completely before refreshing is possible. This point would correspond to the limit of wholistic visualization. While successive elements are added to the display, the preceding elements still need to be refreshed. Increasing the presentation rate, therefore, decreases the time available to refresh each preceding item before the next occurs. Even if the subject adequately reactivates a subset of his images, he may not be left with enough time to refresh the remainder. In this case, why does decreasing the presentation rate below a certain level somewhat paradoxically *decrease* the limit of visualization? Why, in other words, is there an optimum presentation rate? A possible explanation is that faced with a slower speed of presentation, subjects may opt to share the time available between presentations (less the time needed to construct a single item) equally among all the preceding elements. By doing this, it is possible that a subject will spend too long on any particular element during which time, another element might have decayed completely. According to this notion, the optimum presentation rate is the one which allows the maximum refreshing of elements to take place with the proviso that *all* the elements are refreshed in the time available. This explanation seems to demand that people have strategic control over REGENERATE, but on reflection, even a simple, pre-programmed refreshing procedure might evince the same properties. In Kosslyn's simulation, REGENERATE refreshes the image in cycles, starting with the most faded parts, i.e. the "oldest". With a sufficiently long interstimulus interval, more than one, but less than two complete cycles might be completed and by the time the next item was generated a previous one could have disappeared.

3 Maintaining images

In Kosslyn's original simulation, the procedure REGENERATE operated on the surface matrix, but it does not fixate on particular location nor does it scan, i.e. change the location of the image with respect to the processor. Kosslyn has questioned whether or not there really is a relation between scanning and maintenance and in an experiment conducted with Farah and Wallace (cited in Kosslyn, 1980) has tried to investigate this issue. Subjects were asked either to "focus mentally" on the centre of an image of an animal or were given no special instructions about what to do with their images. A property name was then presented immediately, or at either 3 or 6 seconds after the animal name, and, as usual, subjects were to look for the property in the usual way. The time taken to detect a feature increased with property word latency only for the focus group. As for the non-focus group, property verification speeds actually increased with longer property word delays. When questioned later as to their strategies people in the latter condition did report scanning to maintain their images. Kosslyn *et al.* reasoned that when an image is initially constructed, not all of its features are included, and some of these may have to be generated for the property verification task, especially in the focus condition. This was supported by their data which showed that large, highly verbally associated properties were detected fastest and small properties with low association strength the slowest. The results suggest that scanning may be involved in image maintenance and that people held images with but a few elaborated parts, and "flesh out" or add other features only when necessary. Scanning itself, argues Kosslyn, may be used to provide visual prompts which tell the imager what needs to be placed in the representation. This would involve considerable extension of Kosslyn's model, as he realizes, but would fit in well with the theory put forward in Chapter 6 in which BOSS both initiates and checks the results of operations performed on the data base. By appropriate use of BOSS programs, it should be possible for the cognitive system to detect not just the presence but also the absence of a particular, plausible, image feature and to take steps to rectify the situation. Further discussion of the relation between these and the other findings concerning the privileged properties of the image and their relation to the BOSS-consciousness model will be postponed until the end of the chapter.

II   Transforming images

In their different ways William James (1890) and Craik (1943) alert us to the dynamic as well as substantive or representational aspects of cognition. For James, thought consisted of a series of "flights and perchings"; for Craik, somewhat less poetically, new representations can be derived from old using processes of inference. In this section, then, we too must consider ways in which images can be manipulated to derive more information from them, or to make explicit information which was previously tacit. To some extent, all the operations such as constructing, scanning and maintaining images we have just considered are examples of "image transformations", but in the sense used here the term "transformation" is usually reserved for cases where the position of an orientation of the surface image is altered, or where the image is deformed in some way. Some of the most important work in this area has been carried out by Roger Shepard and his colleagues (see for example Shepard and Podgorny, 1979; Metzler and Shepard, 1974; Cooper and Shepard, 1973; Shepard and Metzler, 1971; for reviews; also, Cooper, 1975; Cooper and Podgorny, 1976; Metzler, 1973). This whole research programme developed from Shepard's interest in the "form, formation and transformation" of representations as we discussed in Chapter 6. Early studies (e.g. Shepard and Feng, 1972) investigated transformations, using a mental, paper folding task, which included several spatial operations such as sequences of rotations, reflections or foldings around different axes. Later studies, referenced above, have concentrated on one transformation in particular viz. "mental rotation", examples of which will be discussed here.

A   Mental rotation

The first experiments on mental rotation examined the phenomenon in three dimensions. In their basic experimental task, Shepard and Metzler (1971) presented subjects with perspective drawings of three-dimensional forms, two at a time, and instructed them to decide as rapidly as possible whether or not the two patterns were identical (i.e. had the same three-dimensional configuration) irrespective of their orientation. The stimuli used were line drawings of relatively abstract, unfamiliar objects, which each consisted of ten cubical blocks arranged to form a connected string of cubes with three right angles and two free ends. For each of ten distinct objects, 18 perspective views were constructed corresponding to 18 equally-spaced increments of rotation of the object about a vertical axis in either the picture or the depth plane. Half of the picture pairs consisted of views of identical objects at different orientations. The remainder consisted of views of the object and its mirror image version, again at different angles. The most striking finding of this experiment was that the time needed to perform the task increased as a linear function of the angular difference in the portrayed orientation between the objects. This linearity held for picture plane *and* for depth plane differences in orientation. Evidence was also produced to show that mental rotation times were additive such that the time taken to go from orientation A to C was the sum of the time to go from A to an intermediate orientation B, and then from B to C. An additional finding was that the degree of similarity of the picture pairs as two-dimensional patterns had no independent effect on rotation times. Metzler and Shepard (1974) concluded from all this that subjects were operating mentally on representations that were more like the three-dimensional objects portrayed in the pictures than their two-dimensional portrayals. From these data, it seems not unreasonable to speak of a process of "mental rotation" of an internal representation analogous to the physical rotation of a real object. Metzler and Shepard found that these rotations are performed at speeds of from 55 to 60 degrees per second, although faster rates for solids composed of less sub-cubes were recorded.

Using a similar technique to Metzler and Shepard's, Lynne Cooper and co-workers have very thoroughly investigated the mental rotation of two-dimensional shapes (see for example, Cooper and Shepard, 1973; also Cooper, 1975). The earlier finding of a constant rate of rotation was confirmed with alphanumeric characters. Also, by presenting patterns successively, as opposed to simultaneously, the effects of prior knowledge of the orientation difference between the patterns were determined. Results showed that subjects were able to prepare in advance for the test stimulus, presumably by mentally rotating a stored representation of the original stimulus to the expected orientation of the second. Rotation rates in these experiments were typically much higher than the rotation of three-dimensional representations, and varied considerably from around 800 degrees per second for the fastest subject to around 164 degrees per second for the slowest.

The experiments reported by Cooper (1975) are particularly interesting. To demonstrate that the rotation effects were not phenomena tied to particular stimuli such as block figures or alpha-numeric characters, she showed that computer generated, random, two-dimensional shapes produced similar results. Moreover, on manipulating the complexity of the stimuli (by varying the number of different inflection points in the figure) she discovered that complexity, so defined, had no effect on rotation rates. Cooper and Podgorny (1976) repeated and extended Cooper's third experiment and replaced the mirror image patterns in the mismatch condition with figures which differed to greater or lesser extents from the standard stimulus. They made this modification because they felt that subjects in the earlier experiments might have been using schematic versions of images during rotation, or focussing on selected stimulus features during the match. By selectively perturbing randomly chosen parts of the stimuli in the mismatch condition, it was hoped that a greater degree of uncertainty would be introduced which would force the subject to encode and maintain all of the stimulus feature during rotation. Once again, no effect of complexity on rotation rates was found.

These results are intriguing, but not without their problems. First of all, the possibility that subjects were using schematic images or selected stimulus features still cannot be completely ruled out. As Hochberg and Gellman (1977) have shown, subjects can and do make use of salient stimulus features to speed up rotation. Second, it is highly unlikely, in view of the limitations on processing capacity discussed above, that subjects could adequately encode, let alone maintain the complex images that the figures used in some trials would have necessitated. Third, the finding is counter-intuitive and more important would be predicted explicitly by only the most radical of analogue theories. Most other models, especially those which assert that images are constructed from underlying representations, suggest that complex images will take longer to form than simpler ones (cf. Kosslyn's model, above). Rotation of complex figures, according to these models, might also take longer, either because the trans-formation is effected on the underlying data base or because more parts of the surface image need to be manipulated, (e.g. Palmer, 1975; Kosslyn, 1980). Fourth, if there is no effect of stimulus complexity on two-dimensional mental rotation, why does the rotation of a portrayed three-dimensional object take longer than a two-dimensional representation, even when the three-dimensional rotation is confined to the picture plan? Moreover, why is there a difference in rotation rates between simple and complex three-dimensional forms, but no such difference for two dimensions? Other researchers have added more criticisms to this list. Kosslyn (1980) has pointed out that the subjects used in these experiments were highly practised and that the results might be subject to floor effects, and that as only six different stimuli were used it is possible that psychological complexity was not adequately manipulated. The last criticism seems somewhat unfair, but using more stimuli would have added more weight to Cooper and Podgorny's case. A serious problem has been mentioned by Anderson (1978). Since more complex polygons had more points altered when "different" stimuli were generated from them, subjects needed to remember a smaller proportion of points with complex images, than with simple images, to have the same chance of spotting a "different" test stimulus. This means that our first suggestion above could well have occurred. As Kosslyn rightly points out the crucial experiment is one in which subjects are compelled to maintain all the information about the stimulus during rotation.

Hampson (1979) and Shwartz (1979) using different types of stimuli have attempted to clear up the issue. Hampson used random dot patterns and varied the position of one dot at each level of complexity. An *overall* difference in performance emerged, with complex stimuli taking longer to deal with and resulting in more errors, but no specific effect on rotation *rate* was found. Shwartz' study was also inconclusive using random polygons; he discovered that larger images took longer to rotate than smaller, an interesting effect of size on rotation rates, but a non-significant complexity effect though the difference was in the expected direction. With a different technique, Pylyshyn (1979) has produced some interesting data which suggest that the elusive complexity effect does occur. He has shown amongst other things that good Gestalts can be rotated and judged to be parts of a figure more quickly than poor Gestalts. However, the fact the simultaneous comparisons were used and that therefore the task was generally different from that used in "normal" rotation studies makes comparison with previous work difficult.

Kosslyn and Adelson (reported in Kosslyn, 1980) have performed an experiment using the ambiguous geometric forms previously constructed for the image generation experiment which we considered earlier. These stimuli could be described either in terms of a few superimposed or relatively more adjacent units. Also, different figures could be described in terms of greater number of parts. Two groups of subjects were required to indicate when they had formed an image after being given a particular description and were then cued to rotate their image through either 60 or 120 degrees, transformations which they had previously practised with real objects. The groups differed only with respect to the descriptions they received. Both rotation and generation times were recorded. The results were interesting. More complexly described patterns took longer to generate, replicating previous findings, and once generated took longer to rotate than patterns given simple descriptions (as did patterns with more subparts). One problem however, was that the same amount of time was needed to rotate an additional 60 degrees (presumably after the initial 60 degrees) for both types of patterns. Adelson and Kosslyn wondered if this was because subjects first regenerated and then rotated their images and that although complex forms took longer to regenerate than simple ones, once refreshed they were equally easy to rotate. To test this, they subtracted the mean generation times from the rotation times and correlated the result with the number of units in each figure. The correlation was 0·61 which suggests that complexity did affect rotation *per se*. Unfortunately it is unclear from Kosslyn's brief report of these results whether complexity really did alter rotation *rates* or merely overall rotation times. It is obviously important to demonstrate the former and not just the latter. Rotation rate is, of course measured in units of time per given angle, variation in rate is an interaction between time and angle, and hence must be measured over several angles. We are confident that Kosslyn and Abelson recognized these elementary points, but as reported at present the results of their experiment are ambiguous. Additional evidence that stimulus complexity does affect mental rotation has been provided by Yuille and Steiger (1982) who also suggest that previous failures to find any effect (e.g. Cooper and Podgorny, 1976) were due to subjects focussing on distinguishing features of the stimuli.

Mental rotation studies are frequently cited as outstanding examples of work demonstrating the existence and use of specifically visual images possibly because the latter are often mentioned in subjects' reports. For this reason any experiment which purports to demonstrate mental rotation in the blind cannot be passed over lightly, since it calls into question this visual interpretation. Marmor and Zaback (1976) have attempted to show that the phemonenon occurs with blind as well as sighted subjects using a tactile version of the task originally used by Shepard and Metzler (1971) which involves comparing two stimuli presented side by side at different orientations. Instead of using the mirror image comparison technique, Marmor and Zaback presented teardrop shaped blocks which had curved segments, or "bites", taken out of either the right or left side. All four possible combinations of "bite" pairs were presented with the stimuli at different orientations, and subjects had to determine as rapidly as possible whether both forms had parts missing from the same sides. Three groups of subjects were used, early blind subjects who had lost their sight before age five, late blind subjects who could see until the age of fifteen, and sighted adults who wore blindfolds. The mean rotation rates for the blind groups were not significantly different, at 59 and 114 degrees per second for the early and late blind groups respectively, nor was there a significant difference between the late blind and sighted groups with the latter achieving a rotation rate of 233 degrees per second. An interesting finding was that the reaction time function did not increase linearly with angle for the early blind and sighted groups. Marmor and Zaback suggest that some verbal processing may have been involved here. Finally the introspections of many subjects suggested that they had used some type of mental rotation 63% of the early blind, 94% of the late blind and 69% of the sighted reported using a strategy of this type.

There are at least two ways of interpreting the Marmor and Zaback results. One approach, favoured for example by Kosslyn (1980), is to claim that they are outside the scope of an imagery since there was no need for subjects in this experiment to use an internal representation that was independent or "unhitched" from the perceptual data. Presumably these tasks involve percept–percept comparisons which may well be tactile in form. The advantage of this argument is that it leaves intact the conventional account of rotation studies. The alternative interpretation is to argue that mental rotation involves a massive *spatial* component. In transforming and manipulating images the real work horses are the control processes concerned with their relative positions and orientations. Perhaps even the early blind are able to perform mental rotation type tasks because their spatial control system is still operative. Indeed this may well be the case since in an exploratory study which one of us conducted with Chris Duffy at Manchester Polytechnic, we found that congenitally blind children were as equally susceptible to spatial interference on a Brooks' type letter categorization task as a normally sighted, blindfolded group. It could be that Baddeley (1976) is right to emphasize the importance of imagery's spatial aspects and play down its visual component, but for reasons discussed in Chapter 7, we believe that both are important. A third possibility is to argue that in the Marmor and Zaback study apparently quite large differences in the performance of the various groups were found though they failed to reach significance. A replication of their study with successive presentation of the stimuli would encourage the groups to hold and transform a representation of the standard stimulus and might show up any differences more clearly. As they stand, the differences discovered by Marmor and Zaback look suspiciously large and though found to be not significant in their experiment they might reflect an underlying real effect. It is also quite possible that wide individual variation in symbolic skills between subjects within the groups could swamp any differences in processing ability or style between the groups.

B   Other types of transformation

Two additional types of image transformations that have been investigated involve (1) altering the size of mental images and (2) the (imaginal) processes involved in mental paper folding. Experiments on magnitude alteration have shown, in general, that subjects can change the subjective size of their images in an analogue fashion, and that larger size changes take longer to effect. For example, Sekuler and Nash (1972) had subjects judge whether the height-to-width ratios of rectangles presented in rapid succession were the same. The second rectangle presented was either the same size as the first or one of three smaller, or one of three larger sizes. Times to make the judgement increased linearly with increasing size discrepancy. (The relative orientation of the stimuli was also varied in this experiment with the second stimulus sometimes appearing at 90 degrees from the first, and this variable also affected RTs.) Sekuler and Nash found that around 70 ms was needed to alter the size of an image by 50%. A similar time was found by Hayes (1973) employing a different procedure. Using himself as a subject he imaged capital letters at one of two subjective sizes "large" and "small". On pressing a button he presented a letter to himself which was either the same size as the one imaged or the other size (larger or smaller); also, for each size combination, half of the letters had the same identity half were different. Congruent size verifications were 60 ms faster, on average, than incongruent verifications. Larsen and Bundesen (1978) have recently reported a series of experiments relevant to this issue. In their first experiment, for example, with random, two-dimensional forms as stimuli, they again found that evaluation times increased linearly with the size ratio of the two figures, though their subsequent results were less clear cut.

Experiments involving more specialized image transformations have been reported by Shepard and Feng (1972). Subjects were shown diagrams of interconnected squares, designed to represent unfolded cubes. In two of the squares was an arrow, pointing to one of the squares sides. Subjects were to determine as rapidly as possible if the arrows would meet up, on a common edge, when the paper was folded into a cube. Response times increased with the number of squares that had to be moved to form the solid. Cooper and Shepard (1975) examined another type of transformation. Their subjects had to decide whether pictures of hands in arbitrary positions were of the right or left hand. People in this experiment appeared to "flip over" their images of hands. Shepard (1975) has reported several other additional experiments involving image transformation most of which support an analogue-type explanation of the process, but since many of these experiments involve comparisons made with simultaneously presented stimuli we feel, together with Kosslyn (1980), that there may be considerable, nonmental components in these transformations and hence that they may be outside the domain of a theory concerned specifically with imagery.

C   The theoretical nature of image transformations

So far we have considered several examples of empirical work showing that images can be manipulated in various ways, but have not explored the theoretical nature of these processes in any great detail save to remark that many transformations have been used to show a similarity between imaginal and perceptual operations. It is necessary, therefore, for us to consider transformations more thoroughly from a theoretical perspective if we wish to gain a deeper understanding of the imagery system. Specifically we need to consider first what general varieties of image transformations can be shown to exist, and second the applicability of various transformations to all or part of an imaginal representation. Incidentally, to understand both of these issues it is useful to accept provisionally a type of "mixed" imagery theory, with propositional and analogue aspects, similar to that advanced by Kosslyn (1980) or to our BOSS-consciousness model introduced in Chapter 6. The reason for this is that speculation concerning the varieties of transformations possible and their application has been within the framework of this type of model.

Kosslyn's research group have distinguished between two ways of transforming images. In the first the surface image is manipulated in an analogue fashion such that it passes through a series of intermediate points on its path from position A to position B. For all practical purposes, this transformation can be labelled "continuous" or "shift", though in the Kosslyn and Shwartz simulation the surface image is modified by successive incremental adjustments. (Applying Johnson-Laird's (1978a) point regarding the need to determine the functional level of representations and transformations: the first type of transformation functions "as if" it were continuous and thus should be considered as such.) A second way of transforming images depends less on their links with perception and more with their properties as representations in memory. Kosslyn has labelled this a "blink" transform since it involves allowing a surface image to fade and regenerating a new, modified image in its place from its underlying representation. Blink transforms are assumed by Kosslyn to occur less frequently than continuous modifications since they probably require more effort. In certain circumstances, though, a blink transform may "cost" less than a continuous one especially if the latter involves shifting the image across a large distance.

Evidence supporting the existence of continuous, shift transforms is not hard to find. The mental rotation and size scaling studies which we discussed above are good examples of these. Empirical studies of the blink transform are, however, just emerging. Kosslyn (1980) reports an experiment in which different predictions were generated for shift and blink operations. With a subjectively large image more time should be taken to shrink the image to more and more subjectively smaller sizes if a shift transform is used (e.g. Sekuler and Nash, 1972). On the other hand if the same, subjectively large image is altered using a blink transform, then the *smaller* the final image the *faster* the transformation. This last prediction, although seemingly counter-intuitive, follows naturally from Kosslyn's (1975) finding that subjectively small images take less time to generate than larger ones. Therefore, the smaller the end product of a blink transformation, the more rapidly it will be generated. For increases in size, both types of transformation will take longer for bigger size changes. Kosslyn presented subjects with a letter on a cathode ray tube at either a large or a small size followed by a box at one of five sizes, and instructed them to alter mentally the size of the letter until it would fit into the box using either a shift or a blink transform. The main findings were as follows: overall, blink transforms took longer than shift transforms. Increasing the amount of expanation or contraction resulted in longer shift transforms with a suggestion that it was easier to expand than to contract an image. Results in the blink condition, which were quite different from the shift condition, depended on whether the initial image was large or small as predicted though the exact nature of the interaction was equivocal. Certainly over the first three amounts of size change blink "expansions" took increasingly longer whereas blink "contractions" took less time. Size changes four and five were less clear cut especially when the initial image was large. Quite which components of the interaction are significant is not stated. Until Kosslyn's data and the details of the instructions given to his subjects are reported more fully, therefore, these results must be regarded as tentative. On the positive side, however, the clear-cut overall difference between blink and shift operations does suggest very strongly that the distinction is meaningful.

It is interesting to note that image scanning can be interpreted as a type of image transformation. Research reported by, for example, Kosslyn *et al.* (1978) suggests that scanning is an example of a shift transform. Kosslyn (1980) reports that "blink scans" are also possible. By asking subjects to image faces at one of three sizes, focus their attention on the mouth, and then blink scan to the eyes, he has shown that distance has no effect on such transformations.

Turning now from the types of transformation on to the aspects of the representation on which they are applied, Kosslyn has distinguished between field-general (FG) and region-bounded (RB) transforms. A field-general transformation involves shifting all of the contents of the image display in some specified way. A region-bounded transformation operates on some locally defined area of the display space. Kosslyn exemplifies this distinction by contrasting zooming in on a scene with expanding a particular object. The former is field general in that all the contents of the visual buffer or display area are altered, the latter is region bounded since only a limited aspect is perturbed. Scanning is FG since the entire display is shifted relative to the processor or mind's eye, whereas imaging a mental rotation against a stationary background is RB. This distinction is not an arbitrary one, says Kosslyn, since the two sorts of transformation have different behavioural consequences. Three variables are predicted to lengthen RB transformations but to have no effect on FGs. First, the complexity of the image which is transformed, second, the number of imaged objects to be altered, and third, the number of elements in the background which need to be "held still" while the transformation is taking place. Data supporting these predictions have been presented by Pinker and Kosslyn (1978). No more time was taken to scan between pairs of equidistant objects when an imaged scene contained six as opposed to four objects (scanning is an FG transform), but subjects took longer to move an object when the scene contained six as opposed to four objects. A further prediction, which has not yet been tested, is that zooming in on a scene will be unaffected by the complexity or number of items imaged, whereas imaging one object expanding will take longer when more complex objects are manipulated and when this is done against a greater number of objects in the background, (and possibly against a more complex background).

Kosslyn's taxonomy of transformations might lead us to assume that they can only occur in isolation, but a moment's reflection should convince the reader that intricate combinations and sequences of transformations are used by adults in often the more routine, as well as the more esoteric of cognitive tasks. For example, if a familiar route to work is impassable an alternative could conceivably be worked out mentally using a series of rotations and blink transforms. When a medical student is attempting to build up a composite, three-dimensional picture of the human anatomy from his two-dimensional text book he may frequently have to rotate and zoom in on a particular region after a preliminary blink scan to reach the appropriate area. Whether young children possess these skills is not clear, though Piaget's studies of egocentricity (Piaget, 1926) and the development of imagery (Piaget and Inhelder, 1971) make it appear unlikely. Research into this area is still in the early stages, since the issues are obviously highly complex. To begin with, we are concerned not merely with the transformation of representations, but with the much wider question of the high level *control* of a series of transformations. This will involve such things as assessing the computational cost effectiveness of a set of operations as well as decisions concerned solely with their geometric and topological properties. To do this, it is likely that some sort of hierarchy of control would be necessary so that actions could be initiated, their results checked and modifications made. As was noted in Chapter 3, the notion that the cognitive system is organized into levels like this is widely recognized (cf. Broadbent, 1977; Miller *et al.*, 1960) and is incorporated in our BOSS-consciousness theory, but the detailed applications of this arrangement as far as imagery is concerned still need to be specified. At the moment, we can only speculate that any such system, involving as it must the possibilty of flexible, strategic control over subordinate processes, would need to be in close touch with the plans and intentions of the organism as a whole. Also, when a task is novel and therefore relatively unpractised, the sequence of transformations may have to be verbally guided, or in some way paced by BOSS's main program.

There is some limited evidence that sequences of image transformations can occur, that some series are less error prone and more accurate than others, and that subjects can obey instructions designed to help them use more efficient strategies. In two of the experiments reported by Hampson and Morris (1978b), which we will consider in more detail later, we showed that subjects could make use of the syllabic structure of a word to generate images of groups of its letters in a backward spelling task. When a group of letters had been produced in this way, subjects could inspect each letter in turn for the presence of curved or straight features, before moving on to the next group. We used the terms iteration and scanning for the processes involved in the production of letter groups and the inspection of imaged displays respectively, though to bring our interpretation in line with Kosslyn's terminology, iterations could just as easily be referred to as blink transforms, whereas scanning and inspection may be retained. In one of our experiments we also showed that subjects instructed to use a word's syllabic structure could do so to their advantage during image formation. Strategies in these tasks can be co-ordinated and are flexible.

How does the BOSS-consciousness model cope with the variety and complexity of image transformations? In general, quite well, but one modification appears to be necessary. When we introduced our imagery model in Chapter 6 it was suggested that all image transformations are effected on the long-term representation in the data base, and their results picked up by the goals or expectations constructed by BOSS. After considering Kosslyn's recent data it is more likely that only some transformations are performed in this way and that others involve more direct operations on the surface image itself. As Kosslyn suggests, it is probably better to consider such modifications as scanning and mental rotation as applied directly to the already constructed image, and others, in particular blink transforms as operations of the data base which effectively results in the creation of new surface images. For reasons of computational efficiency it seems more reasonable to allow images a certain degree of processing autonomy and not demand that each and every operation be routed through an abstract data base, though, of course, some may be. Our BOSS-consciousness model needs to be extended to cope with this. The simplest way seems to be for BOSS to be equipped with the facility to "replot" parts of the image display so as to either stretch, contract, shift, rotate or otherwise continuously transform the conscious image. In short, we are prepared to accept Kosslyn's account of image modification as the most appropriate and comprehensive treatment available at present.

III   Imagery and perception

A   Levels of equivalence

In the previous chapter it was pointed out that data from converging sources allow us to distinguish between a visual and a verbal processing system and we suggested, with support from studies of selective interference, that visual images and their associated operations are supported by the visual perceptual and memory system and verbal-auditory images depend on the verbal system. The present chapter, so far, has been concerned with the nature of the visual imagery system, but little has been said about the relation between the imaginal and perceptual systems. All that has been suggested is that certain operations on images appear to mimic operations with real objects, but the primary consideration has been with data obtained from tasks specifically involving imagery, with no direct comparisons with perceptual data. We have ignored the issue of *what* aspects of the perceptual system are tapped by visual imagery. If images do function *as if* they were percepts in certain circumstances at what level or levels of processing does this *functional equivalence* obtain? For example, do images and percepts share (and compete for) the same processing machinery at all stages of analysis from peripheral to central, or is their access to the same systems restricted to higher levels only? Are all aspects of percepts and images dealt with by the same mechanisms; is information specifying shape, orientation and colour all processed equivalently or are only some of these attributes treated similarly? We will try to answer these questions in this section. Before doing so, however, it is worth reminding the reader that to find evidence for a relationship between imagery and perceptual processing does not commit us unequivocally to any particular position on the representation issue. To show some link between imagery and perception does not of itself imply that imagery has, say, analogue characteristics as some sort of equivalence is predicted by all the major theoretical approaches. Neither can we deduce the structure of imagery in a more circuitous fashion from perceptual theory since again, percept–image equivalence does not allow us to infer automatically that any particular model of perception is true. Studies of the structure of imagery, which have just been considered, must stand or fall on their own merits. Despite these *caveats* we must also point out that, used with caution, studies which purport to show certain types of equivalence can give *some* limited support to one version or other of the nature of imagery. Consider the following two possibilities. In case one it is shown that processing systems which normally accept perceptual information can also be stimulated by conscious visual images, and the magnitude of stimulation varies directly with subjectively reported image vividness. In case two, it is shown that images cannot act as the *inputs* to systems normally activated by information at some stage in the stream of perceptual processing but instead are shown to be equivalent to the *outputs* of perceptual processes and reported vividness is shown to be irrelevant. Case one would help support those theories which assert that the surface image can affect the course of future processing; case two would be more in line with propositional theory. Used sensibly and cautiously, studies of equivalence may provide circumstantial evidence for imagery theory.

Finke (1980) has explored these ideas in some detail (see also Finke, 1979; Finke and Schmidt, 1977, 1978). An important aim of his work has been to present data showing functional equivalences between imagery and perception which cannot be subjected to the usual criticisms aimed at this area. Finke has three sorts of criticisms in mind: one frequent complaint is that subjects might respond as they do in imagery tasks using their knowledge of how real objects and events behave. This criticism has been made of mental rotation studies (cf. Pylyshyn, 1978). An associated argument is that subjects' responses might be affected by their *tacit* knowledge about perceptual phenomena. A third problem is that the demand characteristics of imagery experiments may be such that subjects can deduce what results the experimenter expects. The reader will recall that this last criticism has been aimed at experiments in image scanning by Richman *et al.* (1979).

To show that these criticisms can be avoided, Finke reports several experiments in which certain imagery effects concerning objects and their locations are demonstrated whose associated perceptual phenomena are unlikely to be consciously or tacitly known by subjects, nor are they likely to be influenced by demand characteristics since the pattern of both perceptual and imaginal responding is difficult to predict in advance. Finke and Schmidt (1977, 1978) have discovered an interesting phenomenon which could be called a *mental McCullough effect*. The McCullough effect (McCullough, 1965) is a colour after-effect produced when one views horizontal black stripes against a background of one colour alternating with vertical stripes against a background of another colour. After observing this alternation for a period of time horizontal and vertical gratings are seen to be tinged with colours of complementary hues. Finke and Schmidt's subjects had to imagine horizontal and vertical stripes against perceptually presented coloured fields (red or green) or to imagine coloured backgrounds (red or green) around perceptually presented horizontal and vertical bar patterns. Subjects participated in both conditions with the usual counterbalancing, and were then tested for any McCullough effect by having them make forced choice judgements for the presence of red and green hues on the test stripes. The results were intriguing. When subjects imaged bars against real coloured backgrounds they appeared to experience the McCullough effect, but when they imaged colours paired with real bar patterns they responded in the direction opposite to that expected for the McCullough effect. Equivalence with perception was obtained at levels involved in imaging shape and orientation but not colours. In their second study Finke and Schmidt found that mental McCullough effects were more pronounced in those subjects who experienced more vivid imagery as measured by Marks (1973) questionnaire. Finke argues that the results

> provide perhaps the strongest answer so far to criticisms that subjects always use their knowledge about objects or expectations for performance to generate predicted responses in mental imagery tasks. Indeed not only were subjects in these experiments unaware of the McCullough effect but they were evidently biased to expect the opposite effect, falsely believing that the purpose of the studies had been to test their memory for previous associations between pattern orientation and color. (1980, p.121.)

These results have subsequently been replicated and extended by Kunen and May (1980).

A second group of experiments were concerned with the relative acuities of the perceptual and imaginal fields. Finke and Kosslyn (1980) asked subjects to judge, in a perceptual condition, how far out in their peripheral visual fields they could tell that pairs of dots were separate. Subjects in an imagery condition practised forming images of the patterns. They then made acuity judgements by imagining the dots to be present in front of them and moving their eyes away from this central position until the imagined dots appeared to merge. Additionally the vividness of the participants imagery was measured. There were three major findings. For both imagery and perception conditions there was a negatively accelerated relationship between the separation of the dots and the size of their fields of resolution. Fields of resolution for vivid imagers were larger than those of non-vivid imagers but there were no significant differences between the sizes of their perceptual fields. Finally the imaginal fields of resolution of vivid imagers were the same size as their perceptual fields whereas the imaginal fields of non-vivid imagers were smaller than their perceptual fields. Two control experiments were also run. First of all, it was shown that similar effects could be obtained when subjects were instructed to keep their eyes shut in the imagery condition, thereby ruling out the possibility that they were using perceptual cues, tacitly or otherwise, to help them estimate dot separation. Second, to avoid the demand characteristics criticism, an independent group of subjects was asked to try to guess how people would respond. Although they guessed correctly that the size of the fields of resolution would increase with dot separation, they did not anticipate that the relationship was not in the form of a straight line graph. Also, they overestimated the degree of (elliptical) eccentricity of the fields of resolution. Finke concludes from this that:

> Evidently, subjects can use their knowledge about how objects should appear to predict the most general characteristics of fields of resolution, but they cannot use this knowledge to predict the more subtle characteristics that are present when one forms images. (1980, pp.123–124).

A third series of experiments investigated people's images for errors of movements. Finke (1979) has shown that imagined errors of movement in an experiment where subjects had to perform a manual task with prisms which displaced what they saw result in similar types of pointing after effects as perceived errors of movement. The after-effects following imagined errors were less than those following perceived errors but vivid imagers produced larger after-effects than non-vivid imagers.

Taken together the experiments reported by Finke support the proposal that images and information from physical objects and events are treated similarly at many levels in the visual processing system. Moreover, these equivalences can occur at levels where people are unaware of the effects which will be produced. At some levels, functional equivalences do not exist especially where information specifying an object's colour or brightness is processed. Perhaps because these are relatively early levels of analysis.

What can be deduced from this about theories of imagery? Finke suggests that images can act as the *inputs* of perceptual processes, and that the stronger the image the greater the degree of activation of a processing system. As he says,

> According to this view, mental images can stimulate visual processing mechanisms directly. Thus, when mental images are formed, these mechanisms would respond in much the same way as they do when objects and events are observed, resulting in the sensation that an image can be ''seen'' as if it were an actual object or event. Further the more vivid the image, the more strongly these mechanisms would respond, and the more similar to actual objects or events the mental image would appear. (1980, p.130.)

Although propositional theory could be stretched in a somewhat *post hoc* fashion to explain these effects and make these predictions, we believe that models in which the surface image has a functional role to play in processing can account for them more easily (cf. Kunen and May, 1980).

B   Concluding remarks on the nature of the image

We have summarized a considerable amount of data in this chapter concerning the nature of the imagery system. As a great deal of it has been produced by two groups of researchers led by Kosslyn and Shepard, the general tenor of the work reported is that images do have a functional role to play in cognitive processing and can be treated as perceptual analogues. It is possible to recast many of their theoretical explanations in a propositional theory (cf. Anderson, 1978) as we have just stated, but we argue that to do this is to choose the wrong functional level of explanation. As was stated in Chapter 6, many of the important qualities of high level programming languages are dissolved when they are reduced to machine code. So it is with the reduction of images to propositions. Moreover, we seriously doubt whether many of the effects reported in this chapter would have been generated from propositional accounts in advance of their being tested. Analogue models (including mixed analogue and propositional accounts) have a heuristic value if nothing else.

To conclude, we would like to list some major properties of images supported by recent evidence:

1   The information from which images are constructed is represented in long-term memory in an organized and interpreted abstract format.

2   Depictive and descriptive information can be used to generate visual images, a process which will take time, with more complex images taking longer to construct than less complex.

3   Once it has been generated, the surface image can be scanned and inspected. The longer the distance scanned the longer it will take, and the larger the property to be detected the quicker it will be spotted.

4   The processing capacity of the imagery system in general and its ability to display conscious images in particular is limited. (Also, processing involving conscious imagery may be quite effortful (Hasher and Zacks, 1979).)

5   Surface images need to be regenerated continuously to sustain them. Scanning the surface image may help in its maintenance by revealing which parts need to be refreshed.

6   Images can be transformed in a continuous fashion, by operating directly on the display as in mental rotation or scanning.

7   On the other hand, images can be modified by activating different parts of the long-term data base. This process has been labelled a "blink transform" by Kosslyn (1980).

8   Transformations of the surface image can be applied to the whole (field general) or part (region bounded) of the image display.

9   Images tap the perceptual processing system at many levels including those that cannot be consciously monitored. Effects associated with images are often smaller than those associated with their perceptual counterparts.

10 Often, the more vivid the subjective image the stronger are its percept-equivalent effects. Recent data suggests that images can act as the inputs to, as well as being the outputs of perceptual processes.

With the modifications which were noted earlier to cope with property 6 the BOSS-consciousness model can accommodate these data quite easily. Whatever their *fundamental* format images used by BOSS appear to function as if they are mental models and to understand the subsequent operations of BOSS it is theoretically desirable to treat them as such. Indeed, to ask about the *fundamental* basis of representation can lead directly to the reductionist fallacy as we noted in Chapter 6. By functioning as spatial representations, mental images can be used by BOSS as *surrogate* objects; additional information can be made explicit or derived from them by interpretive procedures such as scanning, inspecting, rotation and so on. Note that in many cases propositional type descriptions can be obtained by acting on mental images with components of the perceptual system just as descriptions of the world are obtained by perceiving it. We can analyse and hence talk about our images. These descriptions can then be used by BOSS to report on comparisons of image with image, or image with percept. Note further, however, that such descriptions are couched at a particular level of analysis; they frequently refer to organized perceptual and conceptual aspects of the representation, which will often be sufficiently interpreted to allow them to correlate closely with ordinary language terms. We suspect that one reason that the BOSS-consciousness system has the facility to reprogram itself, select strategies and reflect on previous processing is simply because it is able to describe its images in this way. Images and their descriptions are intimately related but not equivalent. The terms used to describe images must obviously refer to their organized aspects, just as language can be used to refer to organized aspects of the world. Indeed, current thinking would seem to support the theory that many of our linguistic and deeper conceptual categories are perceptual in origin, i.e. structured in the way they are because of real-world structure (see Rosch, 1973; Rosch and Mervis, 1975; Miller and Johnson-Laird, 1976 for example). Language and propositional representation may be constrained by prior perceptual representation.

On evolutionary grounds, it would seem reasonable to assume that the mechanisms originally used solely for perception and the terms used in its description could become internalized, so to speak, and be applied to images as well (Wilton, 1978). It is possible to speculate that images may have evolved from "extended percepts", that is represen-tations which were kept alive for some time after the object or event had disappeared from view. The organism could do this by continuing to use the top-down processes needed to perceive the object, an operation equivalent to visual rehearsal, after the input from the world had ceased. Later, greater flexibility and freedom from the immediate environment would be achieved by any organism which managed to reinstate these top-down perceptual processes in the absence of any relevant stimuli. By reconstructing the state of affairs normally cued by incoming data, the organism would have the luxury of living in an imagined or simulated world, without any of its attendant dangers.

In the next chapter we will consider (more) data which show

that images are implicated in a whole range of cognitive tasks. A good test of our account of the structure and function of the imagery system will be how well it can be used to predict the various ways in which images might be used to aid thinking, problem-solving and reasoning.

9

Uses and functions of imagery

After examining the structure or mechanics of the imagery system, we are now ready to consider its function and investigate its wider role in cognitive processing. Our job is really two-fold. First, we need to discover the types of situations and cognitive processes in which mental imagery has been implicated. Because of its links with perception, for example, we might well expect imagery to be used mainly in dealing with visuo-spatial rather than verbal tasks, though, as we hope to show, its involvement in cognition is much greater than this. The second issue is perhaps more important as it concerns the exact nature of this relationship. Merely to show that reports of imaging correlate with the performance of certain tasks is not sufficient for us to conclude that its use is necessary. The crux of the matter is whether the results obtained from more objective studies really are consistent with a coherent model of imagery, whether people could have performed satisfactorily without using images, and, if there is flexibility in processing, which mode people habitually choose.

The chapter is divided into three main sections. The first is concerned with the use of images in fact-retrieval, question answering and problem solving. The majority, though not all, of the studies reported here will involve visuo-spatial tasks. Next, we show that images may well have an important function in certain types of reasoning tasks, perhaps an area in which some might otherwise consider more abstract processes more likely to be involved. Finally, because its importance is frequently cited in autobiographical and anecdotal accounts, we examine the role of imagery in creativity. A point for the reader to note is that the division between structural and functional studies, between the material in this and the previous chapter, is not a hard and fast one. Work on the nature of the imagery system shades off into work on its use. One reason for this is obvious. The mode of operation of any system will constrain the uses to which it can be put. In natural systems especially, the structure–function relationship is an intimate one because of the process of evolution. A less apparent reason is that to set up experiments to investigate any cognitive process is equivalent to inviting our subjects to participate in a problem-solving exercise. We can only study the nature of imagery by asking subjects to use it for some purpose. Hence, structural studies become functional studies because all cognitive processes can be construed as forms of problem solving (cf. Neisser, 1967). Many of the issues raised by psychologists concerned with the nature of imaginal representation then, have relevance for those who investigate its use. For example, if the surface image has privileged properties which the system cannot deduce from an underlying, abstract representation, then imagery may well have a unique function in problem solving. Also, if the image can be manipulated in some ways more easily than others then this too will have consequences for the situations in which it is used.

I   Imagery and problem solving

A   "Micro" problems

The problems discussed in this section have several things in common: (1) They are relatively simple (if often somewhat artificial) and so they can be solved fairly easily and quickly. (2) Subjects' introspections concerning their strategies have been supplemented with more objective data. (3) These "micro" problems have yielded useful information on the representation issue. (4) Many of these studies have been used to demonstrate that cognition can often mimic perception.

1   Property checking

We have already provided evidence to show that images can be used to retrieve facts about objects and events. As we noted in the last chapter, Kosslyn (1975, 1976) has shown that people can determine whether animals possess various properties by checking images of them. The speed of verification was shown to depend on the size of the property rather than its association with the name of the object when imagery was used. Also, the simple "thought experiment" of counting the number of windows of one's house is often cited as a demonstration that the experience of imaging correlates with solving problems of this type. Our present concern, though, is not *whether* operations of this kind are possible, but *when* (in what circumstances) imagery, rather than a more abstract form of representation, is likely to be used. Once again, Kosslyn's group of researchers has addressed itself to this. Kosslyn (1980) reports a number of experiments in which the likelihood that imagery is used to retrieve factual information is investigated. The basic assumptions of their approach are that certain questions, for example those concerned with object properties or category relationships, can be answered using either imaginal or propositional processes, that the two types of operation may proceed in parallel, and that the faster of the two processes will be the one used to reach a decision. Which procedure is actually the faster, will depend, amongst other things, on the nature of the question. So, if propositional information about an object's property is hard to retrieve, or has to be inferred, then it is more likely that subjects will use imagery. On *a priori* grounds Kosslyn has argued that the more highly qualified a property description is, the harder it will be to verify without recourse to imagery. To test this idea he presented subjects with three types of sentences each referring to features of concrete objects. The first set contained no adjectives, for example, ''Lions have fur''; the second contained one adjective, for example, ''Trucks have big wheels''; the third contained two adjectives ''Donkeys have long furry ears''. Fifty per cent of each type of statement were true, 50% false. Subjects were asked to check the truth of the statements, to rate the degree of difficulty they experienced in so doing, to estimate how much they thought they had used imagery, and to indicate how frequently they believed they had considered the assertion in the past. Rated degree of difficulty and imagery use for the ''true'' statements were positively correlated ($r = 0.84$) and a negative correlation was found between evoked imagery and frequency of consideration ($r = -0.64$). The data comparing imagery ratings with number of adjectives in the statements were less clear-cut though generally in the predicted direction (more adjectives, increased likelihood of imagery). As for the ''false'' statements, statements that were more difficult to check evoked more imagery, though, this time, the more frequently considered assertions were associated with more, not less, imagery. Kosslyn's explanation for this anomaly is that more frequently considered false statements might be checked more often because of their plausibility, and since plausible false properties take longer to evaluate in the propositional process of semantic memory (e.g. Smith *et al.*, 1974), the image processes may have "outraced" the parallel propositional ones. This seems a reasonable explanation especially when it is remembered that participants were providing *subjective* assessments of the number of times they had considered the assertions in the past. It is probable that the more subjects had to use conscious, imaginal strategies to check the assertions in the past, the more likely they will remember dealing with them. The implication of this for Kosslyn's "false" statement data is that the frequency of consideration ratings should correlate with the rated difficulty of checking the assertions. Unfortunately, he does not report this correlation.

In a more ambitious experiment, Kosslyn and Jolicoeur (1980) have extended the use of the ratings method and provided more support for their race model. They varied the association strength between a part or property of an object and the object itself, between an object and its most common superordinate, and between the property and superordinate category. They argued that association strengths would reflect the ease of locating the propositional relationships in question with easier retrieval resulting in higher strength. Subjects, as before, were asked to verify assertions which contained the object-part-superordinate and to rate the extent that they used imagery in the task. As predicted the highest and lowest association values were paired with the least and greatest spontaneous use of imagery.

If Kosslyn's (1980) race model is correct the question still remains as to whether some problems are not resolvable at all using the propositional system but are resolvable by imaging. The commonest class of such problems is, we suggest, that in which the information required is about a component of a concrete object or imageable scene and has not been previously retrieved. The component is a necessary part of the whole, but the whole has normally been experienced without particular attention being directed to its part. As a result, while the necessary specifications to generate an image of the object and its parts have presumably been incidentally learned, and are stored in the data base, no propositional information about the component which can be separately accessed has been provided for or deduced by the abstract or linguistic coding system. Thus the link between the *name* of the object and the component in question is not well established which results in the former acting as a poor retrieval cue for the latter. Retrieval of information about the part requires the generation and inspection of an image of the whole, the structure and content of which can be considered in turn to act as a better set of retrieval cues than the object's name alone. The classic question about the number of windows in one's house is a good example of this sort of problem, as are asking which way the head face on a coin faces and what colour the stars in the Stars and Stripes are. Inspection of the questions which Eddy and Glass's (1981) subjects report as requiring imagery suggests that they all fall within this description. Our suggestion that images must be used to perform some tasks is really the limiting case of the race model where propositional processing is unable to get started because of the lack of adequate descriptions in the data base. Notice that in this special case, when the link between whole and part has *never* been explicitly considered by the majority of subjects in a group, both the rated frequency of consideration and the association value should tend to zero, the task should be noted as being difficult and the group should exhibit a high degree of consensus that imagery is necessary for its execution. When, however, a part–whole relation has been considered at least once before and the results stored, the possibility of some propositional processing arises. The more frequently considered a relation, the faster this processing will be, hence the more likely that it will produce results before the slower, imaginal processing which began at the same time. In this way, our suggestion in Chapter 6 that the *use* of imagery diminishes as a task becomes more practised can be sharpened into a claim that the success of imagery in producing results declines as it is outstripped by faster more abstract processes. As time goes on these abstract systems, relying heavily on verbal mediation, may operate so rapidly and efficiently that even if image processing begins it will scarcely be noted by the problem solver, and will not be mentioned in subjective reports.

One final point is worth noting if our account is correct. It concerns the link between encoding and retrieval which is emphasized by the Encoding Specificity Principle, which asserts that the effectiveness of a cue in a memory task depends on whether or not it is appropriate to or compatible with the information in the episodic trace of the to be remembered item (see for example, Tulving and Thomson, 1973). It has just been argued that when an object's part is first checked a visual image will serve as a better retrieval cue than the object's name. This seems to accord well with the principle since presumably both object and part were encoded via visual perception. Later, however, subjects seem to rely more on the link between the names of the whole and part.

Does this violate the Encoding Specifity Principle? Our guess, in fact, is that it is further strengthened rather than weakened by this phenomenon. The greater facilitation with which descriptive cues can be used following practice reflects both a shift in the nature of the material to be retrieved as well as a difference in the way this new material was encoded. The effectiveness of descriptive cues suggests that the part–whole relation is now descriptively encoded. This laying down of new traces can only be explained by realizing that humans appear to be able to store not only information obtained via the senses but also information about their own previous cognitive episodes. By remembering in descriptive terms the results of past operations with images people can in the future retrieve information using either visual or verbal cues.

2 Mental comparisons

We turn now to an area that has been the subject of considerable investigation in recent years and is known as the study of "mental comparisons" or, less commonly, as internal psychophysics (for good, recent reviews see Richardson, 1980; also Kosslyn, 1980). In this paradigm, subjects are asked to compare pairs of objects along some dimension when the objects are presented as words or pictures. To get the feel for this task consider the following question. "Which of the following is the larger, a fox or a cat?" When answering such a question many people report that they must first form images of the objects and then make a "mental comparison" of their sizes. Not surprisingly several workers have suggested that imagery has an important role to play in these problems (e.g. Moyer, 1973). Moyer, however, reached these conclusions not from subjects' introspections alone but from a potentially more interesting finding. When real objects are compared on some dimension, such as size for example, judgements about their respective magnitudes are made more quickly the larger their absolute difference in size (e.g. Curtis et al., 1973; Johnson, 1939). What Moyer found was that a similar relationship held when subjects made *covert* magnitude judgements when presented, on each trial, with the names of two animals. This finding, at the time, was useful ammunition for analogue theorists (e.g. Paivio, 1975a) who argued that subjects were using concrete, mental images of the objects as a basis for their comparisons. Only half a decade or so later we must be more cautious. Demonstrations that mental operations mimic perceptual operations can no longer be taken as firm evidence that the mental representations used are visuo-spatial images (see Kosslyn, 1980; Finke, 1980 and our discussions in the preceding Chapters 6 and 8). One mistake is to assume that analogous operations in the mental and perceptual domains, defining operations as the workings of control processes on internal representations, necessarily imply that *analogue* representations are used in either or both cases. Both types of representation might be propositional, for example.

Nevertheless, the finding of a functional isomorphism between imagery and perception is interesting in its own right and prompted researchers to look for other instances of the *symbolic distance effect*, as the inverse relation between RT and magnitude difference has been called. Comparisons of roundness, angularity and brightness of colour appear to obey similar laws (Paivio, 1976) as do judgements of the closeness of hue of two colour chips to a named colour (Paivio, 1978a). Also, in a novel task Paivio (1978b) has asked subjects to estimate which of two clock times subtended the smaller angle between the minute and the hour hands. The reader is invited to try this for himself: at which of the following times do the clock hands form the smaller angle 11.15 or 7.55? Once again the larger the angular difference between the times, the faster were subjects' RTs, moreover, most participants claimed to have used visual imagery.

Before we convey the impression that imagery *must* be used in these tasks, we should point out that the symbolic distance effect has been demonstrated for a variety of other dimensions some of which are quite abstract. As these findings have been well reviewed elsewhere (cf. Richardson, 1980) we shall only mention selected examples here. Holyoak and Walker (1976) found a reliable effect with comparisons involving time, quality and temperature and Kerst and Howard (1977) discovered similar relationships with judgements of the cost of cars, the ferocity of animals and the military power of countries. Only devious *post hoc* explanations can implicate imagery in these tasks, but even more serious for proponents of imagery is Friedman's (1978) discovery that the relationship holds for properties of words which are clearly non-imageable. She gave her subjects pairs of abstract words and asked them to decide which made them feel better or worse. Discussing her results, Friedman maintains that imagery is *sufficient* as a representation in these tasks, but is not *necessary* (see also Banks and Flora, 1977; Buckley and Gillman, 1974; Lovelace and Snodgrass, 1971; Moyer and Landauer, 1967; Parkman, 1971; Restle, 1970; Sekuler *et al.*, 1971). It can be argued that the main reason for introducing the imagery construct into explanations of the symbolic distance effect is a chance result of the order in which different types of mental comparisons have been investigated. If the initial experiments had not been on size judgements but upon other not so obviously perceivable dimensions such as value or military power, researchers might not have been tempted to offer quasi-perceptual explanations of the phenomena. However, the subject reports of imaging in some of these tasks must not be ignored.

If imagery is not strictly necessary for performing mental comparisons, what other types of representation might be used? It should come as little surprise that more abstract, propositional systems have been suggested as alternatives (e.g. Banks *et al.*, 1978). As an example of how these "pure" propositional models might work, consider how a typical version (Banks *et al.*, 1978) accounts for size comparisons. They claim that object representations in memory are tagged with information about the rough size category and more detailed information about its precise size. The symbolic distance effect occurs because the probability that both types of propositional tag will need to be retrieved varies. The closer the two objects are in size, the higher the likelihood that both tags would be required, and the longer the retrieval will take. This explanation, of course, rests on the assumption that rough information about size is retrieved first, and if this proves insufficient as a basis for the comparison, the more detailed size information is then sought. Not only is a plausible explanation required for why this should be so, but also why two grades of information on most dimensions should be stored for each representation in memory. As it stands, the model seems implausible. A reason for favouring propositional explanations is that they appear more suitable for certain types of mental comparison. When asked to determine the larger of say an elephant and a flea, the majority of people report that they just "know" the answer, they need not consult a mental image at all. We will, however, suggest reasons for this later.

A related comparison phenomenon, the "congruity" effect, is often cited as further evidence for the use of propositional representations. The mental congruity effect arises when subjects are able to decide which is the larger of two relatively large objects faster than they can decide which is the smaller of two large objects and, conversely, which is the smaller of two relatively small objects faster than the larger of two small objects (see for example, Banks *et al.*, 1975; Jamieson and Petrusic, 1975). Congruity effects are explained in propositional theories in terms of the relationship between the question and the category tags. Thus, two large objects might be tagged as L (large) and L + (indicating the larger of the two). If asked about the size of the two objects it is a fair assumption that the question will be encoded into the same format as the memory tags. If the question is which is the larger then this will be automatically encoded in terms of L, and the check should proceed smoothly. On the other hand, if the question is which is the smaller then its representation must first be translated into the L form before any check can be made. More time is needed when the question and memory representations do not match because of this extra operation. As Kosslyn (1980) has rightly pointed out, this type of explanation is closely related to pure propositional models of mental comparison (e.g. Banks *et al.*, 1976; Clark *et al.*, 1973).

Kosslyn's research group has attempted to develop a model with both analogue and propositional characteristics to explain the various symbolic distance effects and the congruity phenomena. Insight into the way their model works can be gained by reconsidering examples of types of comparison which we introduced earlier. First of all: ''Which of the following is the larger, a fox or a cat?'' Now consider: ''Which of the following is the larger, an elephant or a flea?''. People often say that they use imagery to answer the first question, but just ''know'' the answer of the second, suggesting that more abstract processes are involved. These introspections have been taken seriously by Kosslyn *et al.* (1977) who have put forward a model with both analogue and propositional characteristics to explain mental comparisons and associated effects. Their theory is quite straightforward but its implications are interesting. Instead of claiming that mental comparisons are performed using imagery alone or by relying solely on more abstract propositions, they claim that all comparison problems can be solved using *either* form of representation. In addition, they suggest that solutions using propositions and images are computed in parallel, and whichever process is completed first is used to provide the answer. The various effects associated with these tasks depend on which type of processing wins the race, as was the case with the property checking tasks examined in the last section.

To describe the Kosslyn *et al.* model properly we must explain how it is applied in more detail. One of its underlying assumptions is that when two entities fall into dimensional categories that are clearly distinct, as in the elephant and flea example, the appropriate propositional information will be readily available permitting rapid retrieval and comparison and thereby "outrunning" the processes of image construction and checking. When, however, the entities fall within the same dimensional category, as in the case of the fox and the cat, detailed propositional information is less likely to be easily retrievable and so it is the imagery comparison which will be performed more quickly. Extending this argument slightly, the greater the probability in general that dimensional information can be retrieved directly, the lower the likelihood that imaginal processing will be faster. As was just noted, this idea is related to the property checking work which was mentioned earlier, though there are some differences between the explanations. There, it was the association strength between the object and property names which determined whether imaginal processes would *need* to be used. With mental comparisons it is *which* process runs to completion first that determines the effects. Logically, though, there seems to be no reason why a parallel processing, "race" model should not be proposed for both phenomena.

One way of making it easier to retrieve dimensional information is to learn and encode it more thoroughly in the first place. Overlearning should, therefore, make it more likely that people will use propositions rather than images when making mental comparisons. To test this idea Kosslyn *et al.* (1977), in one of their experiments, presented to their subjects six drawings of matchstick men which ranged in height from 3/4 in. to 4 ½ in. Each figure was drawn in a different hue, and subjects were taught to associate figure size with colour by learning to reproduce the stimuli when given the colour names. The subjects were next taught to categorize the figures by learning to distinguish the three smallest from the three largest. Following these procedures the subjects were tested and had to respond with the name of the category (large or small) when presented with a colour name or to respond with the colours of the category members when given a category name. The amount of overlearning was manipulated by having half of the subjects learn the colour–size–category combination to a criterion of two correct responses in a row, this was referred to as the 200% group, and by requiring the remaining subjects to learn the combinations to a criterion of five correct responses, the 500% group. A mental comparison task was then performed. Subjects heard two colour names in succession and had to decide, by pressing response keys, if the first named colour referred to the larger figure of the two. In all cases RTs decreased as the size difference increased except for the 500% group which showed no effect of size disparity. These findings support a mixed image and propositional processing model in which the ease of retrieving propositional information results in propositions being processed more quickly than images.

It was stated earlier, Kosslyn *et al.* have extended their model to explain the congruity effect. They note, to begin with, that congruity

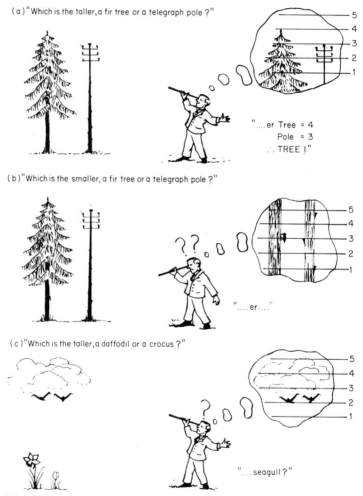

Fig. 11 Illustrates the interaction between question and stimuli which produces the "congruity" effect. In (a) because the question is appropriate, the stimulus sampling mechanism is already calibrated correctly. Some re-calibration is needed, however, in (b) and (c).

effects are most evident when the to-be-compared objects are close in size, and, therefore, it is more likely that imagery will be needed to perform the comparison. The congruity phenomena itself, they believe, arises because the stimulus sampling mechanism, which checks the sizes of the imaged objects, needs to be "recalibrated" when the size referred to in the question and that of the object do not match. Figure 11 shows how this would work. Imagine, for the sake of argument, that the to-be-compared images are accessed in a limited region only. Rather as if two objects are viewed through a limited aperture. To compare the sizes of the objects a series of samples are taken in the region defined by the aperture, at different "heights", represented by the horizontal bars in the diagram. Decisions concerning size disparity are made on the basis of which object achieves more "hits" after a series of samples, i.e. is noted as being present. Now, the stimulus sampling mechanism itself can be pre-set to deal with relatively large or small objects. In the case where question and object sizes match (Fig. 11(a)) the stimulus sampling can proceed immediately, where there is a mismatch, however, re-setting of the mechanism is necessary (Fig. 11(b) and (c)). Now any process which speeds or obviates the need for recalibration should also attenuate the congruity effect. Once again, Kosslyn *et al.* reasoned, overlearning category size tags should allow recalibration to proceed more quickly, before the images are retrieved and sampling begins. Their explanation was supported by an experiment they conducted in which the congruity effect was attenuated for a 500% overlearning group compared with a 200%.

Can we now conclude that imagery does have a functional role in mental comparison? The Kosslyn *et al.* model would seem to suggest so at any rate, but the perspicacious reader will have noted that these experiments embody this as an assumption, rather than actually demonstrate it. What still needs to be done is to show that the *surface* image is used in these tasks, as opposed to the long-term or underlying form of imaginal representation. To do this it is necessary to show that *alterations* in the surface image can cause *alterations* in the comparison process. Requiring subjects to manipulate the size of their images is a useful way to show this. Kosslyn *et al.* have attempted this with a technique originally used by Holyoak (1977). They asked people to image an object at an extremely small, subjective size or at normal size. Next, the name of a second object was presented and subjects were asked to compare mentally the actual sizes of the two objects. As before, half of the subjects learned to group the stimuli into "large" and "small" categories but the remaining half did not learn to sort the objects at all. Kosslyn *et al.* hypothesized that the effects of the initial size of the images would disappear when the categories were well learned, providing that the objects were drawn from different size categories. Propositional information, they reasoned, could be used instead of imagery. Also, as in their previous work, they expected the symbolic distance effect to be reduced for pairs of objects taken from well learned, different categories. As expected, subjects took longer to make judgements when the first object was imaged subjectively small compared with when it was imaged at normal size. Somewhat unexpectedly there was no influence of category learning on the effects of image size though category learning did reduce the symbolic distance effect. Granted that subjects did make use of category information, as is evidenced by the attenuation of the symbolic distance effect, but it is hard to see why the effects of initial image size were so hard to change. Kosslyn (1980) suggests two possible explanations to avoid modifying his parallel processing "race" model. First of all, the fact that subjects had to generate an image of the first object in advance of the comparison might well have given the imagery process a "head start" in the race. A second and perhaps more plausible suggestion is that because certain object comparisons involved decisions about objects which were quite close in size, subjects might have had to use imagery for these pairs, and may have got into the habit of using it for all other pairs. Whatever the final explanation we believe that it would be foolish to abandon the parallel processing model prematurely especially since Kosslyn *et al.* have provided more evidence for it in other experiments. One of its strengths, given that its essential characteristics are correct, is that it indicates the great flexibility of the cognitive system. Particularly interesting as far as the BOSS-consciousness model is concerned, is that imagery makes its appearance (or, at least, its appearance becomes evident) in tasks requiring novel, unpractised responses. Situations which are well learned, on the other hand, can be processed more efficiently using propositions. Moreover, the fact that subjects can give strategy reports about their performance in these type of problems helps support our claim that many of these operations are under the general control of BOSS. Lest the hardheaded should still protest that all this talk of "parallel processing models" is nothing but cognitive psychological moonshine it may reassure them to know that Kosslyn and Johnson have programmed a mental COMPARE process, based on the race model, into their general simulation (see Kosslyn, 1980 for details). Finally, some recent work by Howard (1980) puts one aspect of the Kosslyn *et al.* model on a firmer footing. The finding that the symbolic distance effects could be attenuated was based on the use of over-learned arbitrary categories in the Kosslyn *et al.* work. Howard has shown that subjects can spontaneously use natural categories of occupational status in making mental status comparisons. Between category comparisons were found to be reliably faster than within category comparisons. Howard, however, finds it hard to believe that subjects need use imagery in his task, but argues that at least his results support the notion that subjects *can* use information from categories, whatever other process they employ.

One problem with an imagery explanation is that images can be formed of the objects in any size. This may be countered by claiming that the ''correct'' size is coded with the construction rules for imaging any given object. However, for a given image the correct size will always be relative to any other object that is being imaged. That is, it is a relative not an absolute property. It is hard to believe that while the relative sizes of the objects to be imaged is being computed information about the absolute sizes could not be made available to short circuit the whole complex business.

An alternative possibility is that the images that are reported in symbolic distance tasks are epiphenomenal by-products of the processing involved. Suppose, as a general model of the basis for the distance effect that the more similar two items may be on the dimension involved the larger a sample of instances from memory (or the real world) must be taken before a reliable decision can be made. These may include sampling until some shared yardsticks are encountered. So, for example, comparing ''cat'' and ''fox'' may require activating memories of both in relationship to other cues to size (grass, bushes etc.). Images may be formed either because the delay while such comparisons are made allows the imagery system, as in Kosslyn's race model, to form an image, which turns out to be valueless, or because the search for comparative information on size activates the visual system and actually stimulates images to be formed. In the latter case it might be for the purpose of ''reading off'' comparative information rather than the absolute size of the object itself.

Two aspects of mental comparison research have not yet been considered. The first concerns the modality of presentation of the stimuli in mental comparison tasks. Some investigators (e.g. Paivio, 1975) have used either pictures or words as stimuli and the general finding is that RTs are speeded with pictorial presentation. A finding consistent with Paivio's (1971b) dual code theory in which the image arousing potential of pictures is superior to words. Other work along these lines is reviewed by Richardson (1980) to which the reader is referred but like him we do not believe that these studies shed much light on the nature of the representations used in these problems. The second issue concerns the role of individual differences in mental comparisons, but as we have already discussed this in Chapter 5 we shall not refer to it here.

3   Orthographic memory

We were somewhat at a loss for a label for this section as the body of research does not have a generally accepted name, though the experiments do have something in common. We finally decided on "orthographic imagery" since these tasks have all required subjects to image letters either in groups or in words either as an aid to spelling or as a basis for checking some of their properties.

The research goes back about a decade and was initiated by Weber and his associates (e.g. Weber et al., 1972, 1973), and, although not very well known, it is quite relevant to more recent discussions of the structure and function of imagery. For example, in an early experiment Weber and Bach (1969) asked subjects to go through the alphabet either by silently pronouncing each letter or by forming a visual image of it and found that imaging letters took around 500 ms per item whereas pronouncing them took only 150 ms. One problem with this experiment, as we stated in Chapter 8, is that the task allows no opportunity for checking that the subjects do image each letter and although the results are interesting the later methods used by Weber's group appear to be more reliable. Thus, Weber et al. (1972) asked subjects to categorize mentally lower case letters as either "small" (e.g. the letters a, c, e, i, m etc.) or "large" (b, d, f, g, h, j, k, etc.), a task which they believed would rely heavily on imagery, and found that letters groups which made up words were categorized faster than random strings of letters. A further finding was that subjects who were allowed to write their responses were quicker than those who spoke them, but only in the non-word conditions. They interpreted these results to suggest that images of the words were generated as a whole, before the letters were categorized, whereas images of the random letter strings had to be constructed letter by letter. As the letters of the words were displayed in parallel they could be spatially scanned rapidly and efficiently, the letters of the non-words, on the other hand, had to be produced one at a time under the control of what Weber *et al.* call "verbal sequencing". It was this verbal sequencing, they claimed, which conflicted with verbal responding (cf. Brooks, 1968). Supporting the claim that subjects used visual imagery to perform these tasks, research by Weber *et al.* (1973) demonstrates that when subjects are asked to form visual images of five letter words they can access the perceptual properties of their letters (large or small) faster than their acoustic properties (absence or presence of long ē sound). These results suggest that images of letters can be constructed as organized units or verbally prompted one at a time, a finding that would fit in with the BOSS-consciousness model.

Kelley (1973) extended the study of verbal sequencing using a novel technique. He asked his subjects to spell backwards, a task which is commonly believed to require visual imagery (cf. Hebb, 1949; Paivio, 1971b). Kelley found that by increasing word length he could decrease backward spelling rates without affecting forward spelling rates, which were always faster than backward. More "sequencing problems" were thought to be associated with backward spelling, and these difficulties were worse when longer words were processed. This interpretation receives some support from the interesting "one off" study by Coltheart and Glick (1974), noted in Chapter 5, of a subject abnormally proficient at backward spelling. The authors attributed the ease with which Ms D'Onim performed this task to her unusually large "span of imaginal apprehension", or in Kosslyn's (1975) terms to her large imagery capacity. This implies that she was able to display many more letters at once than normal subjects and, therefore, would need to do much less verbal sequencing.

Hampson and Morris (1978b) attempted to use the technique of backward spelling to relate the concepts of image scanning, capacity and production more closely. The series of experiments (reported fully in Hampson, 1979), began in 1976 when in a seminar on imagery, seven Lancaster undergraduates were asked to spell the word "rocket" backwards and to introspect on how they had performed the task. Without exception the seven students said that they had had to form a mental picture of the word, and had used their image to "read off" the letters of the word in the reverse direction. Several people spoke of "getting lost" in the middle of the word and of having to start again by reconstructing their image afresh from left to right. Two students mentioned that the task was made much easier by splitting the word into its two component syllables and then imaging them one at a time. These introspections suggested that backward spelling might be a valuable technique for studying the interaction of imaginal control processes and perhaps of demonstrating their flexibility. Shortly after this, we unearthed Kelley's work and then proceeded to perform some experiments of our own. The first experiment was very simple and was designed as no more than an exploratory study (see Hampson, 1979). Hampson hypothesized that the generation of the image of a word is at least partially controlled by its underlying verbal structure, such that individual letters, or organized letter sequences, are produced in order from left to right in English, just as some neon signs illuminate in a step-by-step sequence. If the word is only a few letters in length, the whole image may be maintained while the person scans backward through it to give his response. When backward spelling longer words, whose length overloads his image display capacity, the imager has not only to scan backwards but must also periodically regenerate various parts of his image. This suggested that there are at least two control processes at work in backward spelling, firstly one involving scanning similar to that investigated by other researchers (e.g. Kosslyn *et al.*, 1978) and secondly what we called an "iteration process" which generates images of successive components of the word for inspection, operating from left to right. We chose the word "iteration" at the time to relate this work to the claim by Lea (1975) that image scanning was really a form of step-by-step movement through a list structure and whereas Lea's case was that scanning as such did not exist we believed both processes to be complementary (see Chapter 8). We could just as easily have used Weber's term "verbal sequencing" though as we shall argue shortly a third expression might be more appropriate! A second hypothesis which was entertained was that subjects' control strategies were flexible and that if instructed to make use of the syllabic structure of a word when backward spelling they would be able to do so to their advantage. Subjects were randomly allocated to one of three groups involving either forward spelling, backward spelling or backward spelling with instructions to treat the words syllable-by-syllable. All groups were asked to image the words, which were six letters long, and to use their image, if possible, to perform their spelling tasks. The times taken to spell ten such words were recorded. The results of this simple though procedurally loose experiment were encouraging.

Backward spelling times were consistently longer than forward and instructions to use a syllabic strategy speeded up backward spelling though it was still significantly slower than forward.

The next two experiments in this series employed tighter procedures (see Experiments 1 and 3 in Hampson and Morris, 1978b). Instead of presenting the stimuli auditorially, printed words were displayed in a T-scope for 0·5 seconds each. Subjects were instructed to read each word to themselves and maintain a visual image of it from which they were to read off the letters in the appropriate direction. Half of the words in Experiment 1 were four letters long, the remainder were eight letters long. Subjects received both types of stimulus and were randomly allocated to either a forward or backward spelling group. The results partially replicated the experiment performed by Kelley which we mentioned above. The two main effects of spelling direction, backward taking longer than forward, and spelling rates for the four and eight letter words, with the former taking longer than the latter, were highly significant. The crucial interaction between word length and spelling direction was also significant and the effect of spelling direction was shown to affect only the longer words. We interpreted these RT data as suggesting that the longer backward spelling times associated with the eight letter words were caused by more iteration problems when words exceeded subjects' display capacities. Reports from our subjects supported these observations. The forward spelling group reported little or no difficulty with the task, whereas the backward spelling group claimed to have had more difficulty especially with the eight letter words which often had to be regenerated afresh. Experiment 3 investigated the effects of syllabic structure and instructions to make use of it thus replicating and extending the findings of the pilot study. We found that six letter words which could be split into two syllables were backward spelled faster than monosyllabic, six letter words, and that when a group of subjects were expressly told to make use of the stimuli's structure their performance was better than a control group who received no such special instructions.

It appears from these results that subjects are limited in their capacity to display information for scanning and must develop strategies which enable them to generate successive portions of their image in a controlled and orderly fashion. We referred to the latter as an "iteration" process which in the case of the backward spelling experiments is verbally sequenced. We now feel that what we were investigating in these experiments was the interaction between a particular type of blink transformation and the continuous transformation of scanning (see Kosslyn, 1980; also Chapter 8). Iterations are equivalent to blink transforms since they involve constructing portions of the image afresh.

Other research relating imagery and spelling has not been concerned with spelling tasks as means of exploring the imagery system, but with imagery as an aspect of the spelling process. Thus, Radaker (1963) gave children practice at arousing clear visual images of the words they were learning to spell and found that this improved their spelling performance relative to controls. Radaker naturally concluded that imagery was beneficial but, as Sloboda (1981) points out, his control group were allowed to indulge in free sessions of play and conversation before testing, while the experimental group practised their imagery. The spelling improvement could just as well have resulted from concentrated attention to the words than on imaging them. Sloboda himself has investigated this matter. He has found that there are variations in the frequency with which imagery is used by different individuals when spelling, that these differences permit "visualizers" to perform better than "verbalizers" on tasks involving counting the letters of imagined words, but that they have no systematic effect on spelling. Sloboda concludes that images of words must depend on operations carried out on the end products of the processes used in spelling, rather than being directly implicated in these processes. This is an interesting suggestion. Our interpretation of this is that when poor spellers happen to produce images of words, these images are likely to embody spelling errors. If, therefore, a poor speller happens to make frequent use of imagery when spelling it will not be of any particular assistance since he will produce the wrong letters to read off. An important lesson about imagery can be drawn from this after all, though that was not the intention behind the research. Images of words can be produced from verbal information, they do not necessarily have to be stored in pictorial form in LTM. As the BOSS-consciousness model would predict, the surface image is limited by its LTM substrate.

B   Ecological problems and applications

Imagery is spontaneously used in a variety of natural settings to achieve various goals. The problems in which imagery has been implicated discussed here, though diverse, have in common the fact that they have ecological significance. Unfortunately, the evidence for the use of imagery in these tasks is largely circumstantial and rather than give a complete account of each and every situation in which imagery might be used we propose to mention only two or three areas and suggest at the end ways in which some of this research could be firmed up.

1   Cognitive maps

This is a research area which is enjoying considerable popularity at present; it is concerned with the representation of the wider environment in people's minds. Tolman (1948) was the first to use the term "cognitive map" but it has been taken up since by psychologists, geographers and town planners. The use of these representations is evident in a variety of different individuals in many different situations, for example air navigation, Pacific ocean canoeing, map sketching and the perception of inner cities (see Downs and Stea, 1973, 1977, for comprehensive reviews, and Neisser, 1976, for a good critical treatment). However, our concern is not with the details of the many interesting studies in this area, but rather with the relation between imagery and cognitive maps. Perhaps we should stress at the outset that we do not doubt that people build up, possess and use internal representations of their environment (cf. Lynch, 1960, 1972, also Kosslyn *et al.*, 1974). How else would they go to work or to the super-market? The problem is whether "cognitive maps" really are map-like in the sense of spatially extended visual displays. Some workers have been impressed by the representation-as-map notion (e.g. Norman, 1976; Stenning, 1977). Norman suggests that the metaphor, borrowed from the study of cognitive maps, should remind us that no represen-tation is ever completely analogue since though maps represent some information analogically, such as the shape of coastlines and the bends in roads, other information, such as the size of towns or the importance of roads is often noted symbolically. Cartography, Norman believes, can help us understand representations. Ironically, Robinson and Petchenik (1976), two recent writers on cartography have tried to use psychologists' studies of representations to help them understand maps! To compound the issue, even if a physical map provides a useful way of explaining the structure of mental imagery, the problem of whether a cognitive map is the same as an image remains.

How then are the two related? We suspect that the distinction between form of an internal representation and the manner in which it is made public or external is frequently blurred by those who study cognitive maps. There is a tendency to suggest that simply because a person can draw a map of his town or neighbourhood he must have a map-like structure in his head. No such implication necessarily follows. A similar problem arises if we consider children's drawings, it is tempting to make inferences about the form of their representations from the pictures children produce, but there is no justification for this. Peculiarities in drawings by children may depend on problems in the rules which they use in their productions and the conventions which they adopt specifically for drawing. As for cognitive maps, Neisser's (1976) suggestion that they are simply ongoing perceptual anticipations used to predict the arrival of spatial information offers a satisfactory explanation of the use of these representations. No mention of imagery is strictly necessary. However, when generating a cognitive map out of the context of its appropriate, specifying, perceptual information, as in the case of imagining one's drive to work, it is likely that a true mental image will be produced. Otherwise, it is difficult to see how the imager could describe or modify his mental map. (This latter point, of course, relates to our criticisms of Neisser's theory of imagery in Chapter 6.) There are it seems two traps for the unwary: the first is to assume that cognitive maps are nothing but mental images; the second is to assume that images are nothing but cognitive maps understood as perceptual anticipations. The two types of representation are related but not identical.

2   Other applications and suggestions for research

Imagery has been implicated in some situations which, at first, might appear to rely more heavily on verbal processing. Mental arithmetic is one of these. We mentioned in Chapter 7 that Hayes (1973) reported an interesting if somewhat discursive study of mental calculation. He argued that subjects rely heavily on imagery when performing even quite simple mathematical operations and, as we saw in Chapter 5, Professor Aitken, the mental calculator studied by Hunter (1977a) appeared to make extensive use of visualization techniques. The use of internal representations during chess and other board games has also been studied, though it is not clear exactly what form these take (de Groot, 1965; Chase and Simon, 1973). Originally, Binet (1966 translation), who studied blindfolded chess games and interviewed the players, noted a greater dependence by less experienced players on a concrete, well fleshed-out image of the board. Some players, he discovered, claimed to visualize even the nicks and scratches of the pieces in their set. With more experience at the game came less reliance on "literal" visual memories and a shift toward more abstract, schematic and impressionistic representations. As Binet puts it, the images became "stripped of all material and concrete baggage" (p.158). Less anecdotal studies by de Groot and Chase and Simon have shown that remembering a particular configuration of board pieces is a function of game experience. After only 5 seconds exposure to an organized game position, chess experts can almost perfectly reconstruct the arrangement of pieces, a feat that novices find extremely difficult to match. The suggestion that perhaps chess masters just happen to have larger visual or verbal STM capacities is easily ruled out. When presented with a random arrangement of pieces, chess masters are no better than novices at reconstructing the positions. The important factor seems to be that chess masters can make better use of their memories by imposing organizations on the board which they have learned from previous games. Some positions they can label in a shorthand way such as Sicilian Defence, stage 4, a very convenient way of storing a program for constructing either the actual board position or an image of it. Chase and Simon have provided evidence for this view and argued that chess masters can more easily "chunk" sensible board positions, but when faced with random arrangements, like novices, they find it as difficult to structure them. Once again, is imagery used here? From the data we have at present it is difficult to say, but we believe that novices probably do rely more on relatively uninterpreted images which need to be mentally manipulated before a move is contemplated. Chess masters, by contrast, will already "know" (propositionally) that certain board states afford certain transformations, and will only have to resort to image manipulation in less familiar game scenarios. Masters make greater and more economical use of their cognitive systems by sharing work between different subsystems.

Imagery is probably used in a variety of other contexts which have not yet been documented. When an engineer first thinks about the workings of an internal combustion engine, when a medical student imagines the functioning of the heart and when an architect designs a new house it is likely that at least some of the time they will need to use imagery. However, if researchers interested in these matters continue to favour the use of anecdotal reports, apart from their intrinsic interest, such studies will neither furnish strong evidence for imagery's involvement nor tell us very much about its nature. What is needed is to attack the ecological study of imagery with the conceptual and methodological tools used in studying laboratory problems. For example, if imagery really is used in a particular task, then it should be possible to interfere selectively with it by using concurrent or interpolated perceptual tasks (see Chapter 7). If imagery aids but is not strictly necessary in a particular situation, instructing one group of subjects to make explicit use of it should improve their performance. Finally, identifying those who possess particularly relevant imagery abilities should allow us to predict that they will do better on tasks which tap these operations. Until this is done for *ecological* we should read *anecdotal*.

II Imagery and reasoning

Despite their differences the problems discussed in the last section had one thing in common, they were all dependent on real world contingencies. Perhaps because we interact so much both perceptually and behaviourally with our three-dimensional universe, it is not surprising that many of our mental operations should mimic perception and action. Images, or mental models, can be used in place of the world. The problems which we are now to consider, however, are somewhat different. They are concerned less with the correspondence between our ideas and reality and more with the internal consistency and logical implications of the semantic information we possess. We are interested here in studies of reasoning.

Work in this area has progressed through a number of stages which have been well documented elsewhere (e.g. Bolton, 1972; Cohen, 1976). Recently, two major issues have come to the fore: the first, which we will mention but briefly, relates to the logicality or otherwise of human reasoning. So, for example, Wason and Evans (1975) and Evans and Wason (1976) have proposed the so called "dual process" theory, based largely on information derived from studies of "if, then" statements. This approach suggests that reasoning involves a preliminary, alogical process in which conclusions are formed followed by a secondary process of rationalization in which the reasoner attempts to justify them. A critique of the research which led to this theory will be found in Morris (1981b). The second topic, which we will consider in more detail, is concerned with the types of internal representations which people use during reasoning tasks (e.g.

Huttenlocher, 1968). Of course, both of these issues must be intimately related, but until recently, as we shall see, they have, to some extent, been treated quite separately. To caricature research in this area slightly, there seems to have been an emphasis on the overall logicality or otherwise of the operations when subjects generally *fail* to solve the problems they are given as in the case of reasoning with conditionals (e.g. Wason and Johnson-Laird, 1972). When subjects succeed in getting the right answers, however, the logicality of their reasoning tends to be assumed, and attention is transferred to the representations they use. Our main concern in this section will be with the role of internal representations in reasoning, and we shall, therefore, restrict our attention to reasoning with syllogisms in which this matter has been treated and ignore reasoning with conditionals. Within the study of syllogisms, however, we can discern two general areas. The first revolves around the problem of transitive inference; the second involves classical syllogisms.

A   Transitive inference

Sometimes called "three-term series problems" or "linear syllogisms", these problems are presented as two premises, in which a relational argument is specified, from which a conclusion can be drawn. A typical example is:

John is smaller than Bob
Mark is taller than Bob
Who is the smallest?

To which the answer is, of course, John. The issue at stake is how do subjects solve these problems, and three general explanations have been proposed. The first explanation is really more of a description, since it offers few insights into the types of representations and processes employed, the other two are true process accounts.

Hunter (1957) put forward his operational model which embodied two principles to explain why people take longer to deal with certain forms of the linear syllogism. For example a straightforward problem such as: "Jane is richer than Mary; Mary is richer than Sue. Who is the richest?", will generally be solved faster than the logically equivalent: "Mary is richer than Sue; Jane is richer than Mary. Who is the richest?". In the first case the general form of the premises is $A > B; B > C$ (where $>$ signifies richer) and the answer can be "read off" easily since the inference proceeds smoothly from left to right. In the second case the syllogism takes the form B > C; A > B, this time, Hunter argued, the premises need to be re-ordered before the conclusion can be derived from them. Re-ordering will take time. To understand Hunter's second principle consider the following problem. "Jane is richer than Mary; Sue is poorer than Mary. Who is the richest?" (or A > B; C < B) once again this will take longer to solve than the standard version (or A > B; B > C). The reason for this, Hunter argued, is that one of the relational terms, in this case "poorer", must be converted to "richer" and the premise rearranged to read "Mary is richer than Sue". Converting a premise will also take time. Finally, those problems which need to be both re-ordered and converted will take longest of all to solve.

Hunter's model accounted reasonably well for the available data at the time, but it was not able to predict a phenomenon which was soon discovered. If subjects are asked to evaluate linear syllogisms with relational terms such as "taller", "wider" or "better" they do so more quickly than if the terms are "shorter", "narrower" or "worse". Why should this be? Provided that *both* the terms are the same no conversion will be needed, according to Hunter's model; there should be no difference. A theory advanced by De Soto *et al.* (1965) explained this by referring to the representations needed to solve these problems. De Soto *et al.* claimed that subjects construct a visual image of a horizontal or vertical array to do this. The image combines the premises into a unitary representation. Terms such as "better" and "taller" are easier to process than "worse" and "shorter", they argued, because the former allow the image to be constructed from top to bottom (or left to right) which is easier than the latter which forces construction to proceed from bottom to top (or right to left). Also, construction of the image is easier if the first named term can act as an "end-anchor". The evidence certainly seemed to support De Soto *et al.*'s model (see also Handel *et al.*, 1968; Huttenlocher, 1968) and Wason and Johnson-Laird (1972) have illustrated a possible information processing analysis of it.

Very soon, the image model was challenged by Clark (1969) who attempted to account for subjects' performance by purely psycho-linguistic principles. Nowadays, we could call his a propositional interpretation. Clark was interested in treating the solution of a three-term series problem as an example of the process of comprehension. To do this he appealed to two major psycholinguistic principles, the first of which relates to understanding the premises, while the second is to do with the relation between the premises and the question. Clark's first principle is that of lexical marking which asserts that certain comparatives are easier to understand than others. Terms such as "better" and "taller" are easier to process because they are *unmarked*, that is they tell us nothing about the absolute position of items on a scale, only about their relative arrangement. On the other hand, "worse" and "shorter" convey absolute as well as relative information and are considered to be more linguistically complex. Clark's first principle makes similar predictions to De Soto *et al.*'s preferred direction of working. Both postulate that

A is better than B

B is better than C

should be easier to cope with than

C is worse than B

B is worse than A

Clark's theory, however, also predicts that "A is not as good as B" should be easier than "B is not as bad as A", since the former contains an unmarked and the latter a marked term. The image theory generates just the opposite prediction because the former involves working upwards. Clark has also drawn attention to the importance of the form of the question, an issue neglected by the earlier models. Quite simply, if the form of the question matches the form of the premises, that is, if both contain the same relational term, solving the problem will be much easier. This principle of congruence has a parallel in propositional explanations of the congruity effect in mental comparisons which we considered earlier (e.g. Banks *et al.*, 1975). Once again, Wason and Johnson-Laird (1972) have provided an information processing breakdown of Clark's model.

The by now familiar question can be posed. If a linguistic explanation of these problems is available, do we need to posit the use of imagery at all? Is Clark's model sufficient? As in the case of mental comparisons, subsequent research has shown that neither the image nor the linguistic model offers a complete explanation. Both Johnson-Laird (1972) and Wood *et al.* (1974) have suggested compromise positions. For example, Johnson-Laird has argued that subjects switch strategies during the course of solving several problems. Initially, subjects may adopt an imagery mode but shift to a verbal one as they become more adept. This is exactly what we would expect from the BOSS-consciousness model and the earlier discussions of Kosslyn's

(1980) race model. Imagery is likely to make its appearance in tasks which are novel and relatively unpractised, but to be replaced or masked by swifter, more autonomous processes as skill increases. Finally, Shaver *et al.* (1974) have provided converging evidence that imagery can be used to good effect in three-term-series problems. Subjects given special instructions to use imagery, and those with better than average imagery abilities performed better.

B Classical syllogisms

All respectable people wear bowler hats.
Some psychologists are respectable people.
Therefore, some psychologists wear bowler hats.

Like the transitive syllogisms we have been considering, the classical syllogism is made up of two premises and a conclusion. These need not be *true* but the syllogism is *valid* provided that the conclusion follows logically from the premises. Not all syllogisms have valid conclusions, however. Syllogisms also vary in the combination of "mood", "figure" and "order". First of all "mood". The premises and the conclusion can contain either the universal quantifier "all", the particular, "some" and be either affirmative or negative, yielding 64 possible combinations. There are also four different types of figures or arrangements of the three nouns which appear in the premises and conclusions, "psychologist", "bowler hat" and "person" in our example. Finally there are two possible orders of the premises. Johnson-Laird and Steedman (1978) have shown that all three factors —mood, figure and order—can affect the ease with which syllogisms are evaluated unlike earlier work (e.g. Lefford, 1946) which concentrated largely on mood. This is not, however, the place to expand fully on their findings; the interested reader is referred to the original papers and to Dodd and White (1980) for a simplified but excellent coverage. We do, though, wish to describe the basic mechanics of Johnson-Laird and Steedman's theory because it is extremely relevant to imagery research. Their approach is aptly named the analogical theory of reasoning since they believe that a person reading a pair of premises converts them into a unified, concrete, mental model. The theory is best illustrated by means of examples. Assume that a person is presented with a premise which reads "All psychologists are academics". One way to understand and represent this premise is to imagine a small group of psychologists in a SCR wearing academic gowns. The premise has then been represented as

psychologist	———▶	academic
psychologist	———▶	academic
		(academic)

The academic in brackets is there to remind the reasoner that though "All psychologists are academics" according to the premise, this does not mean that "All academics are psychologists". He imagines a physicist as well. The arrows in our representation mean that it is easier to move mentally from psychologist to academic than from academic to psychologist. Three other premises are represented below:

1   Some psychologists are academics.

| psychologist | ———▶ | academic |
| (psychologist) | | (academic) |

Here a clinical psychologist is now in the same room as the physics and psychology teachers.

2   No psychologists are academics.

| psychologist | ————┤ | academic |
| psychologist | ————┤ | academic |

A room of practising clinical psychologists perhaps!

3   Some psychologists are not academics.

| psychologist | ————┤ | academic |
| (psychologist) | ————┤ | (academic) |

The implication is that some psychologists may be academics.

Now, while in general few mistakes are likely to be made in representing the first premise, difficulties can arise in integrating it with the information from the second premise. The main problem is to do with the fact that the common middle term has already been represented.

Using an example similar to one of Johnson-Laird and Steedman's, consider the following syllogism:

> Some psychologists are academics.
> Some academics smoke pipes.

For the first premise we already have:

| psychologist | ———▶ | academic |
| (psychologist) | | (academic) |

One obvious integration would be to mistakenly integrate the premises as follows:

psychologist	———▶	academic	———▶	pipesmoker
(psychologist)		(academic)	———▶	pipesmoker
		(academic)		

From which the invalid conclusion "Some psychologists are pipe-smokers" would be generated. The cautious and skilled reasoner is one who attempts a falsification stage. The trick is to try to break any identities which have been formed between subject and predicate without destroying the representation of the component premises. In the example above:

    psychologist   ———→   academic
    (psychologist)   (academic)   ———→   pipesmoker

From which no valid conclusion may be drawn. A simplified version of this syllogism can be seen in Fig. 12.

Even more problems can arise with the following syllogism because of the directionality of the processing operations.

        Some psychologists are academics.
        All pipesmokers are academics.

The following invalid arrangement could easily be constructed

    psychologist   ———→   academic   ←———   pipesmokers
    (psychologist)   (academic)   ←———   pipesmokers

Here difficulty arises because the second premise has to be directed towards the already existing academics. Two invalid conclusions might be formed, namely, "Some psychologists are pipesmokers" or "Some pipesmokers are psychologists". Again, no valid conclusion is actually possible. The "proof" is left to the reader!

The analogical model of reasoning is very powerful. In particular it can explain not only how certain subjects manage to reach the right conclusions but can also suggest why others reach the wrong ones. In this respect it is far superior to earlier theories based on the atmosphere effect. Perhaps not surprisingly then its implications for theories of imagery and reasoning are considerable. The analogical theory does two things. First, it asserts that reasoning is a skill which depends on mental models. This is sensible empirically in that it allows us to account easily for the available data and theoretically, the theory itself is buttressed by arguments which demonstrate the distinction between models and propositions (see Chapter 6). In so doing, it extends the number of tasks in which images are not only implicated but necessary. Second, it suggests that the logicality or otherwise of reasoning is really dependent on the extent to which an integrated model is subjected to falsification tests. We can also now see why the simple transitive inferences, discussed above, are much easier to cope with than classical syllogisms with quantifiers. As Johnson-Laird (1980b) argues

In the case of simple relational inferences, and propositional inferences, an error-free process of integration guarantees us a valid conclusion provided that we have not forgotten or misinterpreted any of the premises. In the case of quantified assertions, however, the process of integration is under the control of an inferential heuristic that cannot deliver any such guarantee, and it is accordingly necessary to submit the

Fig. 12   A mental model of the premises "Some psychologists are academics" "some academics are pipesmokers" which might be used to evaluate the proposition "Some psychologists are pipesmokers".

model to a series of tests. This qualitative difference is, of course, reflected in the very much greater difficulty of quantified inference over inference with propositions and simple relations. The point to be emphasised is that it is only because we can construct mental models that we are able to make inferences based solely on the meanings of expressions and without recourse to any system of mental logic. (p.27)

Indeed, elsewhere, Johnson-Laird (1980a) has suggested that formal logical systems may have been produced by people reflecting on the invariant properties of their operations with mental models. Even in the abstract area of reasoning, perception seems to influence thought. For a very recent coverage of his views on thinking and reasoning as skills see Johnson-Laird (1982).

III   Imagery and creativity

Compared with the elegant simplicity of the analogical theory of reasoning the theories psychologists have advanced about creativity appear to be much less coherent. Studies of creativity have, of course, burgeoned since Guilford's famous address, some 30 years or so ago, to the A.P.A. (see for example, Guilford, 1950), but during this period, relatively little progress has been made in understanding the creative *process*. Part of the reason for this is doubtless that creativity research grew as an offshoot of the testing movement, as a reaction to traditional measures of mental ability. Indeed, the social histories of the two constructs, intelligence and creativity, are remarkably similar. Just as early intelligence testing got underway during World War One when it was necessary to select men rapidly and efficiently, creativity tests emerged in response to a similar social need, some commentators have argued (cf. Razik, 1967). Razik has linked the rise of creativity studies with the Cold War, the Atomic Age and the Russian "threat". Intelligence tests, whose purpose is to distinguish between criterion groups, are notoriously lacking in theoretical underpinnings, and, perhaps because of their similar heritage, creativity tests tend to suffer from the same flaw. As Golann (1963) has pointed out, creativity studies can be divided into "person", "product" and "process" accounts. Person accounts are investigations of the personality structure of the creative; product studies are concerned with the results of creative activity; while process approaches describe the activity itself. Psychometric investigations of creativity rely on the study of products to the exclusion of all else: Creativity tests are built on the tacit assumption that test protocols represent miniature creations in their own right (Bolton, 1972). Needless to say, this assumption is extremely dubious. Even more dubious is the supposition that identical products, large or small, can be taken as evidence for the same underlying processes. Gilham (1978) reports a study Donaldson (1963) which showed that identical, or very similar responses or products in a verbal reasoning task were sometimes achieved by very different routes. Also, Westerman (1973) and Bennett (1976) have demonstrated similar effects with a figural reasoning test thought to be particularly uniform in context, viz. Raven's Progressive Matrices. Gilham argues that if thinking is a product related process it may be only partially, not completely specified by its products. We believe that there is no *a priori* reason to suspect that the performances underlying creativity tests can be specified more easily than those underlying divergent tests when only test products are examined. If anything, we expect them to be more variable and less predictable.

For these and other reasons, a natural place to look to further one's knowledge of creativity should be the process accounts. Unfortunately, there are problems here too. The main sources of information are the autobiographical accounts of creative individuals (e.g. Poincare, 1924; Spender, 1952). These reports are essentially introspections of the creative process and descriptions of contingent events. As reliable data they are naturally suspect. However, with the usual provisos that introspection is subject to distortions, reflects only conscious processes and provides us merely with beliefs about cognition (see Chapter 2 for a further discussion), such data, used with caution, can play an important role in theory construction and hypothesis formation (cf. Valentine, 1978). Thus, some of the earliest theoretical treatments of creativity (e.g. Rogers, 1959; Wallas, 1926) were process descriptions built around these autobiographical accounts.

Visual imagery has been implicated in creativity by many autobiographers and theorists (Arnheim, 1969; Ghiselin, 1952; Khatena, 1976; Paivio, 1971b; Richardson, 1969; Rugg, 1963; Spender, 1952), but as Ernest (1977) has pointed out, little has been done to link the two in any systematic way. Recently, however, Hargreaves and Bolton (1972) have found a relation between several divergent thinking measures and performance on a pair-associated learning task when subjects were told to form images linking each pair. Also, there have been a few attempts to link individual differences in imagery ability with creativity (see Chapter 5). For the most part, though, all these studies have merely implicated imagery and not gone on to explain how it was used. As we pointed out in Chapter 5, it is likely that imagery control might be important in creativity, though this variable has attracted very little attention in the literature. For a recent, general review linking imagery, creativity and aesthetics the reader is referred to Lindauer (1977). Though suffering from the abundance of description and dearth of explanation that marks this area, the latter does, at least, attempt to integrate three branches of knowledge.

IV   Concluding remarks

We have examined a variety of situations and contexts in which imagery is used. Some surprising, some less so. If we had to pick out what all these have in common it would be that they all capitalize on imagery's function as a mental model. This means that operations which otherwise would have to be performed on real objects can be applied to mental images. On theoretical and empirical grounds propositions seem ill suited to this role. Also, in many of the situations we have considered, imagery makes its appearance when the task is relatively unpractised. BOSS-consciousness is needed to control such operations.

One application of imagery we have not considered, since, strictly speaking, it is to do with the affective rather than informational properties. Many behaviour modification techniques apparently depend on the ability of clients to form and use mental images. Early approaches, such as systematic desensitization (Bandura, 1969; Wolpe, 1973), have been supplemented recently by techniques based on operant theory (see especially Cantela, 1977 for a comprehensive review; also Cantela, 1970, 1971, 1973; Meichenbaum, 1974 and Chapter 5). Marks (1977) also reports that many self-help techniques (e.g. Klausner, 1965) imply that vividly imagined changes in cognition will lead to desirable clinical or personal outcomes. Conversely, as Wolpe (1973) has pointed out, inadequate imagery may be more of a hindrance than a help in desensitization. For a recent review of this area see Strosahl and Ascough (1981). Some evidence that imagery abilities can be modified and improved was discussed in Chapter 5 and this work is obviously relevant to the study of behaviour change. However, we believe, that only a full knowledge of imagery's function will allow us to isolate just which imagery related skills are relevant and malleable. The work reviewed in this chapter will help us to reach that distant goal.

10
Imagery and memory: Voluntary images

This chapter and the following one examine the role of imagery in remembering. The chapters are roughly divided between research on situations where subjects are specifically instructed to form images, and those in which no such instructions are given but where mental images may nevertheless be playing a part.

I Factors which influence memory

It will be easier to understand the research upon imagery and memory if we first review some of the problems inherent in any information processing system, and the main features of human memory.

It is often useful to think of remembering as involving three stages, (1) the encoding or entry of new information, (2) the storage of that information and (3) the retrieval of the information when required. However, encoding and retrieval are inevitably interrelated in that it will only be possible to retrieve what was encoded and to do so on the basis of how the encoding was made, and the information stored at the time.

For any information retrieval system, such as the human memory, a crucial factor is to make available for retrieval as much stored information as possible at appropriate times. A vast amount is entered into our memories. There is a continuous process of storing new information alongside the enormous amount that has been accumulated over decades of life, and for all information storage and retrieval systems sheer quantity of stored entries leads to problems in retrieval.

There have been many attempts to model some aspects of the memory system. Some models assume that retrieval is accomplished by some part of the cognitive system initiating a search through the stored memories whenever retrieval of a particular entry is believed to be desirable. Sometimes such models envisage each memory entry being examined one by one, until the "memory probe" matches the code assigned to the stored information. These models are implausible for several reasons. They assume that the system "knows" in advance much of what is stored so that it is "aware" that it is worth retrieving, and can specify the codes under which it may be found. Secondly, they assume a complex mechanism for initiating the search, and imply that retrieval is a relatively rare activity. Thirdly, they postulate search mechanisms which are implausibly inefficient if large numbers of the millions of memory entries have to examine one by one.

More plausible are models which assume that most entires in memory are associated with a rich set of labels indicating the context of the learning while the entries themselves have features which are accessible. Then, when the current, active processing within the system is dealing with information similar to that in the memory entry, it will activate the similar attributes in the entry (resonance is a suitable analogy) and, in certain circumstances, the memory will be retrieved. The circumstances limiting retrieval include enough total activation to make it accessible and enough specific activation of one memory so that it is sufficiently distinguishable from competing activated memories for it to be selected. Also, the programmes and plans running in the cognitive system must be such that they allow information from memory to be retrieved. This may not happen if, for example, full attention is required by an ongoing task.

It is not necessary to commit oneself to any specific model to accept that the main determinants of memory are (a) what is stored at the encoding stage, which is a function of the activity of the cognitive system at that time, and (b) what information is available, when retrieval would be desirable, to initiate the reactivation of the stored information. The more closely this information at retrieval matches that laid down at encoding, the better will be recall. The more distinctive the encoding, the less problem with competition from similar memory entries. Finally, if the information in one memory that is retrieved closely resembles that encoded for another entry, there will be a high probability it will in turn trigger the recall of that entry.

Recall is normally considerably improved when subjects form

images which link together several of the items to be remembered; we will review the evidence later. Here, we point out that the improvement could result from any of the determinants of memory discussed above. The same image, if recalled, should produce similar activity in the system at retrieval as at the initial encoding and so cue retrieval. Or the image may be, by its specific nature, a good distinct cue selecting a specific entry in memory. Or the image may, by containing within it representations of the items to be remembered, trigger their recall.

Fundamental to encoding, and therefore to subsequent retrieval, is the nature of the material that is being acquired and the activities of the system in acquiring it. In both cases there is what might be called an internal and an external aspect. So, how well some material is remembered will depend upon its external properties — whether it is a prose passage or a picture for example, but these external properties are important insofar as they relate to internal characteristics of the cognitive system. It will usually, for example, by easy to remember a short word list such as *kitchen, cooker, gas, toast,* but this is because the words contact a rich data base of knowledge about kitchens etc. already available in memory. However, the probability that these words will be recalled in the future depends not just upon their nature and the prior knowledge of the subjects, but also upon what they do to activate and reorganize knowledge about kitchens etc. That will depend upon the task demands of the situation: what subjects are required to do. In turn, the requirements of the subjects' current situation, their needs and aims, and the nature of the material with which they are interacting will determine their strategy for handling the task. In the interaction of these internal and external aspects new memory traces will be formed as a by-product of the cognitive activity. It is worth remembering that, however essential a memory system may be for our cognitive functioning, it is, nevertheless, not the central component of the cognitive system. The system has the task of making sense of its environment and controlling behaviour, and the memory system plays its part, albeit a vital one, towards these ends. Often, what is recallable from memory is the result of some earlier process of comprehension, and reflects the deductions and selections that took place at the time.

The present chapter will be mainly concerned with the effect of a demand that the subjects form images, and the influence that this strategy has on subsequent recall. In the next chapter we will consider how the material to be remembered may elicit imaging as a strategy by the subject. When we review research on imagery and memory the importance of the properties of the material being memorized, and the strategies of the subjects elicited by the demands of the situation will be found to play a major part in determining what will be remembered. It will not be adequate to ask simple questions like ''does forming images help remembering?'' It will be necessary to ask specific questions about the type of image, the material to be learned and the way memory is to be tested.

II   Imagery and different memory tasks

A   Imaging and free recall

The need to specify one's question about the influence of imagery is well illustrated if we begin by considering what, superficially, is the simplest of learning paradigms, that of free recall. Here subjects are given a list of words to learn, usually presented one at a time at a fixed rate, and they then recall as many words as they can in any order they wish. Suppose that, to investigate the influence of imagery on recall one group of subjects is instructed to form images of the items named by the words and their performance is compared to a control group not given imaging instructions. Morris and Stevens (1974) reviewed several such studies, and found that some reported that imaging improved recall while others did not. The common features of studies where imaging improved recall was that subjects were encouraged to form images which linked items together, while those which failed to show an imagery effect had subjects forming images to individual items. Morris and Stevens (1974) manipulated the instructions to subjects, so that one group formed images which linked together three times at a time, while others were told to form an image to each item in turn, or were given conventional free recall instructions. They found a 50% improvement in recall when images linked items together, but no difference between the subjects forming images to individual items, and control subjects. Richardson (1976, 1978) found similar results, and observed that the separate image condition led to poorer memory from most of the list but increased the recency effect, that is the normally better recall of the last few items from the list. He suggested, as Morris and Stevens had done, that the formation of separate images disrupts the subjects' organizing of the list so that the emphasis is placed on short-term retention. Morris and Stevens found no difference in the apparent organization of the recall of subjects, but attempts to measure the organization which subjects impose on recall are notoriously insensitive and the suggestion that the formation of separate images interferes with such processes remains plausible.

This research suggests that we must consider the type of image that subjects form. At least for free recall, the mere formation of an image is

Fig. 13 To remember, for example, CAT, HAT, BOOK, forming single images of each has little influence on recall, but an integrated image markedly improves memory.

not necessarily sufficient to increase recall. The image must be one which integrates together the items to be learned. We will discuss why integrated images aid memory shortly. First, notice the qualifications which must be made relating to the material and the activities of the subjects. The experiments just described used common concrete nouns as the items to be learned. They allowed several seconds for each item to be studied. If the interval had been cut to, say, 1 second per item the contribution of imagery would have been markedly reduced, since it takes time to form an integrated image. To form an image linking two objects together requires a couple of seconds (Morris and Reid, 1974; Morris, 1978) and adding a third item complicates matters further. Concrete words easily elicit images, but it is harder and takes longer to form an image to an abstract word. Further, subjects report more variability in their images to abstract than to concrete words (Morris and Reid, 1973) and this may lead to failures in recall if the original image cannot be retrieved. Then there are the interactions which instructions, material and available time will have on the subjects' strategies. Only a limited number may follow the method in which they have been instructed, and the numbers sticking to the given method will depend upon the possibility of putting it into practice. Few subjects will persevere trying to form linking images to rare, abstract nouns presented at a rate of 1 per second. Conversely, subjects in the control group may adopt the strategy given to the experimental groups. So, for example, the control group in Morris and Stevens' (1974) study may have contained subjects who were forming linking images spontaneously, others who were forming single images and others who did not form images at all. This raises important questions for the interpretation and quantification of research on imagery. The main point to note, however, is that statements about the influence of imaging must be couched in terms which specify the learning and testing conditions, and any estimates of the efficacy of imagery must be qualified by reference to the conditions with which it is compared. For example, a statement based upon the Morris and Stevens data that linking images to concrete nouns will improve recall by 50% may be a valuable statement about the practical implications of the strategy, but may underestimate the actual benefit of imaging, since, among the control subjects, some may have formed linking images, while among the experimental group, some subjects may not.

While the main influence of imagery on free recall depends upon the formation of images which link items together, there may be small effects that result from forming single images. This is suggested by experiments by Ritchey and Beal (1980) who used the methodology of Kosslyn (1975) (see Chapter 8). They required subjects to form images to individual nouns, fitting the image within either a large or a small field on a screen. There was significantly better recall for words to which large images had been formed although the actual size of the difference in performance was small. There was also better recall when subjects had to imagine concurrently a simple matrix rather than a complex matrix while imaging to each noun. The difference in recall did not occur with easily categorizable lists of nouns. Ritchey and Beal argue that the bigger images or those concurrent with the simple matrix, are more elaborated than the others and this leads to better recall. However, strong interitem associations can override the effect by providing a different basis for recall. Slightly better recall for items to which single images were formed was also found by Kirkpatrick (1894) in the earliest experimental investigation of imagery. Roediger (1980) found forming single images to lead to better immediate recall than rote rehearsal, but not when compared to performance when no strategy was specified. The difference disappeared for delayed testing, and the imagery groups who linked items together produced far better recall, especially in the delayed test. So, integrative images are probably required for any major improvement in recall, but single images may make small contributions.

B   Imaging and paired-associate learning

In paired-associate learning, when pairs of items are presented, and recall is tested by presenting one of the items to the subject and requiring recall of the other, the task appears potentially appropriate to the use of linking images to associate the stimulus and response items. Using five lists of 20 pairs of concrete nouns, each shown for 5 seconds, Bower (1971) demonstrated that instructions to visualize the named items in an interactive scene led to a 50% improvement in recall compared to control subjects given no specific instructions. As was argued earlier, and as Bower pointed out, this probably underestimates the contribution of imaging, since some of the control subjects reported using imagery to memorize the lists. When Paivio et al. (1966) asked subjects after a paired-associate experiment what, if any, mnemonic methods they had used to learn the pairs, they found that for pairs of concrete, easily imageable nouns, imagery mnemonics were frequently reported.

Bower (1970) had one group of subjects form images linking pairs of concrete nouns, or form images so that the two named objects were imagined "non-interacting, far separated in the left versus right sides of the imaginary visual field". In comparison with a control group who were told to repeat the pairs as their method of learning, the integrated imagers had far better recall, while the separate image group did not do better than the controls. As with free recall, it appears that integration *via* images is the important factor in improving paired-associate performance. There have been many reports of better paired associate performance following such integrated imaging (e.g. Colman and Paivio, 1970; Bugelski, 1970; Bower, 1971). In some studies the experimenters varied the instructions to subjects within the same list, by indicating when the pair was presented whether it was to be learned by forming an image or by repeating the pair. Bower (1971) found 80% recall of imaged pairs and only 33% recall of repeated pairs and Yarmey and Barker (1971) found an effect of similar magnitude. Such experiments are obviously open to criticisms on their demand characteristics, and the choice of rote repetition as a control probably produced the maximum difference between conditions (cf. Morris, 1979), but nevertheless the experiments illustrate the potential contribution of imagery.

One reason for believing that recall improves because of some process associated with imaging is that powerful effects of integrative images occur even when subjects are unaware at the time that they will later be tested for recall. For example, Bower (1971) told subjects that norms were being collected for the English Department on "word pictures". Two groups of subjects were asked to rate the vividness of the image which they attempted to form linking 20 paired-associates. One group knew that recall would later be tested, the other did not. A third group were told to learn the words for a test, but were not given a specific method. The imagery groups did not differ significantly, with 77% recall by those aware of a future test, and 71% by those who were not. The control group, aware of the test but not of a suitable mnemonic method, recalled only 35% of the responses. The ratings of vividness correlated significantly with recall. Yarmey and Ure (1971) similarly found no difference between imaging subjects aware of forthcoming test, and those not forewarned.

C   Imaging and serial recall

Images linking items in a serial list improve serial learning (e.g. Delin, 1969; Roediger, 1980). Roediger (1980) instructed one group of subjects to link adjacent words in three 20-word lists. He found not only superior free recall, but also much better recall of words in their correct positions in the list. At an immediate test on average of 9·6 items per list were remembered in their correct places, compared to 4·8 recalled by subjects imaging each word separately, and 5·8 by those saying the words over to themselves. Twenty-four hours later the single image and control groups could recall only 1 and 1·3 items per list in their correct position, while those who had formed linking images could still place 5 items per list.

D   *Imagery and recognition*

So far, we have seen that images which integrate items together usually improve recall, while single images to items do not. The situation is rather different when we turn to tests of recognition. Winograd *et al.* (1971) found that following instructing subjects to form images to word pairs, the recognition of the pair was subsequently improved, but not the recognition of individual words from the pairs, if presented alone. Similarly, Bower (1970) had found that the subjects who formed either separate or integrated images to paired-associates did not differ in their recognition of the stimulus words from the pair. Morris and Reid (1974b) showed that instructions to form images to single words improved the recognition of concrete words by increasing the numbers of hits in an absolute judgement (yes/no) task. The Winograd *et al.* (1971) improvement for imaged pairs also occurred through changes in hit rate with no alteration in false positives. Morris and Reid (1974b) argued that images may aid recognition by being re-elicited during the recognition test, when the recognition of an old image could supplement performance. An old word may re-elicit an old image and confirm its recognition. A new word will elicit a new image supporting its identification as new, but so, on occasions will an old word so that the use of new images to identify new words will not be a very reliable strategy. Overall the main effect should be to improve the hit rate for old items, as has been observed.

Morris and Reid (1974b) tried to identify why images to concrete words or intact pairs improve recognition, but those to abstract words or single words from pairs do not. They found that while subjects almost invariably reported the same image as being formed to concrete nouns when they were repeated during the experiment, for only two-thirds of abstract words did subjects both succeed in forming an image on both occasions, and report the re-occurrence of the same image. This implies that not only is the formation of images more difficult to abstract nouns, and, as Morris and Reid also showed, takes far longer than to a concrete word, but the images are much less reliable than those to concrete words as indicators of the earlier presentation of the word. Concrete noun pairs normally re-elicited the same image, but on only 22% of occasions did the original image re-occur when only one word from a pair was presented. No doubt subjects could often have re-elicited the original image, with further effort. However, the important point is that in the context of a mixed list of old and new single words, the images that were originally formed when a word was one of a pair are not readily re-elicited by the single word, and a new image is likely to occur. As such a new image is to be expected half the time since half the words are new, the subject is likely to be misled by the new image. They may even decide not to persevere with imagery as a technique for aiding recall, and use other information for their judgement. The non-occurrence of an old image may lure the subject into reporting an old word as being one of the distractor items. Morris and Reid (1974a) found just this, with subjects being more than four times as likely to call a single noun from an old pair a new word, than to report a new word as an old one.

E   Bizarreness of images

Proponents of memory improvement systems that have used imagery have often recommended that the images which are formed should be a bizarre as possible (Lorayne, 1957; Yates, 1966). A bizarre image would be more distinctive than one using conventional representations, and as such might be less susceptible to retrieval problems. However, Morris (1978c) noted that at least 13 studies had found no benefit from the formation of bizarre images, and proceeded to describe a four-teenth! It is possible to suggest reasons why these studies failed, beyond the probability that bizarre images are no more effective than common-place ones. For example, Morris (1978c) reported that subjects took an average of 4 seconds to form bizarre images linking two nouns, twice as long as they took for conventional images. Limited time for imaging may have caused problems in some experiments, and have encouraged subjects to abandon bizarre imaging. Nevertheless, even with 10 seconds allowed per pair and a design which maximized interference, bizarre images did not lead to better recall (Morris, 1978c). It may be that bizarre images help recall over longer times than are normally tested (cf. Andreoff and Yarmey, 1976; Webber and Marshall, 1978). However, bizarreness generally appears to contribute nothing to the efficiency of imagery over and above that supplied by an interactive image.

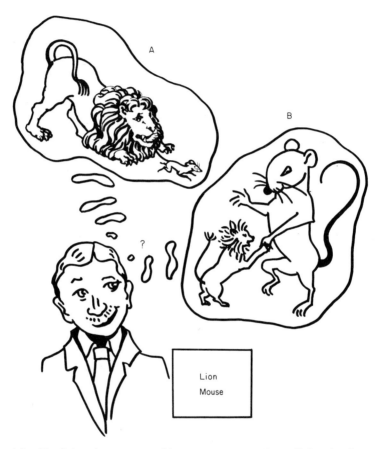

Fig. 14 Traditional accounts of imagery mnemonics call for the formation of bizarre images (B), but most studies have found conventional scenes easier to imagine and just as effective (A).

F Imagery and memory for sentences and prose

Anderson and Bower (1973, p.305) asked subjects to form vivid visual images to sentences such as ''The hippie touched the debutante who sang in the park''. They found that, when cued with one or more of the content words, recall was improved with imagery. Jones (1978) reanalysed the results, and showed that the improvement was relatively specific to the latter part of the sentence (i.e. "the debutante who sang in the park"). He suggested that the coding of information in a locational setting may be particularly improved by imaging.

Pressley (1976) trained 8-year-olds to form mental images as they read prose passages. After practising with sentences and progressively longer passages the subjects read a short story divided into 17 segments, and formed an image to each segment. Control subjects experienced the same practice lists, but without imagery instructions. They were told to "do whatever you can or have to" in order to remember the story. However, the imagery subjects answered significantly more short answer questions about the story when tested later.

III   Why does imagery aid recall?

With the exception of recognition memory, the main influence of imagery upon recall has been associated with images which integrate together the items to be recalled. Why and how, therefore, does the formation of such linking images facilitate memory? We will consider shortly several arguments which might direct our attention in searching for explanations, away from mental images to other processes. Initially, however, thinking in terms of images, it is obvious that the introduction of spatial relationships which mental imagery allows makes possible the linking together of apparently unrelated items. There is no obvious connection between a duck and a typewriter, but a duck can be imaged typing at a typewriter. It therefore becomes possible to enter into memory the codes for the future recreation of this image which incorporates both the duck and typewriter in one representation. If conditions at the recall stage are such that they can retrieve the image, then that image should have a high probability of generating the recall of duck or typewriter, or both as required. If images to single items only are formed, then the recall of the image following recall of the item will do little more than substantiate the initial correctness of recalling the item. It will not help the recall of new items.

It is possible, however, that if imaging leads to two entries in memory, one related to the verbal character of the item, the other as imagery codes, then there will be two possible routes to recall and one would expect performance in such circumstances to improve. The latter is, essentially, the prediction from Paivio's Dual Code theory, described by him as a coding redundancy hypothesis (Paivio, 1971, p.181) which we have already discussed in Chapter 7. As reported earlier, the formation of single images in free recall does sometimes marginally improve performance, and this may occur because of this double opportunity for retrieval. The effect is small, however, much smaller than might be expected if both the images and the words shared equal and independent probabilities of being recalled.

One possibility is that the Dual Code hypothesis is false and that we are wrong to think of two different types of entries being made in memory. However, we argued earlier that the complete rejection of the Dual Code hypothesis could be misleading. A second possibility is that the verbal and imaginal codes are not equally easy to access. It may be, for example, that the retrieval of an image may require a more specific cue than retrieval of the verbal label. This is not a very easy possibility to test because the retrieval of an image may quickly cue the retrieval of the verbal label, and *vice versa*. Consequently, the introspections necessary to identify which came first may be difficult. Another possibility is that even if there are two separate codes, the probability of recall from them is not independent. They may, for example, share such similar retrieval codes that the same active content of the cognitive system will either retrieve both or neither entry. Another possibility is that the memory search must be directed to one or the other type of code, so that effectively only one may be retrieved at any time.

Some researchers have criticized the assumption that imagery and so called verbal coding are qualitatively different. Some, including Anderson and Bower (1973), have disputed the need to propose a separate imagery code. Others have pointed to what appear to be anomalous results for a simple imagery explanation (e.g. Neisser and Kerr, 1973). First, as we have discussed in earlier chapters, the phenomenal experience of the recall of mental images or words is but the tip of a metaphorical iceberg of cognitive processing. Both require the initial encoding and later reactivation of codes for their reconstruction and, for either to be meaningful, rather than just the experience of a visual pattern or a sound, many components of the cognitive system which deal with semantic information must be activated. Although, as we argued in Chapter 7, there is a danger that those who wish to emphasize the similarity of imaging to other cognitive activities may neglect the fact that imaging does have its own distinctive features, it may, nevertheless be the case that what leads to better recall is a feature common to different types of output (i.e. imagery or verbal).

The superiority of interactive imagery for recall implies that it is not imaging *per se* that aids performance, but the processes which underlie interactive imagery, namely the identification and exploitation of potential relationships between the items. If subjects can be encouraged to generate such interactions without imaging, and if their resulting performance does not differ from that which follows interactive imaging, then at the least it has been shown that imaging is not a necessary condition for the memory improvement. A process shared with imaging could explain the performance.

The comparison of imagery instructions with those to form meaningful sentences or stories has sometimes been attempted. Paivio (1971, Ch.11), for example, reviewed such research to that date. There is no doubt that instructions to form stories or sentences can lead to greatly improved recall (e.g. Bower and Clark, 1969). However, although such instructions bring performance up to be comparable with that following interactive imagery instructions, there seems to be a marginal superiority in the imagery condition. While some studies report no difference between imaginal and verbal mediation (e.g. Paivio and Yuille, 1967; 1969; Yarmey and Csapo, 1968; Johnson, 1972; Jansen, 1976), others have found better recall with imagery (e.g. Colman and Paivio, 1970; Bugelski, 1970; Bower, 1971; Bower and Winzenz, 1970). However, there are almost no reports of better performance with verbal mediators than with imagery. The only exception is Paivio and Foth (1970) who required subjects to draw their mediating images or write their sentences, and found that while imagery instructions were superior for concrete nouns they were inferior with abstract nouns.

It could be argued, balancing the evidence for and against the superiority of imagery over sentence mediation, that while imagery does not markedly excel, it does tend to produce a better recall. If so, then the processes of imaginal and sentence mediation would appear to be different. In fact, the complications in interpreting the evidence serve as a useful reminder of the problems in theorizing about subjective processes, but also prevent any reliable conclusion. For instance, there is nothing to prevent subjects from forming images while inventing mediating sentences. It may be that such images

commonly occur spontaneously, and certainly subjects report experiencing them (Bower, 1972). Similarly, when forming images the
subjects may decide upon the way the items are to be interrelated prior
to imaging them. Much that underlies sentence construction may take
place when imaging, and *vice versa*. This would be expected by a
believer in a common code or underlying process, but it could also be
the case even if there is much involved in imaging and composing
verbal statements that uses different processes. Alternatively, even if
the same processes underlie imaging and sentence formation, it is
possible that when a single sentence is devised it contains less relational
information than an image and is therefore a less efficient mediator.
Also, the construction of an image requires full comprehension of the
relationships involved which must be realized in the concrete scene.
There is more potential for incomplete comprehension with verbal
mediators. Especially where they are supplied by the experimenter
rather than the subject they may produce less appropriate coding than
images. Add to these problems the evidence reviewed by Paivio (1971)
that subjects sometimes abandon the method in which they have been
instructed for one which they believe to be more efficient, and it is
apparent that the superiority, or otherwise, of images over sentence
mediators does not provide evidence for evaluating dual and common
code theories.

One awkward finding for proponents of imagery as the basis of the
memory improvement was that of Neisser and Kerr (1973) who asked
subjects to rate the vividness of imagery evoked by sentences which
described three types of situations. They either encouraged interactive
imagery (e.g. "A daffodil is sitting on top of the torch held up by the
Statue of Liberty") or separate images ("Looking from one window,
you see the Statue of Liberty; from a window in another wall, you see a
daffodil") or an interactive relationship in which, if actually physically
pictured, at least one of the items would be concealed (e.g. "A daffodil
is hidden inside the torch held up by the Statue of Liberty"). The
"concealed" condition produced recall that was superior to that for the
"separate" condition and which did not differ significantly from the
"interactive" group. Neisser and Kerr argued that it was the spatial
relationships involved rather than the picturing of the items which
influenced recall. This would be support for the view that it is the
nature of the relationships not some special feature of imagery which
aids recall. However, the majority of subjects in Neisser and Kerr's
experiment reported that they made the concealed object visible in

some way in order to image it (Neisser, 1972). Keenan and Moore (1979) tightened up the experiment by asking one set of subjects to form images, not as though they could see the objects, but exactly as described. These subjects performed worse than those given interactive sentences, and no differently from those with separate image sentences. Using the original instructions of Neisser and Kerr (1973), the latter's initial finding was replicated. It does appear, therefore, that Neisser and Kerr's results do not demonstrate the irrelevance of imaging, but rather the flexibility of the subjects as they tried to comply with ambiguous instructions.

Evidence specifically implicating images, or at least a special spatial form of coding, comes from two experiments by Baddeley and Lieberman (1980). They trained subjects in using the peg and place imagery mnemonics (see below) and examined the influence of concurrently tracking on a pursuit rotor during list learning when subjects did or did not use the mnemonics. When the mnemonics were not employed, the pursuit rotor task did not alter performance. However, when the mnemonic was used, the concurrent spatial task considerably reduced the benefit which the mnemonic contributed. This seems to imply that encoding of spatial information is taking place with mnemonic instructions, but not when the mnemonic is not used. It does suggest that different encoding is taking place.

Richardson (1980) argues that any pictorial representations produced in memory experiments are epiphenomenal, and that what is functional is the propositional description which he sees as logically required for imaging. He states that "A subject who constructs a mental image in response to the appropriate mnemonic instructions does so under an intentional description which must be conceived as an abstract propositional representation of the image" (p.82) and

> Of course, it is possible that the construction of a mental image according to an intentional description when material is presented for learning gives rise both to a propositional representation and to a pictorial representation in long-term memory. However, the identity of any mental image generated at the time of the retention test will depend upon the intentional description on the basis of which it is constructed, and so whether it is the right image will depend upon whether it is constructed on the basis of the right propositional description (cf. Wittgenstein, 1953, 389, p.177; 1967, 650). This means that only the propositional description will be functional in remembering, and that any pictorial representation produced by the original imaging experience will be purely epiphenomenal. (p.83)

This argument derives from one which Richardson presented earlier (p.39). He asserted that mental images are representations. A logical feature of all representations is their intentionality, in that the object of a representation, that is, what is being represented, depends on what is intended by its creator, not upon what it resembles. So, for example, a cross on a map may represent a church, even though it more closely resembles a couple of sticks. If an image did have to resemble what was represented, Richardson argues, we would have to inspect our images to find what they were. Even if an image does resemble what it represents, it could be open to more than one interpretation. For example, a + might be interpreted as a church, as an instruction to add, as two sticks, as a vote, as a signal of a mistake, etc. So, Richardson concludes that "the object of a mental image is not defined by any of the pictorial properties of the image itself, but is carried by the description under which the image is intended" (p.39).

First, it is not obvious that images should only be considered as representations like arithmetical symbols, deliberately scribbled to stand for something else. Memory images can often surprise, hallucinations can horrify and appear to behave autonomously of the hallucinator. Even the images that we deliberately form can cause problems, in refusing to comply with our wishes (cf. Richardson, 1969). There is more to imagery than simple representation.

Second, for representations in the physical world it is always possible to consider the representation and the intentions of the representer separately. A picture may be painted for a purpose by an artist. But whatever its object may be for him at the time, the picture is open to interpretations by others, and even for reinterpretation by the artist in the future. For both the artist and others the picture can have all sorts of influences upon them beyond and independent of the purpose for which it was originally painted. For mental images it could be argued that it is not logically possible to separate the image from the processes which led to its formation. However, the way people can describe their images does make it plausible to regard them as having a separate existence, in some sense. If so, then the image may be valuable in helping recall independent of the intentional description.

Next, it is logically possible that images may sometimes have to be inspected to find what they represent. It is possible that the same processes which allow us to classify our real world perceptions of chairs, tables, etc. may be used to interpret our mental images (see Chapters 8 and 9). The only thing that *is* logically ridiculous is for anyone who has already decided that the representation which they are about to create is to stand for an x to then have to inspect the representation to see if it is an x.

The logic of imaging probably more closely resembles depicting than simply representing. That is, while any symbol may serve to represent something, a depiction requires that the symbol resembles what is depicted. As we described in Chapter 6, images are first order isomorphisms, not second order as Richardson implies (see Shephard, 1975). On Richardson's account, it would be quite possible to ask someone to image a tiger, then to ask them to describe their image, and for them to reply "a circle with a dot in it". To our complaint that that is not an image of a tiger, they could reply "Oh yes it is, I intend it to represent one". Clearly the Humpty Dumpty world of complete freedom of representation applies in only a limited number of situations. Our surprise at the description of the tiger suggests that we normally expect an image to resemble the object it represents. If images usually resemble the objects for which they stand, then it will be highly probable that when the same image recurs, the imager will recognize the objects represented.

Concentrating upon Richardson's specific argument quoted above, if an image is formed following an intention to depict some scene, then the intention and the image are logically separable, and some record of both may be stored in memory. Subsequently, there will normally be no need to equate the image with the one formed earlier, if the image can itself be retrieved and its properties examined. There is nothing illogical about such retrieval and examination.

It is possible that Richardson believes that the intentional description required by the logic of the concept of representation is equivalent to the codes and rules from which an image is generated. This is very unlikely, since the logical requirements for the description are no more than the boundary conditions which determine for the individual whether or not the image meets the specification for the representation which he or she is trying to compose. In that case they are not equivalent to the process required to generate the image. Richardson appears, unnecessarily, to equate the intentional description with the processes which generate the image, a position similar to that of other proponents of a propositional account. Certainly, within the generative process will be information specifying the form the image will take. However, it neither follows that such information would be of the form from which other types of representation (e.g. sentences) could be generated, nor that the information can be accessed in this form. Even if accessible, operators to evaluate answers to questions may not exist at that level. By analogy, one might have the skill to lay a ruler on a map and establish that three points were in a straight line, but not be able to carry out the necessary calculations if given the map coordinates of the towns from which the map had been composed. We may be equipped in some cases with the equivalent of mental rulers but not processors for analytical geometry. The existence of information in the system is not in itself grounds for believing that the information can be used. Its use involves access and the necessary transformation which its format requires. Systems for accessing or transforming the information may not exist. More specifically, while systems for accessing and transforming the information as images may exist, other systems may not. This same point was made in Chapter 6.

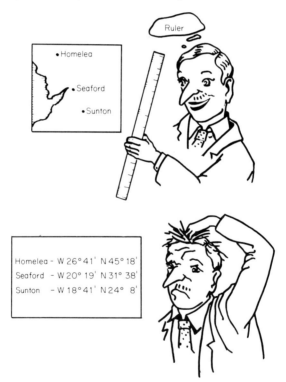

Fig. 15 A map makes it easy to test whether three towns lie in a straight line. Similarly, the usefulness of a representation depends both upon its form and upon the mental operators that already exist to read out information.

It is incidentally worth noting that, if correct, Richardson's argument would demonstrate that sentences and stories used as mediators were equally as epiphenomenal as mental images. We are sympathetic to efforts to localize the point at which memory improvement occurs through changes in the underlying processes. However, the logical nature of images or verbal statements is not a sufficient base for this localization.

IV   Imagery mnemonics

So far in this chapter we have discussed the way in which forming images can contribute to better memory of the sort of word lists used in laboratory investigations. However, the use of imagery to improve memory as a practical aid has an extremely venerable history. Indeed, the research reviewed previously was largely inspired by the claims of systems which offered to equip their students with "super-power memories" (e.g. Lorayne, 1957). Within such systems imagery frequently played a part. The laboratory studies were often carried out to check these claims.

There are several published reviews of the history of imagery mnemonics (e.g. Paivio, 1971, Ch.6; Yates, 1966). The present discussion will be restricted to outlining the common methods, illustrating their effectiveness, and mentioning some extensions of imagery mnemonics to other situations. Other recent reviews of mnemonic methods will be found in Morris (1977, 1979), Bellezza (1981) and Higbee (1977).

A   Method of places or loci

The oldest imagery mnemonic is the place method, devised, according to tradition, by the Greek poet Simonides (c. 500 B.C.), and later described by Cicero and Quintilian. The memorizer selects a series of well known, easily imaged places with their own inherent order. A familiar street might be used, or a well known room. Then, concrete representations of the items to be remembered are imaged one by one around the room or along the street. When recall is required a mental scan of the room or imaginary walk down the street should lead to the recall of the appropriate images. The mnemonic was used in classical times to memorize the points to be made during long speeches, not because the speakers were illiterate but because the free flowing speech without notes was highly valued.

The place method has sometimes been used in modern times by stage memory experts (see e.g. Luria, 1968). In controlled tests it has normally produced massive improvements in recall, compared to control subjects (e.g. Briggs *et al.*, 1970; Bower, 1973; Groniger, 1971). Roediger (1980), for example, found that the place method increased recall of items in their correct position for three lists of 20 words by almost 100% compared to performance on a practice list, and by more still if compared to subjects who either rehearsed the lists or formed single images to each word. Groniger (1971) found 100% better recall of items in their correct positions after five weeks delay.

B Peg method

This method is one of the foundations of many memory improvement systems. Easily imaged words are memorized to represent numbers, usually those from 1 to 100, but sometimes more. These words can then replace the numbers when memorizing a long list in order. The person forms a mental image linking together the peg word and the item to be memorized. Subsequently, when recall is required, the memorizer recalls the peg word, which cues the image which in turn cues the recall of the item. The advantage over the method of loci comes from the relative ease in finding suitable peg words as compared to loci when large numbers are required. Also, the peg method allows recall in any order without problems in losing one's place. The disadvantage is the need to memorize the peg words, but that it minimized by rules such as the phonetic translation system (Morris, 1979, p.40) which specify sounds for digits so that an easily learned logic underlies the construction of most sets of peg words. Long lists of such pegs have been published (e.g. Higbee, 1977; Lorayne and Lucas, 1976). The peg method can be adapted to the learning of playing cards, and other material involving numbers.

As with the place method, many studies have demonstrated the effectiveness of the peg method (e.g. Bugelski *et al.*, 1968; Hunter, 1964). Morris and Reid (1970) found that a peg system doubled recall compared to a control group and did not observe problems when the same pegs were used for learning six consecutive reorderings of the same items. Roediger (1980) found that recall with a peg mnemonic equalled that for subjects using the loci method when examined for recall in the correct position from the original list, but was poorer for recall independent of position, though far better than the control conditions. Bower and Reitman (1972) noted essentially equal recall for the peg method and the method of loci under a variety of test conditions. The peg and place mnemonics require imageable items for memorization. Usually some suitable substitute can be found for abstract words, but numbers or nonsense material, or too short a time to allow for the necessary elements of the mnemonic to be completed will lead to its failing to aid recall (Foth, 1973).

C   Remembering names to faces

A method recommended by Lorayne (1957; Lorayne and Lucas, 1976), for learning people's names involves first converting the name to some imageable substitute, then choosing a prominent feature of the person's face, and forming an image of the name substitute there on the face. So, if, for example, the person is named Isaacs, this might convert to "ice axe" and, if they had an especially large chin, an image would be formed of the ice axe stuck in their chin. Bizarre as this method may seem, it has been shown to markedly increase performance. Morris *et al.* (1978) reported an 80% improvement and McCarthy (1980) found over three times the performance when the mnemonic was used, compared to several control conditions. Interestingly McCarthy observed no benefit from the mnemonic when subjects were instructed to link the name substitute with the whole face rather than a prominent feature.

D   Keyword method of vocabulary learning

Atkinson and Raugh developed a method employing imagery in the acquisition of vocabulary when learning a new language (Atkinson and Raugh, 1975; Raugh and Atkinson, 1975). The technique is intended to aid the initial acquisition of new words from the new language, which is one of the major restraints upon learning a new language. The link between the sound of the foreign word and its meaning is provided by what Atkinson and Raugh called a keyword. An English word which is similar in sound to the foreign word and is easily imaged is selected to be the keyword. This is then visualized in an interactive image with a representation of the meaning of the foreign word. There are thus two links, one between the sound of the foreign word and the keyword, and one between the keyword and the representation of its meaning. An example would be the learning of Spanish word ''carta'' which means letter by selecting *cart* as the keyword, and forming an image of a letter inside a cart.

Several experiments have shown that the keyword system helps subjects, when they are given the foreign word, to retrieve the English equivalent. In one experiment by Atkinson and Raugh 120 Russian words were taught. For keyword subjects, the Russian word was played several times over headphones while the keyword and the English translation was displayed. For control subjects the keyword was omitted. The words were learned in sets of 40 over a period of three days. On the fourth day all 120 Russian words were presented for translation, and six weeks later there was another unexpected test. On the first test, keyword subjects remembered 72% of the English translation, compared to the 46% correct translations by the control group. After six weeks the keyword subjects, who had had no reason to use the words in the interval, could still recall 43% of the translations, compared to the 28% remembered by the controls. Recall was better when subjects generated their own images, rather than being given cartoons or sentences linking the keywords and the English translation. However, perhaps because the discovery of an appropriate keyword can take time and effort, recall was better when keywords were provided than when they were generated by subjects, and if given a choice, the learners asked for prepared keywords on 89% of occasions.

Pressley *et al.* (1980) confirmed the value of the mnemonic in learning English definitions to foreign words, finding a 71% facilitation. However, in several experiments the mnemonic failed to improve the recall of the foreign word, given the English definition.

Pressley and Levin (1981) suggested that the failure of the keyword mnemonic to cue the foreign word occurred because the retrieval of the keyword was not sufficient to retrieve the foreign word. They noted that in the earlier Pressley *et al.* (1980) study the subjects could often remember the component of the foreign word which was cued by the keyword, but, apparently could not remember the rest. Pressley and Levin first considered that this might result from the unfamiliarity of the orthographic and phonological patterns in the foreign language. They therefore used English words instead, teaching the definitions of very low frequency words. So, for example, ''carlin'' meaning ''old woman'' was taught using *car* as the keyword. However, although the keyword subjects could recall far more of the keyword components of the low frequency words (suggesting that the images successfully cued the keywords), they were no better than control subjects at remembering the full word if given the definition. Pressley and Levin then made sure that the low frequency words were cued by the keywords, by prior training in which, for eight trials, the subjects were shown the first syllable of the word and asked to supply the second. After this initial training, subjects using the keyword method did produce markedly better recall than controls who had carried out the pretraining but not the keyword technique. Similarly, better performance was found when unusual meanings were taught to common nouns (e.g. couch–animal's den). Here there was no need to translate from the keyword to the word being memorized. It appears, therefore, that there are limitations upon the scope of the keyword technique which must be taken into account when it is applied. Nevertheless a wide range of situations has now been tackled through the keyword method. Second-language vocabularies have been taught to school children (Pressley, 1977; Pressley and Levin, 1978) and military terms in the difficult Korean language have been taught to American military personnel, with large benefits to all levels of General Technical Aptitude (Griffith, 1981); the names of capital cities have been taught for the appropriate states, (Levin *et al.*, 1980) and the products that are associated with particular cities (Pressley and Dennis-Rounds, 1980).

E   Peg word mnemonics for language learning

Paivio and Desrochers (1979) required subjects to learn 96 French peg words composed using the phonetic translation alphabet. When these were easily retrievable, they asked subjects to learn a further 96 French words, half by repeating the word and peg together and half by forming an image linking the meaning of both words. Recall was three times better in the imagery condition, and a subsequent test of comprehension found twice as good knowledge of the meaning of the words from the imaging condition as from the repetition condition. The act of imaging had apparently encouraged considerable memorizing of the words. While this exact mnemonic seems both artificial and awkward for language acquisition, it does suggest that techniques which require the mental manipulation of the referrent of foreign words in images may improve their retention.

F   Why do the mnemonics work?

Interactive imagery is incorporated into all of the imagery mnemonics, and, as described earlier, that is found to contribute greatly to recall. There are, however, other important elements in the mnemonics. The loci and the pegs provide distinct easily retrieved cues to aid retrieval of the images. The conversion processes of the peg and face-name mnemonics make imageable things which are not normally easily imagined. For the mnemonics to function with any but the most concrete of items it is necessary for a conversion to a concrete item to be made. So, the Greek or Roman speaker using the method of loci had to find a single imageable object to represent his next theme. Clearly, there are chances of mistranslation here, but the success of the mnemonics suggests that, if recall of the concrete object can be accomplished, then there is a good chance of the original being recalled. The probability of memory failure without the mnemonics normally far outweighs the dangers of errors that are inherent in them. However, cuing can fail, even when the images are available and the limitations of the keyword mnemonic which Pressley *et al.* (1980) and Pressley and Levin (1981) explored illustrate that it is not always a possible to retrieve an item if the cue provided in the image is not sufficiently specific.

The mnemonics have shown their value in situations where memorizing is difficult because the processes which normally lead to adequate memory performance are, in this case, lacking. Normally, we encounter information which has an inherent logic and structure, so that when this is recognized and encoded it can direct retrieval. However, sometimes there is no logical connection between the things to be memorized—there is, for example, no obvious connection between someone's face and their name. It is then that mnemonics have been developed to supply artificially the interconnections and specific cues which are missing. The result is that the mnemonics often seem bizarre, and are sometimes criticized for apparently adding to the memory load. They do, nevertheless, work, and help with what would otherwise be an arduous and slow task of rote rehearsal. However, by their nature, the mnemonics are suited to only those situations where the individuals know that they will have to memorize the material and where the material is not connected and meaningful. Also, the forming of interactive images is a problem-solving task which requires effort by the imager. If he or she is willing to invest the effort then their memory will be greatly improved. However, often even people familiar with mnemonic systems will choose not to apply them if the cost of forgetting will not be too great (cf. J. Harris, 1978). A fuller discussion of the conditions under which mnemonics aid memory will be found in Morris (1978, 1979).

11
Imagery and memory: Aroused images

I Imageability

In the previous chapter it was argued that an adequate account of memory required consideration of the task set, the subject, the strategy which the subject adopted, the material to be learned by the subject and the prior knowledge which the subject already possessed of that material. All these factors interact to determine what is encoded and what will be retrieved. The previous chapter concentrated upon subject strategies, or rather, the effect of asking subjects to adopt the strategy of forming mental images. One reason was that this instruction makes it at least highly probable that images are being constructed during the experiments. There were, nevertheless, hints that the ease of imaging the material to be memorized may have an important influence upon the effectiveness of instructions to image, so that, for example, Morris and Reid (1974) found better recognition by subjects when forming images to concrete nouns, but imaging to abstract nouns had no effect.

This chapter will discuss the influences on memory of the nature of the material and its consequent activation of prior knowledge, or strategies. It begins with the more thoroughly researched topic of the imageability of individual words, and then considers recall of connected narrative and pictures.

Common to much of the discussion will be the problem of whether or not the memory differences which are observed really derive from the occurrence of imagery, or whether other explanations are appropriate. Studies of this sort have been carried out in enormous numbers, and the present chapter can offer only a review. Fuller treatments, though with some differences in emphasis and interpretation, will be found in Paivio (1971) and Richardson (1980).

A   *Imagery value and concreteness: the scene is set*

The growth of interest in the role of imagery in remembering, following the desert days of behaviourism when imagery as an explanation was forbidden, is largely thanks to Allan Paivio. For several years his interest was in the successfulness of predictors of the recall and recognition of words, based upon measures of the ease with which the items elicit images.

Paivio (1963) showed that in a paired-associate task concrete nouns were learned more easily than abstract nouns. Subsequently, he demonstrated that the concreteness of the stimulus item in the pair was more important than that of the response item (Paivio, 1965). This resembled earlier research by Lambert and Paivio (1956) on adjective–noun pairs, where they had suggested that the stimulus item forms a "conceptual peg" to which the response is "hooked". In later papers (reviewed in Paivio, 1969; 1971) he developed the conceptual peg hypothesis in the context of learning where he hypothesized that imagery played a major role. He argued that the effect of concreteness reflected the use of imagery by subjects in the different conditions, and explained the importance of the concreteness of the stimulus item by its place as a conceptual peg for re-eliciting the images. He stated that on recall trials, "when the stimulus is presented alone, its image-arousing value would be particularly important for the stimulus member must serve as the cue that reinstates the compound image from which the response component can be retrieved and recoded as a word" (Paivio, 1969; p.244).

B   *Measuring I value*

Paivio (1963, 1965) had used concrete and abstract words, that is, words which did or did not refer to "objects, materials or persons" which could be experienced by the senses. However, he speculated that it was the ease of imaging to a word rather than its concreteness that was the fundamental determinant in his experiments. Some words, such as "parclose" (a screen round a shrine), refer to objects, but may not arouse images because they are unfamiliar; conversely, technically abstract words such as "Christmas" can arouse visual images. Paivio *et al.* (1968b) provided ratings of 925 nouns. Separate groups of subjects rated the ease with which the words elicited images, and the concreteness of the words on seven point scales. The average number of associations to the words which could be thought of in 30 seconds was also measured to give the words "meaningfulness" value abbreviated to m (Noble, 1952a,b). The mean rating of the ease of imaging became known as the words I value, and the mean concreteness rating as the C value. The correlation of I and C was $0\cdot83$ confirming that while concreteness and imageability are closely related properties of words, they are not identical. However, for most subsequent research it has usually been assumed that I and C are alternative measures of the likelihood that mental images will be formed when the word is processed, and that I gives a better estimate than C (e.g. Paivio, 1971, p.201). This may misleadingly undervalue concreteness as a factor in memorizing, as we shall discuss later.

II   Imagery or what?

Paivio's central assumption was that words with high I values were more likely to elicit images than those with low I values. If images were formed, he deduced from his Dual Code hypothesis that there were two opportunities for recall, one based upon the verbal and one upon the imagery representation. Superior performance of high I words could be accounted for in this way, either because they had two codes to draw upon when recall was required and/or because the imagery code was more effective.

The research reviewed in the previous chapter suggests that, at least in situations involving recall, as opposed to recognition, the important factor may be not that images are formed but that those that are formed integrate the items together. Nevertheless, the I value could be considered an indicator of how likely subjects will be to adopt such a strategy of composing linking images, as opposed to other methods of acquiring the words.

However, the words which Paivio (1965) had shown to produce different levels of recall also varied on properties other than the ease with which they elicited mental images. As has already been explained, concreteness was not initially regarded as important, but there were several other leading contenders to explain the apparent influence of I as merely the result of the coincidental co-variation of I with the other variable. Noble (1952a,b; 1953) had extended to real words the concept of *association value* defined by Glaze (1928). The latter found that the percentage of subjects who reported a meaningful association to a nonsense syllable in a 1 to 2 second period was related to the ease with which the nonsense syllables could be memorized. Noble defined his variable of *meaningfulness (m)* as the average number of associations to a given word that could be written in a specified time (normally one minute or 30 seconds). From Noble's early studies onward, this variable was usually related to recall, with words with higher m values being easier to learn. Underwood and Schulz (1960) suggested that there were several other interrelated variables such as pronouncibility which, together with m, were all measures of a major underlying variable. They suggested, as James (1890) had done earlier, that the greater the number of associates which a word elicits the greater the possibility during the learning of paired associates or word lists that the words will ''hook up'' with one another.

Paivio *et al.* (1968b) found that m correlated 0·74 with I so that the two clearly tend to vary together. Of course, the explanations of the underlying processes by which I and m come to be associated with recall are not mutually incompatible. The ability to image to a word may open up possible associations to boost m, while the idea of the associations which m measures providing opportunities for items to be linked together does not exclude the possibility that the link might be through images. Nevertheless, m was assumed to be a measure of processes that were not necessarily imaginal, and given the established acceptances of m and doubts about the subjective nature of I, Paivio proceeded to a series of studies in which I and m were independently varied. Full reviews will be found in Paivio (1969, 1971, Ch.8). The main finding from many experiments was that for paired-associate learning, serial learning and free recall I still predicts recall when m is controlled either by the choice of the items (e.g. Paivio *et al.*, 1968a) or statistically by partial correlation (e.g. Paivio, 1967). The influence of m has been variable but that is another story.

Another recognized variable at the time that Paivio and his associates were conducting their research on I was word frequency. Common words tend to be more easily free recalled than rare words, though the reverse is true for recognition (Gregg, 1976; Morris, 1978b). However, frequency and I were found by Paivio *et al.* (1968a) to be only weakly correlated (0·23) and Paivio's results for I were normally derived from experiments in which frequency was controlled.

We have dealt, so far, with the contenders with I to explain I's correlation with recall which were established when Paivio began his research. There are, however, other possibilities. There may be another dimension on which words vary which really accounts for the I/recall relationship. This has been examined in several studies where many potential variables are examined by techniques of factor analysis or multiple regression. Perhaps, however, there is a more subtle co-variable which has not been included in such studies. Over the years several such variables have been proposed, and we will discuss the more important of them after reviewing the multivariable studies.

A   Multivariable studies

Paivio (1968) factor analysed the values of 96 nouns on 30 variables. These included the free recall of the nouns, and their ease of learning as stimulus and response items in paired-associate learning. He used several measures of imagery, including the latency to report an image, rated vividness and I value. He also included frequency, familiarity and other dimensions such as: concreteness, goodness, impressiveness, complexity, activity, unusualness, specificity, emotionality, hardness, preciseness, interest, tangibility, roughness and colourfulness. Several factors were isolated, the sixth being identified by Paivio as a learning factor. There were loadings of this factor of 0·65 and 0·69 on stimulus and response paired-associate learning and 0·47 on free recall. It loaded about 0·3 on the imagery variables and on m and the other variables did not appear to contribute to it. When the actual correlations of the dimensions with recall are examined, it is the correlations with measures of imagery which appear strongest, with, for example, the I of the stimulus word in paired-associate learning correlating 0·54 with recall. Only the measures of imagery exceeded a correlation 0·4.

All this strengthened Paivio's conviction that it was imagery itself and not some co-variable which was influencing recall.

A similar study by Frincke (1968) on free recall isolated a factor on which free recall performance loaded heavily (0·78) and on which I loaded 0·82 and m 0·58. Frincke had included concreteness, goodness, pleasantness, familiarity and number of associations among his variables, but again it was imagery which was found to be the best predictor of recall.

More recently, Rubin (1980) carried out a factor analysis of 51 scales for 125 words. The overall result was, perhaps, disappointing for the champions of any one variable. Only emotionality loaded significantly upon the factor which was heavily loaded by the main recall measures. However, for recall as a function of the stimuli in paired-associate learning, this variable loaded 0·66 on the imagery factor. Rubin carried out multiple regression analyses to evaluate the power of the variables in the study to predict performance. Overall the resulting predictions were quite good. For present purposes it can be noted that *I* value was required in the multiple regressions for paired-associate learning of both stimulus and response terms and for free recall. For paired-associate stimuli, *only I* was required. For paired-associate responses and free recall three others were required. Interpretation of such analyses must, however, be made with care. They show that performance can be quite well predicted if enough variables are taken into account. there are, however, problems if one hopes to draw causal inferences from the data. The high intercorrelations of the variables combined with the unreliability of memory performance from test to test means that there is a considerable degree of arbitrariness in the choice of variables and in the estimation of their contribution. Rubin deliberately excluded any variables which correlated 0·85 or more with other variables. This carries obvious risks of excluding important variables since the choice is made independently of their correlation with the dependent measures. A discussion of the problems in interpreting multiple regression analyses in this area will be found in Morris (1981c).

Gilhooly and Gilhooly (1979) examined the free recall and recognition of word lists, intercorrelating the results with *I*, *C*, *m*, frequency, familiarity and age-of-acquisition. For free recall, the highest correlation was for *I* (0·42) followed by frequency (0·33) and *C* (0·31). The latter's correlation may have resulted through its co-variation with *I*. For recognition, however, the main correlations were with frequency (0·45) and Age of Acquisition (0·41) and the correlation for imagery was not significant (see also Morris (1981c) for further discussion of these results).

Christian *et al.* (1978) tested 900 of the nouns from the Paivio *et al.* (1968) norms. They then calculated partial correlations with recall, taking out all but one of *I*, *C*, *m* and frequency. The resulting partial correlations were highest for *I* (0·20) next highest for frequency (0·17) and lower for *C* (0·07) and *m* (−0·04). As with most of the other studies discussed in this section, *I* value appeared as the best predictor of free recall.

From all of these studies several important conclusions emerge. First, that the *I* value of words is repeatedly identified as one of the best predictors of the ease of the word's recall. Rubin (1980), for example, concluded that ''unlike many of the other changes in encoding used here, the use of imagery does have drastic effects on what is recalled.'' No other variable shows anything like the consistency with which measures of imageability top the lists of predictors of recall. However, while this gives confidence to the assumption that there is no obvious alternative variable underlying the *I*/recall relationship, it is also a result of the limited value of any of the other variables in predicting recall. With the exception of dimensions of stimulus items in paired-associate learning, where *I* value is a good predictor, the correlations between recall and the variables examined are consistently low. This may reflect our ignorance of the important factors involved, or variability in encoding between subjects, perhaps as a function of different strategies. It does show that we have a lot to learn about learning.

III   Alternative variables, covarying with *I*

Since Paivio first proposed that ease of imaging underlay the better learning of concrete words, several alternative properties of high and low *I* words have been suggested as at least contributing to the effectiveness of *I* as a predictor while some experimental results have cast doubt on an explanation of the relationship of *I* and recall based on imagery. For example, Baddeley and Lieberman (1980) found no evidence of concurrent pursuit rotor tracking selectively interfering with the effect of concreteness, even though the use of imagery mnemonics was markedly disrupted. Four alternatives to imagery will be discussed here. Two have received little subsequent support and will be considered only briefly; the others are worthy of further study.

A   Lexical complexity

Kintsch (1972a,b) claimed that many abstract words are syntactically complex, deriving from other base forms. So, for example *refusal* may be considered as deriving from *refuse*. Concrete words tend to be simple syntactically. Kintsch (1972a) found roughly similar effects for lexical complexity and imageability, implying that at the most lexical complexity could account for only some of the apparent influence of *I*. However, Richardson (1975a,b) when he controlled for both imageability and concreteness found no effect of lexical complexity, and subsequent linguistic accounts cast doubts upon the status of lexical complexity (cf. Richardson, 1980, p.94).

B   Arousal

Butter (1970) in a paired-associate experiment using four words of high *I* and four of low *I* as stimuli and digits as responses, found greater GSR responses to the low *I* words, suggesting that low *I* words are more arousing than high *I* words. Butter obtained an interaction between immediate and delayed recall similar to that reported by Kliensmith and Kaplan (1963, 1964) for items producing high and low arousal, with low *I* words being poor stimuli at an immediate test, but exceeding high *I* words at a late test. Subsequently, however, Butter and Palmer (1970) and Yuille (1971) failed to replicate the interaction. While we will argue later that arousal and emotionality should not be completely neglected when discussing imageability, it is unlikely that the *I*/recall relationship is solely the result of arousal. Indeed, it will soon be suggested that the relationship between emotionality and *I* is the opposite of that implied by Butter, although concreteness and arousal may co-vary negatively.

C   Concreteness

Paivio chose not to try to distinguish between concreteness and imagery in his research following the preparation of the Paivio *et al.* (1968) norms. He argued that it was the imagery which concrete nouns could evoke which led to the correlation of concreteness and recall. Several studies have suggested that *I* value is a better predictor than concreteness. For example, *I* loaded more highly than *C* on the recall variables and factors in all the multivariable studies described earlier. Nevertheless, concreteness should not be too quickly rejected. It is, logically, a distinct variable, and one which might be more important than imagery outside the laboratory. It is assumed, on the imagery account, that high *I* words in memory experiments normally encourage subjects to create images which improve memory. Reports of the use of mediators after such experiments do indicate more imaging to high *I* nouns (e.g. Paivio *et al.*, 1968a). However, imagery is usually a flexible strategy which can be consciously adopted by subjects. High I nouns do not automatically elicit images. The success of instructions to form images, reviewed in the previous chapter, shows that there is considerable opportunity for more images to be composed than are normally produced in experiments with high I nouns. If this were not so, then the instructions would have no effect. It is therefore possible that the power of I as a predictor of performance is restricted to situations in which subjects choose to adopt a mnemonic strategy of imaging. Such strategies are rarely used in real life (Harris, 1978). On the other hand, concreteness concerns the meaning of the word and the perceptual properties of referrents of words. As such it may be an important property outside the limited conditions of intentional list learning.

There have been attempts to separately vary concreteness and imageability. Yuille (1968) prepared paired-associates which were composed of words either high or low in C but medium in I. With imageability controlled in this way, Yuille found recall to be correlated $0·43$ with the concreteness of the stimulus word of the paired-associate. However, Paivio et al. (1968a) had noted that words such as those used by Yuille which were medium in their I rating but low on C were words with emotional connotations. To check whether these results were caused by emotionality, Yuille therefore obtained ratings of emotionality and found not only that, for his sample, emotionality and C correlated $0·83$, but emotionality correlated negatively ($-0·48$) with recall. Partialling out the correlation of either emotionality or C with recall reduced that of the other to insignificance so that either might account for the recall differences. This does not separate the causal from the casual variable, but we will return to the question of emotionality shortly.

To try to separate the effects of concreteness and imagery in free recall, Richardson (1975a,b, 1976) carried out a series of experiments on a set of 80 nouns selected so that all combinations of high and low-concreteness and high and low-imagery were equally represented. When specific instruction to form images were given, higher I value was related to greater recall. However, without such instructions, higher I value was only related to better recall for low C nouns. Richardson argued that, in the absence of specific imagery instructions, imagery was only used with abstract words. In Richardson's experiments Concreteness did not produce a main effect benefitting recall. Subsequently, Christian et al. (1978) claimed to fail to replicate the interaction of I and C, but the method they adopted of subdividing their sample of words failed to control both for other co-variables including frequency, and the average values of I and C in the separate groups of words. Richardson himself has, however, abandoned his original position (Richardson, 1980). Since he had hypothesized that imagery was used only with abstract words, he predicted that for words high on both I and C there should be no correlation between recall and I value when C was partialled out. However, for a sample of concrete, easily imageable words, Richardson actually found a significant correlation for I and recall but no correlation for C and recall, that is, the reverse of his prediction. Therefore Richardson concluded that "conventional accounts, which identify stimulus imageability as the primary determiner of recall performance, are likely to be essentially correct" (Richardson, 1980, p.93).

Unpublished research by the first author may help both to clarify the earlier Richardson findings and to raise again the possibility that concreteness may independently covary with recall. Morris followed up the possibility that Richardson's sample was confounded with emotionality. He obtained ratings of both Richardson's sample, and other nouns on emotionality. When m, I, age of acquisition and frequency were controlled there was a significant relationship between rated emotionality (E) and both recognition and free recall (Morris, 1980). For Richardson's sample, E varied indirectly with I ($r = 0.50$) and negatively with C ($r = -0.42$). The pattern of Richardson's results for free recall was replicated, with the only significant difference being for I value when the words were of low C. It seems, however, that this may be attributable to E, which reaches its maximum for high I, low C nouns. Partial correlations were calculated between recall, and I, C and E, separately for the high C and low C sample used by Richardson. For low C nouns, there was no longer a significant correlation of I with recall when E and C were partialled out. Finally, using the whole sample of words, there was a significant correlation between C and recall when I and E were partialled out.

Two points are worth emphasizing from the research just described, over and above the clarification which they may offer of Richardson's findings and the evidence for E as a variable influencing recall. First, I value is not related to recall in the experiment. Second, there is evidence linking concreteness and recall. Although Richardson designated one of his sets of nouns "high I", in comparison to the rest of those rated in the Paivio *et al.* (1968a) norms, they are not so. The mean *I* value of Richardson's high *I* set is below the mean for Paivio *et al.*'s norms. Virtually all studies of imagery have used the full range of the Paivio norms. It may be, however, that only those words which are given high ratings on *I* normally prompt subjects to adopt an imagery strategy on their own accord. This would mean that *I* as a predictor of performance would be limited to such conditions. When subjects are not led by the instructions or the material to adopt an imagery strategy, then the concrete/abstract nature of the material may still influence what is encoded, with the effect no longer obscured by the imagery strategy. More evidence is needed to support such a claim, but is is a possibility.

D   Semantic similarity

Wickens and Engle (1970) suggested that there is more overlap in meaning between abstract than between concrete words. If this is so, then the clearer distinctions between concrete words may account for the better recall and recognition of high *I* words. Wickens and Engle were led to their proposal following a release from proactive inhibition experiment using words of high and low *I*. Sets of three words, of either high or low *I* were shown to subjects for three seconds, after which the subject had to spend several seconds carrying out mental subtraction before recalling the words. On the fourth trial half the subjects switch from low to high *I* or vice versa. Their performance is compared with controls who do not switch. For many such changes, e.g. between letters and numbers, the normal rapid decline in performance over trials is reversed and recall returns to the high level common on first trials (cf. Wickens, 1972). Wickens and Engle found no such changes which implied for them that the switch between high and low *I* did not alter the form of the encoding. However, they did note that from the second trial onwards performance was better with the high *I* words. This they presumed implied that there was greater interference for low *I* than for high *I* words. More interference would be expected if low *I* words are more similar to one another in meaning than are high *I* words.

If there really was no difference in the form of encoding of high and low *I* nouns, as the failure to find release from proactive interference implies, then the recall difference may not be attributed to the imaging of high *I* but not low *I* words. One problem is that the difference between low and high *I* words in Wickens and Engle's experiment may reflect better encoding of high *I* words rather than problems created by interference at storage or retrieval. If so, the similar performance on the first trial of low and high *I* words must be attributed to a ceiling effect or to naïvety about appropriate strategies.

Paivio and Begg (1971) replicated Wickens and Engle's experiment but also manipulated associative overlap, i.e. the number of common associations shared by a set of items. Their triads of words were composed so that they were either high or low in associate overlap within each triad. Two examples of high within overlap are "corner, square, circle" and "skin, blood, flesh". They also manipulated associative overlap between the lists. Recall was best for triads with high within and low between overlap, and worst for pairs low on both within and between overlap. They therefore argued that inter-item relatedness could not explain the effect of *I*. They did, however, find twice the mean associative overlap for low *I* words as for high *I* words.

Is associative overlap an appropriate measure of semantic similarity? Certainly one would expect the two to be related, and take the greater associative overlap of low *I* words as evidence of their greater similarity. However, the use of close associations by Paivio and Begg probably introduced opportunities for guessing, as well as clearly specifying dimensions for encoding which linked the words. Low *I* words may not be so similar in meaning that they normally match Paivio and Begg's associative overlap condition, yet they may be sufficiently similar in meaning to cause problems.

Morris and Reid (1974) found better recognition of high *I* than of low *I* words. Interestingly, however, the difference occurred in the false positive rates, with twice the number for low *I* nouns. This has been replicated several times (Jones and Winograd, 1975; Winograd *et al.*, 1976) and appears to result from some property associated with *I*. Instructions to image produce increases in hits not changes in false alarms (see Chapter 10). False alarms are often observed where new words that are similar in meaning are presented as distractors (e.g. Anisfeld and Knapp, 1968; Fillenbaum, 1969; Grossman and Eagle, 1970). Morris and Reid therefore suggested that the recognition differences with *I* value resulted from differences in the similarity of meaning of the old words and distractors, with low *I* words being less distinct. When dictionary definitions of a large sample of high and low *I* words were examined, low *I* words appeared far more frequently as synonyms of other (low *I*) words than did high *I* words. It is worth noting that the number of different usages for high and low I words does not differ markedly (Morris, 1978b). It is in the similarity of meaning rather than range of meanings that low I words differ from high I.

Morris (1978b) offered an explanation in terms of semantic similarity of Galbraith and Underwood's (1973) observation that abstract words are reported as being more frequent than concrete words, and of Ghatala and Levin's (1976) finding that when abstract and concrete words are equated on the basis of their perceived rather than objective frequency the usual advantage of concrete words in verbal discrimination experiments (cf. Paivio, 1971, p.288) disappears. Morris argued from the finding that abstract nouns are more semantically similar to one another than are concrete nouns, that abstract (low I) words shared more common attributes associated with their meaning than do concrete (high I) nouns. If sets of abstract and concrete nouns are equated on the basis of their objective frequency, the individual attributes of the abstract nouns will have been encountered more frequently. This will be so because other abstract nouns which share the attributes will have been encountered more frequently than will concrete nouns which share the attributes of the

	Abstract Words			Concrete Words		
	A1	A2	A3	C1	C2	C3
Frequency	20	15	10	20	15	10
Attributes	a	a	a	m	m	n
	b	b	b	n	q	t
	c	c	e	o	r	u
	d	e	g	p	s	v

Attribute frequency   a = 45   b = 45   c = 35   e = 25   etc.

Summed frequencies of attributes

	A1-	A2	A3	C1	C2	C3
	145	150	125	105	80	60

Fig. 16   If the perceived frequency of the abstract words A1-A3 depends on the frequency with which their attributes a,b,c, etc. are encountered, then because concrete words share fewer attributes than abstract words, the concrete words C1-C3 will be reported as less frequent, even though they actually occur with the same frequency as the abstract words.

concrete nouns. The effects is illustrated in Fig. 16 for an example set of three abstract words (A1-A3) and three concrete words (C1-C3) which are equal in their actual frequency of occurrence. However, because more attributes are shared by the abstract words the frequency of occurrence of these attributes is much higher. A necessary assumption is that the number of relatively frequent abstract and concrete words are not grossly unequal. If frequent concrete words many time outnumbered abstract words, then this would counteract the influence of repeated attributes shared by abstract nouns. If judgements of frequency are made, at least in part, on the basis of the frequency with which the attributes have been encountered, then abstract words will be judged more frequent than concrete words. The reverse will happen in Ghatala and Levin's (1976) experiment. If the words are selected on the basis of their perceived frequency, they will be being equated on the basis of the past experience of their attributes. If abstract and concrete nouns are equated in perceived frequency, they will be selected so that they have attributes which are equally common and distinctive. In that case, the usual advantage which distinctive attributes provide for concrete nouns will be eliminated, as Ghatala and Levin observe.

The evidence from dictionary synonyms, and of associative overlap, supported by the results of the experiments on the release from proactive inhibition, recognition and verbal discrimination is all consistent with the distinctiveness of items increasing with I. The very fact that dictionaries of synonyms include few concrete words suggests that few such synonyms exist. If high I words are more distinctive than low I words, then this could account for many of the observed effects of I. Our argument is not that I value is not related to recall through its indication of the likelihood that an imaging strategy will be adopted, but that, concurrent with this, differences in distinctiveness will be influencing recall whether or not imaging takes place. This difference in discriminability may account for the effect of concreteness observed in the research by Morris described in the previous section. Discriminability would be expected to vary with concreteness rather than imageability, given that the other was controlled, and to cause problems in the retrieval of the less easily discriminated, abstract, words in free recall.

IV   Why does *I* value predict recall?

If it accepted that at least part of the relationship between *I* and recall is the result of words of high *I* being involved in more imaging than words of low *I*, the question of why should *I* predict recall remains. For Paivio, part of the answer was that for high *I* words both a verbal and an imaginal entry was stored in memory, so that there were two opportunities for recall. As we discussed in the previous chapter, this dual code hypothesis is not well substantiated by the data from experiments where subjects are requested to form images which do not link items together. In these cases imaging produces only marginal improvements in recall. The powerful effect of instructions to image is associated with the request to link items in the image. The dual code explanation is, therefore, incomplete at the best. Two other assumptions have been suggested. One, especially for paired-associate learning, but extendable to free and serial recall, is Paivio's conceptual peg hypothesis in which he hypothesizes that high *I* words used as stimuli in paired-associates are, because of their ease of eliciting images, more likely to recall the image linking the two items than will low *I* words. The second assumption is that subjects do spontaneously form images linking items together sufficiently frequently to generate the *I*/recall relationship, more frequently with high *I* than with low *I* items.

An implication of the conceptual peg hypothesis which is far from intuitively obvious is that because a stimulus word is of high *I* it will re-elicit the specific linking image formed at encoding. Why a general potential to be imaged should mean that a particular image will be retrieved is not explained. It might be because high *I* words are more distinctive, and provide more specific cues to retrieve the image code.

Morris and Reid (1975) looked at the assumptions of the conceptual peg hypothesis and related explanations. They argued that performance in paired-associate learning should, according to the hypothesis, be a function of the imageability of the stimulus and the ease with which a linking image for stimulus and response could be formed. If the stimulus was of high *I*, then the performance should be closely related to the ease of forming the linking image; if it was of low *I*, then the image was less likely to be retrieved, and recall would be less well related to the ease of composing the linking image. Also, the imageability of the pair should be a function of the ease of imaging the individual words, but other variables such as the meaningfulness of the pairing would play a part.

Morris and Reid (1975) used adjective–noun pairs, half of which formed meaningful phrases (e.g. burning village) and half bizarre pairings (e.g. murdered tweezers). They found that both the I value of the adjective and the noun contributed to the rated imageability of the pair, but the biggest contribution was the compatibility of the pairing. When subjects learned the pairs as paired associates (with the adjectives as stimuli) the predictions from conceptual peg hypothesis were supported. With high I stimuli, the I of the pairs was highly correlated with recall (0·75) suggesting that the high I stimuli did retrieve the images, the formation of which was indexed by the I of the pair. With low I stimuli, pair I correlated only 0·02 with recall, suggesting that the images formed were not retrieved, so that pair I was no longer relevant in predicting recall.

Other evidence for the conceptual peg hypothesis comes from studies in which subjects are unexpectedly given the normal response word from a paired associate and asked to recall the original stimulus words. In these cases, as the hypothesis predicts, it is the imageability of the new stimulus (the old response word), which is normally a better predictor than the former stimulus word (Lockhart, 1969; Yarmey and O'Neill, 1969).

That the ease of forming an image linking the items in paired-associate learning is, as Morris and Reid (1975) argue, one of the important factors when images are formed is illustrated by Richardson (1980, p.86). Subjects who rated the ease of forming interactive images between pairs of nouns were then tested by being given the first of each pair and were asked to recall the second word. There was a correlation of 0·67 between the I ratings of each pair and the frequency of recall. This contrasts with an insignificant correlation of 0·28 for the free recall of individually rated nouns, a result consistent with other evidence on the formation of single images.

V   Memory for connected discourse

So far we have considered the learning of individual words. It is possible that imagery may play a part in the comprehension and encoding of everyday speech. This suggestion goes way beyond the position which regards imagery as a valuable mnemonic technique which is sometimes adopted voluntarily by subjects. In so doing it enters deep waters that surround the problem of the representation of meaning. There are fundamental philosophical objections to any claim that images can represent the meaning of a proposition. It is, for example, impossible for any finite set of images to capture the defining features of a triangle. However, it could be claimed that, while accepting the existence of other codes representing meaning, the formation of images does frequently take place when language is processed, and in so doing contributes to comprehension and recall.

Whenever two words are encountered together there is the potential for an integrated construction of their meanings in which imagery may be involved. As Morris and Reid (1975) reported, the meaningfulness of adjective–noun pairs is a major factor in their ease of imaging. Morris and Reid (1971) showed that noun imagery and meaningfulness of pairing interacted in free recall of the adjective–noun pairs, with recall enhanced only for meaningful pairs with high I nouns.

It seems reasonable to assume that comprehension must normally precede imaging because otherwise the specifications for the image would not exist. It is necessary, however, to be cautious here, given what is known about the interactions of top-down and bottom-up processes in speech recognition (e.g. Norman, 1976). Imaging might provide one way of hypothesizing the meaning of the stimulus. Once an image can be formed rules for its reconstruction may be stored, and the recalled image retrieve other more abstract representations of the meaning.

In the recall of phrases, imageability has proved a good predictor. For example, Paivio (1971a) and Richardson (1975) were able to explain in terms of the ease of imaging Rohrman's (1968) finding that subject nominalizations (e.g. *growling lions*) were easier to remember than object nominalizations (e.g. *digging holes*—which implies a someone who does the digging). Begg (1972) found that with highly imageable material adjective–noun phrases were recalled as if they were stored as functional units, while abstract material had poorer recall which suggested it was stored as separate words. Morris and Reid (1972b) showed that the recall of nouns from a prose passage correlated 0·54 with their I value, and that more high I than low I adjectives were remembered.

Following up the dual code theory, Paivio (1971) argued that concrete phrases and sentences are stored both verbally and as images.

He interpreted the common finding (e.g. Bartlett, 1932; Bransford *et al.*, 1972; Sachs, 1967) that the exact wording of discourse is usually rapidly forgotten even though the meaning is retained, as resulting from problems in translating from the image back to prose.

An experiment by Begg and Paivio (1969) appeared at first to support this hypothesis. Subjects had to detect changes in sentences. The changes were either in the meaning or the wording, and Begg and Paivio predicted that if concrete sentences are stored as images, then retention of meaning should be better than wording, while if abstract sentences are stored in a verbal form lexical changes should be easier to identify than semantic changes. This interaction occurred in their experiment. Begg and Paivio argued for a stronger position than was necessary on a dual code hypothesis, asserting that "concrete sentences are coded and stored primarily as non-verbal images" (p.283) and "under natural conditions, subjects rely exclusively on the imaginal representation of concrete sentences" (p.282).

Such a theory was always implausible. While a few, rare individuals such as S.V. Shereshevskii (Luria, 1968; see Chapters 4 and 5) may have a continuous flow of mental images corresponding to what they are hearing or reading, most people do not report such an experience. The latency and effort apparently involved in image formation (see Chapter 4) all weigh against the claim. If imagery is such an integral part of human thinking, why do instructions to image, which would be superfluous, improve memory? It is not, therefore, surprising that subsequent research has located weaknesses in Begg and Paivio's study which invalidate their conclusion. The abstract sentences have been found to be more difficult to comprehend (Johnson *et al.*, 1972; Klee and Eysenck, 1973) and may be less specific in their meaning. When sentences are matched on comprehensibility, the interaction disappears and concrete sentences lead to better detection of both changes in meaning and wording.

The possibility remains that imageability influences not only storage in memory, but also comprehension itself. It so, then equating for comprehensibility would unfairly weight against the Begg and Paivio account. A less contentious possibility is that imagery is commonly used as a supplement to comprehension by non-imaginal processes, and that imagery may sometimes be employed in the verification of sentences, even though it may not be required for comprehension. Eddy and Glass (1981) and Glass *et al.* (1980) have compared the verification of low and high *I* sentences. For sentences which were rated by subjects as requiring imagery for their verification, Glass *et al.* (1980) found more errors in the recall of a 4 × 4 matrix pattern which subjects had to remember concurrently, suggesting that the memory for the pattern was interfered with by selective interference from the images used in the sentence verification. Eddy and Glass (1981) found slower verification and comprehension times, for sentences which had been rated as requiring images for verification, with visual presentation of the sentences, but no difference with auditory presentation. They suggest that the visual presentation interferes with imaging. They claim that these results support Paivio's dual code theory by showing that information stored in the visual code is not redundant.

Research such as that by Glass and Eddy and that described in Chapter 8 by Kosslyn and his associates is beginning to specify the situations in which subjects do and do not resort to imagery. Imagery does not have the central role in long-term memory which Begg and Paivio claimed, but it does have a place. Many years ago, Shepard (1966) illustrated one condition in which imagery is common by asking how many windows there are on the front of your house? Most people report needing to image the house before answering. Information about such scenes must be stored and can be used. This brings us to memory for pictures and scenes.

VI   Pictures and imagery

The study of memory for pictures is, of course, interesting in its own right, independent of any relationship there may be between pictorial memory and mental imagery. For present purposes, however, the question is whether research on memory for pictures clarifies our understanding of mental imagery. As we described in Chapter 6, Paivio (1971, 1975, 1978) has assumed that there are separate imaginal and verbal codes, and that, while pictures may arouse encoding in either coding system, an imagery code will be most easily available (e.g. Paivio, 1971, p.179). On the other hand, propositional accounts have tended to assume that visually and verbally presented information are encoded in the same basic way. It is not an essential part of a propositional account to hold that there is only one coding system, since separate visual and verbal coding could take place in a propositional form. Nevertheless, one system using one type of coding is the most parsimonious assumption from which to start.

While there are obvious attractions of parsimony in assuming that memory for visual and verbal information employ the same code, there are several reasons for caution in making even the assumption that images and pictures are coded in the same way. Firstly, the high efficiency of recognition memory for pictures contrasts with the demanding, slow task of voluntary imaging, where the resulting images often contain relatively little information (see Chapters 4 and 8). Secondly, as we described in Chapter 5, studies of individual differences have consistently found separate verbal and visual skill factors, but the tests which try to tap the subjective experiences of imagery load on neither factor (Di Vesta et al., 1971; Paivio, 1971, p.495). Thirdly, there is little empirical evidence linking imagery with memory for pictures. It would therefore be unwise to generalize from research on memory for pictures to conclusions about imagery and memory. However, the study of imagery has been much influenced by Paivio's dual-code theory, and the theory itself is concerned with picture memory. The performance of the dual code theory in explaining memory for pictures may therefore indirectly influence our account of imagery. This research will therefore be reviewed. Other reviews will be found in Richardson (1980), and Goldstein and Chance (1974).

If rich, pictorial scenes are used, memory for pictures can be very good. Shepard (1967), for example, using two-item forced choice recognition, found 98·5% performance for the recognition of a sample from 612 pictures which the subjects were shown and there was still 92% correct recognition after one week. Similar, excellent performance has been reported by Standing et al. (1970a) using 2560 pictures, and Standing (1973) with 10,000 pictures. Such experiments have usually found better memory for pictures than for words or sentences similarly tested. For example, Shephard (1967) found recognition rates of 90% and 88% for sentences and words respectively. Proponents of a dual code would like to ascribe this difference to a separate visual code (see Chapter 7). However, the scenes used in the experiments have usually been chosen for their distinctiveness, and it has been argued (e.g. Ellis, 1975; Richardson, 1980) that the pictures are simply more distinctive and less liable to interference and retrieval problems than are words. In other words, the differences are not the result of two types of coding, but of a property common throughout the memory system, that those memories which have richer and more distinct entries are easier to retrieve from among competing alternatives.

If so, it is worth noting that a very rapid encoding of this distinct information must take place.

Goldstein and Chance (1971) argued that visual material can be encoded in both a pictorial and a verbal code, *and* that since pictures vary on many more dimensions than words it is likely that at least some attributes of visual material will be encoded. To test these hypotheses, they manipulated the number of dimensions on which a set of pictorial stimuli varied, as well as altering the ease with which they could be labelled. They asked their subjects to view women's faces, ink-blots or snow crystals. On a later test, recognition performance was much better for faces than for ink-blots, and poorest of all for snow crystals. Recently, Nelson and co-workers have provided evidence which suggests that verbal coding of pictures is less common than implied by Goldstein and Chance (1971) and Paivio (1971) (see for example, Nelson, 1979; Nelson and Brooks, 1973; Nelson *et al.*, 1973). By varying the phonemic similarity of the names of a set of pictures, and using either the pictures or their labels as stimuli and unrelated words as responses in a paired-associate paradigm, Nelson and Brooks were able to show that label similarity disrupted performance only when subjects were explicitly asked to name the pictures during acquisition. When subjects were given no naming instruction, no decrement in pictorial recognition was found. Pictures which were not spontaneously named, therefore, were still easily recognized. However, a limited role for verbal labelling was established in the Nelson *et al.* (1973) study. They showed that high label similarity can disrupt performance on a task involving memory for a sequence of pictures. No specific naming instructions were given in this experiment, though the majority of subjects did report labelling the pictures. This finding fits in well with Paivio's (1971) suggestion that the verbal system may be better suited than the visual for processing sequential information. Nelson (1979) agrees and concludes that picture naming is probably a flexible strategy which people can use in certain tasks and under certain conditions. As such it is similar to the strategy of forming visual images to verbal material.

If dual coding (i.e. two opportunities for recall being better than one) cannot account fully for the pictorial superiority effect, since Nelson has shown that two codes often will not be used, what about Goldstein and Chance's second hypothesis that visual stimuli might be intrinsically more memorable than verbal materials? The distinctiveness of the memory trace has been frequently cited as an important factor aiding both recall and recognition, in verbal memory (e.g. Jacoby and Craik,

1979). Could it be that the relative ease with which pictures are remembered is a function of the greater distinctiveness of either their appearance or their underlying meaning? Nelson *et al.* (1976) have investigated this possibility. Using pictures as paired-associate stimuli, they independently varied high and low conceptual similarity with high and low visual similarity. The idea behind this experiment was that if pictures are easier to remember than words because of the distinctiveness of their visual features, then high visual similarity between the pictures should have had a detrimental effect; on the other hand if the appearance of the stimuli is relatively unimportant then visual similarity should have had little or no effect. Also, by varying the amount of conceptual similarity, Nelson *et al.* were able to investigate whether the underlying semantic representations of words and pictures differed. Their findings were clear cut. High visual similarity eliminated the pictorial superiority effect at slow rates of stimulus presentation and reversed it at fast study rates. Conceptual similarity produced the same decrement in performance when either words or pictures were used at stimuli. Nelson (1979) concludes from this work that the difference between memory for pictures and their verbal equivalents arises because of the inherent superiority of the *visual* code of a picture which is more differentiating than that of its label.

In so far as memory for pictures shares the same properties as memory for verbal information there is no reason for hypothesizing two codes. Many such shared properties can be found. For example, pictures, like words, can be processed more or less "deeply" (cf. Craik and Lockhart, 1972) with corresponding memory effects. Using an incidental learning technique, Bower and Karlin (1974) found that asking subjects to judge whether a set of faces were male or female produced poorer recognition performance than asking them to rate the likeableness or honesty of the faces. Similar results have been reported by Patterson and Baddeley (1977) and Winograd (1978) (see Fig. 17). If depth of processing effects occur in the pictorial domain, it would be interesting to look for other phenomena, such as transfer appropriate processing (Bransford *et al.*, 1979) where the usefulness of an encoding strategy depends on the way in which the representation is to be used. Finding such effects would suggest that despite the important differences associated with the type or content of information stored, the global mechanics of the verbal and visual long-term memory systems may be very similar.

In this context, Kunen *et al.* (1979) have recently carried out an interesting series of experiments designed to test the *spread* of encoding concept in the visual domain. Spread or elaboration of encoding are terms originally used by Craik and Tulving (1975) and Lockhart *et al.* (1976) to refer to the varying degrees or amounts of processing carried out *within* a particular level (see Baddeley (1978) for a critique of this concept). Greater amounts of elaboration generally result in better recall and recognition. Kunen *et al.* have shown that as the amount of contour completeness of a picture decreases the extent to which the subjects must engage in elaborative operations increases, and hence, that incomplete pictures, up to a point, are better recognized than

Fig. 17   The best memory of faces follows decisions like this on the faces shown.

complete pictures. This finding runs counter to the predictions of simple concreteness theory (Paivio, 1971) which would suggest that the more complete pictures will be remembered better, but the results and Kunen *et al.*'s explanation of them fit in neatly with the hypothesized links between imagery and perception discussed in Chapter 6. Kunen *et al.* suggest that elaborative pictorial processing involves constructive operations of image production. The more elaboration performed, the better "fleshed out" is the image, and the better encoded the picture. Images themselves, they argue, embody two types of information, first, the information associated with their construction, second, information concerning their visual structural properties. They conclude that the general superiority of visual recognition tasks may arise because people cannot only compare the presented pictures against visual images but can also note the similarity between the constructive operations needed to interpret the pictures with previous visual syntheses (cf. Neisser, 1967). The BOSS-consciousness model can account easily for these results. Incomplete visual stimuli will require more top-down, constructive processing, which in turn will result in more elaborate image production. Also, we agree with Kunen *et al.* that the imagery system involves more than information about visual properties. Mental models contain or embody the more abstract information concerned with image production and evaluation, as well as the specifically *visual* information available as conscious image. Similarly, the prediction follows that more top-down processing will result in better encoding of the stimulus and hence better recognition in the future. These top-down processes will demand more of the limited capacity BOSS-system and will, in general, be quite demanding. Evidence that effort expended correlates with spread of encoding and recall in the verbal domain has been presented by Eysenck and Eysenck (1979). If the above analysis is correct a similar result should be found with pictorial material.

Opponents of the dual code theory, emphasizing the similarity of pictorial and verbal memory, point to the similar effects upon recall which pictures showing interactions between items have to those for sentences or images describing an interaction (e.g. Kerst, 1976; Wollen and Lowry, 1974). They claim that it is the provision of organization rather than specific pictorial properties which accounts for the improvement in recall.

Instructing subjects to name pictures increases both their recall (Bahrick and Boucher, 1968; Bower, 1970a) and recognition (Nelson and Kosslyn, 1976; Reese, 1975). Supplying supplementary pictures also aids verbal learning (Madigan *et al.*, 1972). A single common code theory therefore has to assume that extra information is encoded in these cases. Richardson (1980, p.63) sees the effects of labelling as a major problem for common code theories. However, since the labels and pictures require separate, extra processing, and since memory is a by-product of perceptual processing, it does not seem a problem to assume that in these cases extra information is encoded which subsequently aids retrieval. Problems only arise if a ''straw man'' common code theory is erected which deduces identical coding of both a picture and a name of an object. However, the assumption of a common form of encoding in no way implies that all that is encoded at any time is a sparse entry recording the mere occurrence of the object. Further details must be encoded if the entry is to be discriminable, and no common code account will exclude them.

Independent tests of dual versus common code theories become very difficult once adequate versions of the theories are permitted. One technique used by Paivio and Csapo (1969) was to present pictures and words at a rate slow enough to allow reading of the words, but fast enough to inhibit naming of the pictures. In comparison with slower rates, pictures suffered on sequential memory tasks, but were superior to words on recognition tasks. Paivio and Csapo argued that this reflected the value of verbal coding for sequential recall, while the richer imaginal code led to better recognition. Other evidence in favour of dual codes has come from the latency to switch between pictures and words when carrying out a semantic categorization task (Harris *et al.*, 1977) and from differential effects of auditory and visual distractor tasks on the retention of pictures and words (Pellegrino *et al.*, 1975; Warren, 1977). There is a paradox in research comparing memory for pictures and words as the basis for deciding between common and dual codes. Comparisons are only possible if pictures of named objects are used. Yet this restricts research to only a small aspect of the visual information with which the imaginal code is supposed to deal. Most scenes cannot be described adequately in words. It would be very risky to generalize from research on pictures of single objects to conclusions on the nature of representation of pictures in general.

On balance, the evidence probably just favours dual code theories, but our knowledge of the nature of memory representation is so sparse that it is easy for saving hypotheses to be constructed to escape the apparent implications of any empirical result. As with the related issue of analogue/propositional coding, the means available to answer the question, and the questions themselves, are not adequately developed and may resist such development. Less grandiose expectations and theories might be more fruitful in the long term.

VII   Conclusions

Chapter 10 began by pointing out that memory depends upon the material to be remembered, the interaction of the properties of the material with the information already stored in the individual's cognitive system, the demands of the task set and the strategies which the person adopts in response to all these other factors. It is easier to form images to some words than to others, and such words are often better remembered. It is reasonable to attribute this better memory to either a strategy of imaging or to images involuntarily elicited by the nature of the material and the task. Some of the results showing better recall of easily imageable words may, however, result from other covarying properties such as the semantic distinctiveness of the words, and/or their concreteness. The strategy of imaging leads to better recognition, and to better recall if items are linked in the images. The interpretation of the place of imagery in these situations depends, as we have said on several occasions, upon one's philosophical position on imagery. Nevertheless, the study of imagery in memory research has played a major part in encouraging the study of subject strategies, mnemonics and other contributions which the conscious actions of the memory make to performance, as well as playing a big part in the study of the influence properties of materials upon their recall.

12
Conclusions and speculations

Whatever your opinion upon the status of mental images, whether you believe them to be playing a central functional part in our cognitions or see them as epiphenomena, we hope that you will agree that the research that we have been able to review in earlier chapters has been interesting and important. Mental images are such a frequent aspect of our conscious experience that it is highly desirable that we come to understand their properties and purposes. We believe that progress in this understanding has been made in recent years, but that the work which has been carried on has been frequently dominated by theoretical assumptions which have restricted the development of research on imagery. For example, the long running dispute over the underlying representation of images has the mark of psychologists trying to run before they can walk. Answers to very fundamental questions are sought when we are ignorant of even the most simple knowledge about mental images such as when they normally occur. Without such information to help resolve and clarify the issues it has always seemed very optimistic to us to believe that questions as abstract as the nature of the representation of images should be answerable. This is not to say that these questions should not be asked; fundamental questions should never be avoided. However, in the hope of resolving the grand and abstract propositional/analogue battle many investigators have been lured away from asking questions about imagery which they might have been able to answer. We hope that as the dust begins to settle that interest in imagery itself rather than its underlying representation may re-emerge so that the properties and the probable functions of imagery can be better understood. Perhaps this book may remind some of its readers of the unanswered questions.

We began by discussing the philosophical and methodological issues associated with imagery. Philosophical questions on the mind–body problem are reflected in attitudes to the functional contributions which mental images may make. Those such as Kosslyn who search for the active place that imagery plays in cognitive processing would, we imagine, be more sympathetic to philosophical accounts such as the identity theory, dual aspect or even interactionism, while those who with Pylyshyn have argued that images cannot be regarded as explanatory concepts are probably more sympathetic to epiphenomenalism. It is not, of course, necessary to be an epi-phenomenalist to hold that mental images do not contribute to cognitive processing, you may believe that images are not causally involved in cognition but that other conscious processes are. You may not be an epiphenomenalist to accept a propositional account, but it probably helps. We suspect that the ease with which the arguments advanced by both sides in the dispute were accepted by their adherents was, in part, bolstered by their philosophical attitudes to imagery. Advocates of propositional theories have contributed very little positive support for their cause, they have usually rested upon attempts to debunk the pictorial models while vaguely outlining what appears to be a logically possible alternative. Advocates of the pictorial positions sometimes seem to accept that the mere co-occurrence of images during some task is enough to demonstrate their functional involvement. Both sides have seemed to have difficulty in quite appreciating the other's position, and, we suspect, this may derive from deeper held philo-sophical attitudes to the mind–body question.

We briefly reviewed arguments for the rejection and counter-arguments in favour of introspection. Since mental imagery cannot be studied without introspections, the rest of the book depended upon an acceptance of introspective data in some situations. We hope that the research that we subsequently reviewed demonstrates that interesting and valuable information can come from subjects' reports of their mental experiences. Many of those who studied mental imagery in the 1960s were worried about the subjective nature of their topic and adapted what they claimed to be operational definitions of imagery. Good criticisms of the use of operational definitions in psychology will be found in Plutchik (1968) and a critique of the post behaviourist "operational" definitions of imagery in Richardson (1980). We hope that the perceived need for "objective" measures of imagery has now withered. The only reliable evidence that someone is having or has had a mental image is their report. This still causes problems, as it will always do in research on imagery. The question of the existence of a special type of imagery called eidetic remains in doubt because the images are experienced by such a small number of people (if they are experienced at all) and because no adequate criteria are available to other people to tell when an image should be classified as eidetic or simply as a memory image. Similarly, some of Kosslyn's research (e.g. Kosslyn, 1978) contains such powerful demand characteristics that sceptics easily reject the results as merely reflecting the compliance of his subjects.

We believe that the dual aspect account of the relationship of conscious experience to physical states is justified in the research which we review. It is not possible to show that images are essential for any cognitive activity because the creation or suppression of mental images independent of other cognitive processing is beyond the means of experimental psychology. However, the accumulation of situations in which mental images reliably occur in forms and occasions which would be perfectly sensible if they did have a functional role, strengthens our suspicion that the sheer coherence and predictability of mental experience makes epiphenomenalism implausible. Yet dualism and some versions of the identity theory remain unsatisfactory alternatives. Dual aspect incorporates the importance of mental experience for the individual with the acceptance of normal physical laws.

In our BOSS-consciousness model we tried to locate the aspects of cognitive processing of which we are conscious. We believe that this provided a suitable framework for the interpretation of the research which we proceeded to review. We are well aware that we have not offered any conclusive evidence to support our model. It remains, at best, a plausible account of the place consciousness occupies in cognition. That is the most that we would hope for it at the present. Proper tests of the theory are perhaps even more hampered by uncertainties over how to model the cognitive system than they are over the difficulties of pinning down what is and what is not consciously experienced. Until one can specify the properties of the systems by which we plan and direct our actions it will not be possible to confirm that consciousness corresponds to information being made available to that system. However, this does not mean that our model should be rejected, but rather that many others remain equally as plausible. It should not be overlooked that the BOSS-consciousness model makes some strong predictions concerning imagery. For instance, one implication of the theory is that BOSS-consciousness becomes less involved in controlling processing as tasks become more practised. This means that interference between processes which largely depend on separate EMPLOYEE systems will diminish to the extent that they require less and less supervision and co-ordination by BOSS programs. Another implication is that imagery will be involved only in high level planning and control and will not play a part in lower level cognition. Images will ''drop out'' from practical processes as BOSS involvement is withdrawn. There are many such predictions from the theory by which its adequacy can be tested. We hope that the book will have been useful, however, to those who find the BOSS-consciousness model implausible. The data remain.

For those who are willing to tolerate the BOSS-consciousness model for a little longer we would like to add these speculations. First, given the BOSS-consciousness account, it is easy to see how philosophers have been attracted to dualism and freedom of the will while behaviourist psychologists have seen no contribution from conscious processes and have preferred determinist accounts which can occasionally approach fatalism. We can conceptualize the relationship of the BOSS, Perceptual EMPLOYEE and Motor EMPLOYEE systems, and the external environment as illustrated by the diagram in Fig. 18. For actions by the person, this can be seen as a cycle (see also Neisser, 1976), with the BOSS plans determining the motor

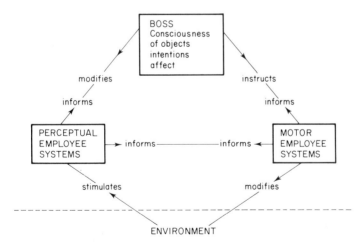

Fig. 18   Where one starts to examine the cycle of BOSS, EMPLOYEES and Environment may influence one's views on dualism and determinism (see text).

programmes, which both modify the environment and set expectations in the perceptual systems. These systems receive stimulation from the environment which is translated and forwarded to BOSS if the input is in a class which normally requires BOSS control. BOSS confirms that the action went as planned and proceeds to future plans. The importance that one places upon conscious experience depends upon where you enter this cycle when considering the relationship of consciousness and actions. To the philosopher such as Descartes the obvious place to start is with the BOSS activity of thinking. It then appears that conscious intentions and acts of will are followed by bodily actions, controlled by the motor components to which we do not have conscious access. We consciously perceive success or failure in our acting upon the world. The result is to place a high value on BOSS operations, to have problems in knowing how the conscious experiences lead to the bodily movements controlled by the motor EMPLOYEE systems, and to postulate some form of dualism. On the other hand, the psychologist who has come to think in terms of stimulus and response or input and output begins the analysis where the environment inputs to the perceptual EMPLOYEES. The BOSS activity is just one part of the chain of internal processing which is difficult to observe and model, but which normally seems to be consistent and predictable. The same types of responses follow the same sorts of stimuli. Consciousness is difficult to observe, impossible to imagine as a causal factor, and consequently likely to be played down and often ignored. If the full cycle is recognized, and if we are correct about the nature of consciousness, then it becomes easier to understand why both the dualist philosopher's and the behaviourist psychologist's accounts can be essentially correct, apparently contra-dictory, and sometimes misleading. No starting point within the cycle is preferable to another and while conscious experience is important, since it reflects the cognitive processing, it does not mysteriously modify that processing, so that it is not necessary to understand it to give an adequate account of the person's cognitive activities.

The second speculation is that the distinction between learning and memory may approximate to the activities of EMPLOYEE and BOSS systems respectively. The concept of learning has been central to experimental psychology since its inception, and relates to any modification in the system as the result of experience. In the last twenty years, however, the concept of memory has been dominant in certain areas of psychology, and with it the metaphors of encoding, storage and retrieval of information. The difference between learning and remembering is that the former assumes a modification of the system at the time learning took place, but requires no special processes when that learning is put into practice; however, remembering assumes the finding of the stored memory among many others, and its re-activation. Some psychologists, too deeply steeped in the memory framework, have sometimes carried the memory model over from the recall of past events, where it seems appropriate, to perceptual and motor processes, where it is probably quite inappropriate. The result is that perceiving is sometimes assumed to involve a search for memories applicable to the experience being processed, and responding is conceived as requiring the search for a similarly applicable motor programme. So, for example, Gregory (1972) argued that ". . . perceptions are constructed by complex brain processes from fleeting fragmentary scraps of data signaled by the senses and drawn from the brain's memory banks . . ." (p.707). Bransford *et al.* (1978) discuss in detail the limitations of "memory" models. Here is not the appropriate place to discuss models of learning and remembering. However, we suspect that it will not be possible to capture both our ability to recall memories, e.g. vivid mental images of past events and our continuous updating of our expectations and responses (e.g. to fashions) within one type of learning process. Rather, we suspect, the updating of appropriate responses and the discrimination and attuning that are fundamental to learning will be mainly properties of the EMPLOYEE systems, while the conscious re-creation of past experience which is what is normally meant by "memory" will be associated with BOSS functioning. Learning will take place for BOSS processes, but the phenomena of memory will be mainly restricted to BOSS. So, the recreation of past experience, while existing to aid the comprehension and control of complex situations, because of its association with consciousness can take on an apparent independence of its own. Then, novelists such as Proust may explore its details, and can even give the impression that recollection in tranquillity is the purpose of memory.

Turning to research on types of imagery we have already stated our hope that the facts about imagery will receive rather more attention in the future. There is scope for considerable research on most forms of imaging which could supply more reliable data than any survey or collection of anecdotes.

It is unfortunate that imagery offers such scope for disagreement, speculation and even exploitation as have been connected with studies of dreaming or attempts at psychotherapy *via* imagery. Shorr *et al.* (1980), for example, provide a collection of papers describing the use of imagery in psychotherapy. Such studies are clearly well intentioned and may provide as much opportunity for the participants to talk about their problems as any other. However, they reveal confidence in the therapist's ability to interpret images and in the assumed motivational control over imagery which leaves considerable scope for the sceptic. The following is just one example of image interpretation from a study of imagery during biofeedback:

> The process of repeatedly submerging into an altered state of consciousness is graphically described in this image reported by Jeff "A guy in a swimming pool, pushed around on a float, and being dunked time after time". (Oliver *et al.*, 1980, p.136).

Possibly, no doubt, but . . .!

The study of the dimensions of imagery is one which remains intriguing. There is no doubt that psychologists have shared with other people a tendency to attribute performance to enduring dispositions when the evidence suggests that much behaviour is situation specific (Nisbett and Ross, 1980). Nevertheless, it is usually possible when discussing the occurrence of imagery during, say, reading a novel, with a group of people to find that some claim to "see" the events and cannot imagine what reading would be like if they did not, while others find the notion of such a mental theatre peculiar. We still believe that there are individual differences in the habitual use of imagery which have been overlooked partly because of the emphasis on vividness, which need have nothing to do with image frequency and is in any case difficult to quantify, and the use of tasks in which all but those who have a pathological failure in their imagery systems will turn to imagery. It is to tasks where imagery may be an optional choice that one should look for individual differences.

Chapters 10 and 11 confirmed that the contribution of imagery to the remembering of verbal material is well established. We hope that the future may provide more information upon the recall of images themselves. To many people, the re-arousal of the mental images associated with a place, sound, smell or such like is one of the most fascinating aspects of their memories. While general principles about memory encoding and retrieval can provide a general explanation of these memories, there are probably special features to be illuminated by direct research. For example, we suspect that there is no equivalent common recurrence of special words or sentences to be the verbal equivalent of spontaneous memory images, although memories of songs or rhymes may be similar.

Throughout our survey of imagery we have been aware of two competing tendencies. One is to dismiss imagery as irrelevant, an epiphenomenon with no purpose or place in cognition, the other is to ascribe to imagery properties and powers which it could not possibly possess. The former position is, of course, represented in the propositional account of the basis of imagery, but it has been present in the philosophy of behaviourism and sometimes seems to underlie the writings of reviewers who have been overimpressed by some experimental failures in imagery research (e.g. Wingfield and Byrnes, 1981). The other position has appeared in the writings of some philosophers of knowledge, been carried into psychology by Titchener and others, and appears in some experimental reports including, for example, the imagery explanation of the symbolic distance effect. We hope that if the topic of mental imagery is examined without too many pre-suppositions, beyond that it is an interesting phenomenon, the true place of imagery will gradually become apparent. We hope that this book has helped to find a place for imagery and to put imagery in its place.

References

Ahsen, A. (1977). Eidetics: An Overview. *Journal of Mental Imagery* **1**, 5–38.

Allport, D. A. (1979). Conscious and unconscious cognition: A computational metaphor for the mechanism of attention and integration. In L. G. Nilsson (ed.) *Perspectives on Memory Research*. Hillsdale N.J.: Lawrence Erlbaum.

Allport, D. A. (1980). Attention and performance. In G. Claxton (ed.) *Cognitive Psychology: New Directions*. London: Routledge and Kegan Paul.

Allport, G. W. (1924). Eidetic imagery. *British Journal of Psychology* **15**, 99–110.

Anderson, J. R. (1976). *Language, Memory and Thought*. Hillsdale N.J.: Lawrence Erlbaum.

Anderson, J. R. (1978). Arguments concerning representations for mental imagery. *Psychological Review* **85**, 249–277.

Anderson, J. R. and Bower, G. H. (1973). *Human Associative Memory*. Washington: Winston.

Anderson, J. R. and Paulson, R. (1978). Interference in memory for pictorial information. *Cognitive Psychology* **10**, 178–202.

Andreoff, G. R. and Yarmey, A. D. (1976). Bizarre imagery and associative learning: A confirmation. *Perceptual and Motor Skills* **43**, 143–148.

Anisfield, M. and Knapp, M. (1968). Association, synonymity and directionality in false recognition. *Journal of Experimental Psychology* **77**, 171–179.

Annett, J. (1981). Action, language and imagination. *Bulletin of the British Psychological Society* **35**, 211.

Antaki, C. (1981). *The Psychology of Ordinary Explanations of Social Behaviour*. London and New York: Academic Press.

Antrobus, J. S., Antrobus, J. S., and Singer, J. C. (1964). Eye movements accompanying daydreaming, visual imagery and thought suppression. *Journal of Abnormal and Social Psychology* **69**, 244–252.

Armstrong, D. M. (1968). *A Materialist Theory of the Mind*. London: Routledge and Kegan Paul.

300

Arnheim, R. (1969). *Visual Thinking*. Berkeley: University of California Press.

Asch, S. E. (1956). Studies of independence and submission to group pressure. 1. A minority of one against a unanimous majority. *Psychological Monographs*, Vol. 7, Series No. 416.

Aserinsky, E. and Kleitman, N. (1953). Regularly occurring periods of eye mobility and cocomitant phenomena during sleep. *Science* **118**, 273–274.

Ashton, R. (1979). Eidetic imagery and stimulus control. *Behavioral and Brain Sciences* **2**, 596.

Ashton, R. and White, K. D. (1980). Sex differences in imagery vividness: An artifact of the test. *British Journal of Psychology* **71**, 35–38.

Atkinson, R. C. and Raugh, M. R. (1975). An application of the mnemonic keyword method to the acquisition of a Russian vocabulary. *Journal of Experimental Psychology: Human Learning and Memory* **1**, 126–133.

Atkinson, R. C. and Shiffrin, R. M. (1968). Human memory: a proposed system and its control processes. In K. W. Spence and J. T. Spence (eds.) *The Psychology of Learning and Motivation: Advances in Research and Theory*, Vol. 2. London and New York: Academic Press.

Atwood, G. E. (1971). An experimental study of visual imagination and memory. *Cognitive Psychology* **2**, 290–299.

Baddeley, A. D. (1976). *The Psychology of Memory*. London: Harper.

Baddeley, A. D. (1978). The trouble with levels: A reexamination of Craik and Lockhart's framework for memory research. *Psychological Review* **85**, 139–152.

Baddeley, A. D. and Hitch, G. (1974). Working memory. In G. H. Bower (ed.) *The Psychology of Learning and Motivation*, Vol. 8. New York and London: Academic Press.

Baddeley, A. D. and Lieberman, K. (1980). Spatial working memory. In R. S. Nickerson (ed.) *Attention and Performance VIII*. Hillsdale, N.J.: Lawrence Erlbaum.

Baddeley, A. D., Grant, S., Wight, E. and Thomson, N. (1974). Imagery and visual working memory. In P. M. A. Rabbitt and S. Dornic (eds.) *Attention and Performance*, Vol. V. London and New York: Academic Press.

Bahrick, H. P. and Boucher, B. (1968). Retention of visual and verbal codes of the same stimuli. *Journal of Experimental Psychology* **78**, 417–422.

Bandura, A. (1969). *Principles of Behavior Modification*. New York: Prentice Hall.

Banks, W. P. and Flora, J. (1977). Semantic and perceptual processes in symbolic comparisons. *Journal of Experimental Psychology: Human Perception and Performance* **3**, 278–290.

Banks, W. P., Clark, H. H. and Lucy, P. (1975). The locus of the semantic congruity in comparative judgements. *Journal of Experimental Psychology: Human Perception and Performance* **1**, 35–47.

Banks, W. P., Fujii, M. and Kayra-Stuart, F. (1976). Semantic congruity effects in comparative judgements of magnitudes of digits. *Journal of Experimental Psychology: Human Perception and Performance* **2**, 435–447.

Banks, W. P., Yu, H. and Lippincott, W. (1978). Semantic coding in comparative judgements of serial order. Unpublished manuscript, Claremont College.

Barber, T. X. (1971). Imagery and "hallucinations": Effects of LSD contrasted with the effects of "hypnotic" suggestions. In S. J. Segal (ed.) *Imagery: Current Cognitive Approaches.* New York and London: Academic Press.

Barrat, P. E. (1956). Use of the E.E.G. in the study of imagery. *British Journal of Psychology* **47**, 101–114.

Bartlett, F. C. (1932). *Remembering.* Cambridge: Cambridge University Press.

Bartram, D. J. (1978). Post-iconic visual storage: chunking in the reproduction of briefly displayed patterns. *Cognitive Psychology* **10**, 324–355.

Beaumont, G. (Ed.) (1982). *Divided Visual Field Studies of Cerebral Organization.* London and New York: Academic Press.

Beech, J. R. (1976). The limitation of wholistic visualisation. *Perceptual and Motor Skills* **42**, 1271–1275.

Beech, J. R. (1977). Wholistic visualisation: a comparison of techniques. Paper presented at the B.P.S. Annual Conference, University of Exeter.

Beech, J. R. (1978). Image scanning: more problems for a pure propositional interpretation. Paper presented at the B.P.S. Annual Conference, University of York.

Beech, J. R. (1979). *The Scanning of Visual Images.* Unpublished PhD thesis, New University of Ulster, Coleraine.

Beech, J. R. and Allport, D. A. (1978). Visualisation of compound scenes. *Perception* **7**, 129–138.

Begg, I. (1972). Recall of meaningful phrases. *Journal of Verbal Learning and Verbal Behavior* **11**, 431–439.

Begg, I. and Paivio, A. (1969). Concreteness and imagery in sentence learning *Journal of Verbal Learning and Verbal Behavior* **8**, 821–827.

Bellezza, F. S. (1981). Mnemonic devices: Classification, characteristics and criteria. *Review of Educational Research* **51**, 247–275.

Bennett, B. (1976). *The Invisible Features: an Exploration of Children's Difficulties in Solving Figural Relation Problems, namely Matrices.* Unpublished M.A. Project.

Bennett, G. K., Seashore, M. and Wesman, A. G. (1947). *Differential Aptitude Tests.* New York: The Psychological Corporation.

Berger, R. J. (1969). Oculomotor control: A possible function of REM sleep. *Psychological Review* **76**, 144–164.

Berger, R. J. and Oswald, I. (1962). Eye movements during active and passive dreams. *Science* **137**, 601.

Betts, G. H. (1909). *The Distribution and Functions of Mental Imagery.* New York: Teachers College, University of Columbia.

Bexton, W. H., Heron, W. and Scott, T. H. (1954). Effects of decreased variation in the sensory environment. *Canadian Journal of Psychology* **8**, 70–76.

Binet, A. (1966). Mnemonic virtuosity: a study of chess players. *Genetic Psychology Monographs* **74**, 127–162. (Translated by M. L. Simmel and S. B. Barron.)

Bolton, N. (1972). *The Psychology of Thinking*. London: Methuen.

Boring, E. G. (1942). *Sensation and Perception in the History of Experimental Psychology*, New York: Appleton-Century.

Boring, E. G. (1946). Mind and mechanism. *American Journal of Psychology* **59**, 173–192.

Bower, G. H. (1970). Imagery as a relational organiser in associative learning. *Journal of Verbal Learning and Verbal Behavior* **9**, 529–533.

Bower, G. H. (1972). Mental imagery and associative learning. In L. W. Gregg (ed.) *Cognition in Learning and Memory*. New York: Wiley.

Bower, G. H. (1973). How to . . . Uh . . . Remember! *Psychology Today* **7**, 63–70.

Bower, G. H. and Clark, M. C. (1969). Narrative stories as mediators for serial learning. *Psychonomic Science* **14**, 181–182.

Bower, G. H. and Karlin, M. B. (1974). Depth of processing pictures of faces and recognition memory. *Journal of Experimental Psychology* **103**, 751–757.

Bower, G. H. and Reitman, J. S. (1972). Mnemonic elaboration in multilist learning. *Journal of Verbal Learning and Verbal Behavior* **11**, 478–485.

Bower, G. H. and Winzenz, D. (1970). Comparison of associative learning strategies. *Psychonomic Science* **20**, 119–120.

Bradshaw, J. L. and Nettleton, N. C. (1981). The nature of hemispheric specialization in man. *Behavioral and Brain Sciences* **4**, 51–91.

Bransford, J. D., Barclay, J. R. and Franks, J. J. (1972). Sentence memory: A constructive versus interpretive approach. *Cognitive Psychology* **3**, 193–209.

Bransford, J. D., McCarrell, N. S., Franks, J. J. and Nitsch, K. E. (1977). Toward unexplaining memory. In R. Shaw and J. Bransford (eds.) *Perceiving, Acting and Knowing*, Hillsdale, N.J.: Lawrence Erlbaum.

Bransford, J. D., Franks, J. J., Morris, C. D. and Stein, B. S. (1979). Some general constraints on learning and memory research. In L. S. Cermak and F. I. M. Craik (eds.) *Levels of Processing in Human Memory*. Hillsdale, N.J.: Lawrence Erlbaum.

Broadbent, D. E. (1958). *Perception and Communication*. London: Pergamon.

Broadbent, D. E. (1977). Levels, hierarchies and the locus of control. *Quarterly Journal of Experimental Psychology* **29**, 181–201.

Brooks, L. (1967). The suppression of visualisation by reading. *Quarterly Journal of Experimental Psychology* **19**, 280–299.

Brooks, L. (1968). Spatial and verbal components of the act of recall. *Canadian Journal of Psychology* **22**, 349–368.

Brown J. (1958). Some tests of the decay theory of immediate memory. *Quarterly Journal of Experimental Psychology* **10**, 12–21.

Buckley, P. B. and Gillman, C. B. (1974). Comparisons of digits and dot patterns. *Journal of Experimental Psychology: General* **108**, 1131–1136.

Bugelski, B. R. (1970). Words and things and images. *American Psychologist* **25**, 1002–1012.

Bugelski, B. R., Kidd, E. and Segmen, J. (1968). Image as a mediator in one trial paired-associate learning. *Journal of Experimental Psychology* **76**, 69–73.

Bull, R. and Clifford, B. (1979). Eyewitness memory. In Gruneberg, M. M. and Morris, P. E. (eds.) *Applied Problems in Memory*. London and New York: Academic Press.

Butter, M. J. (1970). Differential recall of paired-associates as a function of arousal and concreteness-imagery levels. *Journal of Experimental Psychology* **84**, 252–256.

Butter, M. J. and Palmer, O. S. (1970). Effects of imagery on paired-associate recall as a function of retention interval, list length and trials. *Journal of Verbal Learning and Verbal Behavior* **9**, 716–719.

Byrne, B. (1974). Item concreteness vs. spatial organisation as predictors of visual imagery. *Memory and Cognition* **2**, 53–59.

Cautela, J. R. (1970). Covert reinforcement. *Behavior Therapy* **1**, 33–50.

Cautela, J. R. (1971). Covert extinction. *Behavior Therapy* **2**, 192–200.

Cautela, J. R. (1973). Covert processes and behavior modification. *Journal of Nervous and Mental Disease* **157**, 27–36.

Cautela, J. R. (1977). Covert conditioning, assumptions and procedures. *Journal of Mental Imagery* **1**, 53–64.

Chapman, L. J. and Chapman, J. D. (1959). Atmosphere effect re-examined. *Journal of Experimental Psychology* **58**, 220–226.

Chase, W. G. and Simon, H. A. (1973). Perception in chess. *Cognitive Psychology* **4**, 55–81.

Christian, J., Bickley, W., Tarka, M. and Clayton, K. (1978). Measures of free recall of 900 English nouns: Correlations with imagery, concreteness, meaningfulness and frequency. *Memory and Cognition* **6**, 379–390.

Chowdhury, K. R. and Vernon, P. E. (1964). An experimental study of imagery and its relation to abilities and interests. *British Journal of Psychology* **55**, 355–364.

Clark, H. H. (1969). Linguistic processes in deductive reasoning *Psychological Review* **76**, 387–404.

Clark, H. H., Carpenter, P. A. and Just, M. A. (1973). On the meeting of semantics and perception. In W. G. Chase (ed.) *Visual Information Processing*. New York and London: Academic Press.

Clifford, B. R. and Scott, J. (1978). Individual and situational factors in eyewitness testimony. *Journal of Applied Psychology* **63**, 352–359.

Cohen, G. (1977). *The Psychology of Cognition*. London and New York: Academic Press.

Cohen, D. B. (1979). *Sleep and Dreaming: Origins, Nature and Functions*. Oxford: Pergamon.

Colman, F. and Paivio, A. (1970). Pupillary dilation and mediation processes during paired-associate learning. *Canadian Journal of Psychology* **24**, 261–270.

Coltheart, M. (1980). Iconic memory and visible persistence. *Perception and Psychophysics* **27**, 183–228.

Coltheart, M. and Glick, M. J. (1974). Visual imagery: a case study. *Quarterly Journal of Experimental Psychology* **26**, 438–453.

Conrad, C. (1974). Context effects in sentence comprehension: A study of the objective lexicon. *Memory and Cognition* **2**, 130–138.

Cooper, L. A. (1975). Mental rotation of random two-dimensional shapes. *Cognitive Psychology* **7**, 20–43.

Cooper, L. A. and Podgormy, P. (1976). Mental transformations and visual comparison processes: effects of complexity and similarity. *Journal of Experimental Psychology: Human Perception and Performance* **2**, 503–514.

Cooper, L. A. and Shepard, R. N. (1973). Chronometric studies of the rotation of mental images. In W. G. Chase (ed.) *Visual Information Processing*. New York and London: Academic Press.

Cooper, L. A. and Shepard, R. N. (1975). Mental transformation in the identification of right and left hands. *Journal of Experimental Psychology: Human Perception and Performance* **1**, 48–56.

Cornsweet, T. N. (1970). *Visual Perception*. New York and London: Academic Press.

Corteen, R. S. and Wood, B. (1972). Autonomic responses to shock-associated words in an unattended channel. *Journal of Experimental Psychology* **94**, 308–313.

Craik, K. (1943). *The Nature of Explanation*. Cambridge: Cambridge University Press.

Craik, K. J. W. (1966). *The Nature of Psychology*. Cambridge: Cambridge University Press.

Craik, F. I. M. and Lockhart, R. S. (1972). Levels of processing: A framework for memory research. *Journal of Verbal Learning and Verbal Behavior* **11**, 671–684.

Craik, F. I. M. and Tulving, E. (1975). Depth of processing and the retention of words in episodic memory. *Journal of Experimental Psychology: General* **104**, 268–294.

Curtis, D. W., Paulos, M. A. and Rule, S. J. (1973). Relation between disjunctive reaction time and stimulus differences. *Journal of Experimental Psychology* **99**, 167–173.

Dale, H. C. A. (1973). Short term memory for visual information. *British Journal of Psychology* **64**, 1–8.

Day, R. H. (1958). On interocular transfer and the central origin of visual after-effects. *American Journal of Psychology* **71**, 784–790.

Deffenbacher, K. A., Brown, E. L. and Sturgill, W. (1978). Some predictors of eyewitness memory accuracy. In M. M. Gruneberg, P. E. Morris and R. N. Sykes (eds.) *Practical Aspects of Memory*. London and New York: Academic Press.

De Groot, A. D. (1965). *Thought and Choice in Chess*. New York: Basic Books.

Delin, P. S. (1969). Learning and retention of English words with successive approximations to a complex mnemonic instruction. *Psychonomic Science* **17**, 87–89.

Dennett, D. C. (1979). *Brainstorms*. Sussex: Harvester.

Dement, W. C. (1960). The effect of dream deprivation. *Science* **131**, 1705–1707.

Dement, W. and Kleitman, N. (1957). The relationship of eyemovements during sleep to dream activity: an objective method for the study of dreaming. *Journal of Experimental Psychology* **53**, 339–346.

De Soto, C. B., London, M. and Handel, S. (1965). Social reasoning and spatial paralogic. *Journal of Personality and Social Psychology* **2**, 513–521.

Di Vesta, F. J., Ingersoll, G. and Sunshine, P. A. (1971). A factor analysis of imagery tests. *Journal of Verbal Learning and Verbal Behaviour* **10**, 471–479.

Dixon, N. F. and Henley, S. H. A. (1980). Without awareness. In M. Jeeves (ed.) *Psychology Survey No. 3*. London: Allen and Unwin.

Dodd, D. H. and White, R. M. (1980). *Cognition: Mental Structures and Processes*. Boston: Allyn and Bacon.

Donaldson, M. (1963). *A Study of Children's Thinking*. London: Tavistock.

Doob, L. W. (1965). Exploring eidetic imagery among the Kamba of Central Kenya. *Journal of Social Psychology* **67**, 3–22.

Downs, R. M. and Stea, D. (eds.) (1973). *Image and Environment*. Chicago: Aldive.

Downs, R. M. and Stea, D. (1977). *Maps in Minds: Reflections on Cognitive Mapping*. New York: Harper and Row.

Durndell, A. J. and Wetherick, N. E. (1976). The relation of reported imagery tests to cognitive performance. *British Journal of Psychology* **67**, 501–506.

Eddy, A. L. and Glass, J. K. (1981). Reading and listening to high and low imagery sentences. *Journal of Verbal Learning and Verbal Behavior* **20**, 333–345.

Ericsson, K. A. and Simon, H. A. (1980). Verbal reports as data. *Psychological Review* **87**, 215–251.

Ernest, C. H. (1976). Verbal and non-verbal processing systems in high and low imagers: a study of system differentiation. Study in progress, 1976 (cited in Ernest, 1977).

Ernest, C. H. (1977). Imagery ability and cognition: a critical review. *Journal of Mental Imagery* **2**, 181–216.

Ernest, C. H. (1979). Visual imagery ability and the recognition of verbal and non-verbal stimuli. *Acta Psychologica* **43**, 253–269.

Ernest, C. H. and Paivio, A. (1971). Imagery and sex differences in incidental recall. *British Journal of Psychology* **62**, 67–72.

Evans, C. R. and Newman, E. A. (1964). Dreaming: An analogy from computers. *New Scientist* **24**, 577–579.

Evans, J. St. B. T. (1980a). Introspective reports of cognitive processes: A critique. *Bulletin of the British Psychological Society* **33**, 32–33.

Evans, J. St. B. T. (1980b). Thinking: Experimental and information processing approaches. In G. Claxton (ed.) *Cognitive Psychology: New Directions*. London: Routledge and Kegan Paul.

Evans, J. St. B. T. (1980c). Current issues in the psychology of reasoning. *British Journal of Psychology* **71**, 227–239.

Evans, J. St. B. T. and Wason, P. C. (1976). Rationalization in a reasoning task. *British Journal of Psychology* **67**, 479–486.

Eysenck, M. W. (1977). *Human Memory: Theory, Research and Individual Differences*. Oxford: Pergamon Press.

Eysenck, M. W. and Eysenck, C. (1979). Processing depth, elaboration of encoding, memory stores and expended processing capacity. *Journal of Experimental Psychology, Human Learning and Memory* **5**, 472–484.

Falk, G. (1972). Interpretation of imperfect line data as a 3-dimensional scene. *Artificial Intelligence* **3**, 101–144.

Fernald, M. R. (1912). The diagnosis of mental imagery. *Psychological Monographs*, No. 58.

Fillenbaum, S. (1969). Words as feature complexes: False recognition of antonyms and synonyms. *Journal of Experimental Psychology* **82**, 400–402.

Finke, R. A. (1979). The functional equivalence of mental images and errors of movement. *Cognitive Psychology* **11**, 235–264.

Finke, R. A. (1980). Levels of equivalence in imagery and perception. *Psychological Review* **87**, 113–132.

Finke, R. A. and Kosslyn, S. M. (1980). Mental imagery acuity in the peripheral visual field. *Journal of Experimental Psychology: Human Perception and Performance* **6**, 126–139.

Finke, R. A. and Schmidt, M. J. (1977). Orientation-specific color after effects following imagination. *Journal of Experimental Psychology, Human Perception and Performance* **3**, 599–606.

Finke, R. A. and Schmidt, M. J. (1978). The quantitative measure of pattern representation in images using orientation-specific color after effects. *Perception and Psychophysics* **23**, 515–520.

Fishbein, W. and Gutwein, B. M. (1977). Paradoxical sleep and memory storage processes. *Behavioural Biology* **19**, 425–464.

Forisha, B. L. (1978). Mental imagery and creativity. *Journal of Mental Imagery* **2**, 209–238.

Forisha, B. L. (1981). Creativity and mental imagery in men and women. *Journal of Mental Imagery* **5**, 85–96.

Forster, P. M. and Govier, E. (1978). Discrimination without awareness? *Quarterly Journal of Experimental Psychology* **30**, 282–295.

Foth, D. L. (1973). Mnemonic technique effectiveness as a function of word abstractness and mediation instructions. *Journal of Verbal Learning and Verbal Behavior* **12**, 239–245.

Foulkes, D. (1962). Dream reports from different stages of sleep. *Journal of Abnormal and Social Psychology* **65**, 14–25.

Foulkes, D., Spear, P. S. and Symonds, J. D. (1966). Individual differences in mental activity at sleep onset. *Journal of Abnormal Psychology* **71**, 280–286.

Freud, S. (1900). *The Interpretation of Dreams*. New York: Avon (1965).

Freud, S. (1927). *The Ego and the Id*. Republished. New York: Norton, 1960.

Freud, S. (1949). *Collected Papers*. New York: Basic Books.

Friedman, A. (1978). Memorial comparisons without the "mind's eye". *Journal of Verbal Learning and Verbal Behavior* **17**, 427–444.

Frincke, G. (1968). Word characteristics, associative-relatedness, and the free-recall of nouns. *Journal of Verbal Learning and Verbal Behavior* **7**, 366–372.

Galbraith, R. C. and Underwood, B. J. (1973). Perceived frequency of concrete and abstract words. *Memory and Cognition* **1**, 56–60.

Gale, A., Morris, P. E., Lucas, B. and Richardson, A. (1972). Types of imagery and imagery types: an E.E.G. study. *British Journal of Psychology* **63**, 523–531.

Galton, F. (1883). *Inquiries into Human Faculty*. London: Dent.

Gauld, A. and Shotter, J. (1977). *Human Action and its Psychological Investigation*. London: Routledge and Kegan Paul.

Gazzaniga, M. S. (1970). *The Bisected Brain*. New York: Appleton-Century-Crofts.

Gazzaniga, M. S. and Le Doux, J. E. (1978). *The Integrated Mind*. New York: Plenum.

Gazzaniga, M. S., Bogen, J. E. and Spery, R. W. (1962). Some functional effects of sectioning the cerebral commisures in man. *Proceedings of the National Academy of Science, U.S.A.* **48**, 1765–1769.

Gengerilli, J. A. (1930). Some quantitative experiments with eidetic imagery. *American Journal of Psychology* **42**, 399–404.

Ghatala, E. S. and Levin, J. R. (1976). Phenomenal background frequency and the concreteness/imagery effect in verbal discrimination learning. *Memory and Cognition* **41**, 302–306.

Ghiselin, B. (1952). *The Creative Process*. Berkeley: University of California Press.

Gibson, J. J. (1966). *The Senses considered as Perceptual Systems*. Boston: Houghton Mifflin.

Gilham, W. E. C. (1978). Measurement constructs and psychological structure. In A. Burton and J. Radford (eds.) *Thinking in Perspective*. London: Methuen.

Golann, S. E. (1963). The psychological study of creativity. *Psychological Bulletin* **60**, 548–565.

Gilhooly, K. J. and Gilhooly, M. L. (1979). Age of acquisition effects in lexical and episodic memory tasks. *Memory and Cognition* **7**, 214–233.

Glass, A. L., Eddy, J. K. and Schwanerflugel, P. J. (1980). The verification of high and low imagery sentences. *Journal of Experimental Psychology: Human Learning and Memory* **6**, 692–704.

Glaze, J. A. (1928). The association value of nonsense syllables. *Journal of Genetic Psychology* **35**, 255–267.

Goldstein, A. G. and Chance, J. E. (1971). Recognition of complex visual stimuli. *Perception and Psychophysics* **9**, 237–241.

Golla, F. L. and Antovitch, S. (1929). The respiratory rhythm in its relation to the mechanism of thought. *Brain* **52**, 491–509.

Golla, F. L., Hutton, E. L. and Walker, W. G. (1943). The objective study of mental imagery. 1. Physiological concomitants. *Journal of Mental Science* **89**, 216-223.

Goodenough, D. R., Shapiro, A., Holden, M. and Steinschriber, L. (1959). A comparison of 'Dreamers' and 'Nondreamers'. *Journal of Abnormal Social Psychology* **59**, 295-302.

Gordon, R. A. (1949). An investigation into some of the factors that favour the formation of stereotyped images. *British Journal of Psychology* **39**, 156-157.

Gordon, R. A. (1950). An experiment correlating the nature of imagery with performance on a test of reversal of perspective. *British Journal of Psychology* **41**, 63-67.

Gralton, M. A., Hayes, Y. A. and Richardson, J. T. E. (1979). Introversion extraversion and mental imagery. *Journal of Mental Imagery* **3**, 1-10.

Gregg, V. (1976). Word frequency, recognition and recall. In J. Brown (ed.) *Recall and Recognition*. London: Wiley.

Gregory, R. L. (1972). Seeing as thinking: An active theory of perception. *The Times Literary Supplement* 707-708.

Gregory, R. L. (1973). The confounded eye. In R. L. Gregory and E. H. Gambrick (eds.) *Illusion in Nature and Art*. London: Duckworth.

Griffith, D. (1981). An evaluation of the keyword technique for the acquisition of Korean vocabulary by military personnel. *Bulletin of the Psychonomic Society* **17**, 12-14.

Groniger, L. D. (1971). Mnemonic imagery and forgetting. *Psychonomic Science* **23**, 161-163.

Gross, J., Byrne, J. and Fischer, C. (1965). Eye movements during emergent stage I: E.E.G. in subjects with lifelong blindness. *Journal of Nervous and Mental Disease* **141**, 365-370.

Grosser, G. S. and Siegal, A. W. (1971). Emergence of a tonic-phasic model for sleep and dreaming: Behavioral and physiological observations *Psychological Bulletin* **75**, 60-72.

Grossman, L. and Eagle, M. (1970). Synonymity, antonymity and association in false recognition responses. *Journal of Experimental Psychology* **83**, 244-248.

Guilford, J. P. (1950). Creativity. *American Psychologist* **5**, 444-454.

Guilford, J. P. (1967). *The Nature of Human Intelligence*. New York: McGraw Hill.

Gurney, E. (1886). *Phantasms of the Living*. London: Society for Psychical Research.

Haber, R. N. (1979). Twenty years of haunting eidetic imagery: Where is the ghost? *Behavioral and Brain Sciences* **2**, 583-629.

Haber, R. N. and Haber, R. B. (1964). Eidetic imagery I: Frequency. *Perceptual and Motor Skills* **19**, 131-138.

Haber, R. N. and Standing, L. G. (1969). Direct measures of short-term visual storage. *Quarterly Journal of Experimental Psychology* **21**, 43-54.

Hale, S. M. and Simpson, H. M. (1970). Effects of eye movements on the rate of discovery and vividness of visual images. *Perception and Psychophysics* **9**, 242–246.

Hampson, P. J. (1979). *The Role of Imagery in Cognition*. Unpublished PhD thesis, University of Lancaster.

Hampson, P. J. and Morris, P. E. (1977). Distance effects in visual images: evidence for scanning. *IRCS Medical Science: Psychology and Psychiatry* **5**, 455.

Hampson, P. J. and Morris, P. E. (1978a). Unfulfilled expectations: a criticism of Neisser's theory of imagery. *Cognition* **6**, 79–85.

Hampson, P. J. and Morris, P. E. (1978b). Some properties of the visual imagery system investigated through backward spelling. *Quarterly Journal of Experimental Psychology* **30**, 655–664.

Hanawalt, N. G. (1954). Recurrent images: New instances and a summary of the older ones. *American Journal of Psychology* **67**, 170–174.

Hanney, A. (1971). *Mental Images: A Defence*. London: Allen and Unwin.

Handel, S., De Soto, C. B. and London, M. (1968). Reasoning and spatial representation. *Journal of Verbal Learning and Verbal Behavior* **7**, 351–357.

Hargreaves, D. J. and Bolton, N. (1972). Selecting creativity tests for use in research. *British Journal of Psychology* **63**, 451–462.

Harré, R. (1979). *Social Being: A theory for Social Psychology*. Oxford: Blackwell.

Harris, P. (1978). Developmental aspects of children's memory. In M. M. Gruneberg and P. Morris (eds.) *Aspects of Memory*. London: Methuen.

Harris, P., Morris, P. E. and Basset, L. (1977). Classifying pictures and words: Implications for the dual coding hypothesis. *Memory and Cognition* **5**, 242–246.

Harvey, N. and Greer, K. (1980). Actions: the mechanisms of motor control. In Claxton, G. (ed.) *Cognitive Psychology: New Directions*. London: Routledge and Kegan Paul.

Hasher, L. and Zacks, R. T. (1979). Automatic and effortful processes in memory. *Journal of Experimental Psychology: General* **108**, 356–388.

Hayes, J. R. (1973). On the function of visual imagery in elementary mathematics. In W. G. Chase (ed.) *Visual Information Processing*. New York and London: Academic Press.

Hebb, D. O. (1949). *The Organisation of Behavior*. New York: John Wiley.

Henderson, S. E. (1975). Predicting the accuracy of a throw without visual feedback. *Journal of Human Movement Studies* **1**, 183–189.

Henley, S. H. A. (1976). Responses to homophones as a function of cue words on the unattended channel. *British Journal of Psychology* **67**, 559–567.

Heron, W. (1961). Cognitive and physiological effects of perceptual isolation. In P. Soloman *et al.* (eds.) *Sensory Deprivation*. Cambridge, Mass.: Harvard University Press.

Higbee, K. L. (1977). *Your Memory: How it works and how to improve it*. Englewood Cliffs, N.J.: Prentice Hall.

Hilgard, E. R., Atkinson, R. L. and Atkinson, R. C. (1979). *Introduction to Psychology* (7th Edition). New York: Harcourt Brace and Jovanovich.

Hiscock, M. and Cohen, D. B. (1973). Visual imagery and dream recall. *Journal of Research in Personality* **7**, 179–188.

Hitch, G. J. (1980). Developing the concept of working memory. In G. Claxton (ed.) *Cognitive Psychology: New Directions*. London: Routledge and Kegan Paul.

Hochberg, J. E. (1964). *Perception*. Englewood Cliffs, N.J.: Prentice Hall.

Hochberg, J. and Gellman, L. (1977). The effect of landmark features on "mental rotation" times. *Memory and Cognition* **5**, 23–26.

Holt, R. R. (1972). On the nature and generality of mental imagery. In P. W. Sheehan (ed.) *The Function and Nature of Imagery*. New York and London: Academic Press.

Holyoak, K. J. (1977). The form of analog size information in memory. *Cognitive Psychology* **9**, 31–51.

Holyoak, K. J. and Walker (1976). Subjective magnitude information in semantic orderings. *Journal of Verbal Learning and Verbal Behavior* **15**, 287–299.

Horowitz, N. J. (1970). *Image Formation and Cognition*. New York: Appleton-Century-Crofts.

Howard, R. (1980). Category use in abstract mental comparisons. *Quarterly Journal of Experimental Psychology* **32**, 625–633.

Hubel, D. H. and Wiesel, T. N. (1963). Receptive fields of cells in the striate cortex of very young visually inexperienced kittens. *Journal of Neurophysiology* **26**, 994–1002.

Hughlings Jackson, J. (1880). On aphasia with left hemiplegia. *Lancet* **1**, 637–638.

Hull, C. L. (1931). Goal attraction and directing ideas conceived as habit phenomena. *Psychological Review* **38**, 487–506.

Hume, D. (1748). *An Enquiry Concerning Human Understanding*. Chicago: Open Court.

Humphrey, G. (1951). *Thinking*. London: Methuen.

Hunt, E. and Love, T. (1972). How good can memory be? In A. W. Melton and E. Martin (eds.) *Coding Processes in Human Memory*. Washington: Winston.

Hunter, I. M. L. (1957). The solving of three-term series problems. *British Journal of Psychology* **68**, 155–164.

Hunter, I. M. L. (1962). An exceptional talent for calculative thinking. *British Journal of Psychology* **53**, 243–258.

Hunter, I. M. L. (1964). *Memory* (2nd edition). Harmondsworth: Penguin.

Hunter, I. M. L. (1977a). An exceptional memory. *British Journal of Psychology* **68**, 155–164.

Hunter, I. M. L. (1977b). Imagery, comprehension and mnemonics. *Journal of Mental Imagery* **1**, 65–72.

Hunter, I. M. L. (1979). The easel procedure and eidetic characteristics. *Behavioral and Brain Sciences* **2**, 605.

Huttenlocher, J. (1968). Constructing spatial images: a strategy in reasoning. *Psychological Review* **75**, 550–560.

Huxley, T. H. (1894). *Methods and Results*. London: Macmillan.

Jackson, D. N. and Messick, S. (1967a). Response styles and the assessment of psychopathology. In D. N. Jackson and S. Messick (eds.) *Problems in Human Assessment*. New York: McGraw Hill.

Jackson, D. N. and Messick, S. (eds.) (1967b). *Problems in Human Assessment*. New York: McGraw Hill.

Jacoby, L. L. and Craik, F. I. M. (1979). Effects of elaboration of processing at encoding and retrieval. In L. S. Cermak and F. I. M. Craik (eds.) *Levels of Processing in Human Memory*. Hillsdale, N.J.: Lawrence Erlbaum.

Jaensch, E. R. (1930). *Eidetic Imagery*. Translated by O. Oeser. New York: Harcourt Brace.

James, W. (1890). *Principles of Psychology*. New York: Holt, Rinehart and Winston.

Jamieson, O. G. and Petrusic, W. M. (1975). Relational judgements with remembered stimuli. *Perception and Psychophysics* 18, 373–379.

Janssen, W. (1976). *On the Nature of the Mental Image*. Soesterberg: Institute for Perception TNO.

Jeannerod, M. and Mouret, J. (1903). Etude comparative des mouvements oculaires observes chez le chat de la veille et du sommeil. *Compte Rendu des Séances de la Societé de Biologie* (Paris) 156, 1407–1410.

Jenkin, A. M. (1935). Imagery and learning. *British Journal of Psychology* 26, 149–164.

Johannson, G. (1971). Visual motion perception: a model for visual motion and space perception from changing proximal stimulations. University of Uppsale, Department of Psychology, Report 8.

John, E. R. (1976). A model of consciousness. In G. E. Schwartz and D. Shapiro (eds.) *Consciousness and Self-Regulation*, Vol. 1. London: Wiley.

Johnson, D. M. (1939). Confidence and speed in the two-category judgment. *Archives of Psychology* 241, 1–52.

Johnson, R. B. (1972). More on "bizarre" images in artificial memory *Psychonomic Science* 26, 101–102.

Johnson, M. K., Bransford, J. D., Nyberg, S. E. and Cleary, J. J. (1972). Comprehension factors in interpreting memory for abstract and concrete sentences. *Journal of Verbal Learning and Verbal Behavior* 11, 451–454.

Johnson-Laird, P. N. (1980a). Mental models in cognitive science. *Cognitive Science* 4, 71–115.

Johnson-Laird, P. N. (1980b). *Propositional Representation. Procedural Semantics —Mental Model*. Paper presented at the C.N.R.S. Conference, Royaumont.

Johnson-Laird, P. N. (1982). Ninth Bartlett Memorial Lecture. Thinking as a skill. *Quarterly Journal of Experimental Psychology* 34A, 1–29.

Johnson-Laird, P. N. and Steedman, M. (1978). The psychology of syllogisms. *Cognitive Psychology* 10, 64–99.

Johnston, W. A. and Heinz, S. P. (1978). Flexibility and capacity demands of attention. *Journal of Experimental Psychology: General* 107, 420–435.

Jones, G. V. (1978). Tests of a structural theory of the memory trace. *British Journal of Psychology* 69, 351–367.

Jones, S. and Winograd, E. (1975). Word imagery in recognition memory. *Bulletin of Psychonomic Society* **6**, 632–634.

Kahneman, D. (1973). *Attention and Effort*. Englewood Cliffs, N.J.: Prentice-Hall.

Kamiya, J. (1969). Operant control of the EEG alpha rhythm and some of its reported effects on consciousness. In Tart, C. S. (ed.) *Altered States of Consciousness*. New York: Wiley.

Kamiya, J. and Zeitlin, D. (1963). Learned EEG alpha wave control by humans. Report No. 183, Department of Mental Hygiene, Research Division, California.

Keenan, J. M. and Moore, R. E. (1979). Memory for images of concealed objects: A re-examination of Neisser and Kerr. *Journal of Experimental Psychology: Human Learning and Memory* **5**, 374–385.

Kelley, J. R. (1973). *Visual Imagery and Eye Blinking*. Unpublished PhD thesis, Oklahoma State University.

Kennedy, A. (1978). Personal communication.

Kerst, S. M. (1976). Interactive visual imagery and memory search for words and pictures. *Memory and Cognition* **4**, 573–580.

Kerst, S. M. and Howard, J. H. (1977). Mental comparisons for ordered information on abstract and concrete dimensions. *Memory and Cognition* **5**, 227–234.

Khatena, J. (1976). Autonomy of imagery and production of original verbal images. *Perceptual and Motor Skills* **43**, 245–246.

Kimura, D. (1967). Functional asymmetry of the brain in dichotic listening. *Cortex* **3**, 163–178.

Kinsbourne, M. (1972). Eye and head turning indicates cerebral lateralisation. *Science* **176**, 539–541.

Kintsch, W. (1972a). Abstract nouns: Imaging versus lexical complexity. *Journal of Verbal Learning and Verbal Behavior* **1**, 59–65.

Kintsch, W. (1972b). Notes on the structure of semantic memory. In E. Tulving and W. Donaldson (eds.) *Organization of Memory*. New York and London: Academic Press.

Kintsch, W. (1977). *Memory and Cognition*. New York: Holt, Rinehart and Winston.

Kirkpatrick, E. A. (1894). An experimental study of memory. *Psychological Review* **1**, 602–609.

Klausner, S. Z. (ed.) (1965). *The Quest for Self-Control*. New York: Free Press.

Klee, H. and Eysenck, M. W. (1973). Comprehension of abstract and concrete sentences. *Journal of Verbal Learning and Verbal Behavior* **12**, 522–529.

Kliensmith, L. J. and Kaplan, S. (1963). Paired associate learning as a function of arousal and interpolated interval. *Journal of Experimental Psychology* **65**, 190–193.

Kliensmith, L. J. and Kaplan, S. (1964). Interaction of arousal and recall interval in nonsense syllable paired-associate learning. *Journal of Experimental Psychology* **67**, 124–126.

Kline, P. (1982). *Fact and Fantasy in Freudian Theory* (2nd edition). London: Methuen.

Kluver, H. (1926). An experimental study of the eidetic type. *Genetic Psychology Monographs* **1**, 71.

Kocel, K., Galin, D., Ornstein, R. and Merrin, E. L. (1972). Lateral eye movements and cognitive mode. *Psychonomic Science* **27**, 223–224.

Koestler, A. (1967). *The Ghost in the Machine*. London: Hutchinson.

Kosslyn, S. M. (1973). Scanning visual images: some structural implications. *Perception and Psychophysics* **14**, 90–94.

Kosslyn, S. M. (1975). Information representation in visual images. *Cognitive Psychology* **7**, 341–370.

Kosslyn, S. M. (1976). Can imagery be distinguished from other forms of internal representation? Evidence from studies of information retrieval time. *Memory and Cognition* **10**, 291–297.

Kosslyn, S. M. (1978). Measuring the visual angle of the mind's eye. *Cognitive Psychology* **10**, 356–389.

Kosslyn, S. M. (1980). *Image and Mind*. Cambridge, Mass.: Harvard University Press.

Kosslyn, S. M. (1981). The medium and the message in mental imagery. *Psychological Review* **88**, 46–66.

Kosslyn, S. M. and Johnson, M. (1980). Cited in Kosslyn (1980) *Image and Mind*. Harvard: Harvard University Press.

Kosslyn, S. M. and Jolicoeur, P. (1980). A theory-based approach to the study of individual differences in mental imagery. In R. E. Shaw, P. A. Federico and W. E. Montague (eds.) *Aptitude Learning and Instruction: Cognitive Processes Analysis of Aptitudes, Vol. 1*. Hillsdale, N.J.: Lawrence Erlbaum.

Kosslyn, S. M. and Pomerantz, J. R. (1977). Imagery, propositions and the form of internal representations. *Cognitive Psychology* **9**, 52–76.

Kosslyn, S. M. and Shwartz, S. P. (1977). A simulation of visual imagery. *Cognitive Science* **1**, 265–295.

Kosslyn, S. M., Murphy, G. L., Bemesderfer, M. E. and Feinstein, K. J. (1977). Category and continuum in mental comparisons. *Journal of Experimental Psychology: General* **106**, 341–375.

Kosslyn, S. M., Pick, H. L. and Fariello, G. R. (1974). Cognitive maps in children and men. *Child Development* **45**, 707–716.

Kosslyn, S. M., Ball, T. M., and Reiser, B. J. (1978). Visual images preserve metrical spatial information: evidence from studies of image scanning. *Journal of Experimental Psychology: Human Perception and Performance* **4**, 47–60.

Kosslyn, S. M., Pinker, S., Smith, G. E. and Shwarts, S. P. (1979). On the demystification of mental imagery. *The Behavioral and Brain Sciences* **2**, 535–581.

Kripke, S. (1971). Identity and necessity. In M. K. Munitz (ed.) *Identity and Individuation*. New York: New York University Press.

Kroll, N. E. A., Kellicut, M. H. and Parks, T. E. (1975). Rehearsal of visual and auditory stimuli while shadowing. *Journal of Experimental Psychology: Human Learning and Memory* **1**, 215–222.

Kulpe, O. (1902). Uber die objectivirung und subjectivirung von sinnesein-drucken. *Philosophische Studien* **19**, 508–556.

Kunen, S. and May, J. G. (1980). Spatial frequency content of visual imagery. *Perception and Psychophysics* **28**, 555–559.

Kunen, S., Green, D. and Waterman, D. (1979). Spread of encoding effects within the non-verbal visual domain. *Journal of Experimental Psychology: Human Learning and Memory* **5**, 574–584.

Lambert, W. E. and Paivio, A. (1956). The influence of noun-adjective order on learning. *Canadian Journal of Psychology* **10**, 9–12.

Latane, B. and Darley, J. M. (1970). *The Unresponsive Bystander: Why Doesn't he Help?*. New York: Appleton-Century-Croft.

Larsen, A. and Bundesen, C. (1978). Size scaling in visual pattern recognition. *Journal of Experimental Psychology: Human Perception and Performance* **4**, 1–20.

Lea, G. (1975). Chronometric analysis of the method of loci. *Journal of Experimental Psychology. Human Perception and Performance* **2**, 95–104.

Leaning, F. E. (1925). An introductory study of hypnagogic phenomena. *Proceedings of the Society for Psychical Research* **35**, 289–409.

Leask, J., Haber, R. N. and Haber, R. B. (1969). Eidetic imagery in children: II Longitudinal and experimental results. *Psychonomic Monograph Supplements* **3**, 25–48.

Lefford, A. (1946). The influences of emotional subject matter on logical reasoning. *Journal of General Psychology* **30**, 127–151.

Leibniz, G. W. (1934). *Philosophical Writings*. Translated by M. Morris. London: Dent.

Lenneberg, E. H. (1967). *Biological Foundations of Language*. New York: John Wiley.

Leuba, C. (1940). Images as conditioned sensations. *Journal of Experimental Psychology* **26**, 345–351.

Levin, Schriberg, Miller, McCormick and Levin (1980). The keyword method in the classroom: How to remember the states and their capitals. *The Elementary School Journal* **80**, 185–191.

Levy, P. (1973). On the relation between test theory and psychology. In P. Kline (ed.) *New Approaches in Psychological Measurement*. London: John Wiley.

Lewis, J. L. (1970). Semantic processing of unattended messages using dichotic listening. *Journal of Experimental Psychology* **85**, 225–228.

Likert, R. and Quasha, W. H. (1941). *Revised Minnesota Paper Form Board Test* (Series A.A.). New York: The Psychological Corporation.

Lindauer, M. S. (1977). Imagery from the point of view of psychological aesthetics, the arts and creativity. *Journal of Mental Imagery* **2**, 343–362.

Lindsay, P. H. and Norman, D. A. (1977). *Human Information Processing*. New York and London: Academic Press.

Locke, D. (1968). *Myself and Others*. Oxford: Clarendon.

Lockhart, R. S. (1969). Retrieval asymmetry in the recall of adjectives and nouns. *Journal of Experimental Psychology* **79**, 12–17.

Lockhart, R. S., Craik, F. I. M. and Jacoby, L. L. (1976). Depth of processing, recognition and recall: some aspects of a general memory system. In J. Brown (ed.) *Recall and Recognition*. London: John Wiley.

Long, G. M. (1980). Iconic memory — a review and critique of the study of short-term visual storage. *Psychological Bulletin* **88**, 785–820.

Lorayne, H. (1958). *How to Develop a Super Power Memory*. Preston: Thomas.

Lorayne, H. and Lucas, J. (1974). *The Memory Book*. New York: Ballantine.

Lorens, S. A. and Darrow, C. W. (1962). Eye movements, E.E.G., G.S.R. and E.K.G. during mental multiplication. *Electroencephalography and Clinical Neurophysiology* **14**, 739–746.

Lovelace, E. A. and Snodgrass, R. D. (1971). Decision times for alphabetic order of letter pairs. *Journal of Experimental Psychology* **88**, 258–264.

Luria, A. R. (1967). *The Mind of a Mnemonist*. New York: Basic Books.

Lynch, K. (1960). *The Image of the City*. Cambridge, Mass.: M.I.T. Press.

Lynch, K. (1972). *What Time is this Place?* Cambridge, Mass.: M.I.T. Press.

Madigan, S., McCabe, L. and Itatani, E. (1972). Immediate and delayed recall of words and pictures. *Canadian Journal of Psychology* **26**, 407–414.

Malcolm, N. (1959). *Dreaming*. London: Routledge and Kegan Paul.

Mandler, G. (1975). *Mind and Emotion*. New York: Wiley.

Marks, D. F. (1973a). Visual imagery differences in the recall of pictures. *British Journal of Psychology* **64**, 17–24.

Marks, D. F. (1973b). Visual imagery and eye movements in the recall of pictures. *Perception and Psychophysics* **14**, 407–412.

Marks, D. F. (1977). Imagery and consciousness: a theoretical review from an individual differences perspective. *Journal of Mental Imagery* **2**, 275–290.

Marmor, G. S. and Zaback, L. A. (1976). Mental rotation by the blind: does mental rotation depend on visual imagery? *Journal of Experimental Psychology: Human Perception and Performance* **2**, 515–521.

Marr, D. (1976). Early processing of visual information. *Philosophical Transactions of the Royal Society of London* Series B, **275**, 483–519.

Marshall, J. C. and Fryer, D. M. (1978). Speak memory! An introduction to some historic studies of remembering and forgetting. In M. M. Gruneberg and P. E. Morris (eds.) *Aspects of Memory*. London: Methuen.

Maury, L. F. A. (1861). *Le Sommeil et les Rêves*. Paris.

McCarthy, D. L. (1980). Investigation of a visual imagery mnemonic device for acquiring face-name associations. *Journal of Experimental Psychology: Human Learning and Memory* **6**, 145–155.

McCullough, C. (1965). Color adaptation of edge-detectors in the human visual system. *Science* **149**, 1115–1116.

McGrath, M. J. and Cohen, D. B (1978). REM sleep facilitation of adaptive waking behavior: A review of the literature. *Psychological Bulletin* **85**, 24–57.

McKellar, P. (1957). *Imagination and Thinking*. London: Cohen and West.

McKellar, P. (1968). *Experience and Behaviour*. Harmondsworth: Penguin.

McKellar, P. (1972). Imagery from the standpoint of introspection. In P. W. Sheehan (ed.) *The Function and Nature of Imagery*. New York and London: Academic Press.

McKellar, P. (1977). Autonomy, imagery and dissociation. *Journal of Mental Imagery* **1**, 93–108.

McKellar, P. and Simpson, L. (1954). Between wakefulness and sleep: Hypnagogic imagery. *British Journal of Psychology* **45**, 266–276.

McKelvie, S. J. and Gingras, P. P. (1974). Reliability of two measures of visual imagery. *Perceptual and Motor Skills* **39**, 417–418.

Medlicott, R. W. (1958). An inquiry into the significance of hallucinations with special reference to their occurrence in the sane. *International Journal of Medicine* **171**, 664–677.

Meichenbaum, D. (1974). *Cognitive Behavior Modification*. Morristown, N.J.: General Learning Press.

Menninger, K. A. (1949). *The Human Mind*. New York: Knopf.

Merritt, J. O. (1979). None in a million: results of a mass screening for eidetic ability using objective tests published in newspapers and magazines. *Behavioral and Brain Sciences* **2**, 612.

Metzler, J. (1973). Chronometric studies in semantic and modal logic. *Dissertation Abstracts International* **34**, (6-B), 2973.

Metzler, J. and Shepard, R. N. (1974). Transformational studies of the internal representation of three-dimensional objects. In R. L. Solso (ed.), *Theories of Cognitive Psychology: the Loyola Symposium*. Hillsdale, N.J.: Lawrence Erlbaum.

Michael, L. I. (1966). A factor analysis of mental imagery. Unpublished doctoral dissertation. Auburn University.

Miller, G. A. (1956). The magical number seven, plus or minus two: some limits on our capacity for processing information. *Psychological Review* **63**, 81–97.

Miller, G. A. and Johnson-Laird, P. N. (1976). *Language and Perception*. Cambridge, Mass.: Harvard University Press.

Miller, G. A., Galanter, E. and Pribram, K. (1960). *Plans and the Structure of Behavior*. New York: Holt, Rinehart and Winston.

Milner, B. and Taylor, L. (1972). Right hemisphere superiority in tactile pattern recognition after cerebral commisurotomy: evidence for non verbal memory. *Neuropsychologia* **10**, 1–15.

Minsky, M. (1977). Frame system theory. In P. N. Johnson-Laird and P. C. Wason (eds.) *Thinking: Readings in Cognitive Science*. Cambridge: Cambridge University Press.

Moore, T. V. (1915a). The temporal relations of meaning and imagery. *Psychological Review* **22**, 177–225.

Moore, T. V. (1915b). Image and meaning in memory and perception. *Psychological Monographs* **27** (Whole No. 119).

Moray, N. (1959). Attention in dichotic listening: Affective cues and the influence of instructions. *Quarterly Journal of Experimental Psychology* **11**, 56–60.

Moray, N. (1967). Where is capacity limited? A survey and a model. In A. Sanders (ed.) *Attention and Performance*. Amsterdam: North-Holland.

Morris, P. E. (1972a). *Imagery in Remembering, Recall and Recognition*. Unpublished PhD thesis, University of Exeter.

Morris, P. E. (1972b). Methodology and two early approaches. In *An Introduction to Psychology: Approaches and Methods*. London: Open University Press.

Morris, P. E. (1978a). Encoding and Retrieval. In M. M. Grunberg and P. E. Morris (eds.) *Aspects of Memory*, London: Methuen.

Morris, P. E. (1978b). Frequency and imagery in word recognition: Further evidence for an attribute model. *British Journal of Psychology* **69**, 69–75.

Morris, P. E. (1978c). Sense and nonsense in traditional mnemonics. In M. M. Gruneberg, P. E. Morris and R. N. Sykes (eds.) *Practical Aspects of Memory*. London and New York: Academic Press.

Morris, P. E. (1979). Strategies for learning and recall. In M. M. Gruneberg and P. E. Morris (eds.) *Applied Problems in Memory*. London and New York: Academic Press.

Morris, P. E. (1980a). Recent developments in memory research. *Psychological Teaching* **8**, 1–4.

Morris, P. E. (1980b). Rated emotionality, recognition and free recall. Paper presented at the Cognitive Psychology Section Conference on Arousal and Memory. Bedford College.

Morris, P. E. (1981a). Age of acquisition, imagery, recall, and the limitations of multiple-regression analysis. *Memory and Cognition* **9**, 277–282.

Morris, P. E. (1981b). Why Evans is wrong in criticizing introspective reports of subjects' strategies. *British Journal of Psychology* **72**, 465–468.

Morris, P. E. (1981c). The cognitive psychology of self reports. In C. Antaki (ed.) *The Psychology of Ordinary Explanations of Social Behaviour*. London and New York: Academic Press.

Morris, P. E. and Gale, A. (1974). A correlational study of variables related to imagery. *Perceptual and Motor Skills* **38**, 659–665.

Morris, P. E. and Reid, R. L. (1970). The repeated use of mnemonic imagery. *Psychonomic Science* **20**, 337–338.

Morris, P. E. and Reid, R. L. (1971). Imagery and the compatibility of pairing in the free recall of adjective-noun pairs. *Quarterly Journal of Experimental Psychology* **23**, 393–398.

Morris, P. E. and Reid, R. L. (1972). Imagery and the recall of adjectives and nouns from meaningful prose. *Psychonomic Science* **27**, 117–118.

Morris, P. E. and Reid, R. L. (1973). Recognition and recall: Latency and recurrence of images. *British Journal of Psychology* **64**, 161–167.

Morris, P. E. and Reid, (1974). Imagery and recognition. *British Journal of Psychology* **65**, 7–12.

Morris, P. E. and Reid, R. L. (1975). The role of stimulus and pair imagery in paired-associate learning. *British Journal of Psychology* **66**, 153–156.

Morris, P. E. and Stevens, R. (1974). Linking images and free recall. *Journal of Verbal Learning and Verbal Behavior* **13**, 310–315.

Morris, P. E., Jones, S. and Hampson, P. J. (1978). An imagery mnemonic for the learning of people's names. *British Journal of Psychology* **69**, 335–336.

Morsh, J. E. and Abbott, H. D. (1945). An investigation of after-images. *Journal of Comparative Psychology* **38**, 47–63.

Moyer, R. S. (1973). Comparing objects in memory: evidence suggesting an internal psychophysics. *Perception and Psychophysics* **13**, 180–184.

Moyer, R. S. and Landauer, T. K. (1967). The time required for judgments of numerical inequality. *Nature* **215**, 1519–1520.

Mundy-Castle, A. C. (1957). The electroencephalogram and mental activity. *Electroencephalography and Clinical Neurophysiology* **9**, 643–655.

Murdock, B. B. (1971). Short-term memory. In G. Bower (ed.) *The Psychology of Learning and Motivation*, Vol. 5. New York and London: Academic Press.

Myers, F. W. H. (1903). *Human Personality and its Survival of Bodily Death*. London: Longmans, Green.

Neisser, U. (1967). *Cognitive Psychology*. New York: Appleton-Century-Croft.

Neisser, U. (1972). Changing conceptions of imagery. In P. W. Sheehan (ed.) *The Function and Nature of Imagery*. New York and London: Academic Press.

Neisser, U. (1976). *Cognition and Reality*. San Francisco: Freeman.

Neisser, U. (1978). Anticipations, images and introspection. *Cognition* **6**, 167–174.

Neisser, U. and Becklen, R. (1975). Selective looking: attending to visually specified events. *Cognitive Psychology* **7**, 480–494.

Neisser, U. and Kerr, N. (1973). Spatial and mnemonic properties of visual images. *Cognitive Psychology* **5**, 138–150.

Nelson, D. L. (1979). Remembering pictures and words: appearance significance and name. In L. S. Cermak and F. I. M. Craik (eds.) *Levels of Processing in Human Memory*. Hillsdale, N.J.: Lawrence Erlbaum.

Nelson, D. L. and Brooks, D. H. (1973). Functional independence of pictures and verbal memory codes? *Journal of Experimental Psychology* **97**, 1–7.

Nelson, D. L., Brooks, D. H. and Borden, R. C. (1973). Sequential memory for pictures and the role of the verbal system. *Journal of Experimental Psychology* **101**, 242–245.

Nelson, D. L., Reid, V. S. and Walling, J. R. (1976). The pictorial superiority effect. *Journal of Experimental Psychology: Human Learning and Memory* **2**, 49–57.

Nelson, K. E. and Kosslyn, S. M. (1976). Recognition of previously labeled or unlabeled pictures by 5-year-olds and adults. *Journal of Experimental Child Psychology* **21**, 40–45.

Newcombe, F. (1969). *Missile Wounds of the Brain*. Oxford: Oxford University Press.

Newell, A. and Simon, H. A. (1972). *Human Problem Solving*. Englewood Cliffs, N.J.: Prentice Hall.

Nisbett, R. and Ross, L. (1980). *Human Inference: Strategies and Shortcomings of Social Judgments*. Englewood Cliffs, N.J.: Prentice-Hall.

Nisbett, R. E. and Wilson, T. D. (1977). Telling more than we can know: Verbal reports on mental processes. *Psychological Review* **84**, 231–259.

Noble, C. E. (1952a). An analysis of meaning. *Psychological Review* **59**, 421–430.

Noble, C. E. (1952b). The role of stimulus meaning (m) in serial verbal learning. *Journal of Experimental Psychology* **43**, 437–446.

Noble, C. E. (1953). The meaning–familiarity relationship. *Psychological Review* **60**, 89–98.

Norman, D. A. (1976). *Memory and Attention* (2nd edition) New York: Wiley.

Norman, D. A. and Bobrow, D. G. (1979). Descriptions: An intermediate stage in memory retrieval. *Cognitive Psychology* **11**, 107–123.

Oatley, K. (1978). *Perceptions and Representations.* London: Methuen.

Oliver, G. W., Breger, L. and Zanger, R. (1980). Symbolic aspects of hypnagogic imagery associated with theta EEG feedback. In J. E. Shorr, G. E. Sobel, P. Robin and J. A. Connella (eds.) *Imagery: Its Many Dimensions and Applications.* New York: Plenum Press.

Ornstein, R. E. (1972). *The Psychology of Consciousness.* San Francisco: Freeman.

Osgood, C. E. (1953). *Method and Theory in Experimental Psychology.* New York: Oxford.

Osgood, C. E., Suci, G. J. and Tannenbaum, P. H. (1957). *The Measurement of Meaning.* Urbana, Illinois: University of Illinois Press.

Oswald, I. (1957). After-images from retina and brain. *Quarterly Journal of Experimental Psychology* **9**, 113–118.

Paivio, A. (1963). Learning of adjective-noun paired-associates as a function of adjective-noun word order and noun abstractness. *Canadian Journal of Psychology* **17**, 370–379.

Paivio, A. (1965). Abstractness, imagery and meaningfulness in paired-associate learning. *Journal of Verbal Learning and Verbal Behavior* **4**, 32–38.

Paivio, A. (1966). Latency of verbal associations and imagery to noun stimuli as a function of abstractness and generality. *Canadian Journal of Psychology* **20**, 378–387.

Paivio, A. (1967). Paired-associate learning and free recall of nouns as a function of concreteness, specificity, imagery, and meaningfulness. *Psychological Reports* **20**, 239–245.

Paivio, A. (1968). A factor-analytic study of word attributes and verbal learning. *Journal of Verbal Learning and Verbal Behavior* **7**, 41–49.

Paivio, A. (1969). Mental imagery in associative learning and memory. *Psychological Review* **76**, 241–263.

Paivio, A. (1971a). Imagery and deep structure in the recall of English nominalizations. *Journal of Verbal Learning and Verbal Behavior* **10**, 1–12.

Paivio, A. (1971b). *Imagery and Verbal Processes.* New York: Holt, Rinehart and Winston.

Paivio, A. (1973). Psychophysiological correlates of imagery. In F. J. McGuigan and R. A. Schoonover (eds.) *The Psychophysiology of Thinking*. New York and London: Academic Press.

Paivio, A. (1975a). Perceptual comparisons through the mind's eye. *Memory and Cognition* **3**, 635–647.

Paivio, A. (1975b). Imagery and synchronic thinking. *Canadian Psychological Review* **16**, 147–163.

Paivio, A. (1976). Imagery, language and semantic memory. *Research Bulletin No. 398*, Department of Psychology, University of Western Ontario.

Paivio, A. (1978a). Imagery, language and semantic memory. *International Journal of Psycholinguistics* **5**, 31–47.

Paivio, A. (1978b). Comparisons of mental clocks. *Journal of Experimental Psychology: Human Perception and Performance* **4**, 61–71.

Paivio, A. and Begg, I. (1970). Imagery and comprehension latencies as a function of sentence concreteness and structure. *Research Bulletin No. 154*, Department of Psychology, University of Western Ontario.

Paivio, A. and Begg, I. (1971). Imagery and associative overlaps in short-term memory. *Journal of Experimental Psychology* **80**, 40–45.

Paivio, A. and Cohen, M. W. (1977). Eidetic imagery and figural abilities in children. Paper presented at Annual Convention of the American Psychological Association, San Francisco.

Paivio, A. and Csapo, K. (1969). Concrete-image and verbal memory codes. *Journal of Experimental Psychology* **80**, 279–285.

Paivio, A. and Desroches, A. (1979). Effects of an imagery mnemonic on second language recall and comprehension. *Canadian Journal of Psychology* **33**, 17–28.

Paivio, A. and Foth, D. (1970). Imaginal and verbal mediators and noun concreteness in paired-associate learning: The elusive interaction. *Journal of Verbal Learning and Verbal Behavior* **9**, 384–390.

Paivio, A. and Yuille, J. C. (1967). Mediation instructions and word attributes in paired-associate learning. *Psychonomic Science* **8**, 65–66.

Paivio, A. and Yuille, J. C. (1969). Changes in associate strategies and paired-associate learning over trials as a function of word imagery and type of learning set. *Journal of Experimental Psychology* **79**, 458–463.

Paivio, A., Yuille, J. C. and Smythe, P. C. (1966). Stimulus and response abstractions, imagery and meaningfulness and reported mediators in paired-associate learning. *Canadian Journal of Psychology* **20**, 362–377.

Paivio, A., Smythe, P. C. and Yuille, J. C. (1968a). Imagery versus meaningfulness of nouns in paired-associate learning. *Canadian Journal of Psychology* **22**, 427–441.

Paivio, A., Yuille, J. C. and Madigan, S. (1968b). Concreteness, imagery and meaningfulness values for 925 nouns. *Journal of Experimental Psychology Monograph Supplement* **76**, (1, Pt.2).

Palmer, S. E. (1975). Visual perception and world knowledge. In D. A. Norman and D. E. Rumelhart (eds.) *Explorations in Cognition*. San Francisco: Freeman.

Palmer, S. E. (1978). Fundamental aspects of cognitive representation. In E. Rosch and B. Lloyd (eds.) *Cognition and Categorisation*. Hillsdale, N.J.: Lawrence Erlbaum.

Parks, T. E., Knoll, N. E. A., Salzberg, P. M. and Parkinson, S. R. (1972). Persistence of visual memory as indicated by decision time in a matching task. *Journal of Experimental Psychology* **92**, 437–438.

Parkman, J. M. (1971). Temporal aspects of digit and letter inequality judgements. *Journal of Experimental Psychology* **91**, 191–205.

Paterson, A. S. (1935). The respiratory rhythms in normal and psychotic subjects. *Journal of Neurology and Psychopathology* **16**, 36–53.

Patterson, K. E. and Baddeley, A. D. (1977). When face recognition fails. *Journal of Experimental Psychology: Human Learning and Memory* **3**, 406–417.

Pellegrino, J. W., Siegel, A. W. and Ohawan, M. (1975). Short-term retention of pictures and words: Evidence for dual coding systems. *Journal of Experimental Psychology: Human Learning and Memory* **1**, 95–102.

Perky, C. W. (1910). An experimental study of imagination. *American Journal of Psychology* **21**, 422–452.

Peterson, L. R. and Peterson, M. J. (1959). Short-term retention of individual verbal items. *Journal of Experimental Psychology* **58**, 193–198.

Phillips, W. A. (1974). On the distinction between sensory storage and short-term visual memory. *Perception and Psychophysics* **16**, 283–290.

Phillips, W. A. and Baddeley, A. D. (1971). Reaction time and short-term visual memory. *Psychonomic Science* **22**, 73–74.

Phillips, W. A. and Christie, D. F. M. (1977). Interference with visualization *Quarterly Journal of Experimental Psychology* **29**, 637–650.

Piaget, J. (1926). *The Language and Thought of the Child*. New York: Harcourt Brace Jovanovich.

Piaget, J. (1971). *Structuralism*. London: Routledge and Kegan Paul.

Piaget, J. and Inhelder, B. (1971). *Mental Imagery in the Child*. New York: Basic Books.

Pinker, S. and Kosslyn, S. M. (1978). The representation and manipulation of three-dimensional space in mental images. *Journal of Mental Imagery* **2**, 69–84.

Place, U. T. (1956). Is consciousness a brain process? *British Journal of Psychology* **47**, 44–50.

Plutchik, R. (1968). *Foundations of Experimental Research*. New York: Harper and Row.

Podgorny, P. and Shepard, R. N. (1978). Functional representation common to visual perception and imagination. *Journal of Experimental Psychology: Human Perception and Performance* **4**, 21–35.

Poincaré, H. (1924). *The Foundations of Science*. London: Science Press.

Popper, K. R. and Eccles, J. C. (1977). *The Self and its Brain*. Berlin: Springer International.

Posner, M. I. (1973). *Cognition: An Introduction*. Glenview, Ill.: Scott, Foresman.

Posner, M. I. (1978). *Chronometric Explorations of Mind.* Hillsdale, N.J.: Lawrence Erlbaum.

Posner, M. I. and Boies, S. J. (1971). Components of attention. *Psychological Review* **78**, 391–408.

Posner, M. I. and Keele, S. W. (1967). Decay of visual information from a single letter. *Science* **158**, 137–139.

Posner, M. I. and Mitchell, R. F. (1967). Chronometric analysis of classification. *Psychological Review* **74**, 392–409.

Posner, M. I., Boies, S. J., Eichelman, W. H. and Taylor, L. (1969). Retention of visual and name codes of single letters. *Journal of Experimental Psychology* **97**, 1–16.

Posner, M. I., Nissen, M. J. and Ogden, W. C. (1978). Attended and unattended processing modes: The role of set for spatial location. In H. L. Pick and L. Saltzman (eds.) *Modes of Perceiving and Processing Information.* Hillsdale N.J.: Lawrence Erlbaum.

Potter, S. (1948). *Gamesmanship.* Harmondsworth: Penguin.

Pressley, G. M. (1976). Mental imagery helps eight-year-olds remember what they read. *Journal of Educational Psychology* **68**, 355–359.

Pressley, M. (1977). Children's use of the keyword method to learn simple Spanish vocabulary words. *Journal of Educational Psychology* **69**, 465–472.

Pressley, M. and Dennis-Rounds, J. (1980). Transfer of a mnemonic keyword strategy at two age levels. *Journal of Educational Psychology* **72**, 575–582.

Pressley, M. and Levin, J. R. (1978). Developmental constraints associated with children's use of the keyword method of foreign language vocabulary learning. *Journal of Experimental Child Psychology* **26**, 359–372.

Pressley, M. and Levin, J. R. (1981). The keyword method and recall of vocabulary words from definitions. *Journal of Experimental Psychology: Human Learning and Memory* **7**, 72–76.

Pressley, M., Levin, J. R., Hall, J. W., Miller, G. E. and Berry, J. K. (1980). The keyword method and foreign word acquisition. *Journal of Experimental Psychology: Human Learning and Memory* **65**, 163–173.

Putnam, H. (1973). Reductionism and the nature of psychology. *Cognition* **2**, 131–146.

Pylyshyn, Z. W. (1973). What the mind's eye tells the mind's brain: a critique of mental imagery. *Psychological Bulletin* **80**, 1–24.

Pylyshyn, Z. W. (1975). Do we need images and analogues? Paper presented at the Conference on Theoretical Issues in Natural Language Processing. Cambridge, Mass.: M.I.T.

Pylyshyn, Z. W. (1978). Imagery and artificial intelligence. In W. Savage (ed.) *Minnesota Studies in the Philosophy of Science Vol. 9.* Minneapolis: University of Minnesota Press.

Pylyshyn, Z. W. (1979). The rate of "mental rotation" of images: a test of holistic analogue hypothesis. *Memory and Cognition* **7**, 19–28.

Pylyshyn, Z. W. (1980). Computation and cognition: issues in the foundations of cognitive sciences. *Behavioral and Brain Sciences* **3**, 111–133.

Pylyshyn, Z. W. (1981). The imagery debate: analogue media versus tacit knowledge. *Psychological Review* **87**, 16–45.

Quillian, M. R. (1969). The Teachable Language Comprehender: A simulation program and theory of language. *Communications of the ACM* **12**, 459–476.

Radaker, L. D. (1963). The effect of visual imagery upon spelling performance. *Journal of Educational Research* **56**, 370–372.

Raugh, M. R. and Atkinson, R. C. (1975). A mnemonic method for learning a second language vocabulary. *Journal of Educational Psychology* **67**, 1–16.

Razik, T. A. (1967). Psychometric measurement in creativity. In R. L. Mooney and T. A. Razik (eds.) *Explorations in Creativity*. New York: Harper and Row.

Reddy, R. (1975). *Speech Recognition: Invited Papers Presented at the IEEE Symposium*. New York and London: Academic Press.

Reese, H. W. (1975). Verbal effects in children's visual recognition memory. *Child Development* **46**, 400–407.

Reese, H. W. (1977). Toward a cognitive theory of mnemonic imagery. *Journal of Mental Imagery* **2**, 299–344.

Rehm, L. P. (1973). Relationships among measures of visual imagery. *Behavior Research and Therapy* **11**, 265–270.

Reinhold, D. B. (1957). Effect of training on perception of after-images. *Perceptual and Motor Skills* **7**, 198.

Restle, F. (1970). Speed of adding and comparing numbers. *Journal of Experimental Psychology* **83**, 274–278.

Richardson, A. (1969). *Mental Imagery*. New York: Springer.

Richardson, A. (1977a). Verbalizer-Visualizer: A cognitive style dimension. *Journal of Mental Imagery* **1**, 109–126.

Richardson, A. (1977b). The meaning and measurement of memory imagery. *British Journal of Psychology* **68**, 29–43.

Richardson, A. (1978a). Subject, task and tester variables associated with initial eye movement responses. *Journal of Mental Imagery* **2**, 85–100.

Richardson, A. (1978b). Personal Communication.

Richardson, A. (1979). Dream recall frequency and vividness of visual imagery. *Journal of Mental Imagery* **3**, 65–72.

Richardson, J. T. E. (1975a). Imagery, concreteness and lexical complexity. *Quarterly Journal of Experimental Psychology* **27**, 211–223.

Richardson, J. T. E. (1975b). Concreteness and imageability. *Quarterly Journal of Experimental Psychology* **27**, 235–249.

Richardson, J. T. E. (1975c). Imagery and deep structure in the recall of English nominalizations. *British Journal of Psychology* **66**, 333–339.

Richardson, J. T. E. (1976). Procedures for investigating imagery and the distinction between primary and secondary memory. *British Journal of Psychology* **67**, 487–500.

Richardson, J. T. E. (1978a). Imagery and concreteness in free recall. Paper represented to the London Conference of the British Psychological Society.

Richardson, J. T. E. (1978b). Mental imagery and the distinction between primary and secondary memory. *Quarterly Journal of Experimental Psychology* **30**, 471–485.

Richardson, J. T. E. (1980). *Mental Imagery and Human Memory*. London: Macmillan.

Richman, C. L., Mitchell, D. B. and Reznick, J. S. (1979). Mental travel: some reservations. *Journal of Experimental Psychology: Human Perception and Performance* **5**, 13–18.

Ritchey, G. H. and Beal, C. R. (1980). Image detail and recall: Evidence for within-item elaboration. *Journal of Experimental Psychology: Human Learning and Memory* **6**, 66–76.

Roberts, L. G. (1965). Machine perception of three-dimensional solids. In J. T. Tippet, D. A. Berkowitz, L. C. Clapp, C. J. Koester and A. Vanderburgh (eds.) *Electro-Optical Information Processing*. Cambridge, Mass.: M.I.T. Press.

Robinson, A. H. and Petchenik, B. B. (1976). *The Nature of Maps: Essays towards Understanding Maps and Mapping*. Chicago: University of Chicago Press.

Roediger, H. L. (1980). Effectiveness of four mnemonics in ordinary recall. *Journal of Experimental Psychology: Human Learning and Memory* **6**, 558–567.

Roffwag, H. P., Muzio, J. and Dement, W. C. (1966). The ontogenetical development of the human sleep dream cycle. *Science* **152**, 604–618.

Rogers, C. R. (1959). Toward a theory of creativity. In H. H. Anderson (ed.) *Creativity and its Cultivation*. New York: Harper and Row.

Rohrman, N. L. (1968). The role of syntactic structure in the recall of English nominalizations. *Journal of Verbal Learning and Verbal Behavior* **7**, 904–912.

Rosch, E. (1973). Natural categories. *Cognitive Psychology* **4**, 328–350.

Rosch, E. (1975). Cognitive representations of semantic categories. *Journal of Experimental Psychology: General* **104**, 192–223.

Rosch, E. and Mervis, C. B. (1975). Family resemblances: studies in the internal structure of categories. *Cognitive Psychology* **7**, 573–605.

Rossi, G. E. and Rosadini, G. (1965). Cited in G. Cohen *The Psychology of Cognition*, Academic Press, London and New York, 1977. Also in F. L. Darley and Millikan (eds.) *Brain Mechanisms Underlying Speech and Language*. Grune and Stratton, New York.

Rubin, D. C. (1980). 51 properties of 125 words: A unit analysis of verbal behavior. *Journal of Verbal Learning and Verbal Behavior* **19**, 736–755.

Rugg, H. (1963). *Imagination*. New York: Harper and Row.

Ryle, G. (1949). *The Concept of Mind*. London: Hutchinson.

Sachs, J. S. (1967). Recognition memory for syntactic and semantic aspects of connected discourse *Perception and Psychophysics* **2**, 437–442.

Sakitt, B. (1976). Iconic memory. *Psychological Review* **83**, 257–276.

Sarbin, and Juhabz (1967). The historical background of the concept of hallucinations, *Journal of the History of the Behavioral Sciences* **3**, 339–358.

Sasson, R. Y. (1971). Interfering images at sentence retrieval. *Journal of Experimental Psychology* **89**, 56–62.

Sasson, R. Y. and Fraisse, P. (1972). Images in memory for concrete and abstract sentences. *Journal of Experimental Psychology* **94**, 149–155.

Schacter, D. L. (1976). The hypnagogic state: A critical review of the literature. *Psychological Bulletin* **83**, 452–481.

Schmeidler, G. R. (1965). Visual imagery correlated to a measure of creativity. *Journal of Consulting Psychology* **29**, 78–80.

Segal, S. J. (1971). Processing of the stimulus in imagery and perception. In S. J. Segal (ed.) *Imagery: Current Cognitive Approaches.* New York and London: Academic Press.

Segal, S. J. and Fusella, V. (1970). Influence of imaged pictures and sounds on the detection of auditory and visual signals. *Journal of Experimental Psychology* **83**, 458–464.

Segal, S. J. and Glicksman, M. (1967). Relaxation and the Perky effect: the influence of body position on judgment of imagery. *American Journal of Psychology* **80**, 257–262.

Segal, S. J. and Gordon, P. (1969). The Perky effect revisited: blocking of visual signals by imagery. *Perceptual and Motor Skills* **28**, 79–197.

Segal, S. J. and Nathan, S. (1964). The Perky effect: incorporation of an external stimulus into an imagery experience under placebo and control conditions. *Perceptual and Motor Skills* **18**, 385–395.

Sekuler, R. and Nash, D. (1972). Speed of size scaling in human vision. *Psychonomic Science* **27**, 93–94.

Sekuler, R., Rubin, E. and Armstrong, R. (1971). Processing numerical information: a choice time analysis. *Journal of Experimental Psychology* **89**, 75–80.

Selfridge, O. G. (1959). Pandemonium: a paradigm for learning. In *The Mechanisation of Thought Processes.* H.M.S.O.: London.

Shaffer, L. H. (1975). Control processes in typing. *Quarterly Journal of Experimental Psychology* **27**, 419–432.

Shallice, T. (1972). Dual functions of consciousness. *Psychological Review* **79**, 383–393.

Shatzman, M. (1982). *The Story of Ruth.* Harmondsworth: Penguin.

Shaver, P., Pierson, L. and Lang, S. (1974). Converging evidence for the functional significance of imagery in problem solving. *Cognition* **3**, 359–375.

Sheehan, P. W. (1967). A shortened version of Betts' questionnaire upon mental imagery. *Journal of Clinical Psychology* **23**, 386–389.

Sheehan, P. W. (ed.) (1972a). *The Function and Nature of Imagery.* London and New York: Academic Press.

Sheehan, P. W. (1972b). A functional analysis of the role of visual imagery in unexpected recall. In P. W. Sheehan (ed.) *The Function and Nature of Imagery.* New York and London: Academic Press.

Sheehan, P. W. and Neisser, U. (1969). Some variables affecting the vividness of imagery in recall. *British Journal of Psychology* **60**, 71-80.

Shepard, R. N. (1964). Attention and the metric structure of the stimulus space. *Journal of Mathematical Psychology* **1**, 54-87.

Shepard, R. N. (1966). Learning and recall as organization and search. *Journal of Verbal Learning and Verbal Behavior* **5**, 201-204.

Shepard, R. N. (1967). Recognition memory for words, sentences and pictures. *Journal of Verbal Learning and Verbal Behavior* **6**, 156-163.

Shepard, R. N. (1975). Form, formation and transformation of internal representations. In R. L. Solso (ed.) *Information Processing and Cognition: the Loyola Symposium*. Hillsdale, N.J.: Lawrence Erlbaum.

Shepard, R. N. and Feng, C. (1972). A chronometric study of mental paper folding. *Cognitive Psychology* **3**, 228-243.

Shepard, R. N. and Metzler, J. (1971). Mental rotation of three-dimensional objects. *Science* **191**, 952-954.

Shepard, R. N. and Podgorny, P. (1979). Cognitive processes that resemble perceptual processes. In W. K. Estes (ed.) *Handbook of Learning and Cognitive Processes*. Hillsdale, N.J.: Lawrence Erlbaum.

Shorr, J. E., Sobel, G. E., Robin, P. and Connella, J. A. (eds.) (1980). *Imagery: Its Many Dimensions and Applications*. New York: Plenum Press.

Short, P. L. (1953). The objective study of mental imagery. *British Journal of Psychology* **44**, 38-51.

Shwartz, S. P. (1979). *Studies of Mental Image Rotation: Implications for a Computer Simulation of Visual Imagery*. Unpublished PhD Dissertation, The Johns Hopkins University.

Sidgwick, H. A. (1894). Report on the census of hallucinations. *Proceedings of the Society for Psychical Research* **26**, 25-422.

Siipola, E. M. and Hayden, S. D. (1965). Exploring eidetic imagery among the retarded. *Perceptual Motor Skills* **21**, 275-286.

Simpson, A. J. (1979). Hemispheric differences in cognitive processes: evidence from experimental psychology. In K. Connolly (ed.) *Psychology Survey No. 2*. London: Allen and Unwin.

Simpson, H. M. (1970). Inferring cognitive processes from pupillary activity and response time. Colloquium presented at the University of Western Ontario, January.

Simpson, H. M., Paivio, A. and Rogers, T. B. (1967). Occipital alpha activity of high and low visual images during problem solving. *Psychonomic Science* **8**, 49-50.

Singer, J. (1966). *Daydreaming*. New York: Random House.

Singer, J. L. and Antrobus, J. S. (1965). Eye movements during fantasies. *Archives of General Psychiatry* **12**, 71-76.

Singer, J. L. and Antrobus, J. S. (1972). Daydreaming, imaginal processes and personality: A normative study. In P. W. Sheehan (ed.) *The Function and Nature of Imagery*. New York and London: Academic Press.

Skinner, B. F. (1953). *Science and Human Behavior*. New York: MacMillan.

Skinner, B. F. (1976). *Particulars of my Life*. New York: Knopf.

Slatter, K. H. (1960). Alpha rhythm and mental imagery. *Electroencephalography and Clinical Neurophysiology* **12**, 851–859.

Slee, J. (1980). Individual differences in visual imagery ability and the retrieval of visual appearances. *Journal of Mental Imagery* **4**, 93–113.

Sloboda, J. A. (1981). Visual imagery and individual differences in spelling. In U. Frith (ed.) *Cognitive Processes in Spelling*. London and New York: Academic Press.

Smart, J. J. C. (1963). *Philosophy and Scientific Realism*. London: Routledge and Kegan Paul.

Smith, E. R. and Miller, F. D. (1978). Limits on perception of cognitive processes: A reply to Nisbett and Wilson. *Psychological Review* **85**, 355–362.

Smith, E. E., Shoben, E. J. and Rips, L. J. (1974). Structure and process in semantic memory: a feature model for semantic decisions. *Psychological Review* **81**, 214–241.

Smithells, J. and Marks, D. F. (1977). Rotary pursuit tracking following mental practice as a function of visual imagery ability. Cited in D. F. Marks (1977) *Op. cit.*

Smyth, M. M. (1975). The role of mental practice in skill acquisition. *Journal of Motor Behaviour* **7**, 199–206.

Snodgrass, J. G., Volvovitz, R. and Walfish, E. R. (1972). Recognition memory for words, pictures, and words and pictures. *Psychonomic Science* **27**, 345–347.

Snyder, F. (1966). Toward an evolutionary theory of dreaming. *American Journal of Psychology* **123**, 121–136.

Snyder, F. (1971). Psychophysiology of human sleep. *Clinical Neurosurgery* **18**, 503–536.

Snyder, C. R. (1972). Individual differences in imagery and thought. Unpublished PhD thesis, University of Oregon.

Somekh, D. and Wilding, J. M. (1973). Perception without awareness in a dichotic viewing situation. *British Journal of Psychology* **64**, 339–349.

Spender, S. (1952). The making of a poem. In B. Ghiselin (ed.) *The Creative Process: a Symposium*. University of California: University of California Press.

Sperling, G. (1960). The information available in brief visual presentations. *Psychological Monographs* **74**, (Whole No. 498).

Standing, L. (1973). Learning 10,000 pictures. *Quarterly Journal of Experimental Psychology* **25**, 207–222.

Standing, L., Conezio, J. and Haber, R. N. (1970a). Perception and memory for pictures: single trial learning of 2500 visual stimuli. *Psychonomic Science* **19**, 73–74.

Standing, L., Sell, C., Boss, J. and Haber, R. N. (1970b). Effect of visualisation and subvocalisation on perceptual clarity. *Psychonomic Science* **18**, 89–90.

Start, K. B. and Richardson, A. (1964). Imagery and mental practice. *British Journal of Educational Psychology* **34**, 280–284.

Stenning, K. (1977). On remembering how to get there: how we might need something like a map. Paper presented at the International Conference on Cognitive Psychology and Instruction, Amsterdam.

Stern, L. W. (1939). The psychology of testimony. *Journal of Abnormal Social Psychology* **34**, 3–20.

Sternberg, R. J. (1977). *Intelligence, Information Processing and Analogical Reasoning: The Componential Analysis of Human Abilities*. Hillsdale, N.J.: Lawrence Erlbaum.

Stevens, S. S. (1951). *Handbook of Experimental Psychology*, London: Wiley.

Stricklin, A. B. and Penk, M. L. (1980). Vividness and control of imagery in personality types. *Journal of Mental Imagery* **4**, 111–114.

Stromeyer, C. F. and Psotka, J. (1970). The detailed texture of eidetic images. *Nature* **225**, 346–349.

Strosahl, K. D. and Ascough, J. C. (1981). Clinical uses of mental imagery: experimental foundations, theoretical misconceptions and research issues. *Psychological Bulletin* **89**, 422–438.

Sumner, F. C. and Watts, F. P. (1936). Rivalry between unicular negative after-images and the vision of the other eye. *American Journal of Psychology* **48**, 109–116.

Sutherland, J. D. (1937). Phenomenal memory and calculating ability: with illustrations from Dr Aitken. Unpublished MS cited in I. M. L. Hunter (1977) *Op. cit.*

Teasdale, H. H. (1934). A quantitative study of eidetic imagery. *British Journal of Educational Psychology* **4**, 56–74.

Thomson, J. J. (1969). The identity thesis. In S. Morgenbesser (ed.) *Philosophy, Science and Method: Essays in Honour of Ernest Nagel*. New York: St. Martin's Press.

Thurstone, L. L. and Jeffrey, T. E. (1956). *Flags: a Test of Space Thinking*. Chicago: Education Industry Service.

Tilley, A. J. (1981). Retention over a period of REM or non-REM sleep. *British Journal of Psychology* **72**, 241–248.

Titchener, E. B. (1896). *An Outline of Psychology*. New York: MacMillan.

Titchener, E. B. (1909). *Lectures on the Experimental Psychology of the Thought Processes*. New York: MacMillan.

Tolman, E. C. (1917). More concerning the temporal relations for meaning and imagery. *Psychological Review* **24**, 114–138.

Tolman, E. C. (1948). Cognitive maps in rats and men. *Psychological Review* **55**, 189–208.

Traxel, W. (1962). Kritische untersuchungen zur eidetik. *Archive fur die gesamte Psychologie* **114**, 260–336.

Treisman, A. M. (1960). Contextual cues in selective listening. *Quarterly Journal of Experimental Psychology* **12**, 242–248.

Treisman, A. M. and Gelade, G. (1980). A feature integration theory of attention. *Cognitive Psychology* **12**, 97–136.

Treisman, A., Squire, R. and Green, J. (1974). Semantic processing in dichotic listening? A replication. *Memory and Cognition* **2**, 641–646.

Tulving, E. and Thomson, D. M. (1973). Encoding specificity and retrieval processes in episodic memory. *Psychological Review* **80**, 352–373.

Underwood, B. J. and Schulz, R. W. (1960). *Meaningfulness and Verbal Learning.* Chicago: Lippincott.

Valentine, E. (1978). Perchings and flights: introspection. In A. Burton and J. Radford (eds.) *Thinking in Perspective.* London: Methuen.

Vernon, J. A. (1963). *Inside the Black Room.* New York: Clarkson Potter.

Wagman, R. and Stewart, C. G. (1974). Visual imagery and hypnotic suggestibility. *Perceptual and Motor Skills* **38**, 815–822.

Wallas, G. (1926). *The Art of Thought.* London: Jonathan Cape.

Walsh, F. J., White, K. D. and Ashton, P. (1978). Imagery training: Development of a procedure and its evaluation. Unpublished manuscript. University of Queensland.

Walters, W. G. (1953). *The Living Brain.* London: Duckworth.

Waltz, D. L. (1979). Commentary on: "On the demystification of mental imagery". *The Behavioral and Brain Sciences* **2**, 535–581.

Ward, J. (1883). Psychology in *Encyclopaedia Brittanica* **20**, 37–85.

Warren, M. W. (1977). The effects of recall-concurrent visual-motor distraction on picture and word recall. *Memory and Cognition* **5**, 362–370.

Warren, R. E. and Warren, N. T. (1976). Dual semantic encoding of homographs and homophones embedded in context. *Memory and Cognition* **4**, 586–592.

Wason, P. C. and Evans, J. St. B. T. (1975). Dual processes in reasoning? *Cognition* **3**, 141–154.

Wason, P. C. and Johnson-Laird, P. N. (1972). *Psychology of Reasoning: Structure and Content.* London: Batsford.

Wassermann, G. D. (1979). Reply to Popper's attack on epiphenomenalism. *Mind* **88**, 572–575.

Watson, J. B. (1913). Psychology as the behaviorist views it. *Psychological Review* **20**, 158–177.

Watson, J. B. (1930). *Behaviorism.* New York: Norton.

Waugh, N. C. and Norman, D. A. (1965). Primary memory. *Psychological Review* **72**, 89–104.

Weber, R. J. and Bach, M. (1969). Visual and speech imagery. *British Journal of Psychology* **60**, 199–202.

Weber, R. J. and Castleman, J. (1970). The time it takes to imagine. *Perception and Psychophysics* **8**, 165–168.

Weber, R. J., Kelley, J. and Little S. (1972). Is visual image sequencing under verbal control? *Journal of Experimental Psychology* **96**, 354–362.

Weber, R. J., Kelley, J. and Headley, D. (1973). Visual and acoustic imagery for letters and words. Unpublished manuscript, Oklahoma State University.

Webber, S. M. and Marshall, P. H. (1978). Bizarreness effects in imagery as a function of processing level and delay. *Journal of Mental Imagery* **2**, 291–299.

Westerman, I. C. (1973). *An Investigation of Children's Attempts to solve the Problems of Raven's Progressive Matrices.* Unpublished MA Thesis, University of Nottingham.

White, K. D. (1978). *Salivation: the Significance of Imagery in its Voluntary Control.* Unpublished MS. University of Queensland.

White, K. D. and Ashton, R. (1976). Correlational study of the relationship between Betts'' Q.M.I. and Gordon's test. Unpublished MS. University of Queensland.

White, K. D. and Ashton, R. (1977). Visual imagery control: one dimension or four? *Journal of Mental Imagery* **1**, 245–252.

White, K., Ashton, R. and Law, H. (1974). Factor analyses of the shortened form of Betts' questionnaire upon Mental Imagery. *Australian Journal of Psychology* **26**, 183–190.

White, K., Ashton, R. and Brown, R. M. D. (1977a). The measurement of imagery vividness: normative data and their relationship to sex, age and modality differences. *British Journal of Psychology* **68**, 203–211.

White, K., Sheehan, P. W. and Ashton, R. (1977b). Imagery assessment: a survey of self report measures. *Journal of Mental Imagery* **1**, 175–180.

White, K. D., Ashton, R. and Law, H. (1978). The measurement of imagery vividness: Effects of format and order on the Betts' Questionnaire Upon Mental Imagery. *Canadian Journal of Behavioral Science* **10**, 68–78.

White, P. (1980). Limitations on verbal reports of internal events: A refutation of Nisbett and Wilson and of Bem. *Psychological Review* **87**, 105–112.

Wickens, D. D. (1972). Characteristics of word encoding. In A. W. Melton and E. Martin (eds.) *Coding Processes in Human Memory.* Washington: Winston.

Wickens, D. D. and Engle, R. W. (1970). Imagery and abstractness in short-term memory. *Journal of Experimental Psychology* **84**, 268–272.

Wilkins, A. and Stewart, A. (1974). The time course of lateral asymmetries in the visual perception of letters. *Journal of Experimental Psychology* **102**, 905–908.

Williams, R. L., Agnew, H. W. and Webb, W. B. (1964). Sleep patterns in young adults: An EEG study. *Electroencephalograph and Clinical Neurophysiology* **17**, 376–381.

Wilton, R. N. (1978). Explaining operations in an imaginal format. *Perception* **7**, 563–574.

Wingfield, A. and Byrnes, D. L. (1981). *The Psychology of Human Memory.* New York and London: Academic Press.

Winograd, E. (1978). Encoding operations which facilitate memory for faces across the life span. In M. M. Gruneberg, P. E. Morris and R. N. Sykes (eds.) *Practical Aspects of Memory.* London and New York: Academic Press.

Winograd, E., Karchmer, M. A. and Russell, I. S. (1971). Role of encoding unitization in cued recognition memory. *Journal of Verbal Learning and Verbal Behavior* **10**, 199–206.

Winograd, E., Cohen, C. and Barresi, J. (1976). Memory for concrete and abstract words in bilingual speakers. *Memory and Cognition* **4**, 323–329.

Wittgenstein, L. (1953). *Philosophical Investigations*. Oxford: Blackwell.

Wittgenstein, L. (1967). *Zettel*. Oxford: Blackwell.

Wittkower, E. (1934). Further studies in the respiration of psychotic patients. *Journal of Mental Science* **80**, 692–704.

Wollen, K. A. and Lowry, D. H. (1974). Conditions that determine effectiveness of picture-mediated paired-associate learning. *Journal of Experimental Psychology* **102**, 181–183.

Wolpe, J. (1973). *The Practice of Behavior Therapy*. New York: Pergamon Press (2nd ed.).

Wood, E., Shotter, J. and Godden, D. (1974). An investigation of the relationships between problem solving strategies, representation and memory. *Quarterly Journal of Experimental Psychology* **26**, 252–257.

Woodworth, R. S. (1931). *Contemporary Schools of Psychology*. London: Methuen.

Woodworth, R. S. (1938). *Experimental Psychology*. New York: MacMillan.

Woodworth, R. S. and Sheehan, M. R. (1965). *Contemporary Schools of Psychology*. London: Methuen.

Yarmey, A. D. and O'Neill, B. J. (1969). S-R and R-S paired-associate learning as a function of concreteness, imagery, specificity and association value. *Journal of Psychology* **71**, 95–109.

Yates, F. A. (1966). *The Art of Memory*. Chicago: University of Chicago Press.

Yarmey, A. D. and Barker, W. J. (1971). Repetition versus imagery instructions in the immediate and delayed retention of picture and word paired-associates. *Canadian Journal of Psychology* **25**, 56–61.

Yarmey, A. D. and Csapo, K. G. (1968). Imaginal and verbal mediation instructions and stimulus attributes in paired-associate learning. *Psychological Record* **18**, 191–199.

Yarmey, A. D. and Ure, G. (1971). Incidental learning, noun imagery-concreteness and direction of associations in paired-associate learning. *Canadian Journal of Psychology* **25**, 91–102.

Yuille, J. C. (1968). Concreteness without imagery in P.A. learning. *Psychonomic Science* **11**, 55–56.

Yuille, J. C. (1971). Does the concreteness effect reverse with delay? *Journal of Experimental Psychology* **88**, 141–148.

Yuille, J. C. and Catchpole, M. J. (1977). The role of imagery in models of cognition. *Journal of Mental Imagery* **1**, 171–180.

Yuille, J. C. and Steiger, J. H. (1982). Non holistic processing in mental rotation: some suggestive evidence. *Perception and Psychophysics* **31**, 201–209.

Zikmund, V. (1972). Physiological correlates of visual imagery. In P. W. Sheehan (ed.) *The Function and Nature of Imagery*. New York and London: Academic Press.

Zubreck, J. P., Pushkar, D., Sanson, W. and Gowing, J. (1961). Perceptual changes after prolonged sensory isolation (darkness and silence) *Canadian Journal of Psychology* **15**, 83–100.

Subject index

A

Abstract approach to imagery, *see* Description theories of mental imagery

Abstractness; *see* Concreteness

Action systems; *see* Shallice

After-images, 66, 74–76

Allport,
model of consciousness, 56

Altered states of consciousness, 44–45

Alternatives to imagery; *see* "Arousal to words" theory, Concreteness, Lexical complexity theory, Semantic similarity theory

Analogue approach to imagery, *see* Picture theories of imagery

Analogue–propositional controversy; *see* Imagery debate

Anti-image approach to imagery; *see* Description theories of imagery

Apperception, 46

Arousal and imaging; *see* Physiological measures of imaging

"Arousal to words" theory, 273

Articulatory loop, 114, 147

Associative overlap between words; *see* Semantic similarity theory

Attention; *see also* Automaticity of skills, Apperception, Central processor, BOSS-consciousness model, Interference studies

in introspective tasks, 35

limited aspect of, 29, 51

Automaticity of skills, 45, 55, 61

Autonomic control via imagery; *see* Behaviour modification

B

Backward spelling, 221–223

Behaviour modification,
use of images, 107–108

Behaviourism, 6, 28, 31; *see also* Philosophical behaviourism

and dualism matched, 296

Bizarreness, 249–250, 281

BOSS-consciousness model, 46, 57–62, 67, 294–297

and cognitive processing, 59

and dreaming, 77–78, 82

and emotions, 60

and hallucinations, 84–85

and homunculi, 62

and image transformation, 197

and imagery, 60, 68, 74, 144–148, 178, 203–204

and interference, 169–170

and introspection, 62

learning and employee systems, 296

memory and BOSS systems, 297

and parallel processing, 218

and perception, 145–146